CHRISTIAN RECONSTRUCTION

THE AMERICAN MISSIONARY ASSOCIATION AND SOUTHERN BLACKS, 1861–1890

Joe M. Richardson

THE UNIVERSITY OF GEORGIA PRESS
ATHENS AND LONDON

To Twyla Richardson,
my first and best teacher

© 1986 by the University of Georgia Press
Athens, Georgia 30602
All rights reserved

Designed by Sandra Strother Hudson
Printed and bound by Braun-Brumfield, Inc.
Set in 10 on 13 Century Expanded
by the Composing Room of Michigan

The paper in this book meets the guidelines for
permanence and durability of the Committee on
Production Guidelines for Book Longevity of the
Council on Library Resources

Printed in the United States of America

90 89 88 87 86   5 4 3 2 1

Library of Congress Cataloging in Publication Data
Richardson, Joe Martin.
Christian reconstruction.

Bibliography: p.
Includes index.
1. American Missionary Association. 2. Missions to
Afro-Americans. 3. United States—History—Civil War,
1861–1865—Civilian relief. 4. United States—History—
Civil War, 1861–1865—Religious aspects. 5. Freedmen—
Education. 6. Freedmen—Religion. 7. Reconstruction.
I. Title.
BV2360.A8R53 1986   266'.022'08996073   85–13946
ISBN 0–8203–0816–1 (alk. paper)

Contents

Preface

ON 3 September 1846 the Union Missionary Society, the Committee for West Indian Missions, and the Western Evangelical Missionary Society united to form the American Missionary Association as a protest against the silence of other missionary agencies regarding slavery.[1] The association leadership was staunchly antislavery. Prominent leaders and supporters Lewis Tappan, Simeon S. Jocelyn, Gerrit Smith, Joshua Leavitt, George Whipple, and William Jackson were all evangelical abolitionists who believed that the gospel was a powerful weapon against slavery. As a part of the Tappan wing of the antislavery movement, the AMA advocated political activity, insisted upon the essentially antislavery nature of the Constitution, and was dedicated to purging the churches of the stain of slavery.[2]

In its early work the association strengthened the existing missions of its parent societies in Africa and Jamaica and created or accepted the care of others in Hawaii, Egypt, the Sandwich Islands, and Siam. In 1847 it began to provide clothing for slave refugees who had fled to Canada, and later it sent teachers and preachers among the refugees to establish schools and churches and to administer relief. It maintained its Canadian missions until after the Emancipation Proclamation. The AMA's largest activity, however, was in the United States, preaching the gospel "free from all complicity with slavery and caste." By the mid-1850s it had financed more than one hundred missionaries in the Northwest and the slave states of Missouri, North Carolina, and Kentucky.

Antislavery churches were founded in the Northwest, and in the South the AMA began education and religious instruction "on an avowedly antislavery basis." In Missouri, Stephen Blanchard, an AMA worker, was indicted for circulating "incendiary" books, and the Reverend Daniel Worth was imprisoned in North Carolina for the same offense. A Kansas missionary barely escaped proslavery violence in 1856. A Kentucky mob viciously whipped an association agent and drove another missionary, John G. Fee, out of the state. After being disinherited by his slaveholding father for his antislavery views, Fee in the mid-1850s moved to a small plot of land given him by the notorious antislavery figure Cassius M. Clay. He called his new home Berea. Fee built a rude log cabin and organized a church and school that recognized no distinction of race, caste, or color. The school later became Berea College. At different times Fee was dragged from the pulpit to be ducked in the river, hunted through the mountains to be whipped, and shot at in his home, but he, like other AMA agents, persisted in his antislavery teaching.[3]

When the Civil War erupted, the AMA was probably more an antislavery than a missionary society, yet its experience, organization, and fund-gathering capability enabled it to lead the way in providing systematic relief and education for slaves escaping from Confederate lines. It sent agents to Fortress Monroe, Virginia, in September 1861. The number of teachers and missionaries sent to assist freedmen increased to 250 in 1864 and to 320 in 1865. By 1868 the AMA had 532 agents in the southern and border states. The association provided relief, attempted to help blacks acquire land, demanded civil and political rights for former slaves, established schools and churches, and fought for a system of public education in the South.

The first AMA schools were elementary, but from the beginning the association planned to establish normal schools and colleges. It early decided that blacks should eventually furnish their own teachers. No race, AMA officials thought, should be permanently dependent upon another race for its development. Though whites should assist, and initially would provide leadership and teachers, blacks must eventually play a major role in working out their future with their own educators and leaders. As soon as the southern states began to establish public schools, the AMA deemphasized common schools and concentrated on graded schools, normal schools, and colleges. Although its elementary training and relief were significant, the AMA's most lasting contribution was the establishment of normal schools and colleges.

Association officers were motivated by religion and patriotism, and an educated, moral, industrious black citizenry was their goal. Equality before the law was "the gospel rule," the AMA concluded, and the country's "political salvation" depended upon its implementation. Unfortunately the association sometimes failed to live up to its own lofty ideals. It failed to recognize the richness and vitality of black culture and institutions and only belatedly to comprehend black insistence on self-determination. Paternalism and racial prejudice were too often present in its agents. Nevertheless, the AMA became the most significant of the many benevolent societies assisting blacks during the Civil War and Reconstruction, and it came closer to a full recognition of black rights and needs than did most nineteenth-century Americans. This study is an attempt to portray the strengths and weaknesses, successes and failures of the American Missionary Association in its efforts to bring blacks into the mainstream of American life.

Many people assisted in the preparation of this book. I appreciate the courtesies extended to me by the library staffs at Dillard University, Fisk University, Talladega College, Berea College, Florida State University, the Johns Hopkins University, the University of South Carolina, Louisiana State University, the University of Texas, the University of Arkansas, Yale University, Bowdoin College, the Arkansas Historical Commission, Syracuse University, the South Carolina Department of Archives and History, the Alabama Department of Archives and History, the National Archives, and the Library of Congress.

I am especially grateful to Clifton H. Johnson, executive director of the Amistad Research Center, New Orleans, and his efficient staff. Cliff's encouragement and advice were invaluable. Maxine D. Jones cheerfully shared her knowledge of and enthusiasm for the American Missionary Association. My son, Joseph, patiently listened to stories about the association, even when he was not interested. I have been fortunate in having Charles East copyedit the manuscript. He also offered advice on the use of illustrations. Portions of chapter 9 appeared in an article in the spring 1979 issue of *Southern Studies: An Interdisciplinary Journal of the South* and are herein used with permission. I am indebted to Patricia Richardson, Clifton H. Johnson, W. Augustus Low, Leslie Richardson, and Maxine D. Jones for reading the manuscript and giving me advice on both style and content. It is not their fault if I sometimes failed to follow their advice.

A Grand Field
for Missionary Labor

THE ROAR of Confederate cannons shelling Fort Sumter had hardly faded when the American Missionary Association exulted that the war would open "one of the grandest fields for missionary labor" the world had ever known. By June of 1861 the association proposed to do its part in the "circulation of spelling books" among escaping slaves, and in September of that year it sent its first missionary to Virginia.[1] Shortly after the commencement of hostilities slaves had begun fleeing to Federal lines. Since emancipation was not yet a war aim, puzzled commanders often returned escaped slaves to their masters until on May 23 General Benjamin F. Butler at Fortress Monroe, Virginia, declared three such slaves contrabands of war and set them to work on Union entrenchments at Hampton.[2] News of Butler's decision spread quickly through the black "grapevine," and on May 26 eight more "Virginia Volunteers" arrived. The next day forty-seven, including babies and frail elderly women, straggled into Butler's backyard. Soon the trickle became a flood.[3]

Lewis Tappan, treasurer of the AMA, had avidly followed newspaper accounts of the increasing number of contrabands at Fortress Monroe.[4] On August 8 he wrote commending Butler for his treatment of the fugitives and asking his advice about bringing the "self-emancipated" blacks to the free states where they could find employment. If they could be removed and given jobs, Tappan suggested, the commander would be relieved of great "care and anxiety." Butler replied that the "contrabands" were better off in Virginia, but that if people wished to show sympathy they could send clothing. Tappan, who feared that the fugitives might be remanded to slavery if they remained in the South, questioned Butler's right to "control the movement of colored people, bond or free." He further objected to the army working contrabands without pay, and added that philanthropic people

3

would gladly send relief if they could be assured that the government would not allow the escapees to be returned. Three days later Tappan again corresponded with Butler, asking whether "an intelligent, discreet and good man . . . would have facilities at . . . Fortress Monroe to distribute useful publications, preach to the 'contrabands,' converse with them, ascertain their physical & other necessities and be the medium of distributing clothing etc." Although Butler informed Tappan that the fugitives were being well cared for and that their religious needs were being met, the AMA sent the Reverend Lewis C. Lockwood to Virginia to investigate the condition of contrabands.[5]

Lockwood, who arrived in Hampton on 3 September 1861, was a providential choice as the association's first missionary to contrabands. His sensitivity toward and acceptance of blacks, combined with his remarkable energy and endurance, made him unusual among the missionaries. His expense accounts were often inaccurate, he was unsystematic, and, much to the association's dismay, he sometimes used tobacco for his asthma, but he filled an indispensable role during the thirteen months he remained in Virginia. Lockwood discovered that Hampton blacks were "uniquely prepared" to take advantage of his assistance. Many had been skilled craftsmen, fishermen, and foremen on nearby farms. They had "a great thirst for knowledge" and were anxious for schools. Lockwood gave books to those who could read and organized several Sabbath schools, including one in ex-President John Tyler's house. He immediately began advising blacks, marrying those who had "taken up with each other," and planning the construction of a school and church at Fortress Monroe. But perhaps his most important action was to start a day school at Hampton on 17 September 1861 and to employ the remarkable Mrs. Mary Peake as teacher.[6]

Mary Peake had been born Mary Smith Kelsey in Norfolk, Virginia, in 1823, the daughter of a free black mother and a white European father. At six she was sent to Alexandria, where she attended "a select colored school" for ten years. Upon her return to Norfolk she became active in a black Baptist church and founded the Daughters of Zion to aid the poor and ill. She also spent much of her time secretly teaching slaves. In 1851 she married an "intelligent and pious" former slave, Thomas Peake. She was teaching in Hampton when the Confederates burned the town on 7 August 1861.[7]

Mrs. Peake conducted her AMA school with a strong religious emphasis, much as later association teachers would. Classes began with prayer and scriptures, and students were taught the Bible and religious songs as well as the ABC's. In addition to the day school, Mrs. Peake began night classes for adults, despite her increasing infirmity caused by tuberculosis. In January 1862 she rejected her physician's advice to abandon her work or soon be "lost to earth." Association agent William L. Coan remembered watching her "when too sick to sit, lying upon her bed, surrounded by her scholars, teaching them to read, and by her sweet patient submission to the hand of God upon her, most earnestly teaching them that religion can support the soul even if the body dies." Weakness soon compelled her to suspend her school, and she died 22 February 1862.[8]

Association officials believed that Mrs. Peake's efforts on behalf of the contrabands aggravated her illness and hastened her death, and in their view she became almost a saint. Lockwood called her "a queen among her kind" and badly missed. Her successor, George Hyde, was thankful that he had been privileged to meet her. "Even in death," Hyde said, "the radiance of her life . . . illumined the society of her race." Even hardened military surgeon Rufus K. Browne wrote of her: "In no other woman, however light the skin, have I seen a more comprehensive sense of duty or more activity of self-sacrifice for the benefit of others." Mrs. Peake gave him, Browne added, "a new revival of my respect for human character." Sensitive, unselfish, fragile yet strong, Mary Peake became the first and one of the most admirable casualties in the AMA's war against ignorance. Her school marked the beginning of the AMA's movement to educate freedmen.[9] Hampton blacks and the AMA were partners in the latter's initial educational efforts.

Peake's school was only one of several opened by Lockwood. Mary Bailey, a free woman, and two assistants taught about fifty children at Fortress Monroe. Fugitive Peter Herbert began afternoon classes at Tyler's house, and Lockwood arranged for a private school for black patients at Hygeria Hospital. Lockwood continued to establish schools, but for the next several months his primary duty was to relieve suffering and protect contrabands from the military. The original Hampton residents such as the Peakes often had homes and jobs, but most fugitives flocked to military camps with little clothing, no food, and no place to live. Hundreds were crowded into rudely built split-log huts in

"Slabtown," while others lived in tents or outside. Since many of the men were impressed by the military, most of those squeezed into camps were women and children. A *Harper's* correspondent was touched to see slaves "throwing themselves on the mercy of yankees, in the hope of getting permission to own themselves and keep their children from the auction block." In the process they suffered terribly. Already mal-nourished, without adequate food, clothing, shelter, or medical care, the contrabands were decimated by measles, mumps, whooping cough, respiratory ailments, and dysentery. In late 1862 Fortress Monroe averaged seven deaths daily.[10]

Initially the military was not particularly helpful. Contrabands were an unwelcome nuisance. Almost without exception, commanding of-ficers were more concerned with control than with assistance. There-fore, the AMA attempted to provide relief. Lockwood determined need and the association energetically collected clothing and supplies. By December 1861 a single agent had forwarded nineteen barrels of clothing to Fortress Monroe. After a two-week investigating trip to Virginia in November, Corresponding Secretary Simeon S. Jocelyn wrote President Lincoln of the contrabands' industry, orderliness, and religious character, but, he added, they needed medical attention, and he requested an interview. In a subsequent meeting Jocelyn persuaded the president to assign a military surgeon to the refugees.[11]

The AMA organized a relief system that extended into the postwar era, but it was less successful in protecting contrabands from the mili-tary. Almost from his arrival Lockwood complained about army abuse of contrabands. Indeed, Lockwood charged that "contrabandism" was synonymous with government slavery.[12] Blacks were forced to work for quarters, rations, and perhaps a few dollars' worth of clothing. Some were brutally treated. On one occasion General John E. Wool gave a fugitive a pass permitting him to work for himself. A sergeant tore up the pass and had the man severely whipped and sent back to the gang. Others already working independently had been impressed into government service. Quartermaster G. Tallmadge, assigned to care for contrabands, was unconcerned and dishonest, but, Lockwood wrote, "What more could you expect of old Pharaoh slavery revived under the Stars & Stripes."[13]

Upon his return from a northern tour during which he vigorously criticized the military, Lockwood was refused admission to Fortress

Monroe, but in the meantime his disclosures had propelled association officers into action. They decided that Congress, the president, and the "whole North" must be informed of "how little freedom & humanity have to hope for from such men." Corresponding Secretary George Whipple went to Washington to interview several congressmen in addition to cabinet members Edwin M. Stanton and Salmon P. Chase. From there he went to Fortress Monroe to see Wool, who agreed to appoint an investigating committee which later verified Lockwood's charges. Tallmadge and his assistant were relieved of responsibility for contrabands. The association managed to secure the appointment of one of its agents, Charles B. Wilder, as superintendent of contrabands around Hampton. Wool further ordered that all wages owed former slaves be paid. This order was aimed at transforming contrabands into free wage earners.[14]

Wilder, an antislavery Boston businessman, had been sent to Virginia in early 1862 as the AMA's superintendent of relief operations. The contrabands apparently were impressed with him, but military men, who were more concerned with ending AMA complaints than with blacks, were not. Even though he was given the rank of captain, they correctly viewed him as more a missionary than a soldier and constantly interfered with his work.[15] The AMA and Wilder hoped to do far more than provide relief and protection for contrabands. Lewis Tappan believed that, if treated fairly and given an opportunity, blacks would prove themselves capable, industrious, and educable, which in turn would "give a great impulse to the cause of emancipation." First those who worked for the government should be paid reasonable wages. Others should be allowed to seek available jobs or to farm abandoned land. Wilder persuaded Wool to authorize contrabands to settle on lands near Hampton. The AMA encouraged the move by sending farm managers and teachers, but General John A. Dix, who replaced Wool in June 1862, was less sympathetic to the plan. Whipple's visits with Dix failed to alter the latter's views. Moreover, war uncertainty interfered with settlement. Still, blacks occupied about fifty farms in 1863 under Wilder's supervision.[16]

Contrabands continued to cultivate vacant farms, but the association never succeeded in completely safeguarding them from military abuse and exploitation. AMA officers wrote letters to congressmen and met with cabinet members and army commanders. They demanded that contrabands working for the government receive "just and equal" pay and "receive it punctually." Yet in December 1862 the army still owed Fortress Monroe contrabands $31,435 in back pay. Even more distressing, soldiers beat, robbed, and sometimes murdered fugitives. An AMA teacher claimed that soldiers seemed "to have lost sight of the Rebellion, & are fighting the ex-slaves, determined if possible to prevent them from making a living." He described the military as a mob robbing everyone too weak to defend themselves. Blacks were "stripped of everything eatable, houses broken open, pigs stolen, men seized in the street in open day and their money taken from them, and still the commanders make no effort to stop it," he said. Association agents could apply pressure against commanders, occasionally gaining concessions, but they could not control the troops.[17]

Wilder wrote of soldiers perpetrating "beastly barbarities" upon black women while guards assigned to protect them stood by indifferently. When soldiers armed with pistols and swords broke into a contraband's house near Fortress Monroe and raped his wife and daughter, Jocelyn furiously wrote that "such soldiers like Devils are not to be trusted in armies" and demanded that they be discovered and punished. A group of contrabands planted and cultivated sixty acres near Newport News, Virginia, at their own expense, asking only government protection. What they needed was protection from Union soldiers. In July 1862 General Ambrose Burnside's troops came through and destroyed nearly all of their early crops. The following month part of General George McClellan's retreating force camped nearby and destroyed more than half of their remaining produce. The black AMA teacher there, John Oliver, feared to leave his lodging at night. A contraband exclaimed to Oliver: "Good God, if this is the way we are to be treated we may just as well be in slavery." A teacher at Portsmouth feared that blacks' experience with the army might teach them to distrust all northern whites, "and much worse . . . they will begin to think honesty is only another name for self-interest."[18]

By late 1862 AMA officers almost despaired of securing protection for blacks, and they placed much of the blame on President Lincoln. Tappan thought Lincoln might be honest "on a low scale but he is not honest toward God or the suffering poor," and he prayed that the president's eyes would be opened. The old abolitionist believed his prayers had been partially answered when Lincoln issued the preliminary

Emancipation Proclamation in September 1862. The association praised the decision but lamented that delaying it until January 1863 would be "productive of evil." Tappan was ecstatic when emancipation was finally proclaimed. He rejoiced that Lincoln did not accompany his proclamation with schemes for colonization, compensation to masters, or transitional apprenticeship for slaves. Tappan attended the great emancipation celebration at Cooper Union and made a short speech. It was fitting that he should be there as he, more than anyone else, symbolized antislavery in New York. While the proclamation was less sweeping than he had wished, Tappan was hopeful that it would alter the treatment of blacks, since they were now freedmen rather than contrabands of war. Unfortunately, however, government policy changed too little. In mid-1863 Secretary of War Stanton himself gave orders to impress Virginia freedmen for work in the Quartermaster Department of the District of Columbia.[19]

Although the association was pleased with the Emancipation Proclamation, it believed Lincoln was too slow in recruiting black soldiers and endorsing racial equality. In September 1862 Jocelyn had said that Lincoln ought to accept blacks in the army and added that he hoped the president would "no longer play the fool" with the matter of border states. When the government began actively recruiting freedmen, the AMA praised the policy in an editorial in the *American Missionary*, the association's journal. The decision to incorporate blacks in the army, it said, "creates a new era in their history, it recognizes their manhood, gives them a status in the nation and is an open acknowledgement of their value to the country in time of peril." Moreover, enlisting blacks necessitated "measures for the protection of large masses of women and children, and for their employment, and, thereby their subsistence, while the men are in the army." The association assumed that the country was finally recognizing blacks as worthy of fair treatment. It deplored later methods of recruitment, however, including indiscriminate impressment of all available ablebodied men. This disastrous policy caused suffering and some "bitter feelings" toward the government.[20]

When General Benjamin F. Butler replaced General Dix as commander of eastern Virginia in November 1863, the association believed that the freedmen's position there would improve appreciably. Wilder claimed that some of Butler's orders were essentially what the AMA had been fighting for for the past two years.[21] Although Butler was more sympathetic and helpful than some previous commanders he seemed more interested in enlistments than in helping the freedmen. In 1864 the association was still complaining in Washington of mistreatment of blacks. No matter who was in command, the AMA's aid to freedmen was always limited by uncertainties of war and by the fact that black needs were subordinated to those of the military.[22]

Although the AMA directed much of its energy toward relieving and sheltering contrabands, it did not ignore education. In early January 1862 Lewis B. Hardcastle, an experienced New York teacher, was sent to Fortress Monroe. A few days afterwards "he fell whole length to the ground, and was taken up senseless" to be sent home to die. George Hyde arrived to assist Mrs. Peake, but shortly returned to New York ill. Finally, in April, Charles P. Day, the first long-term northern teacher to Virginia freedmen, opened a school at Woods Mill near Hampton.[23] Day, in his own words, was "but a plain farmer boy, without extra polish" but with an urgent desire to aid blacks. Ever since "the traitors struck the first blow at Ft. Sumter," he wrote, "it has been my earnest . . . prayer to God that [the war] might be the means in the hand of the Governor of the whole universe of the overthrow of that sum of all evils—*slavery*." He believed that the country owed "a work of love to their colored brothers at the South, for the part we have all taken (for I believe the North as well as the South are to blame in this) in helping to tread down him who is our brother." Day, who was so anxious to teach contrabands that he offered his services for travel expenses only, was too modest in his self-description as just a "plain farmer boy." Teaching was his profession. He was kind, patient, a strict disciplinarian, and "a most vigorous and enthusiastic teacher."[24]

Day's school opened with ninety students, and enrollment increased so rapidly that within a few days he divided it into morning and afternoon sessions. At first he thought his "little contrabands" were quarrelsome, dirty, thievish, and "seemingly inclined to almost every species of wickedness," but he noted a decided improvement by the end of the first week, and after a month his classes compared favorably with those he had formerly taught in Lebanon, New York. By mid-summer Day had moved his school to the recently renovated Hampton courthouse. As Lockwood said, "We built a church and schoolhouse out of the ruins of the old courthouse—a place of injustice and oppression; thus being converted into a place for the education and salvation of the oppressed. There in sight of the whipping tree," he added, "with its bark lacerated with the same strokes that fell on quivering flesh, we are teaching a free education and a free religion." Day divided his school into primary and advanced students with new teacher Mary Greene instructing the former. In addition, Day and Greene conducted a Sabbath school of 250 and an adult Bible class of about 100.[25]

The number of contrabands increased so during the summer that Day began classes in September with 500 students. Almost daily, he said, "mothers are having restored to them children whom they never expected to see again this side of eternity" and wives "were brought upon their knees in praise" at the sight of husbands long since sold away. Obviously, more teachers were needed. Day temporarily used advanced students as monitors until the AMA could dispatch more personnel. By October there were eighteen missionaries and teachers at Hampton, Fortress Monroe, Craney Island, Newport News, and Norfolk. In January 1863 black teacher John Oliver opened a school in recently recaptured Portsmouth. Oliver soon was instructing 130 students in a black Methodist church, even though local whites were "exceedingly bitter" about the school. Teachers continued to trail the Union Army into almost every new territory. By May 1863 the association had more than sixty teachers in the field and the number increased monthly. It was teaching approximately four thousand people in day and evening classes.[26]

Most AMA personnel had had prior teaching experience, but nothing that would prepare them for what they would endure in Virginia. They were in a war zone that could be entered only with a military pass. A Norfolk teacher "heard distinctly all day . . . rapid and heavy cannonading," while a Craney Island class was disturbed by the firing of gunboats. Lockwood and his Sabbath school class stood on the shore and breathlessly watched as the *Monitor* dueled the hulking iron-plated monster *Virginia* to a draw. After Confederate troops were driven out, the teachers still had to contend with hostile local whites. When James F. Sisson went to church the first Sunday after his arrival, a pretty, well-dressed teenager stepped up and "administered a dose of spit" upon him.[27]

The endless work was more enervating than fear of Confederates.

Day taught morning, afternoon, and night sessions as well as Sabbath school, yet was denounced for wanting recreation on Saturday nights rather than prayer meetings. Nearly all teachers conducted day, night, and Sabbath school classes. If they had any leisure it was often used in administering relief. James Sisson's activities at Portsmouth were not unique. He taught school, visited the needy daily, and preached on Sundays. Since there was no available physician for freedmen, he prescribed for them to the best of his ability and attended the ill. Additionally, he acted as an attorney in disputes between blacks and whites, secured government wages for those not being paid, furnished hundreds of families with rations and fuel, acted as policeman to punish white boys who stoned black schoolchildren, vaccinated many people for smallpox, handed out AMA clothing and shoes, gave private lessons to black preachers, and obtained coffins for destitute families in which there had been a death.[28]

Marcia Colton thought she had the most difficult task of all the teachers. Captain Orlando Brown, superintendent to freedmen at Norfolk, set up a camp on Craney Island for young freedwomen who were fornicating with white soldiers. Colton was assigned to the camp to teach and rehabilitate them and then place them in good Christian homes. She had not expected chastity among the freedwomen. "Why should I," she asked, "their masters they well know, do not practice it, & often after laying aside their *manhood* for mere animal gratification, they sell their *own* children into bondage." But she began work optimistically, assuming that she could easily teach the wayward girls the virtue of purity. She had almost a hundred girls and only white army guards for help. She reported that the guards made absolutely no contribution to rehabilitation and that the "old men" at the lighthouse "indulged themselves disgracefully" with the "prisoners."[29] The miscreants were unimpressed when Colton wrathfully told them that she "despised the man that would stoop so low."

The soldiers underestimated Colton's determination. She complained to military authorities about their behavior, and they were sent to the front lines, but the "prisoners at once commenced" with the new guards. After she warned them that she was determined to make herself "a terror to evil doers" and threatened them with battle duty, the guards became more careful, but by this time fourteen carpenters had been sent to work on the island hospital, "every one of which needed a guard" to keep him from the women. Colton's troubles never seemed to end. One Saturday evening she caught some of the women running outside "entirely destitute of clothing." Assuming that their rooms were too warm for them, she sent them to the guardhouse for forty-eight hours to cool off. Colton complained that her life was "a sore trial." There were no Christians on the island and "Alas, Alas! that *sin*, the sin of Sodom is so common." Many of her tribulations, she added, had been "too *dark* to be repeated to anybody's ears."[30]

Other teachers had different, though perhaps no less perplexing, problems than Colton. Most of the classes were too large to be taught effectively. A Norfolk school had an enrollment of 457 students of all ages and at various levels with only three teachers. Moreover, the war had created a transient student population. In a six-month period Day had approximately 800 different pupils. Hundreds of refugees might descend upon Hampton, enroll their children in school, and then in a few weeks be removed to Craney Island. Occasionally changing tides of war forced both teachers and pupils to evacuate.[31]

When the student body was stable, school buildings were still frequently inadequate. Adequate facilities such as those at Hampton were rare. Helen M. Dodd began class in a barn loft over a stable. Although the loft was cold and the stable odor unpleasant, she concluded that it was no "less suitable for a dispensary of knowledge and righteousness than for the birthplace of our blessed Saviour." The school building on Wise Farm admitted wind and rain and had no stove to warm the half-clothed children, but it was better than W. O. King's facility on Craney Island. His class met out-of-doors, and during the winter months the children hugged the outside of a barracks building for shelter against the wind.[32]

Under the circumstances the AMA's educational efforts met remarkable success. Several Hampton blacks, already literate, were anxious for further training, and the unlettered refugees were no less eager for learning. Few teachers have had more responsive students than those who went among the contrabands. H. S. Beals wrote of Norfolk freedmen: "The children . . . hurry to school as soon as their work is over. The plowmen hurry from the field at night to get their hour of study. Old men and women strain their dim sight with the book two and a half feet distant from the eye, to catch the shape of the letter. I call this heaven-inspired interest." A man reputedly one hundred and eight and only a few weeks out of bondage attended black teacher Clara Duncan's school in order to learn to read. As already noted, Day was able to place some of his pupils in advanced classes, and by September 1862 a few had progressed enough to serve as monitors. By the following year Day was holding classes in the first, second, and third readers, mental arithmetic, written arithmetic, geography, and grammar. When in 1865 Lee's surrender brought greater stability to the region, students progressed even more rapidly.[33]

Despite the multitudinous problems it encountered during its early years in Virginia, the AMA made meaningful contributions to blacks aside from education. It made northern people and politicians slightly more sensitive to black needs. Its constant harassment of military officials brought fairer, if not yet equitable, treatment of contrabands. The government was encouraged to accept greater responsibility for fugitives, as indicated by the assigning of surgeons and construction of shelters. The military decision to furnish rations for teachers and to permit them to travel on military transports at reduced rates was a tacit recognition of a partnership with the freedmen's aid societies.[34]

The association's relief activities ameliorated the suffering of thousands and undoubtedly saved some lives. Its great success in education and its constant propagandizing of that accomplishment in the *American Missionary* and in speeches and correspondence helped incline the North toward emancipation. Perhaps as important, the Lockwoods and Sissons showed blacks that whites were not necessarily all alike. Often going from old masters to military commanders brought little improvement, but AMA personnel encouraged education, hired Hampton blacks as teachers, sent black missionaries from the North, helped to organize black churches, provided relief, reminded blacks that they were free, taught them the ways of free people, and intervened on their behalf against the government. Blacks appreciated the assistance. On the other hand, most missionaries were less tolerant of the blacks' life-style than Sisson and Lockwood, and some tension developed between freedmen and their benefactors. As Robert F. Engs has indicated, the missionaries were frequently unable to correlate "the right to be free with the right to be different."[35]

2

Wartime Expansion

LTHOUGH the AMA focused its initial efforts upon contrabands in Virginia, it was intimately involved in the Port Royal experiment that Willie Lee Rose so perceptively treated in *Rehearsal for Reconstruction*. In January 1862 association officers Lewis Tappan and George Whipple dispatched the Reverend Mansfield French to Port Royal, South Carolina, to investigate the condition of blacks there. French, a Methodist evangelist, abolitionist, educator, and editor, easily secured a permit for the exploratory visit since he was a close friend of Secretary of the Treasury Salmon P. Chase. French quickly determined that contrabands needed relief and medical care and that they earnestly desired "religious instruction, as well as all the common means of civilization and enlightenment." After discussing the Port Royal field with French, Tappan and Whipple decided that the job was too big for the AMA to handle alone. Or perhaps, as Rose suggested, they concluded "that there was no better way to advance antislavery in the opinion of the public at large than to enlist public interest in preparing the slave to be a free man." At any rate, they called a public meeting at Cooper Institute for 20 February that resulted in the organization of the New York National Freedmen's Relief Association. They acted in concert with the Boston Educational Commission, which had been organized on 7 February.[1]

A committee of six clergymen, with Whipple as chairman, was appointed to screen applicants for South Carolina. After three days of "faithful labor" the committee approved twenty-five men and six women. These teachers and missionaries were among those whom Boston businessman John Murray Forbes described as odd-looking men and odder-looking women. "You would have doubted," he said, "whether it was the adjournment of a John Brown meeting or the fag end of a broken down phalanstery." On 3 March the New York and Boston agents boarded the *Atlantic* and steamed through the fog and freezing rain to the Sea Islands "to strike a blow for freedom."[2]

It was a disparate group that embarked on the *Atlantic*. The Boston contingent included hardheaded businessmen and young university graduates, many of whom were Unitarians. The New Yorkers tended to be older, more nondescript, and evangelicals. Many of the Bostonians had an obvious disdain that bordered on contempt for their evangelical partners. Susan Walker found French gentle and kind, with the right spirit but with small business capacity and executive talent. When he asked her to act as his secretary, she confided to her diary that she did not wish to be "mixed up" with the New Yorkers as "there is no congeniality of taste and sentiment."[3] Walker snidely remarked that she discerned a "discordant strain" when the evangelicals gathered on the deck and sang religious songs. For their part, some of the evangelicals believed that too many of the Massachusetts men viewed the trip as a money-making venture.[4] That they drew such conclusions based on discussions during the trip was not surprising.

The Bostonians seemed obsessed with farming and business, though they were not necessarily seeking personal profit. Edward Philbrick occupied his leisure time during the voyage reading about cotton culture. Edward Pierce, leader of the Boston Commission, warned his men that blacks must be taught responsibility and that any new possessions they gained must be paid for by their own labor. If it became necessary for them to punish blacks, he said, they should be punished by locking them up rather than by whipping. Pierce and his associates were trying to prove a free-labor thesis, to show they could successfully raise cotton with free black workers. They intended to organize farms and bring Yankee industriousness to the Sea Islands. What better way to demonstrate that blacks should be free, they asked, than by growing more cotton with free rather than slave labor? Of course, the Bostonians were interested in education and religion as well, but that apparently was not their major aim. To the AMA teachers and missionaries, on the other hand, growing cotton was secondary to inculcating good morals and faithful family life and teaching the alphabet to the freedmen. While the Boston Educational Commission stressed teaching blacks industriousness and acquisitiveness, the missionaries emphasized the debt owed blacks because of their enslavement. They, as much as the Bostonians, wished blacks to become independent landholders, but they thought land should be provided by the government at minimal cost. Slavery had entitled blacks to considerable assistance in the transition to freedom. "Paradoxical though it may appear," Rose concluded, "the preaching evangels frequently espoused the most radical program for the freedmen."[5]

Despite their differences, the AMA and the Boston Educational Commission worked together relatively well. The association was always the junior partner in the Port Royal experiment, but it did its share in sending teachers, ministers, books, and relief. In late 1862 the association had fifteen agents in the area teaching, preaching, and supervising relief activities. By October 1864 there were thirty-one AMA teachers and missionaries in South Carolina conducting fourteen schools with 1,115 students. Additionally the AMA operated ten Sabbath schools with 800 pupils and two night schools with 300 adult students in attendance. Association officers appreciated the concern and work of the Massachusetts "Gideonites," although they were distressed at their lack of evangelical labor among blacks.[6]

When the AMA sent teachers and missionaries to Virginia, South Carolina, and other Union-occupied areas in 1861 and 1862, its aim had been to assist contrabands by providing relief, protection, and education and in the process to show northern doubters that slaves deserved to be free. From the beginning of the Civil War the association had hoped that the war would result in emancipation. Lockwood had been sent to Virginia in anticipation that it would "open to the friends of the colored man multiplied opportunities of usefulness, compared with which their past efforts were but preparatory work." The AMA eagerly looked to the day when there would be available to it a missionary field among blacks "which in some of its aspects would be of paramount importance to almost any other." Still, in the early months of the war its southern work had necessarily been viewed as temporary. By late 1862, however, emancipation had become an obvious war aim. That battle had been won and the AMA believed it had played an appreciable role in the victory. But emancipation signaled that its mission work had just begun. Tappan and Whipple clearly saw that education was essential if "social emancipation" was to be realized from the legal emancipation already achieved. The association's responsibility was no longer temporary relief but permanent transformation, reconstruction, and redemption. The nation was still "on trial before God &

the universe," since universal emancipation was not yet guaranteed. The association hoped for the best and dramatically increased its activities among those already freed.[7]

In its efforts for the freedmen the AMA was motivated by religion and patriotism and its aim was full citizenship for blacks. Association leaders called themselves "Christian abolitionists," and to them abolition meant not merely "striking off the fetters of the slave" but freeing him "of the shackles of ignorance, superstition and sin." They viewed the war as a God-sent punishment for the sin of slavery. Both North and South were guilty—the latter because it held slaves and the former because it had acquiesced. An "alliance of New England commerce with Southern slavery greed" had, as Augustus F. Beard said, "corrupted the conscience of Northern society and succeeded in making the caste of color about as rigid in the North as Southern assertion could demand." Some northerners had recognized their errors and changed their views. As a result, God had "prospered" the Union Army, but He would "vouchsafe" complete victory for the North only when freedmen were recognized before the law as equals of whites. Blacks had suffered the hell of slavery. The country owed them for the wrongs it had inflicted. It was the nation's Christian duty to help pay this debt to freedmen by providing agencies for moral and intellectual development. The association was fully aware that a majority of northerners were yet to be convinced that blacks were worthy of equality, but it firmly, if naively, believed that equality could be gained through Christian education. If blacks acquired knowledge, were temperate and good Christians, they could eventually gain status equal to their merit. In 1863 Tappan advised a discouraged young American-educated African who was thinking of returning home that the "spirit of caste" would diminish as black men became educated and refined. Emancipation itself would ameliorate caste prejudice, Tappan added, since "caste is the twin brother of slavery, and they die together, in a great degree."[8]

Tappan, who was the driving force behind the AMA from its inception throughout the Civil War, was strongly committed to equality. To those who favored expatriation after emancipation, he responded that blacks must remain in the United States. It was both morally and physically impossible to deport millions of "our people." Most blacks were native Americans with "more natural rights to remain here unmolested and in pursuit of happiness," he said, than many immigrants who had "a peaceful habitancy" in the country. When discussing Mrs. Peake and other black teachers in Virginia with Gerrit Smith, Tappan exclaimed: "Colonize such persons! Why, they are to be the teachers of our children . . . and exemplars of all that is beautiful and excellent— for aught we know." When others charged that blacks were licentious and that they were liars and thieves, Tappan admitted that was true of some freedmen, which, he said, proved conclusively that they were men and brothers in the human family.[9]

Equality before the law was "the gospel rule," he wrote, and the "political salvation" of the United States depended upon its implementation. To Tappan, equality necessitated the right of suffrage. The freedman would never have his rights, he informed Senator Charles Sumner, until "he has a musket in one hand and a ballot in the other." In a July 1865 editorial the *American Missionary* reflected Tappan's views in calling for black suffrage. Blacks were brothers and fellow citizens. Their valor had added to the country's renown and had helped achieve victory over the Rebels. The rights of citizenship, the editorial continued, were not privileges to be bestowed upon the freedmen by whites. They had "inherited them as other men do." They were a God-given birthright, not to be withheld with impunity by their more powerful neighbors. The *American Missionary* naturally mirrored Tappan's views, but at its 1865 annual meeting the general AMA membership approved black suffrage and full citizenship. Emancipation that failed to bring protection of person and property and equal and impartial advantages of the laws and institutions was called "delusive and pernicious." There was no meaning to liberty that left a people stripped of civil rights. "Emancipation and liberty," the association added, "were but empty and mocking words if they do not convey the idea and rights of citizenship; and we protest against excluding men from the rights of citizenship, civil or political on account of their color."[10]

The association opposed any legal restrictions based on color. When Tappan lobbied for a Pennsylvania bill which would end segregation on state railroads, he firmly reminded a state senator that "the absurdity of excluding people from cars on account of their complexion is such that it ought to be condemned by every humane and generous mind." Indeed, Tappan prayed that the daily mingling of races from childhood would banish color prejudice. Unlike many abolitionists, Tappan was not offended by interracial marriage. When asked about a white missionary in Africa marrying a native woman, he said, "If he finds one of any race, who is educated, refined, converted & whom he loves he could marry her without offending God or anyone who sympathizes with God." Being educated, refined, and religious was more important than color. The association employed several interracial couples, both in Africa and the United States. Tappan's views were admittedly in advance of those of many AMA supporters, yet, as Jacqueline Jones has said, the association "soon gained a well deserved reputation for radicalism on the race issue." Unfortunately it sometimes failed to live up to its own ideals.[11]

After emancipation the AMA assumed the dual responsibility of convincing the North to accept blacks as equals and of training blacks up to citizenship. Good citizens, association officers believed, would likely think and behave as they did. That was what Tappan meant when he said that all abolitionists wanted blacks freed, but that Christian abolitionists desired something more. "They wished the slaves to be free citizens, and good men and women also . . . free from sin as well as free from slavery. Christ Jesus is then the Great Abolitionist." Without Christian education, slaves could degenerate into a menace to the country. With such training, they would become a valuable asset. The goals of the association officers were educational, religious, and political. They longed for a literate, thoughtful, temperate, godly society which, they believed, could be produced only through religious education. Therefore, the AMA went South with the book, the Bible, and the New England Way.[12]

In late 1862 the association began to close its other home missions and concentrate on the freedmen. By 1863 it had schools at several points in Virginia, in the District of Columbia, on the South Carolina Sea Islands, and in Cairo, Illinois, and had sent an advance agent to Memphis, Tennessee. It proposed to establish missions and teachers along the Mississippi from St. Louis to New Orleans as quickly as the river was controlled by Union forces, and was setting up "efficient committees" in Chicago and Cincinnati to assist in that endeavor.[13]

Of the many areas where the AMA opened schools during the war, none was judged more important than the District of Columbia, where the association hoped to attract the attention of both congressmen and

executive officers and thereby create the opportunity to make suggestions for the permanent welfare of blacks. Several societies and
individuals established black schools in the District, but the association
was increasingly viewed as the most effective agency. On the other
hand, there is little evidence that this caused the association officers'
suggestions to be received with greater gravity than previously. The
AMA sent its first teachers to the District of Columbia in September
1862, and by 1864 it employed sixteen teachers and missionaries in the
area. Most were teaching, although Rachel Patten became matron of a
small orphanage and the Reverend Danforth B. Nichols, in addition to
his other duties, was assisting freedmen in farming. Sixty acres and a
large vegetable garden had already been planted in an attempt to feed
freedmen and demonstrate "that these people can labor hard and well
and need no lash either."[14]

Perhaps the AMA's most interesting work in the capital was conducted by William J. Wilson. Wilson had been raised in the District of
Columbia, but for the past two decades had been teacher and then
principal of Public School No. 1 for black children in Brooklyn, New
York. He was an active abolitionist lecturer, a correspondent for *Frederick Douglass' Paper*, and a frequent contributor to other black newspapers and magazines under the name "Ethiop." However, a series of
antislavery speeches at Cooper Institute in 1862 and 1863 had so annoyed the school board that he lost his position. "The truth is," Wilson
wrote, "my course was too antislavery for some of these gentlemen to
longer remain & so I resigned." He went to Washington and offered his
services to the AMA. Since the association was actively seeking
qualified blacks, it happily accepted his offer.

Wilson, with his wife and daughter as assistants, took charge of the
Camp Baker school. When the enrollment grew too large he asked for
more teachers, but he rejected white assistants. He wished "good
competent earnest devoted *colored persons*," and he knew several
such people seeking employment. His school should be promoted, he
thought, as black-taught and supervised. "Give us a chance," he wrote
Whipple, "not as an experiment, but as an act eminently proper at this
stage of the progress of colored people themselves." Wilson said he
desired to inculcate in the black mind black ability and self-elevation.
Blacks, he added, must be taught to do their own work, only being
assisted by the "dominant class." As long as whites filled the "first

places" and blacks were regarded as "minors," blacks would remain a helpless and dependent class. Wilson preferred black teachers for all black youth, but since that was impossible, he said, "Let one school in Washington at least be so conducted though it be the largest." When the AMA failed to respond to his demands for another teacher, Wilson simply hired Julia Landre and asked the association to pay her.[15]

The association officers sought black teachers, but they apparently were nonplussed by this confident, sometimes quarrelsome black man. He constantly chided them for their late salary payments, demanded more pay for himself and his wife and daughter, hired teachers without authorization, broached no interference from the local white superintendent of AMA missions, and complained at his lack of authority to purchase supplies and to contract for repairs. Yet he usually won his battles with the association, and a new superintendent in 1865 claimed that Wilson had "succeeded admirably in spite of opposition and deliberate attempts" by a former AMA agent to prejudice him in the eyes of the association Executive Committee. Corresponding Secretary Michael E. Strieby visited Washington in 1865 and was "much pleased" with Wilson's school. It was perhaps the best in the District. Unfortunately, however, Wilson accepted a position with the Freedman's Savings Bank and neglected his school. There were constant complaints that it was badly managed and that discipline was poor. In response to these charges, Wilson said that people who "ought to be better occupied" were creating *dissatisfaction of me & my school.*" When he eventually resigned, the association made no effort to retain him. It would have benefited from making greater efforts to work with Wilson. Though never specifically indicated in correspondence, the impression remains that he was not tractable enough and chafed too much under AMA restraints, which injured his usefulness in the association's view. Greater patience and understanding were called for. Too few black teachers and principals was a major AMA weakness.[16]

Although the AMA viewed its Washington schools as "showcases" to impress federal officials, it placed as much emphasis on training black soldiers. Once the North started recruiting blacks, the association began sending teachers and arranging for its missionaries to serve as chaplains. Education would enable blacks to become better, more confident soldiers, but, more important, AMA leaders assumed that noncommissioned officers and others in leadership positions would have great influence in their communities when the war was over. They expected the military experience to strip blacks of many negative slave characteristics, to enhance self-confidence and independence. Teacher reports reinforced that view. A South Carolina missionary who saw freedmen enlisted into the Second Regiment, South Carolina Volunteers, commented on the effect of soldiering: "Some who left here a month ago . . . cringing, dumpish, slow, are now here as picket guards, and are ready to look you in your face, are wide awake and active. I am astonished at the change." In short, soldiers would realize their "manhood," thereby becoming natural leaders for their race. If they were taught to read and write and were exposed to association values, they would become even more efficient and useful.

C. B. Whitcomb and Thomas A. McMasters, both white, were sent to Port Hudson, Louisiana, in early 1864 to instruct the Corp d'Afrique. The black soldiers attended class as much as consistent with their duties. "I am sure that I have never witnessed greater eagerness to study," wrote a Corp d'Afrique chaplain. He added that "a majority of the men seemed to regard their books an indispensable portion of their equipment, and the cartridge-box and spelling book are attached to the same belt." During his free time McMasters taught an additional school for children living within Union lines. When part of the corps was transferred to Baton Rouge, Whitcomb followed. Since the soldiers were so occupied with training or fatigue duty, Whitcomb opened a night school for adults.[17]

Teachers followed black soldiers everywhere except into battle, and they almost uniformly claimed that the soldiers were eager to learn. Jonathan J. Wright, a black who instructed Negro troops in Beaufort, South Carolina, wrote: "I have taught in the North several terms, but I had not the least idea with what rapidity persons could learn, till I began to teach these freed soldiers. They made me think of half starved men sitting at the table of plenty." Fannie Scott was similarly impressed with the Twelfth Louisiana Volunteers in Vicksburg, Mississippi. She admitted that attendance was necessarily irregular, but advance was still rapid. "I have taught in the North," she wrote, "and have *never* seen such zeal on the part of pupils, nor such advancement as I see here among these dusky sons . . . of Ham." Maturity and desire enabled many of the soldiers to progress rapidly. Their greatest impediment was constant activity. Training, fighting, transfers from post to post, and routine duties severely limited the soldiers' instruction. Nevertheless, hundreds of them learned at least to read and write.[18]

John G. Fee considered working with Kentucky soldiers so important that he temporarily abandoned his beloved Berea. By 1863 Fee, an abolitionist fugitive from Kentucky, had returned to resume his antislavery preaching and teaching. When he heard that black soldiers were being gathered at nearby Camp Nelson, he decided to go preach to them and to secure suitable chaplains from among AMA missionaries. When he arrived there were five thousand soldiers present. The opportunities for assisting and influencing the soldiers were so great that Fee, with association approval, decided to remain. Never, he said, had he been so intensely interested in his work. "Here are thousands of men, made in the image of God, just emerging from the restraints of slavery into the liberty of free men, and of soldiers."[19]

Fee saw his work at Camp Nelson as more than teaching soldiers. Since Kentucky was a Union state, the Emancipation Proclamation had not freed its slaves. Those who enlisted in the army were presumed free, but what of their wives, children, and relatives? Fee used Camp Nelson as a platform from which he could attack slavery. He encouraged slaves to escape to the camp and resisted when the military tried to return them. He held up the troops as examples of black manhood and intellectual ability. After a Kentucky senator claimed that Kentucky slavery was not the horrible institution that abolitionists described, Fee told of badly lacerated women coming into the camp, and reminded the public that of the first three thousand men examined at Camp Nelson three out of five "bore on their bodies marks of cruelty." This was an opportunity, he asserted, "to knock the starch out of slavery." After all, it was slavery that stood between Kentucky and loyalty. Fee designated Camp Nelson as the "cradle of liberty to central Kentucky."[20]

The soldiers were easily susceptible to Fee's guidance. Many of them knew him personally, and nearly all had heard of him as their friend. Thousands gathered to hear him speak. When he and his son, Burritt, began a school to teach noncommissioned officers, it was crowded with eager men. Fee was impressed with his unique opportunity. "When we consider that this people . . . are manifestly capable of rapid intellectual development, that they are humble, grateful, trusting, religiously inclined—that they are destined to occupy an important place in the army and agriculture of this nation I feel that it is blessed to labor with such people," he wrote. There is no evidence that Fee believed that the soldiers' destiny was limited to military and agricultural pursuits. He was pleased with their progress in school, concluding that "perhaps no slaves in the nation are superior in intellectual development to those Kentucky ex-slaves—few their equals." Fee was more a preacher than a teacher, and the AMA soon sent additional teachers and ministers, including blacks whom Fee especially wanted.[21]

Closely connected to the AMA's work with black soldiers was that with contrabands or fugitives, since they tended to flee to military posts. Refugee "camps" dotted the South by 1864. Fee spent much of his time assisting women and children collected at Camp Nelson. Hundreds were crowded into barracks without proper food or clothing, with the result that the mortality rate, especially among children, was fearful. "Four deaths last night," Fee wrote sadly, "four the night before. The ward system is horrible." Association missionaries did what they could to make fugitives comfortable and opened schools when possible.[22]

By May 1863 nine association teachers and missionaries were providing relief and teaching refugees at Corinth, Mississippi. Teachers marveled at the freedmen's uncomplaining attitude and their desire to learn. A. D. Olds described families enduring a cold spring storm in tents without blankets or proper clothing. "But thru it all," he continued, "I do not remember that I heard a murmur. On the other hand there was uniform cheerfulness & even joy at the thought that they had escaped from the thralldom of slavery." A missionary at the Memphis contraband camp said some mothers had lost four and even six children by death since their arrival, "but notwithstanding all these trials, very few are heard to speak of their former life but with horror. They almost without exception declare they would prefer to all die here, rather than go back to slavery." The suffering failed to dull black enthusiasm for learning. One teacher said young and old alike "pant for knowledge as the thirsty beast for the brook. I have mothers in my school, whom I have to excuse at intervals, to nurse their children." As soon as the children learned, they became teachers at home. The AMA sent teachers to several other refugee camps throughout the South. By October 1863 it had eighty-three teachers and missionaries plus nineteen local black "monitors or assistants" in the field.[23]

Far more important in the long run than teaching in military and contraband camps was the AMA's establishment of scores of common schools throughout the South. Teachers tracked Union forces so closely that they sometimes became casualties of the fighting. Mrs. S. F. Venatta was literally torn to bits near Helena, Arkansas, when a six-pound Confederate cannon ball struck her between the shoulders and passed through the length of her body. Her husband was wounded in the thigh by a rifle bullet. Most teachers were not injured by the war, but they were often discomforted. Rose Kinney was compelled to flee Corinth in late 1862, and in 1864 the local commander ordered teachers near Pine Bluff, Arkansas, to pack their belongings and go into Union fortifications for protection. Soon afterwards these teachers were caught in a skirmish between Union pickets and Confederates. Fortunately none were hurt. Mrs. E. A. Lane's Beaufort, South Carolina, school was interrupted several times by troops and contrabands being moved in and out. At times her building was taken over to house wounded soldiers. One battle raged so close that she could see the smoke and cannon reports rattled the school windows. After the courageous but suicidal charge on Battery Wagner by the famous Fifty-fourth Massachusetts Regiment, William T. Richardson temporarily suspended his Beaufort school to attend the wounded.[24]

Confederate raids in North Carolina in 1864 made permanency in freedmen's schools almost impossible. The Trent River School, which opened 1 February 1864, was dismissed by noon owing to the continuous firing of nearby cannons. A few days later a Confederate attack on New Bern and Beaufort forced teachers to evacuate. Schools were resumed as soon as Union reinforcements arrived, but Emily Gill could not shake her nervousness, knowing that 15,000 Confederate troops were camped within a mile. Schools were constantly dislocated at Plymouth, which changed hands five times in two years. Confederate forces temporarily closed AMA schools in New Bern, Washington, Plymouth, Roanoke Island, Camp Totten, and Beaufort in 1864. As William T. Briggs, association superintendent in North Carolina, explained, "Under military sway we must live chiefly in the present for our educational interests & plans for promoting them, are liable at any moment to be disturbed & defeated." Briggs added that the teachers "bravely meet the emergency & seem very calm & trustful."[25]

Many teachers discovered that Rebels not in uniform presented a greater danger to their schools than Confederate soldiers. In mid-1864 the AMA began a school at Clumfort's Creek, North Carolina, established by a small free-black colony before the war. George N. Greene had helped the community build a school and church house. Later ruffians set fire to the building and unsuccessfully tried to extort from the teacher a promise that she would "never again teach niggers to read." Three days after John L. Richardson opened a school in Ebenezer Church in St. Louis, "a few low wicked boys likely backed by Secsh men" burned it. Richardson transferred his students to another building without missing a day of class.[26]

Mrs. Caroline A. Briggs was "persecuted and treated with the utmost contempt" because she taught those "unfortunate ones" in Warrensburg, Missouri. A local editor charged that Mrs. Briggs had "negro on the brain" and put blacks *above the whites.* In Jefferson City Mrs. Lydia A. Montague was called a "nigger teacher" and her school was stoned several times. Soon after her arrival in the "den of copperheads" some "white boys" broke out the windows, destroyed books, and wrecked school furniture. She had to protect her students from stoning by white youths. On the other hand, a number of masters permitted their slaves to attend her classes after their day's work was completed.[27] Local whites managed to make life difficult for teachers in Louisiana also. In Thibodaux Mr. and Mrs. Joseph Parks were subjected to a series of insults and annoyances. They were pelted with dirt on the way to and from school and threatened with death. Opponents continuously broke into the schoolhouse, destroyed books, and defaced furniture. As a final outrage, an opponent entered the school building at night and defecated on Mrs. Parks's desk. He watched at the window the next morning, laughed, and uttered obscenities when Mrs. Parks discovered what he had done. He repeated the incident that night. Mrs. Parks became ill in consequence of her terror.[28]

Despite its problems with Confederates, the AMA sometimes considered the Union Army and federal officials as the greatest obstacle to teaching blacks during the Civil War. The Reverend W. T. Richardson charged that in Beaufort, South Carolina, the army and navy had a shameful, demoralizing effect on blacks, especially the women. A provost marshal, when asked by a teacher in Louisiana for assistance, refused, saying that he did not enlist to help "nigger schools." In Corinth, Mississippi, and New Bern, North Carolina, the military broke up contraband camps and scattered refugee students. A. W. Kelly, health officer at Natchez, Mississippi, with the approval of General J. M. Tuttle, district commander, ordered that after 1 April 1864 no contraband not employed by "some *responsible white person*, in some legitimate business, and who does not reside at the domicile of his or her employer" should be allowed to remain in the city. Kelly defined contrabands as any former slaves who were not employed by their former masters. The order was issued, he said, because blacks were lazy, profligate, thriftless, and improvident and because they crowded into hovels "which soon become dens of noisome filth . . . hotbeds fit to engender and rapidly disseminate the most *loathsome and malignant diseases.*"[29]

Association Superintendent Selig G. Wright vigorously protested to General Tuttle that black women were being driven from "comfortable" homes because they supported themselves and were not dependent on whites. "And it seems strange that just now when the government is fighting for the principles of universal liberty," he continued, "that a distinction should be made in this district in favor of those who have been slaveholders and against well-doing and self-supporting colored people." Wright's protest was unavailing. Children in AMA schools were rounded up by Union soldiers and marched to contraband camps. Approximately one-third of the students never returned. Wright believed that Tuttle's intention was to force blacks to work for their former masters and break up the schools.[30] Dr. Kelly was heard to remark that he would have "all those nigger schools broken up in a few days." It was especially unjust, Wright thought, that many of those driven from Natchez were wives and children of black soldiers.[31]

Military interference with AMA schools obviously was not universal. While the commander at Natchez said he "wished the missionaries and teachers would let the niggers alone," that there were too many freedmen teachers in the South and "they were nothing but a bore," many other officers assisted the association in any way they could. Reports from South Carolina in mid-1863 indicated that the "hatred and jealousy" of white soldiers toward blacks was "dying away" and that they were attending black religious services and assisting in Sabbath schools. But even the most sympathetic officers sometimes thought missionaries and teachers were so obsessed with freedmen that they failed to recognize the complexity of the problems faced by the military. The AMA experience in Louisiana illustrated the often tenuous cooperation between the army and civilian missionaries.[32]

In August 1863 General Nathaniel P. Banks, commander of the federally controlled Louisiana parishes, created the Enrollment Commission, which had education as one of its many responsibilities. Soon afterward Lieutenant W. B. Stickney was appointed superintendent of public colored schools in New Orleans. By mid-October Stickney supervised seven schools with sixteen teachers and 576 students. The military's halting efforts at education were supplemented by the AMA in December of that year when it commissioned Isaac G. Hubbs, "a gentleman of large experience," to establish schools in New Orleans and neighboring towns. In January 1864 General Banks, at Hubbs's request, granted transportation to fifteen association teachers, ten of whom were to go to the interior where there were few schools.[33]

Hubbs opened the first AMA school in New Orleans in early January. More significantly, in mid-February the association took possession of the former New Orleans School of Medicine building and established the School of Liberty, which became the showcase institution in Civil War New Orleans. By May it was graded and had nine teachers and an average attendance of nearly five hundred. Many of the students had been free before the war and had prior education. A number of them were "well advanced in the common English branches—some so far as to be able to enter stores as clerks." The AMA began other schools in several smaller towns and on plantations. By the summer of 1864 it had twenty-five agents in Louisiana.[34]

At first the association was pleased by Banks's cooperation and support. In January 1864 the general had "cheerfully" promised all the facilities, rations, and shelter the teachers needed. But soon relations between Hubbs and military officers became strained.[35] Hubbs discovered that promises made were more common than promises fulfilled. More important, Banks and Hubbs clashed over the question of plantation schools. Hubbs viewed them as essential in reaching the majority of school-age black youth. Local planters aggressively opposed the plan, and Banks capitulated to planter pressure. Moreover, the association was troubled by the military's treatment of blacks. Hubbs complained that plantation hands were "maltreated and defrauded, . . . abused by Northern men, . . . murdered by our own soldiers, . . . thrust out of provost marshals' offices," imprisoned simply for entering complaints, and then "robbed by the jailers who expelled them when they had been frightened into silence."[36]

The clash over plantation schools and abusive treatment of blacks reflected the differing views of the status of freedmen. Banks was responsible for protecting them and at the same time pacifying the white population. The association's only concern in Louisiana was freedmen. As a result, the missionaries' perception of emancipation was generally more expansive than that of the military. They heartily disapproved the "tutelage" period imposed upon blacks by Banks's labor program. Banks sought black submission and peace with the planters. His experience with northern teachers convinced him that southern white teachers would generate less hostility than northern ones and also make subordination of the black population easier.[37] In this atmosphere of increasing friction and hostility between the AMA and General Banks, the system of black schools was reorganized. In early March 1864 Banks appointed a three-man board of education with power to levy taxes, establish district schools, and examine and appoint teachers. The board members were Chaplain Edwin M. Wheelock, B. Rush Plumly, and Hubbs.[38]

Within a few weeks the board was split over personalities and policies. Wheelock and Hubbs distrusted each other. Hubbs advocated plantation schools, while Wheelock and Plumly supported district schools, which reached fewer students. Banks and Plumly viewed AMA teachers and plantation schools as a threat to the military labor program, and Wheelock, a Unitarian, despised the association's self-righteous evangelical teachers. By May the board was attempting to take over AMA schools, but the association resisted giving up the foothold which its persistent efforts had gained. Eventually a compromise was negotiated whereby the board would retain and pay teachers if they agreed to sever ties with the AMA.[39] By summer the transfer was complete and the association's work in Louisiana was temporarily ended. When schools opened in the fall, more than 80 percent of the teachers were white southerners. In the meantime the AMA had provided teachers when few were available, and schools where none existed.[40]

Obdurate southerners and uncharitable military officers impeded but did not halt the AMA movement into the South. By May 1864 the association employed 180 missionaries and teachers among freedmen, and the number increased to 250 by October. The association was instructing 12,000 pupils in day schools, a like number in Sabbath schools, and thousands were in night classes. Dozens of missionaries were providing relief and attending to the freedmen's personal needs. Few areas occupied by Union forces were left uncovered by the association or one of the other education societies. By 1865 the Confederacy was collapsing. There was a question of whether the association could secure the resources to furnish more teachers. On 3 April Mrs. J. N. Coan, a missionary in eastern Virginia, wrote: "Petersburg is ours, Richmond will soon be. . . . Who shall go in this citadel of secession & gather up the pieces of ebony ready for the workman." The AMA and other benevolent agencies rose to the challenge. On 10 April William H. Woodbury started toward Richmond with three teachers, one of whom appropriately was black. Seventeen days after Union forces entered the Confederate capital the AMA had schools organized there with a daily attendance of 1,500 students.[41]

AMA Common Schools
After the War

HE AMA rapidly expanded its educational work after the war. In mid-1865 it had 250 teachers and missionaries in the field. The number increased to 353 in 1866, to 451 in 1867, and to 532 in 1868. In June 1867 the association was teaching 38,719 students in day and night classes and 18,010 in Sabbath schools. It had teachers in every southern and border state, but it concentrated its efforts on certain areas.[1] Because of proximity most societies had many teachers in Virginia, but the AMA virtually dominated benevolent activity in Georgia, Tennessee, Alabama, and Louisiana. In 1867 northern benevolence sustained eighty-four schools in Georgia, seventy-six of which were established by the AMA.[2]

Wherever teachers went they were greeted by enthusiastic students. In the first flush of freedom, grandparents and grandchildren surged to the crude schoolhouses to secure the magic of reading and writing. Their demand for training crowded almost every available facility. Families pinched with hunger asked more eagerly for learning than for food. Thomas W. Higginson, white commander of the black First Regiment of South Carolina Volunteers, said the soldiers' love of their spelling book was "perfectly inexhaustible." Black Philadelphia teacher Charlotte L. Forten had never seen children so anxious to learn as those in South Carolina. "Coming to school was a constant delight and recreation to them," she wrote. "They come here as other children go to play." When the Storrs School opened in Atlanta in 1872, many more students attempted to enroll than could be admitted. "The excitement was intense," a teacher reported. "It was a riot for an education; starved minds were claiming and fighting for food; the sight was pitiful beyond description. To see children go away weeping because they had been refused admission to school was too much even for my hard heart."[3]

Harriet Beecher Stowe distributed spelling books to Florida freedmen which they "accepted and treasured with a sort of superstitious veneration." They appeared evenings after work, earnestly begging to be taught. A North Carolina teacher marveled at the black's "greed for letters. . . . Frock coat or shoes, he takes as his due; but every step of his creeping progress into the mysteries of letters elevates his spirit like faith in a brilliant promise." When a schoolhouse in Nansemond County, Virginia, was burned, approximately forty-five black men met amid the ashes, sent for the teacher, and told her if she would remain they would "build her a larger and better house of timber *so green that it could not burn,* and would keep her supplied with green schoolhouses as long as she would stay."[4]

The craving for learning was not limited to youth. Gray-haired, dim-sighted men pored over the spelling books with bright-eyed youngsters. In Jacksonville, Florida, Harriet Greely had sixty-one diligent and persevering students ranging in age from twenty to seventy-five. A bent, half-blind man of over seventy attended school in Nashville. His uppermost desire was to read the Bible for himself. He made commendable progress because his zeal was so great, his teacher said. His advancement was rivaled by that of Lizzie Smith, who had been a slave for more than fifty years. An Arkansas teacher wrote that he found "well-thumbed" primers in tents, hovels, shops, and kitchens, and often it was a gray head bent over the books.[5]

Many of the elderly students were fascinated by the novelty of going to school or were trying to learn to read the Bible, and numerous adults were motivated by a wish to improve their position or to become responsible citizens. After blacks were enfranchised, Harriet Greely found an increasing interest in night school among young men in Florida. They said they wished to read what names they were placing in the ballot box. Some of them were studying the U.S. Constitution. In 1869 a District of Columbia night school had an enrollment of 232, nearly all of whom worked during the day. After a hard day's work in the broiling sun "these brawny, hard-handed men" hastened home for a bite of food and then hurried off to school. Among the most regular and hardworking students in a Jacksonville night class were a number of masons and carpenters between forty and fifty years old. A Savannah teacher claimed that her class contained cooks, laundresses, ironers, cigar makers, cotton pickers, nurses, and milk carriers as well as playful girls and boys. The efforts for education made by N. B. James of New Orleans were not unusual. He studied at Straight University during the day and attended theological lectures at night. His wife complained that he was no "comfort" to her since he would not leave his book long enough to sit and talk with her. "I tell her," James wrote, "that I can't lose any time, for time is gold with me at present."[6]

Most adults were unable to attend school, and those who did sometimes quickly gave up, but freedmen almost universally wished to see their children educated. Harriet Beecher Stowe claimed that many of the older people on her Florida plantation "never got through the wilderness of the spelling-book into the promised land of the first-reader," but consoled themselves with the thought that their children would learn. An Arkansas teacher noted that blacks were "very proud" of the opportunity to educate their youth. Harriet Lynch Wright walked from Cuthbert, Georgia, to Atlanta, nearly two hundred miles, with three children so that her son Richard could enroll at Storrs School. Tennessee blacks petitioned for schools on the grounds that "the war has set us free; but as yet, we are without the means of making this freedom a blessing to us. In order to use our freedom for our own good, and for the good of society, we must be educated." Freedmen in North Carolina stressed the need for schools so that their youngsters might become more useful in all the relations of life. Throughout the South blacks gave of their scanty means to establish schools.[7]

Northern teachers may have exaggerated black ardor for education. In their public pronouncements, at least in the early years, they tended to present freedmen in the best possible light, but southern whites often corroborated their testimony. A former Louisiana slave-holder said black adults expected to remain no more than laborers, but they anticipated more for their children. "Education . . . is to develop them into gentlemen equal to their old . . . masters. They see them in their imagination, reading the Bible and writing letters—a consummation which they think to be the height of human bliss." Blacks, he added, had "erected education into almost a divine institution." An Alabama white lamented that in his neighborhood freedmen, old and young, big and little, had "all gone crazy about schools." Alexander H. Stephens, former vice-president of the Confederacy, agreed that blacks urgently sought training. Indeed, some southern whites were alarmed lest blacks surpass them in literacy.[8]

A Cape Girardeau, Missouri, editor noticed that education had given new life and energy to the local black community. Children were in school and were teaching their parents. Through their own efforts blacks had recently purchased a large, commodious schoolhouse. "We should blush," the editor scolded, "to permit a poor, ignorant, oppressed people, that has been in bondage over two hundred years, and then turned loose without a dollar in their pockets or even a good suit of clothes on their backs," to have the largest Sunday school in the city and to buy a good schoolhouse while "we, a people who call ourselves the lords of the earth, cannot show manhood, intelligence, and energy enough" to procure a suitable building in which to educate white children. An editor in New Iberia, Louisiana, claimed that almost every black child in the community was learning to read. When public schools were unavailable, their parents secured tutors, while whites seemed uninterested. He feared that, even though whites "were by nature superior," when the present generation became adults some whites might have to lower themselves and go to blacks to have letters read and written for them.[9]

There was no chance that blacks as a group would soon outstrip whites in a literacy race, but their desire for education was both genuine and unsurprising. A Mississippi freedman vowed to send his children to school because, he said, education was next best to liberty. The U.S. commissioner of education asserted that blacks "instinctively" associated the absence of educational opportunities with bondage and the privilege of learning with freedom. That persuasion alone sent thousands of freedmen to school. Learning was viewed as the greatest hedge against reenslavement. Moreover, according to AMA teachers, freedmen thought that knowledge was power, that mental improvement was synonymous with their elevation. W. E. B. DuBois agreed that blacks connected learning with power, that they believed "education was the stepping-stone to wealth and respect." Jacqueline Jones has observed that in their quest for autonomy "schooling was of great symbolic and practical importance to blacks," a means of breaking free from the ignorance which had served whites so well. "Throughout the South," Jones maintained, "going to school—or building, supporting, or teaching in a school—became a political act for black people."[10]

What were the AMA's aims for the thousands of students flocking to their schools? Its ultimate goal was "the incorporation of blacks into a casteless American society," which, given the widespread and strongly

entrenched white notion of racial inferiority, could require generations. In the meantime it intended to demonstrate that with equal advantages blacks were equal to whites, and also to prepare freedmen
for life, work, and citizenship. Most freedmen teachers and missionaries assumed that the prerequisites for a full, good, and productive
life were the esteemed virtues which they taught in northern schools
and pulpits—"industry, frugality, honesty, sobriety, marital fidelity,
self-reliance, self-control, godliness and love of country." As Lewis
Tappan said, the association was laboring for the bodies, souls, and
minds of blacks. George Whipple reminded an AMA agent that he was
a "missionary teacher." Both words were emphatic. Teaching literacy
or the rudiments of science, though enviable, was but a portion of the
freedmen's wants, Whipple said. "They need to be taught how to direct their own energies for their own support, their elevation, their
growth in holiness. . . . They need kindly, gently, lovingly," Whipple
continued, "to be counselled (not lectured or scolded) in relation to the
proper exercise and development of true manhood and womanhood,
and a pure practical Christianity." The AMA hoped such training
would enable freedmen to move toward a more useful and enriching
life and give them as much advantage as possible for survival in a
highly competitive America. The association planned to imbue freedmen with Yankee values overlaid by evangelical Protestantism.[11]

Another association aim was the preservation of the American system of government. The AMA had advocated black suffrage and proclaimed black enfranchisement in 1867 as cause for "thanksgiving to
God." But while this enlarged the freedmen's liberty, it also increased
the necessity for education and improvement. Ignoring black education created a danger, the association thought, not only to freedmen
but to the entire country. Black voting and office-holding must prove a
blessing or a curse as blacks were or were not "fitted to occupy and
cultivate the new and wide field" opened to them. If they were instructed in letters and religion, given sympathy and temporary aid,
they would "become an important element" in national welfare. If left
in poverty, ignorance, and vice, which slavery had forced upon them,
their very freedom might be used to the destruction of the country and
themselves. In the parochial view of many northern church people, as
Ronald E. Butchart has shown, "only evangelical protestantism could
serve as the foundation of the republic." The evangelical assumption of

the total depravity of man taught them that "the pure republic was dangerous except as bound tightly with constraints" of a conservative Protestant morality. The "depraved" could not be trusted to lead the nation. It was not just freedmen who needed evangelical Protestantism and northern values. After all, the white South had attempted to destroy the republic. The AMA and other benevolent societies dreamed of constructing a civil society in the South on a "true basis."[12]

Association aims and beliefs obviously dictated the curriculum. Subjects taught were similar to those in northern common schools: reading, writing, arithmetic, spelling, grammar, geography, singing, and history. Standard textbooks were ordinarily used in AMA schools. Wilson's *Primary Speller*, Fetter's *Primary Arithmetic*, Goodrich's *Pictorial History of the United States*, Montieth's *United States History*, McGuffey's *Reader*, Greenleaf's *Arithmetic*, and *Webster's Speller* were popular.[13] In addition to the usual texts, special books were written for freedmen in primary grades. The American Tract Society (ATS) published a series of readers, primers, and spellers directed to black audiences: *The Freedmen's Primer, The Freedmen's Spelling Book, The Lincoln Primer*, and the first, second, and third *Freedmen's Reader*. These texts stressed morals and good citizenship. Abraham Lincoln, Paul Cuffee, and Toussaint L'Ouverture were used to illustrate the virtues of thrift, hard work, philanthropy, and loyalty. Butchart claims that the evangelical societies, including the AMA, employed these special books "to produce a safe working class for the South and a pious and moral membership for their churches." Although the ATS publications were generally moderate in tone, they still irritated many southerners. Slavery and rebellion were condemned, abolitionists were praised, civil rights advocated, and freedmen were told that all mankind was of "one blood." The *Freedman*, a monthly newspaper-textbook, favored black rights and took a stand against the pro-white policies of President Andrew Johnson. In late 1866 it even contained an article on Congress's impeachment authority. It is unclear how extensively ATS literature was used in AMA schools. Tappan supported the *Freedman*, frequently submitted articles to its editor, Israel P. Warren, and suggested that the association subscribe for five hundred copies to be sent to the South, but he viewed it more as a newspaper for freedmen than as a school book. Also popular in some schools was Lydia Maria Child's *The Freedmen's Book*, which was generally viewed as more strident than ATS literature.[14] However, Mrs. Child also taught moderation, charity, industry, morality, and humility through biographical sketches of blacks.[15]

Whatever the text, many teachers assumed that their duty to apprise black youth of their responsibilities to God, country, family, and society was as important as teaching academics. Most subjects were combined with lessons in religion, thrift, punctuality, and honesty. John W. Alvord, Bureau superintendent of schools, Congregational minister, and an ardent supporter of AMA efforts, wrote in 1870: "Above all, let there be moral training, virtuous principles, and noble aspirations inculcated in school and out, as bringing their own constant reward; while every mean, low passion or deed is to be frowned upon as debasing and inflicting only pain." The pastor of a New York Presbyterian church reflected the views of many association supporters. He sent the Union Sabbath School of New Orleans a Bible and a United States flag. There was nothing, he told black students, that northerners prized more than these two objects, "nothing that you need more that will give you greater comfort, joy and protection." The Bible, he added, was their "only hope for the hereafter, and a true and steadfast adherence to the good old flag, your only hope for the present life."[16]

Love of country was generally taught and schools were often opened or closed with patriotic songs. Charles P. Day exulted that his Hampton, Virginia, students constantly sang "This Universal Yankee Nation Beats in Some Things All Creation," a quite "lively and patriotic" tune. When Salmon P. Chase informed a Fernandina, Florida, school of Jefferson Davis's capture, the students began to sing "We'll Hang Jeff Davis to a Sour Apple Tree." "John Brown's Body" and "Rally 'Round the Flag" were other popular songs. These tunes, not surprisingly, often angered southern whites. A white woman listening to students at Francis L. Cardozo's Charleston school exclaimed bitterly, "Oh, I wish I could put a torch to that building! the niggers." An exhibition in a Georgia school was closed by seven hundred students singing "The Battle Cry of Freedom." The song was accompanied by the waving of flags and an enthusiasm which convinced a local editor that "*patriotism*, as well as other virtues, is taught in our schools."[17]

Manners, truthfulness, punctuality, and industry were stressed in all classes.[18] An 1867 list of rules and regulations for Fisk in Nashville admonished students to be "polite to one another and to strangers and respectful and obedient to instructors." The course of study for the fall 1877 session at a school in Macon, Georgia, included elementary algebra, English composition, and "Good morals and Gentle manners." Harriet Townsend, a St. Louis teacher, attacked deceitfulness, hypocrisy, and untruthfulness, the "bitter fruits of slavery," among her students. In Savannah, Cornelia A. Drake not only taught reading, writing, and arithmetic, but attempted to infuse her students with "some grains of yankee energy and ingenuity." After school she went from house to house giving "little lectures on tidiness and industry." The AMA's obsession with thrift and industry resulted in the formation of "industrial" classes in many schools. Fannie Gleason taught sewing and household work in Norfolk, Virginia. Teachers in St. Augustine, Florida, and scores of other schools gave periodic sewing classes to train students to make their own garments. At Portsmouth, Virginia, Susan Drummond taught economy, industry, and sewing, but admitted that she had not properly attended to the needlework because she refused to neglect the more important book lessons. More often classes for homemakers were held in the evening for adults. For example, in Savannah "The Mother's Meeting and Sewing Class" was designed to help women better perform their household duties.[19]

Basic to the virtues that the AMA wished to instill in black youth was "a pure practical Christianity"; consequently, religion was an integral part of the curriculum. Many teachers followed the example of Mary Peake in the association's first school and began the day with religious exercises. In Corinth, Mississippi, G. M. Carruthers opened school at 8:00 with students reading scriptures in concert. He discussed the passages read, prayed, and all united in repeating the Lord's Prayer. Students then sang religious songs until 9:00, when classes really began. A Galveston, Texas, teacher daily began and ended school with Bible reading and prayer. But scriptures and prayer were insufficient for some teachers. Religious conversion of new students was confidently expected and sought as eagerly as progress in letters. Teachers' reports sometimes announced with greater thankfulness the number of souls saved than the material gifts received. A Virginia teacher wrote that her students manifested an increasing interest in their studies and appeared to realize the importance of education. "And what is still more hopeful," she added, "some of them are earnestly inquiring the way to Jesus." Blanche V. Harris, a black Mississippi teacher, proudly reported that "a deep seriousness seems to have settled over my whole school, and many with streaming eyes" are asking "what shall I do to be saved." A Memphis teacher apologized for writing headquarters again so soon, "but I have such Glad Tidings that I cannot withhold it. Some of our dear pupils have found Jesus, and others are seeking him." Nearly every student "of responsible age" at Fisk in 1868 was "either a professor of religion or seeking it."[20]

Religious work apparently sometimes interfered with instruction in reading and writing. "During the past week when I have been talking to them of righteousness and of judgement," a New Orleans teacher said, "I have seen the tears start, and then my soul would go out after them to lead them to Jesus." In Hampton, Virginia, Palmer Litts temporarily suspended his evening class to hold religious services. The reason she and her colleagues had taught so little the past month, another Virginia teacher, Emily Stuart, confessed, "is that God has been visiting us with a powerful Revival of Religion, and we have felt quite unlike teaching. Have . . . rather felt it a duty to give the whole time, and our hearts to the work." Teachers at LeMoyne Institute in Memphis began thrice daily prayers in 1875 with the result that "nearly seventy of our dear students . . . found Christ as *Saviour*." A "remarkable outpouring of the Spirit" in Woodbridge, North Carolina, in 1880 caused school to be suspended two afternoons because so many pupils were "weeping over their sins."[21]

Association officials did not advocate dismissal of classes for proselytizing and such action was unusual, but they did strongly encourage the more common practice of holding religious services after school and evenings. A visitor to Ely School in Louisville, Kentucky, noted "the tender interest" teachers took in their students' religious welfare at after-school meetings. Dora Ford led a prayer group each Friday for those who wished to remain. In 1871 Selma, Alabama, teachers began a daily prayer service at which much interest was "manifested by the more intelligent part of the school." Several students who had been converted stood up "determinedly in the face of ridicule" and prayed for those who laughed at them. Prolonged prayer meetings were held nightly at Trinity School in Athens, Alabama, in the winter of 1873. There were also noonday prayers and "a short season of prayer, as occasion seems to demand." After-school religious services were not

obligatory, and although the AMA was closely associated with the
Congregationalists there was little attempt in most schools, at least
during the early years, to place students in a particular sect. In 1867
association teachers came from thirteen different Protestant denominations.[22]

Many teachers were uncomfortable with such active soul-seeking,
but nearly all were zealously pious. Walter White remembered that
"the heavy hand of a strict Puritan Sunday" which his father had ab-
sorbed at Atlanta University "patterned the Sabbath" in his home. A
rigid code of personal conduct was advocated. Lying, stealing, sexual
laxity, drinking, smoking, gambling, and profanity were severely condemned. Many schools organized temperance societies. Students who
joined the Brookhaven, Mississippi, Band of Hope pledged to refrain
from intoxicating liquors, tobacco, and profane language. Most association students readily signed the liquor pledge, but there were
greater problems with tobacco. After learning that her students drank
beer and wine, a Kentucky teacher began holding temperance meetings. Sixty youths agreed to abstain from alcohol, but "five deluded
young men clung to the weed." The teacher persuaded some of her
students to give up tobacco only by convincing them that the habit
would hinder them from someday owning a home.[23]

Whether they were teaching spelling or warning of the evils of tobacco, most instructors preferred quiet, attentive students, which was
no easy accomplishment. Many classes were quite large, with students
at various levels and ranging in age from five to the teens. Moreover,
most black youths, having never attended school, had little conception
of what school was like or how they were expected to behave. While
some teachers reported unusually good deportment, others viewed
black students as rambunctious and rowdy, wild "as the Mexican mus-
tang." But most probably agreed with Samuel S. Ashley that black
students were very much like those of other colors, often wayward and
obstinate. How to discipline students in freedmen's schools was a "delicate matter." Many association agents were hesitant to use physical
punishment because of its reminders of slavery. The Reverend B. F.
Jackson said Charleston teachers believed that their strongest hold on
scholars was through "their religious nature. As slaves they were
ruled by brute force. The debasing influence of that system can be
overcome only by an appeal to their higher faculties. They recover

their self-respect and manhood only in this way." One teacher who at first used the rod abandoned it entirely because, she said, her students had been whipped so much in the past that any chastisement which she was disposed to inflict would have no visible effect. Two North Carolina women avoided using the paddle by employing an elderly black minister to keep order.[24]

Perhaps the most widely used method of discipline was the threat of expulsion, which reputedly was "sufficient to tame the most mounting spirit." When confronted with a group of rebellious boys, however, Mary Williams, a North Carolina teacher, disdained suspension. She "conquered" insubordination with kindness which, she claimed, answered "a better purpose than severity." Other teachers effectively used praise, reward, shame, and censure in front of others. When several Nashville students skipped class to view a public execution, they were compelled to make public confession and promises of amendment. Students in Talladega, Alabama, who missed school to attend a circus were reprimanded before the entire school. Abby Clark and Mary Brownson attempted to suppress "the spirit of mischief, which prevailed most extensively" in their North Carolina school by "constant watching, patience & perseverance," and "concert recitations of portions of scripture bearing upon this matter."[25]

Those teachers unable to love, cajole, or praise their impulsive, talkative, restless students into quiet, diligent scholars occasionally resorted to corporal punishment. Antoinette L. Etheridge, who taught in Morehead City, North Carolina, thought it "better to lead than to drive, to win by gentle entreaty than to intimidate by threats," yet she was at times compelled to employ "severe measures." There were pupils everywhere, she added, "to whom the rod is a more potent incentive to duty than any appeal to the affections or reason." In Vicksburg, Mississippi, Clara Spees administered the rawhide in cases of exceptional misbehavior and put a stop to whispering by inserting a wooden peg (more than an inch long) between the teeth, "bringing the lips into an obtuse angle." William Treadwell transformed a disorderly class in Beaufort, North Carolina, into a well-regulated one by switching. He "took right hold" of two of the worst offenders and thoroughly applied the "oil of birch," which produced a decorous class with an "intense" desire to learn. Parents seldom objected to teachers' using physical punishment. Antoinette Etheridge said parents were invariably disposed to uphold teachers in matters of discipline, an encouragement she thought was often lacking in northern schools. Lizzie S. Dickinson, who taught in Hempstead, Texas, reported that when mothers brought their children to school "they charged me to whip them 'powerful' for they were used to it and wouldn't mind without the stick." Dickinson seldom whipped her students, however, and most other association teachers, including Jane McNeil, never struck children. McNeil's Dougherty County, Georgia, students had "willing minds to learn," she said, but they needed "the most, stern, inflexible *rod using* discipline." She simply could not inflict corporal punishment, even though she deemed it an "imperative duty." She asked to work with someone who could attend to the discipline.[26]

For most teachers discipline was a minor problem compared to others they encountered. Organizing and teaching a freedmen's school was not for the fainthearted. Simply securing a suitable building in an often hostile South was difficult. Frequently whites refused to rent or sell property for black schools. Within a few years the AMA owned comfortable buildings in urban areas, but country schools more frequently remained primitive and crowded. At Fort Totten, North Carolina, a barn without heat or lighting became a schoolhouse. There were no windowpanes and students had "to be *chilled* as well as *lighted* by opening the board shutters." An Arkansas teacher instructed in a cabin minus windows and with no light except from the open door. On some days water froze in the room. David Todd began classes in the lint room of an abandoned Arkansas cotton gin, and Harriet Billings taught in a poultry house in Georgia. "Had the comfort of the feathered tribe been more thought of in its erection," Billings wrote, "mine would have been better secured at present." The cracks were so large in a Fayetteville, Arkansas, schoolhouse that snow fell on the occupants. An Athens, Alabama, school was described as an "old house with wide-open cracks, through which pea-shooters and pop-guns were often introduced to the great discomfort both of teachers and pupils." Black teacher Edmonia G. Highgate taught in a half-completed church in Enterprise, Mississippi, with no stove or windows. There was snow on the ground and students were suffering horribly. She begged for a chimney so that a stove could be installed, but local residents told her it was unnecessary since spring would arrive in a few months.[27]

Inadequate housing complicated almost every aspect of teaching.

Numerous instructors blamed crowded, unsuitable, uncomfortable class-rooms for their disciplinary problems. The North Carolina children who cried "bitterly from the pain of frost bitten hands and feet" surely did not learn well. In the Fort Totten school described above the teacher dressed in a hood, blanket shawl, and thick gloves, but most of her students were less fortunate. "The poor children do suffer so with the cold," a South Carolina teacher wrote of her improperly dressed students. She allowed them to warm themselves three or four at a time in front of a small fireplace. Emma B. Eveleth was forced to dismiss a class of nearly two hundred in Jacksonville, Florida, because some of the pupils had no coats and only thin clothing. There was no stove in the classroom.[28]

Poverty was an even greater impediment to black education than poor schoolhouses. Association teachers viewed irregular attendance as a serious problem, and class size was almost universally reduced during cold spells. Attendance declined in Baton Rouge, Louisiana, when some of the "little ones" could no longer go to school with "bare feet and almost naked bodies." Others, ragged and barefoot, were present when the temperature was so low that teachers required heavy winter clothing.[29] Many students arrived not only scantily clad and cold but also hungry. A Virginia teacher reported that some of her students walked to school barefooted over frozen ground and "we sometimes find tears running down their cheeks, caused by actual hunger." Eliza A. Summers, an AMA teacher on a plantation near Hilton Head, South Carolina, discovered on one occasion that several of her pupils had eaten nothing but wild blackberries for two days. "Rents behind, heavy doctor's bills, poor health, scanty clothing, almost nothing to eat and *no work*—this is the summary of the destitution I find among very many of the poor people," lamented a Macon, Georgia, teacher in 1868. During the panic of 1873 some New Orleans families were near starvation. Many students dropped out of school because education, "which means leisure for children and money for parents[,] must be deferred when bread and clothing are wanting." A Beaufort, North Carolina, class was so poorly fed and clothed that the teacher purchased straw and taught them to make straw hats. Five cents was retained from each sale to buy more straw. The teacher believed that many of the students would have suffered from lack of food without these earnings.[30]

The parents' need of children to work during planting and harvest seasons kept even more black youth away from school than cold weather and improper clothing. Children over ten usually worked in the field, and many of those younger had to "mind child" or scare birds away from the seeds. Others cooked for workers who stayed in the field from sunrise to sunset. Harriet B. Greely lost a majority of her St. Augustine, Florida, class at planting time. In Texas absences were so common that many schools were suspended in November and December for cotton picking. Two Alabama sisters managed to keep up with class by alternating at work and school so that one could always teach the day's lesson to the other. Most parents were anxious to have their children educated, but they also needed their labor for survival. Moreover, many parents, both black and white, failed to realize how much time, study, and perseverance were required to get an education. But there were others such as the Florida father who had nine children whom he insisted remain in school. He needed them to work, but he considered their education more important.[31]

When black children managed to be in school, learning was often inhibited by lack of books and school equipment and by crowded classrooms. Lizzie Welsh began a class at Natchez, Mississippi, in 1864 under a large magnolia tree with few supplies except the handful of books freedmen already had. She used a primer with large letters to teach all who could get close enough to see. Teaching conditions were seldom that primitive, but freedmen's schools commonly lacked for books. The 1872 school term began in Woodbridge, North Carolina, with eight barefooted, ragged students and three worn-out, outdated books. Soon there were seventy-six students, but few more texts. A black Sunday school, after several months of collecting, purchased an eight-dollar library for the Monticello, Florida, school of one hundred students. One reason American Tract Society publications were popular was because of their low price. The AMA sometimes furnished texts, but in some schools students were required to buy their own. Generally city schools were better supplied than those in the country, where textbooks varied widely in quality and quantity. Students at a South Carolina plantation school paid for their books with eggs, sweet potatoes, and other produce and by cutting wood to heat the schoolroom. Mary Wells, a longtime teacher at Athens, Alabama, accepted wood, eggs, cabbage, chickens, and squirrels as payment.[32]

Scarcity of books was accompanied by a dearth of other school supplies. Black teachers Robert and Cicero Harris had a good school building in Fayetteville, North Carolina, but no desks or benches. There were seldom enough maps and blackboards. The AMA, always having limited resources, expended its funds on instructors and buildings and "made do" with available furnishings and school materials. Even so, there were too few teachers. It was a fortunate association teacher who had a manageable-sized class of 30 or 40. Monthly school reports for Georgia in February 1866 list classes of 71, 90, 74, 78, 94, 140, 110, and 135 each with a single teacher. Such large classes made almost any teaching method except concert recitations difficult. Certainly children in such schools were given limited, when any, personal attention.[33]

Despite poor facilities, poverty, white hostility, and occasionally inadequate teachers, black students apparently made rapid progress. Teacher testimony concerning black learning must be treated with some skepticism, however, because in their eagerness to demonstrate that blacks deserved freedom the teachers publicly exaggerated black advancement, sometimes attributing to freedmen talents greater than ordinary people possessed. During and immediately after the war, teachers frequently used superlatives when speaking of their pupils. John G. Fee was only one of many who found their progress "astonishing." Students in Baton Rouge "did better than white children usually do, when they first attend school." An Arkansas teacher enrolled students who "knew nothing," yet within ten days they had learned the alphabet and were reading easily. Augustus C. Stickle, an experienced teacher, reported that he had never seen people learn so quickly. Blacks learned in ten to fifteen days what it had taken him three months to teach whites. The difference, he added, was intense application. Frank Greene, who also was impressed with black ability, was probably correct when he complained that a great fault of some freedmen's schools was the tendency to advance children too rapidly. Teachers, he said, strongly desired to report scholars starting in the alphabet and advancing to the *Fifth Reader* in as many months.[34]

In private discussions teachers were more restrained in their evaluations of freedmen. They recognized that slavery was a poor preparatory school and that the legacy of bondage would be difficult to overcome. Nevertheless, they claimed that if allowances were made for the absence of educated parents and educational experience black aptitude was marvelous. No doubt some were genuinely surprised because they had not expected blacks to learn as quickly as whites. Teachers naturally compared black students with their former white pupils, and a majority, sometimes reluctantly, concluded that there was no appreciable difference in inherent ability. "I was astonished," Frank Greene wrote of closing exercises in Baton Rouge. "I have attended many exhibitions in the North far inferior to ours. The parents were so delighted *that they wept for joy.*" The only distinction between black and white was skin color, said Hattie C. Foote, a teacher in Augusta, Georgia. A few such as S. K. Hyde believed that whether black children could master the same studies taught in northern schools could "only be certainly known by trial. But whatever they are capable of becoming is not now the question," he wrote. "We believe they can be improved which is foundation enough for me. I will not say that I think them a whit inferior to white children—but simply that if they prove to be I should not despair." Other observers agreed with Charles P. Day that blacks "could be brought to a certain point very rapidly and then their progress is more slow." Although his students quickly learned to read, Day said, they took "hold of the niceties of articulations with less vim."[35]

Numerous teachers thought that blacks actually surpassed northern white youth in memorizing, and given the long oral tradition in the black community, such an assumption may not have been unreasonable. On the other hand, some of the teachers believed that blacks were more deficient in deductive reasoning. But such shortcomings, they asserted, resulted from environment rather than innate inability. An Alabama teacher suggested that when judging black students' reasoning ability they should be compared not with Brooklyn students but with children of the frontier or backwoods.[36]

Initially many northerners suspected that mulattoes might be more intelligent than their darker brethren. One of the questions asked on early AMA monthly reports was: "Do the mulattoes show any more capacity than blacks?" An overwhelming majority of agents responded with an emphatic no. Some claimed that "true Africans" were mentally quicker. Many of the more advanced students in city schools were light-skinned, but Francis L. Cardozo, principal of Avery Institute in Charleston and himself a mulatto, quickly pointed out that this was true only because they had been free before the war and had prior education.[37]

Although the testimony of most freedmen teachers may have been biased in favor of their students, that of southern whites was not and the latter were alternately amazed and alarmed at black aptness in the classroom. School exhibitions which featured recitations, debates, speeches, and dialogues convinced them of black progress. Hundreds of students, while obviously not well trained, learned enough in common schools to teach in country districts. Others advanced to secondary and normal schools. Richard R. Wright of Storrs School in Atlanta was correct when he gave General O. O. Howard the following message for northern supporters of black education: "Tell them we are rising, sir."[38]

Freedmen's Relief

"I FOLLOWED scores of children to their graves, who, but for cold and hunger, would have been here today," H. S. Beals wrote from Virginia in 1863. Nearly every teacher had a similar story. Tens of thousands of slaves fled to the blue-coated Union soldiers seeking freedom and found death instead. Huddled together in contraband camps or in makeshift shelters, many died from disease, exposure, and malnutrition. The misery was so great that instruction often became secondary to teachers who were preoccupied with providing physical relief. They became medical directors, sanitary commissioners, and welfare agents, "angels of mercy" whose errand was preservation of life.[1]

A stream of letters from the South gave the same horrifying message of ragged, emaciated, suffering refugees. After Confederate General Nathan Bedford Forrest led a cavalry raid into southwestern Kentucky in late 1862, many slaves fled to Columbus, where they were crowded into a stable without food or blankets. Through intrigue and violence, kidnappers carried some of the escapees back to slavery despite the efforts of an AMA agent. Frederick Law Olmsted said the contrabands at Cairo, Illinois, were either inefficiently or badly treated, ill fed, poorly clothed, dirty, and sickly. In June there were three thousand refugees in Corinth, Mississippi, with more arriving each day. Some lived in tents. Others were without shelter. "Nearly one thousand have come in during the last week, many sick and destitute of even a change of undergarments," wrote Helen Luckey from North Carolina. J. L. Richardson said the fugitives coming into St. Louis were "most of them fearful, timid, not knowing whether they are among friends or foes." Richardson met them with assurances that they had nothing to fear, "that they have now but one master, who is in heaven," but he could not cover their nakedness. W. T. Richardson took a small supply of clothing to a camp near Beaufort, South Carolina, for those who had followed Sherman's army. "Such a company of ragged chld. I never saw before," he wrote. "Mothers begging & pleading for something to cover their poor shivering little ones. My supply was soon exhausted & I was obliged to turn from them with a sad heart."[2]

The military provided shelter and some rations, and most area commanders appointed superintendents of contraband to assist and supervise fugitives. But even when inclined to do so, the military could not adequately meet the needs of contrabands and carry on a successful war effort simultaneously. General John A. Dix, who admitted in September 1862 that the contrabands at Fortress Monroe were "a very great source of embarrassment to the troops . . . and to the white population of their neighborhood," decided to communicate with state authorities about the feasibility of sending them North. He wrote the governors of Rhode Island and Massachusetts that contrabands could not be defended outside the fort in case of a Confederate attack. Moreover, about 1,300 were living in exposed tents and dying at a rate of four to six each day. In the face of the privations and perils of camp, Dix added, a number of contrabands had asked permission to return to their masters. Return of fugitives when masters demanded them was prohibited, but when refugees asked to return, Dix believed he had no authority to deny it and he had repeatedly given such permission. Had they been in the North with reasonable care and comforts, he said, the refugees would not have chosen to go back to slavery. The governor of Rhode Island agreed to care for some of the fugitives. Governor John A. Andrews of Massachusetts declined, saying that the contrabands would become demoralized, wandering vagabonds in the North. He suggested they be kept in the South and armed.[3]

The military could not properly care for contrabands, and the North generally wanted them to remain in the South. Nevertheless, northerners were concerned about the slaves' plight. Scores of relief agencies were formed which sent tons of clothing and food to refugee camps. The AMA made a public appeal for clothes, bedding, Bibles, food, missionaries, and teachers. In 1863 it pleaded in the *American Missionary*: "Christian friends, are there not, in many towns, those who can serve the freedmen and please the Savior by gathering up a box of clothing for these destitute ones. Don't delay, we pray you; but for Christ's sake, help these poor, and help them quickly." The association also cooperated with several superintendents of contrabands. In 1863 General U. S. Grant detailed Chaplain Asa S. Fiske to represent the freedmen's needs to northern philanthropy. Fiske went to AMA headquarters in New York, where Michael E. Strieby was assigned to travel with him. Strieby introduced Fiske to a Quaker merchant in Philadelphia who, after listening for a few minutes, wrote a check for $5,000. Another introduction resulted in a $2,500 check for Fiske. A mass meeting the next day brought $75,000 worth of clothing. The association arranged similar meetings in Massachusetts, Connecticut, and New York. Fiske's association-assisted campaign brought three quarters of a million dollars for Mississippi Valley blacks.[4]

The AMA sent collection agents throughout the North. One of the most efficient collecting teams was William L. Coan and William Davis, the latter a black Virginian. In the first half of 1862 they collected and forwarded to Fortress Monroe and Port Royal more than two hundred barrels of clothing. These gifts, Superintendent of Contrabands Charles B. Wilder said, sometimes literally meant the difference between life or death. During a seven-month period ending in May 1863 Coan and Davis collected almost five hundred barrels of clothing in Ohio and western New York. The AMA also became the forwarding agency for hundreds of churches and relief societies. In February 1864 the Freedmen's Relief Society of Worcester, Massachusetts, sent the AMA two barrels of clothing for Virginia freedmen. Three days later the people of Northbridge Center, Massachusetts, forwarded an additional two barrels. The Sewing Circle of Henry Ward Beecher's Plymouth Congregational Church in Brooklyn, New York, sent several bags and barrels almost monthly. Association Treasurer Lewis Tappan reported that by the end of 1863 approximately three thousand containers of goods and clothing for freedmen had passed through his office.[5]

Much of the clothing was sent to AMA teachers for distribution. In Virginia, Charles P. Day first clothed his students and then sought out destitute adults. Katherine A. Dunning's sole responsibility in St. Louis was to parcel out clothes and food. In New Bern, North Carolina, teacher Susan Hosmer was a relief agent after the school day ended. She refused to hand out charity randomly—first she visited in the community to determine those in greatest need. In a three-month period in 1864 she and her colleagues gave out 1,200 garments. Most AMA agents apparently enjoyed their missionary duties. Another North Carolina teacher, Elizabeth James, declared it a "privilege to distribute thousands of garments among those who could make no return but gratitude and love." Charles B. Wilder wrote from Fortress Monroe, Virginia: "If you could be here and witness the gratitude of thousands relieved and made comfortable by these generous donations—a gratitude not infrequently expressed by the eloquence . . . of tears—you would be constrained to say with me that it is good to be here, notwithstanding . . . the deprivation of the comforts of home." Harriet Beals, however, viewed charity work as the least agreeable of her responsibilities. She wrote that she disliked "playing detective to distinguish the truly needy from liars and deceivers."[6]

Letters from compassionate teachers to friends, newspapers, and journals detailing the freedmen's trials spurred northern giving. Frequently goods sent to the AMA were designated for a certain area in response to a letter received or one read in the *American Missionary.* Northern relief diminished the suffering of thousands of refugees, but it was never enough. Clothing and food usually were exhausted before need. Despite the distribution of numerous barrels of clothing in Norfolk, there remained much destitution. William S. Bell said that freedmen continued to suffer and even die. A Roanoke Island, North Carolina, teacher reported seven burials on Saturday, four on Sunday, and five more on Monday, "and these not from any prevailing diseases, but from 'deep colds. . . .' They take severe colds from lack of shoes and stockings." Materials in which to bury the dead were urgently needed. Ella Roper requested cloth for shrouds, enough to last for quite some time. Mumps, measles, whooping cough, dysentery, and pneumonia decimated the freedmen in Pine Bluff, Arkansas, in early 1864. During a later two-month period, 117 of 650 people died in the same camp. The military surgeon ascribed four-fifths of the deaths to privation, exposure, and malnutrition. William T. Briggs estimated that two thousand people were killed by a yellow fever scourge in New Bern, North Carolina, in 1864. Upon his return to New Bern, Briggs wrote: "The city looks strangely & wears the gloom & silence of 'a city of the dead.' I look in vain for old familiar faces. I ask & almost invariably the reply is, *Dead*—Dead!"[7]

H. S. Beals wrote of distress in Portsmouth, Virginia, in 1864. He said that nearly one hundred women and children had come to him

recently seeking clothing, but that he had little to give. Children huddled together to prevent freezing. Many were without food, fuel, or
clothing. In one house sat a woman suffering with dropsy. "Her son, a
soldier, at home for a single hour, stands by her side, while tears run
down his bronzed face." In another house lay a disconsolate sufferer,
speechless and paralyzed. Nearby sat three blind women. Children of
all ages were dying of exposure. Beals recently had written an order
for the fourth coffin for the same father. Conditions were no better in
South Carolina. At Beaufort, W. T. Richardson doubted that anyone
not present could form an accurate conception "of the wretched, for-
lorn condition" of many of the blacks who followed Sherman's army.
Several were dying daily, in large part because of lack of clothing and
fuel to warm them. By 1865 Union forces were moving into the South
so rapidly and liberating slaves in such large numbers that the need for
assistance increased manyfold. In March of that year the AMA made a
new appeal for northern charity.[8]

Although freedmen were grateful for northern assistance, they did
not idly wait for charity. Many energetically tried to provide for themselves. In a Port Royal church Susan Walker saw contraband women
wearing discarded tablecloths and shawls and men with trousers and
vests fashioned from cast-off floor carpets. Men went to work for the
government, and hundreds of women became laundresses for soldiers.
Teacher D. T. Allen said freedmen around Little Rock, Arkansas,
were "industrious and scorn the thought of being dependent upon the
Gov. for support." Approximately two hundred freedmen were found
living upstream from Vicksburg in fifty neat log huts. Uniontown, a
village of 170 small shelters constructed of logs and split pine, was
built outside Suffolk, Virginia, by freedmen in 1863. They even planned
streets, set out trees, and planted wheat and corn. A shift in military
lines compelled them to relinquish their crops and crowd together pen-
niless and suffering in a freedmen's camp. As C. Peter Ripley and Louis
Gerteis have shown, the military and cotton speculators put many freedmen to work on plantations, but thousands of blacks squatted on and
diligently worked deserted farms without supervision. The association
and other societies encouraged freedmen to cultivate such land. It sent
seeds, tools, harness, and sometimes farm supervisors along with
clothing and food. One AMA shipment to Charles B. Wilder at Fortress
Monroe contained twenty-four plows and cultivators.[9]

Blacks not only tried to support themselves, but those who were able helped the less fortunate. Freedmen in Norfolk, Virginia, led by black AMA teacher John Oliver formed an association in 1862 to aid contrabands coming to the area. Within a short time they collected five barrels of clothing and forty dollars. Portsmouth, Virginia, blacks formed the Human Aid Society in early 1863. A society leader said: "After all the trouble we've had, the Lord is working for us now, and we must work for ourselves. We must show our enemies that we are *men*, that we can take care not only of ourselves, but also of our poor brothers who have no work, and nothing to eat or wear." The speaker was an energetic man who had redeemed himself and his five children from slavery with his own earnings and had managed to purchase a house and garden plot. The society took a weekly collection for the poor which averaged about twenty dollars. In 1866 Nashville freedmen organized a provident association "managed exclusively by themselves" for the "systematic relief of the poor, irrespective of color." Black churches probably provided the most assistance, however. A Virginia teacher claimed that every black church, "no matter how poor and beggarly their membership," had several societies whose members pledged themselves "to help each other in sickness or want, to make regular contributions for the support of the poor in their church or neighborhood, and to provide for the respectable burial of their members."[10]

After the war the AMA hoped to deemphasize freedmen's relief and give greater attention to education as a more effective and lasting method of assisting blacks. It managed to accelerate its educational activity, but was unable to abandon its relief work altogether. Even the vast relief effort of the Freedmen's Bureau failed to end the destitution caused by the war, emancipation, and dislocation of the southern economy. In May 1865 Bureau agent Thomas W. Conway appealed for northern aid for 30,000 pauperized Alabama freedmen. Many had starved to death, he said. "I see freedmen every day who come scarred, mangled, bleeding from the brutal treatment of their oppressors." Florida freedmen were living in a "most wretched manner." Everything in "the shape of a house, hut or hovel" available to freedmen in Jacksonville was overflowing. In the District of Columbia freedmen lived in improvised shanties in alleyways or in abandoned army fortifications.[11]

A Norfolk, Virginia, teacher reported in August 1866 that two-thirds of the local blacks were "near a state of starvation." Children ate lunch early at school because it was their first meal of the day. A Macon, Georgia, teacher described the condition of freedwoman Sally Franklin: "She is starving—the day is cold but she lies without covering, in an open building . . . a baby is wailing at her side, and the mother's bosom is bare, as though her last conscious act had been an effort to nurse her child; it is Tuesday, and I learn, after she has tasted a little gruel, that since Saturday she has had but a morsel of bread." When a Kentucky woman begged the Reverend A. Scofield for a blanket, he followed her home to see if she was really in need. "But, oh me! What a house!," he wrote. "Slabs nailed in the form of a pen, about eight feet square. With a rude fireplace on one side, one bench and a pail, comprised the whole furniture. On a few loose boards . . . lay a pile of rags which served for a bed. A loose board answered for a door, and open cracks and corners supplied the place of windows!" Two women and six children were living there without food. Scofield gave them two blankets. In Slabtown, a community near Fortress Monroe, Susan Clark discovered an elderly woman and her grandchild "lying in bed, with snow drifted in . . . about the neck and shoulders of the little boy." They were in bed for warmth since they had no food or fuel. Under such conditions AMA teachers were constrained to continue doubling as relief agents. Indeed, many of them used part of their paltry salaries for freedmen.[12]

In June 1866 Atlanta teachers gave out 345 articles of clothing including 36 dresses, 39 skirts, 44 pairs of trousers, and 41 coats, plus farina, dried apples, grits, beans, and other food. During the winter of 1866–67 the association assisted an average of one hundred people daily in Richmond. The same winter was so severe in Beaufort, North Carolina, that H. S. Beals gave food and wood to the needy, including whites. In 1865 the AMA sent $61,674 worth of supplies to freedmen. The amount increased the next year to $105,441. From July 1864 to July 1869 the association contributed $350,894 to destitute blacks. It was still providing relief on a smaller scale in the 1870s and 1880s.[13]

As will be discussed in a later chapter on the black community, the AMA did more than merely feed the hungry and clothe the naked. Benton Barracks in St. Louis was transformed into "a school, a hospital, a refuge, a *Home*." An observer in Kentucky doubted whether the association had another agent who had "come so many times between the poor & death" by starvation and exposure as A. Scofield. He had also "saved many widows & orphans their entire claims against the gvt. for the services of a dead father or husband." Other agents visited freedmen's homes, wrote and read letters, and gave counsel when it was sought. In 1866–67 Beaufort, North Carolina, teachers and missionaries made more than three hundred home visits among freedmen. The association also placed blacks in contact with Bureau agents, tried to protect them from brutality, and helped make the northern public aware of how blacks were treated. In 1866 the *American Missionary* reported sixty cases of outrages against Kentucky freedmen "unparalleled in their atrocity and fiendishness."[14]

Among the more pitiful victims of the fearful conditions during and after the war were black children. Thousands were deprived of parents by migration, dislocation, war, exposure, and disease. Every major black population center had hundreds of orphans, many of whom were taken in immediately by other blacks. Teachers took the remaining children into their own homes, placed them with other black families, and occasionally sent them North. In 1864 a teacher gathered approximately fifty children and found homes for them in white families in Pennsylvania, New York, and New Jersey. A few months later most of the children were reportedly doing well, but the association considered it an experiment and orphans were never sent in large numbers to the North. Rather, the association established a number of temporary orphanages.[15]

In 1863 AMA agents James F. Sisson, Rachel Patten, and Mary Doxey opened an orphanage at Ferry Point, Virginia. The first inhabitant was Margaret Ann Monday, who had run away from her mistress. She arrived in a thin, tattered calico dress and worn-out shoes with a ragged kerchief on her head and with "no undergarments, whatsoever, on, or in her bundle." Her only change of clothing was a worn muslin dress. Margaret had no mother and her father was a Confederate conscript. Patten became the head of the orphanage, and she soon gathered in numerous other homeless children, twelve of whom died between 16 September and 14 November even though they enjoyed better food, clothing, and shelter than the freed children in refugee camps. By April 1864 there were ninety-four orphans. Classes were held for those old enough to attend. A black minister who visited Ferry Point in May proclaimed the orphanage "one of the star interests" in eastern Virginia. "Too much," he added, "could not be said concerning the good" Rachel Patten and her colleagues were doing.[16]

In 1866 the AMA established orphanages in Wilmington, North Carolina, and Atlanta, Georgia, in response to appeals from its teachers and missionaries. Two years earlier General William T. Sherman had moved 12,000 refugees to the Wilmington area. An estimated one-third of them died before the summer was over, leaving the city crowded with parentless children. Previous pleas for an orphanage were renewed by Samuel S. Ashley. He told of a policeman who saw several children clustered in front of a house crying. When asked what disturbed them, they replied that they were hungry and could not awaken their mother. Upon entering the house the officer found the mother "cold in death" and the father near dead with smallpox. The father died soon afterwards, leaving the children homeless. A few months later Ashley wrote of a father and mother who had died, leaving four children under ten living alone. They contracted smallpox. When an AMA missionary arrived, one had died and the corpse was still lying in the room. Another seriously ill child lay beside the body, and the other two were sick. "There they are, the dead and the living—the dead unburied,—the living, starving, naked, sick and none to care for them," Ashley wrote. The dead child was buried and the other three were placed in a smallpox hospital. But, Ashley asked, what would become of them when they were discharged?[17]

The association responded to his plea for an orphanage by authorizing the purchase of a lot and measures for the temporary relief of needy children. It then invited "special" contributions for an asylum through the *American Missionary*. Within a month $1,600 had been pledged, but before the pledges could be collected J. J. H. Gregory of Marblehead, Massachusetts, asked the privilege of assuming the full cost of an asylum. The association quickly purchased fourteen acres outside Wilmington and opened the orphanage 29 May 1866.[18] The $1,600 previously subscribed, combined with a donation by Ichabod Washburn, a Worcester, Massachusetts, manufacturer, was used to establish an orphanage in Atlanta. The AMA opened an additional orphanage in Adrian, Michigan, which served primarily as temporary quarters for southern black children until northern homes could be found for them.[19] There is no clear statement in AMA records of how many black orphans were placed in northern families, but it apparently was no more than a few hundred.[20] Rebecca Crawford, the second matron at Atlanta, was especially zealous in seeking northern sponsors for children. She wished to send them to the North, where, she said, they would be better cared for and *"taught how to live."* She once sent out a group of eighty-five children. Her eagerness to ship orphans North earned her a severe rebuke from the AMA. She preferred transferring them to the Adrian asylum to returning them to relatives who had temporarily placed them in the institution because they were unable to care for them. The relatives' initial action, she protested, had severed all their claims to the children—she had as much right to find homes for them as if they had no relatives.[21]

Although not an orphanage, the Hathaway Home for the Poor and Friendless in New Orleans cared for many children. This home was established in 1871 when Elisha Hathaway of Bristol, Rhode Island, deeded property worth $20,000 to care for ill and destitute freedmen. The property was transferred to independent trustees, but in cooperation with the AMA. It was operated locally by a board of trustees which reported to the association. Hathaway Home provided food, clothing, temporary quarters, and medical treatment. In 1872 Dr. James T. Newman, a black physician connected with Straight University's medical department, prescribed for 2,609 people. Although it was established for freedmen, Hathaway Home gave refuge and medical care to indigent whites as well. In 1872 Dr. Newman treated 924 foreign-born patients, only 9 percent of whom were African. The largest numbers came from Ireland, Germany, Russia, France, and Mexico.[22]

The AMA orphanages seldom had as many as one hundred inmates, a fact that bears strong testimony to the freedmen's willingness, even determination, to care for their own. The turnover rate of orphans was high as black families adopted them and they were reunited with relatives who had been separated by the war. A few of the older children became servants in white homes. From the beginning the association had viewed the orphanages as temporary. After the South was restored, the AMA decided that asylums should not be permanently maintained by northern benevolence. The Adrian orphanage was closed in the late 1860s. In 1869 the Atlanta institution was also closed, and the remaining twenty children removed to Wilmington, North Carolina. In 1872 the Wilmington property was sold and the proceeds transferred to Greenwood, South Carolina, to support the Brewer Normal School.[23] Teachers continued to support orphans, occasionally sending children to northern homes. They provided relief especially to association students, but by 1870 this was only a minor part of AMA activity.

The association saw not only orphanages but all of its relief efforts as temporary expedients necessary because of the perilous times. It believed that under normal circumstances all who were able to work should care for themselves. Naturally, there were always some incapable of self-support, but they were a local responsibility. Even some of those who most aggressively sought aid for freedmen feared that too much unnecessary charity demoralized the recipient. Such people suggested that blacks who could afford to should be asked to pay a small amount for goods they received. Association officials generally agreed. Charity was obviously essential for the present, but they wished to inculcate in freedmen the "obligations of earning their own living by lawful industry." In 1864 the association informed teachers and missionaries of its relief policy. If, after furnishing their "urgent necessities," freedmen could pay from their earning a little for clothing, it was best to require it "in order that they may feel a laudable independence" and at the same time provide the means to supply the more destitute. Teachers were urged to inspire blacks with the "desire to live on the profits of their own labor . . . so that they might feel the necessity of being frugal, industrious, and self supporting." The greatest assistance that could be given the poor, the association continued, was to teach them to help themselves, and "the sooner the freedmen realize the necessity and advantage of self support, the better it will be for themselves, their families and the country."[24]

The AMA was never able to escape completely the need to furnish assistance to blacks during Reconstruction. The weak southern economy and black lack of property and capital combined with discrimination guaranteed that most blacks would remain impoverished. After the war, however, the Freedmen's Bureau assumed the major responsibility for providing physical relief to freedmen, which permitted the association to focus its resources and energies on black education. In the meantime the AMA in cooperation with other relief agencies had eased the suffering of thousands of freedmen. Even larger numbers would have perished from hunger, exposure, and disease without its timely aid.

Friends and Allies

HE CIVIL WAR spawned dozens of freedmen's aid societies with which the AMA alternately cooperated and feuded. Fortunately differences were subordinated during the war, and the diverse societies worked together for the relief and education of former slaves. In 1862 George Whipple and Lewis Tappan helped found the National Freedmen's Relief Association in New York, which coordinated its activities in Port Royal, South Carolina, with the Boston Educational Commission. The latter agency's clothing and supply committee sent tons of goods to its southern stations through the AMA.[1]

In 1864–65 Freewill Baptist and Boston Educational Commission teachers lived in the association mission home in Norfolk, Virginia. Teachers from different societies worked in the same schools in Savannah without rivalry, and the superintendent of Negro affairs in North Carolina, Horace James, marveled at the cooperation in his state. "It is like soldiers of the regiments fighting side by side, though gathered from the east and from the west, from the north and from the south," James said. When Richmond fell to Union forces, William H. Woodbury, AMA superintendent in Norfolk, was one of the first men to secure a pass to the Confederate capital. He opened a school there for each association represented in Norfolk so that all could have an equal start. In Missouri, Isaac T. Gibson, agent for the Iowa Yearly Meeting of Friends, also represented the AMA and the Northwestern Freedmen's Aid Commission. Occasionally societies held joint public meetings to solicit funds.[2]

The association also worked closely with the African Methodist Episcopal church. In 1864 the AMA proposed to the A.M.E. annual conference that the latter furnish buildings for schools and board for teachers, when possible, and the association would pay the teachers' salaries. The conference accepted the proposal, probably because of the influence of Bishop Daniel A. Payne, who was on good terms with Whipple. The following year Payne visited Whipple and consummated an arrangement even more profitable to the A.M.E. church whereby the church and the association jointly paid A.M.E. southern missionaries. The presumably nonsectarian AMA helped plant African Methodist Episcopal churches in the South. When Bishop Payne went to England on a fund-raising tour, Whipple gave him letters of introduction to English friends. Whipple was also friendly with Bishop John Mifflin Brown, who had been one of his students at Oberlin. Despite Whipple's closeness to Payne and Brown, cooperation turned into competition when the AMA later began to establish Congregational churches in the South.[3]

Not surprisingly, the AMA cooperated with the nation's most important all-black freedmen's aid organization, the African Civilization Society, since they shared several officers and members. Moreover, both were nondenominational and required their members and teachers to be evangelical. That the society contended that blacks were best able to educate former slaves seemed to create little friction. The association and other white-dominated societies would have done well to learn from the African Civilization Society, which aimed to prove the fitness of blacks to teach and lead their own people. Probably more than any other, this society taught racial pride.[4]

As the number of societies increased and their work expanded, jealousy and friction became more apparent. Teachers preferred the safest localities, and societies tried to occupy places where success would be most obvious. John Eaton, superintendent of freedmen for the Department of Tennessee, observed that agents' loyalty to their organization "led occasionally to forms of self-seeking strangely at variance with the heroic self-sacrifices which the same individuals were constantly making." Even when rivalry was absent, there was still a lack of systematic cooperation and direction. Several societies might compete in major cities while smaller towns were ignored. The AMA's aggressive and often successful attempts to occupy desirable points created resentment. A teacher from the New England Freedmen's Aid Society referred to the AMA as "that modest association, which, having appropriated to itself the worlds above, claims as its own also the Whole of the United States." Although the statement was made in anger, there was some substance to the charge. The AMA, no less than other societies, sought to expand its influence and it was becoming more concerned about what was taught and who did the teaching. As Lewis Tappan said, "No matter who does the work if it be well done but there is the rub."[5]

Most of the aid societies recognized the need for coordination, and under the leadership of General Oliver O. Howard, commissioner of the Freedmen's Bureau, considerable unification occurred soon after the war. A majority of the secular agencies, together with western religious organizations, unified in the American Freedmen's Union Commission. The AMA declined an invitation to join the AFUC, however, and continued to receive support from denominations that did not have their own aid organizations. The Methodist Episcopal church, the Presbyterians, and the American Baptists established their own societies. By 1866 the AFUC and the AMA dominated black education, and this set the stage for petty rivalry, infighting, and even public attacks upon fellow laborers.[6]

To an unusual degree the AMA and the AFUC reflected two contending antebellum abolitionist traditions that had been apparent since the National Freedmen's Relief Association and the Boston Educational Commission (AFUC) began work in South Carolina in 1862. The AMA was evangelical abolitionist and emphasized religion in its schools. The Educational Commission was dominated by the secular reformism of the Garrisonians and by Universalism, Rationalism, and Unitarianism, principles the AMA pointedly rejected. The AMA was nonsectarian and evangelical. The AFUC was nonsectarian and nonevangelical. From the beginning there had been competition as well as cooperation between these two groups. They had competed for northern funds and endorsements, and their teachers were sometimes incompatible. An association teacher wrote that he had found some "good Christian Ladies" among AFUC teachers, but that there were others who made "no pretensions to piety & some who are evidently infidel in their creed. It must be demoralizing upon the colored people to have their professed friends and teachers engage in cardplaying & dancing & such like amusements." A black AMA teacher and A.M.E. minister, William D. Harris, said after touring North Carolina and Virginia that he wished "to God" the association "possessed the whole ground." He deplored "the Unitarian seed, now being sown hitherto unknown among this people." Other societies not only failed to care for the spiritual needs of freedmen but paralyzed AMA efforts, he added. Harris had visited many teachers' homes from other societies and had seen "no Bibles, heard no prayer—saw no family altar erected."[7]

Differences which had been subdued during the war sharpened in 1866–67 when the association publicly gave new emphasis to the need for evangelical education. The AFUC responded by accusing the AMA of establishing parochial schools and of placing proselytizing above education. These AFUC statements angered its own western branches, which had required its teachers to be Christian. In 1866 the Western Freedmen's Aid Commission at Cincinnati withdrew from the AFUC and "became cooperative" with the AMA. It was followed by the Cleveland branch in 1868. This resulted in a serious loss for the AFUC and a strengthening of the AMA.[8]

Although the AMA and the AFUC frequently cooperated, exchanged ideas and teachers, even shared members, and met in 1867 to discuss dividing fields for normal schools, the deleterious rivalry continued. In 1866 the AFUC accused the AMA of being the Congregational organ for denominational work, perhaps forgetting that there were two purely Congregational missionary agencies for organizing churches. It slyly added that Congregationalists should support the AMA just as other denominations aided their missionary boards. The association angrily denied that it was a denominational society, pointing out that several denominations and even secular groups supported it. Later the AFUC inaccurately charged that the AMA was a missionary society to plant churches, that its schools were only incidental. It was "actuated by no jealousy, either of the American Missionary Association or the church which it represents," the AFUC virtuously claimed, adding that it was the one society that was "both undenominational and unecclesiastical." Continued charges caused Whipple to complain that "a prominent officer of a branch of the A.F.U. Com. seems to think their existence conditional on ruining our reputation." The association usually did not publicly attack the AFUC by name, but it emphasized the necessity of religious education.[9]

The AMA enjoyed a distinct advantage in this somewhat shabby rivalry. It was an older organization with relatively stable sources of income. Since it was a religious organization it could depend upon church support. The AFUC had to rely on northern enthusiasm for

black education, which was short-lived. Moreover, association teachers often were able to develop greater rapport with freedmen "because their own evangelical piety was more akin" to the former slaves'
"religious experience than was the secularism of the A.F.U.C. teachers." As one teacher said, the surest way to black "affection and confidence" was "through their religious feelings. In fact, they distrust no
one so soon as he who *depreciates religion.*"[10] Sadly, the AFUC's expenditures and the number of its teachers gradually declined until it
disbanded in 1869, when its officers concluded that its work was done.
In the meantime, it had made significant contributions as one of the
outstanding educational societies for freedmen.[11]

The greatest ally of the AMA and other societies struggling to provide relief and education for former slaves was the Freedmen's Bureau, created in March 1865. Association officials and leaders of other
organizations vigorously lobbied for a federal agency to assist blacks in
their transition to freedom. Freedmen's education was not at first a
major Bureau responsibility, but Commissioner Howard believed that
education was "the true relief" for blacks and by 1871 he had channeled more than $4 million into schools. Soon after his appointment as
commissioner, Howard invited the "continuance and cooperation" of
educational societies and promised to assist them as well as state
authorities in "the maintenance of good schools for refugees and freedmen" until a system of public schools could be sustained by local gov-
ernments. He reminded existing societies that it was not his purpose
to supersede them but to "systematize and facilitate them." In order to
coordinate the work, Howard appointed superintendents of schools for
each state.[12]

Initially Whipple feared that the AMA's religious orientation would
injure it with the Bureau. An AFUC officer, apparently with a view of
inducing the AMA to join, told Whipple that Howard had said denominational attempts to share the educational work were unnecessary, uneconomical, and unwise. Whipple assured the Bureau that
though it advocated religious education the association was not denominational. Still, he believed there was a conspiracy to "shut us out
from cooperation with the Bureau, or compel us to work" through the
AFUC. Whipple's fears were unfounded. The association received
more Bureau funds than any other society. Indeed, contemporaries
alleged that Howard, a Congregationalist, favored the AMA because

of its Congregationalist ties. Apparently even some of Howard's friends believed that. Rebecca Bacon, a Hampton teacher, wrote her father at the behest of her principal, Samuel Chapman Armstrong, asking him to urge Howard to award $25,000 to Hampton. "I judge he is particularly open to influence from Congregational ministers like yourself," she said. Howard hotly denied the accusations, claiming that the AMA received funds in proportion to its activity. There is little evidence that Howard preferred the association because of denominational prejudice. In fact, he at first dealt mainly with the AMA and the AFUC, the latter a publicly proclaimed secular society. Nevertheless, the association became Howard's favorite society because of the extent and type of its work and because of his growing friendship with Whipple.[13]

Whipple and Howard's first meeting was arranged by John W. Alvord, the general Bureau superintendent of education. Alvord, an evangelical abolitionist, and Whipple had been friends since their days as Lane rebels. The association had considered employing Alvord as corresponding secretary in 1864, and he was obviously sympathetic with its aims. Whipple had advised Alvord about selection of state superintendents of education, and it was to him that he confessed his fears that the secular societies were trying to prevent AMA cooperation with the Bureau. "I have written to you my dear Brother freely," Whipple stated, "as we are accustomed to show each other our hearts." After receiving Whipple's letter, Alvord had a "long talk" with Howard and concluded that Whipple should talk with Howard personally. "Better come soon," Alvord wrote. "I shall be here for the week to come. Will expect you."[14] It was undoubtedly at this September 1865 meeting that Howard and Whipple became acquainted.

Within a few months Whipple and Howard, the latter known as the "Christian General," had become good friends. They were both evangelical Christians and preoccupied with the future of former slaves. With negligible previous experience and no precedent to follow in directing the Bureau, Howard was understandably impressed with Whipple's vast knowledge of freedmen's affairs, and he often relied on his advice. Soon after their first meeting Whipple urged the retention of confiscated lands and homesteads for freedmen. Howard responded that Whipple's suggestions were practical and in accord with his own "spirit and practice." In 1866 Whipple sent Howard a detailed letter specifying a way by which he could assist the aid societies. The Bureau's eventual transportation, ration, and rental policies were curiously close to Whipple's suggestions. In 1867 Howard referred Peabody Fund officials to Whipple as "an excellent man to consult with, from his extensive and practical knowledge of the South." Later, when Whipple was seriously ill, Howard anxiously inquired about his health, adding, "We all have enjoyed your counsel so long and it has been given so freely that we hardly realize the wisdom God has vouchsafed to you until we come to the fear of losing it." The commissioner once called Whipple "my beau ideal of wisdom."

Whipple, on the other hand, was certain that General Howard was the best possible choice for Bureau commissioner. Howard was offered the presidency of Lincoln College in Kansas in 1866, and Whipple was asked to urge him to accept. He wrote Howard that as president of Lincoln he would exert a strong force upon the formation of western character and influence, but added: "Every Christian heart in our land rejoices in the belief that you have been providentially placed where you now are; and there would be a general mourning at any thought of your removing or being removed from your present position, while the Bureau lasts." Whipple and Howard developed a relationship sufficiently secure to enable them to give candid and sometimes unpleasant assessments of each other's work and staff. Both gave advice freely and both fired subordinates at the other's request. By seeking favors for all freedmen's aid societies rather than for his alone and by carefully subordinating the association's connection with the Congregationalists, Whipple was able to gain the confidence of Alvord and Howard and thereby greatly benefit the AMA financially.[15] Perhaps too much should not be made of the Whipple-Howard friendship. Howard also relied on Erastus M. Cravath for advice and knew AMA Treasurer Edgar Ketchum well enough to stay in his home several times. More important, Howard considered the association's methods of starting and maintaining schools practical and effective, and its aims for freedmen were compatible with his. Moreover, on a day-to-day basis Whipple's friendship with Alvord may have been more significant for the AMA than his relationship with Howard.[16]

As Bureau commissioner, Howard could not afford to appear partial to the AMA, and probably he was not during his first year in office. But as he learned more about freedmen's education he became more impressed with the association, its goals, efficiency, and management, and took a greater personal interest in its success. He attended AMA annual meetings, often at association expense, and became acquainted with teachers and principals who told him of their need. The Freedmen's Bureau gave $18,000 to Berea College shortly after Howard met its leaders at an annual conference. Cravath persuaded Howard to make a speaking tour of the Midwest to stimulate "a new impulse" in collection work. Whipple wrote soon thereafter bluntly asking the commissioner to speak on behalf of freedmen and the association. At a meeting with Secretary of War Edwin M. Stanton, Howard "said all I could in the interest" of the AMA. Of course, Howard spoke for and visited other societies as well, but not as often. He was more comfortable with evangelic AMA leaders than with officers of the AFUC, who constantly scolded him for aiding sectarian societies.[17]

The AMA's relationship with assistant commissioners and Bureau state superintendents of education were almost as important to its work as the friendship with Howard. After all, many of the decisions to give or withhold aid were made on the state level. Most of the assistant commissioners were sympathetic to the association, but there were a few exceptions. General Davis Tillson of Georgia had "about the same regard for negro elevation that planters generally entertain," and as a result AMA representatives were hesitant to press him for funds. He was soon replaced by a friendlier officer. In South Carolina, Bureau Superintendent of Education Reuben Tomlinson was judged "an estimable and impartial" man, but he preferred the AFUC and secular education. He and his assistant superintendent, B. F. Whittemore, engaged in a "pointed controversy" over religious influence in the schools. Whittemore wanted to place the entire state under the AMA's "strong influence."[18]

The importance of good relations with the Freedmen's Bureau is illustrated by the AMA's experience in Texas. General Edgar M. Gregory appointed E. M. Wheelock as superintendent of education and George W. Honey, an AMA agent, as assistant superintendent, an arrangement that pleased the association. Gregory was soon replaced by General J. B. Kiddo, whose drinking was interfering with his duties, Honey reported. After Howard reprimanded him, Kiddo became more amenable, but Honey was summarily fired by Jacob R. Shipherd, AMA corresponding secretary in Chicago, because Kiddo did not wish to work with him. Shipherd now concluded that Kiddo had "taken hold right nobly," but he criticized Superintendent of Education Wheelock for being anti-AMA and asked that he be dismissed.[19]

Indeed, Wheelock favored the AFUC, despised the association, and was unhappy with what he perceived as Bureau partiality toward the association. He wrote the Boston *Recorder* in 1866 that the Bureau was "now wholly on sectarian evangelical grounds. I am the only unitarian who has a position in the Bureau and am expecting my dismissal at any moment. The state is filled with hungry wolfish bigots who are indorsed by the various freedmen aid societies and who come to fleece the freedmen." Wheelock added that he had tried to oppose the "wolfish bigots," but with little success. In fact, he had effectively poisoned other Bureau agents, one of whom denounced association officers as Jesuits and hypocrites.[20]

Upon receiving Shipherd's charges against Wheelock, Howard intimated he would be fired, but after communicating with the most recent assistant commissioner, General Charles Griffin, Howard decided that Wheelock would be retained and that D. T. Allen, an AMA agent, would be appointed assistant superintendent of education. Soon afterwards Wheelock was relieved as superintendent of education, but became inspector of schools. Shipherd still was not satisfied. He complained that school affairs were now referred to the inspector of schools rather than to the Bureau superintendent. Wheelock treated AMA teachers disdainfully and sent them to unpopular and unprotected posts, he said. Allen concluded that if Wheelock stayed the AMA might as well withdraw.

In early April 1867 Shipherd begged Howard to fire Wheelock. Certainly, he wrote, "you do not wish to pay a man $150 a month to slander you in the newspapers, and to upset the work you are so generously helping us to do." Two weeks later Shipherd again demanded Wheelock's dismissal, which, he said, was "vitally essential to the prosperity of the work." He reminded Howard that he had fired Honey upon Kiddo's request but with the assurance that the courtesy would be reciprocated by the removal of Wheelock. "What possible end can be served," he asked, "by retaining to control evangelical Christian schools, a profane, indolent, scoffing ex-Unitarian preacher, whose record for five years is one continuous narrative of malfeasance and misfeasance?" Shipherd then added a statement that undoubtedly irritated Howard: "If you do not regard him more truly your friend than the Secretaries of the A.M.A., you will at length give us proofs of so much." By this time both Howard and General Griffin were weary of Shipherd, and the former suggested to Whipple that the association review its Texas operation "with reference to adjusting the difficulties that have arisen." The Texas controversy played a major role in Shipherd's eventual dismissal by the association.[21] Although Shipherd annoyed Griffin and Howard, his constant carping improved the AMA's position in Texas. In mid-1867 Bureau Superintendent A. H. M. Taylor met with Whipple in New York to arrange school affairs in Texas. Whipple agreed to send necessary teachers, and Taylor promised to have schoolhouses ready upon the teachers' arrival. Taylor's successor also worked closely with the association.[22]

The Texas controversy was unusual as the AMA ordinarily managed to maintain amicable relations with state and local agents. Some of the state superintendents were frankly partial to the association. E. W. Mason of Louisiana proclaimed that the AMA accomplished more, with less government aid, than any other society in his state. Its "unsectarian character," he said, which enabled it to embrace all denominations, largely increased its influence. Mason, who even advertised Straight University on his letterhead stationery, admitted that he made the AMA "a favorite channel for Bureau aid." Arkansas Superintendent William M. Colby sought primarily AMA teachers, and Georgia Superintendent Edmund A. Ware wrote the association: "The interests of the A.M.A. are our interests." Ware's predecessor, G. L. Eberhart, offered to commission all AMA agents as his assistants without pay, "thus bringing them into official connection with the Bureau." Bureau Superintendent H. R. Pease of Mississippi reported in 1868 that the AMA had done more than all the other societies combined and that its teachers were "among the most earnest and competent." In Tennessee, General Clinton B. Fisk, though an officer of the Freedmen's Aid Society of the Methodist Episcopal church, claimed that the association had "a No. 1 warm place in my heart." The Kentucky assistant commissioner asked Erastus M. Cravath to select the Bureau superintendent of education.[23]

A number of men served as Bureau agents and AMA representatives simultaneously, the most prominent example being Charles H. Howard, the commissioner's brother. Howard, who was Bureau in-

spector of schools, retained his position when he replaced Shipherd as
AMA district secretary in Chicago. The Bureau continued to pay
Howard's salary, and his dual position certainly enhanced his usefulness to the association. At least a dozen AMA principals and agents
were appointed to minor Bureau positions. Others were made agents
without pay, enabling them to travel on Bureau funds. In 1886 Commissioner O. O. Howard identified Whipple as an unpaid Bureau
agent, and in 1870 E. P. Smith was commissioned by the Bureau to
tour southern schools at Bureau expense. He promised to report to
Howard on conditions in the South.[24]

It is not surprising that other agencies accused the Bureau of favoritism toward the association. Officers of the Methodist Episcopal
church's Freedmen's Aid Society, aware that both Alvord and Commissioner Howard were Congregationalists, "saw a settled design to
place the whole work of educating the colored men . . . under Presbyterian and Congregational influences through federal encouragement" of the AMA. James B. Simmons of the American Baptist Home
Missionary Society complained that both the AMA and the AFUC had
received more funds than the Baptists. After an explanation from
Howard, Simmons apologized, saying that Howard had been fair. He
now realized that the Bureau aided those who worked and that those
who worked most received the greatest support.[25]

The AFUC made the bitterest charges of favoritism. Even though
the AFUC was itself a favored agency for Bureau aid, one of its officers, J. Miller McKim, early warned Commissioner Howard about
the dangers of supporting religious education. Howard coolly replied
that McKim was aware that his major objective was merely to promote
freedmen's education and to dampen any controversy "between what
you are pleased to call 'undenominational' and other societies, for it is a
work in which we want union, or cooperation, and not division."
Howard continued to work closely with the AFUC, even making fund-
raising speeches for it, but he was unable to soothe their fears of sectarianism. In March 1867 McKim forwarded a clipping of Wheelock's
article to Howard, adding that it was well known that he and Alvord
were Congregationalists, and suggested that they leaned toward the
AMA. He further accused the association of refusing to "cooperate
with us in the work of education on a common platform" and of effort to
"embarrass our Commission with the *odium* theologicum." In July,

Lyman Abbott chastised Howard for aiding Episcopalians, who were even more denominational in their schools, Lyman thought, than the AMA and the American Baptist Home Missionary Society.[26] Howard testily denied that he was "disposed" to grant public funds for sectarian purposes and added that in his view "the so called liberal Christians," meaning the AFUC, were as sectarian as Episcopalians. "It does seem to me," he continued, "that some of our friends take too much pains to search out and worry themselves about the forces that separate the different lots, instead of . . . caring for the sheep in the lot."[27]

Howard was unswayed by Abbott and McKim's claims that separation of church and state was a cardinal American principle which he was violating by supporting the AMA. He gave funds to Episcopalians, Methodists, and Baptists, who were clearly denominational. Alvord reflected Howard's views when he told a Bureau agent who had asked about aiding Catholics that all denominations were inclined to engage in freedmen's work and that all were encouraged not to teach "things of sect technically." At the same time, he said, "They will undoubtedly give them [freedmen] a broad elementary and practical education. If the Catholics will do this, encourage them certainly." Of course, the AMA, the AFUC, and the Protestant denominations would have objected to aiding Catholics. But at that time in the United States there were few objections outside the AFUC to Howard's "intermingling of Church and state" as long as it was Protestants, not Catholics, he assisted.[28]

The 1865 act creating the Freedmen's Bureau did not mention education and no appropriation was made for that purpose, yet Howard imaginatively found ways to assist educational societies. Bureau agents helped place teachers and protected them from hostile whites. Confiscated and surplus buildings were transferred to teachers for use as schools and dwellings. Moreover, teachers were permitted to purchase government rations, and this notably reduced their cost of living in a war-torn South. The right of teachers to buy rations soon ended, but the Bureau continued to provide rations for orphanages. The Bureau furnished so much fresh beef to the AMA orphanage in Atlanta in 1867 that its director sold some to buy cornmeal which the Bureau could not provide. Howard further undertook to relieve the societies of a great expense by providing government transportation to and from the North for teachers. When the military returned railroads to their owners, Howard assisted with Bureau money. In February 1867 the association received $1,557.27 for transporting teachers to Georgia. The expense was so great that Howard limited the AMA and AFUC to $1,000 and "no more" for returning teachers the following summer. For some reason he automatically granted transportation to AFUC and AMA teachers, but other societies had to make special application. As previously seen, the Bureau further benefited the educational associations by appointing a few principals as Bureau agents and paying their salaries.[29]

Far more significant to the AMA than transportation and rations was Bureau support for construction of school buildings. In 1866 Congress appropriated $500,000 for rent and repair of schoolhouses and asylums, but as interpreted by the Bureau the money could be used for constructing new facilities. Howard's policy was that the society purchase the property and the Bureau would help complete the building. Almost every association college, normal, and secondary school was partially built with Bureau funds. At least $80,000 was received in 1867 alone. The Bureau ultimately contributed no less than $300,000 for buildings and property for the AMA and its institutions.[30] In addition, the Bureau in 1869–70 began to deed school property it owned to the AMA, other educational societies, and the states. Property so deeded was to be devoted forever to educational purposes.

By 1868, due to Bureau largess, many educational societies were better equipped with buildings than with teachers. Lack of funds was forcing them to retrench. The Bureau was not authorized to pay teachers, although Assistant Commissioner Wager Swayne had done so illegally in Alabama in 1866–67. Howard devised a clever subterfuge to help pay salaries. The Bureau could legally rent school buildings for freedmen's education. In November 1868 Howard authorized the societies to charge the Bureau rent for the buildings they owned. The rent could then be used to pay teachers. Based on Howard's promise the association sent a larger corps of teachers South in 1869. When Whipple received $9,990 for rentals from Alvord in April 1869, he responded with *"Thanks, many thanks."*[31] In 1869–70 the Bureau paid the association approximately $23,000 in rentals. The importance of the rentals can be seen by examining the number of AMA teachers sent to the field. In 1870 the association had 461 teachers. The next year, after Bureau aid was withdrawn, the number dropped to 309.[32]

It is almost impossible to determine the total amount that the Bureau spent on the AMA and its institutions, since expenditures for association schools were not always separated in Bureau accounts of gross expenditures. The *American Missionary* indicated that the Bureau channeled approximately $213,000 into the AMA treasury, but the total was considerably larger. More than that was spent on construction, repairs, and property. If rations, transportation, rentals, salaries paid those who were employed jointly by the Bureau and the AMA and property deeded to the association are added to construction costs, the total probably exceeds a half million dollars. If funds awarded to the semi-independent Hampton Institute, which was the Bureau's favorite institution, are counted, the total is higher still. Whatever the total sum, the AMA was well aware of its indebtedness to General Howard and the Bureau. Association annual reports commended Howard and expressed gratitude for Bureau aid. Whipple once wrote Howard: "The success of our work, depends under God, much on the success of yours." The Bureau defended the association in times of danger, often provided wise counsel, and greatly increased its potential for educating freedmen. The AMA could not have accomplished as much as it did without the Bureau and other freedmen's educational societies.[33]

Administration and Fund Collecting

THE EFFECTIVENESS of the AMA's southern work depended largely on the efficiency of its central administration, which collected money, hired and supervised agents, and made and implemented policy. The association's initial constitution provided for a president, five to seven vice-presidents, a corresponding secretary (two after 1853), a treasurer, and an executive committee of twelve with the corresponding secretaries and treasurer as ex-officio members. The presidents and vice-presidents were honorary, selected with a view to enhancing the AMA's prestige and fund-raising potential. The primary governing body was the annual meeting constituted of officers and members. It reviewed activities and policies and elected officers. In reality, however, the executive committee, which met monthly in New York, was more influential. Rarely did an annual meeting reverse an executive committee decision, and until 1883 the committee was dominated by the corresponding secretaries and the treasurer.[1] Although the AMA was democratic in organization, its direction and strength came from Simeon S. Jocelyn, George Whipple, and Lewis Tappan.[2]

Jocelyn had a long career of working with and for blacks. As pastor of a black New Haven, Connecticut, church, he had drawn up plans for a black college which was abandoned when local officials refused to cooperate. Later he was a missionary to New York blacks and served on the executive committee of the New York Antislavery Society. It was a Jocelyn speech in 1833, Lewis Tappan claimed, which converted him to immediate emancipation. He was chairman of the Amistad Committee and helped to organize the AMA. In 1853 he became corresponding secretary of the AMA's home department. Jocelyn's gentle nature and reluctance to injure feelings made him much loved by teachers and missionaries, but also rendered him less effective than he should have been. "Father Jocelyn" often gave kindly lectures when severe censure or dismissal was needed.[3]

Whipple had studied at Onedia Institute and at Lane Seminary and was one of the Lane rebels who went to Oberlin in 1835 after the seminary closed its doors to them. Although an ordained minister, he was never a pastor. Rather, he became principal of the Oberlin preparatory department upon graduation and was appointed professor of mathematics in 1838. At Oberlin, Whipple developed close friendships with black students including John Mercer Langston, who lived in his home. While at Oberlin, Whipple continued his involvement with the abolition movement, working for the American Anti-Slavery Society in Ohio and New York. He was a recognized abolitionist figure when he became corresponding secretary for the AMA in 1846. Later he became chief editor of the *American Missionary* and supervisor of foreign missions. When the association began to emphasize missions to freedmen, he shifted his attention to the home department. Whipple was patient with the petty conflicts among teachers and missionaries and generally won their respect and esteem. He wrote thousands of letters of encouragement and, when needed, gentle rebuke. Whipple often worked in the office until after midnight, curling up on his desk to sleep in order to take up the pen at daybreak. At his death he was referred to as "a discreet and sleepless friend of the Freedmen, a trusted counsellor in the trying time of Emancipation, of Lincoln, the Emancipator."[4]

Lewis Tappan, an ardent abolitionist since the early 1830s, was clearly the most influential AMA officer from 1846 until his retirement in 1866.[5] His business acumen and shrewd management were influential in the association's growth and strength. As Bertram Wyatt-Brown has shown, Tappan "scored all too well on the familiar checklist of Yankee do-gooder's grave defects: moral arrogance, obstinacy, cliquish conformity, provincial bigotry, and abrasive manners—with a streak of unpleasant opportunism when circumstances allowed." But he was also courageous, a splendid organizer, a gifted publisher, administrator, and financier of reform causes. He had a "remarkable empathy" for blacks, "an understanding that, while paternal and rather abstract, far exceeded that of most white Americans." He spent much of his seemingly unlimited energy in forwarding the antislavery movement. He lectured, wrote letters and articles, organized societies, financially assisted abolitionists and black vigilance committees, and occasionally hid slave fugitives in his home.

Tappan apparently relished defiance of danger and the hatred of slaveholders. Once he opened a package which contained a black person's ear and a note recommending that it be added to his "collection of natural curiosities." In 1834 a mob vandalized his New York home and made a huge bonfire of his furniture and personal belongings. Threats merely strengthened his resolve. Although intolerant and quick to judge, he could be gentle and thoughtful with old friends, the less fortunate, and children. He believed in hard work, frugality, and keeping his family in material comforts, but he thought amassing and hoarding property with a view to becoming rich was disobedience to God's commands. Christians, he believed, were obligated to give to the poor, to the needy, to hospitals and schools, and to spread the gospel.[6]

As AMA treasurer the irascible Tappan assumed his was the most important office and undertook to supervise and direct Jocelyn and Whipple. He was fond of both men and respected Whipple's judgment and ability. Although he admired Jocelyn's devotion to abolition and the AMA, Tappan regarded him as too much a man of feeling and too unbusinesslike. In 1862 he reproved Jocelyn for being late in getting out the *American Missionary*. When Jocelyn blamed the delay on Whipple's trip to Fortress Monroe, Tappan replied that he doubted Whipple was doing anything more important than getting the publication out on time. "Either I have an imaginary estimate of the disadvantage of delay," he wrote, "or brother W. has an inadequate idea of its disadvantages." Tappan proofread the *American Missionary* and read and criticized the secretaries' articles for publication "in the manner of a pedagogue with a student's composition." When the AMA's teaching force dramatically increased during the war, Jocelyn and Whipple were pressed to keep up with their work. Tappan complained of their want of system, inattention or delay in meeting teachers' requests, failure to answer promptly and thoroughly, and general lack of order. He reminded them that Franklin's motto "A place for everything and everything in its place" would serve them well. He asked for more system, general good housekeeping, proper filing, and a more businesslike atmosphere. Despite his abrasive and authoritarian manner, however, Tappan worked harmoniously with Whipple and Jocelyn. Both possessed remarkable forbearance and appreciated Tappan's

enormous contributions to the association. He in turn had genuine affection for them and frequently apologized for his interference and
temper. Tappan worked less cordially with missionary-teachers. He
thought the secretaries rebuked wrongdoers too gently, and he often
assumed their responsibilities when he deemed severe action necessary. No doubt many teachers agreed with the one who wrote: "I have
been a good deal tried of late by the spirit & manner of LT in New
York, if he is not a centurion it is because he cannot find the number of
one hundred to command. . . . I think him quite too arbitrary and
dictatorial."[7]

All three officers worked hard and for minimal pay. For years Tappan accepted no salary as treasurer.[8] He could afford to volunteer his
services, but Jocelyn and Whipple could not. Neither were wealthy
and both gave up better paying positions to join the association for a
$1,200 annual salary. They had to draw upon their "little property" to
eke out expenses. Whipple was forced to sell his home and board his
family in Jersey City because he could not afford to keep them in New
York. When he informed Tappan in 1862 that he needed a larger salary
to compensate for the rising cost of living, Tappan denied that the
price of bread, meat, and vegetables had increased appreciably and
added, "Considering the small amount of receipts, and the force we
have in the office I do not think we should stand justified in giving
larger salaries to the officers." But it was Tappan, knowing that the
secretaries' salaries had never been sufficient for their support, who
engineered an increase to $1,800 in 1864. Although he considered the
salary still quite low, he objected to more because part of the AMA's
influence, he believed, resulted from the knowledge that it was eco-
nomically conducted.[9] In 1870 Simeon Jocelyn and Michael E. Strieby
said Whipple remained so destitute "that if he were to die today he has
not the means left to bury him." Despite their poverty Whipple and
Jocelyn generously contributed to the AMA from their limited funds.[10]

Although all AMA officers were poorly paid and Tappan sometimes
bullied Jocelyn and Whipple, the three men became an efficient,
smoothly functioning team. Unfortunately, the administration changed
at a critical time. In 1864 Strieby replaced Jocelyn, who resigned because of ill health.[11] An Oberlin graduate and a Congregational pastor in
Syracuse, New York, Strieby was a longtime opponent of slavery and an
eloquent speaker with considerable executive capacity, but he was less

effective than Jocelyn and Whipple in dealing with teachers. He lacked their patience, too often reached conclusions on the basis of insufficient data, and on occasion encouraged teachers to tattle on each other.[12] On the other hand, he was more efficient than Jocelyn, was devoted to the AMA's work, and eventually became a competent, if sometimes erratic, administrator.[13]

The association suffered a more severe blow when Tappan resigned as treasurer and member of the executive committee in 1866 after concluding that poor hearing unfitted him for such duties. Tappan's firm and vigorous leadership was removed at a time when the AMA was rapidly expanding its work and had just instituted a new scheme of district secretaryships in Boston, Chicago, and Cincinnati to assist in collections and in supervising southern fields. The Reverend C. L. Woodworth, who assumed central control of the Boston office, was limited to fund raising. He had no southern field to supervise. The Reverend Edward P. Smith directed the Cincinnati branch until mid-1866, when he became AMA field secretary. The Reverend Erastus M. Cravath, one of the association's most effective school organizers, succeeded Smith. The Reverend William D. Love headed the Chicago office for a few months, with limited results, before being supplanted by the Reverend Jacob R. Shipherd, formerly secretary of the Northwest Freedmen's Commission and the Chicago branch of the American Freedmen's Union Commission. Shipherd was designated western secretary rather than district secretary since he refused to accept the Chicago office unless he was recognized as a full equal to Whipple and Strieby. The Cincinnati office administered missionary operations in Kentucky, Tennessee, Alabama, and parts of Georgia. The Chicago secretary supervised agents in Kansas, Illinois, Missouri, Mississippi, Arkansas, Louisiana, and Texas. Other teachers reported to Strieby and to the recently appointed superintendent of schools, Samuel Hunt, in New York.[14]

Tappan's bookkeeping duties were ably assumed by Edgar Ketchum and William E. Whiting, but they could not fill the leadership vacuum left by his departure.[15] The decision-making responsibilities lay with the professional staff, and it was essential that someone take command. Whipple was the only officer with the experience to take charge, and at first it seemed that he was not up to the task. Lack of firm, decisive leadership led to jurisdictional wrangling among the district secretaries, bickering between Strieby and Hunt, and generally inefficient administration. Teachers complained bitterly about the AMA's slowness in responding to their needs and requests. However, Whipple eventually overcame his early indecisiveness and assumed control. Hunt and Shipherd, the greatest irritants to the other officials, were fired.[16] Strieby took responsibility for personnel complaints and supervising collection agents. Cravath and Smith became skillful field directors, and Whipple dabbled in all these areas, acted as liaison with the Freedmen's Bureau, and was the final authority in administrative matters. Whipple's decade of leadership—1866 until his death in 1876—was probably the most significant in the AMA's history.[17] Naturally, there were still problems. Salaries were often late, teachers' letters sometimes went unanswered, school and college leaders were given little authority, and, most important, there was a constant shortage of funds. Efforts to raise money to support its wide-ranging mission work remained the most pressing responsibility of the AMA.

The lifeblood of the American Missionary Association was the money that flowed into its treasury, and since it had negligible dependable income there was a constant struggle to raise funds sufficient to support its southern workers.[18] Success or failure in collections depended not only upon association exertions but also upon the nation's variable attitude toward blacks, the political climate, and the economy.

Most of the early wartime contributors were association members, abolitionists, or those touched by the plight of escaping slaves. By October 1861 the AMA was receiving money specifically for the benefit of contrabands. A New York woman sent a draft with a postscript: "I pray this may be the beginning of the emancipation of the African race." Another sent two dollars for Lockwood's mission for contrabands with advice to "be sure and take good care of the poor 'contrabands' for God has opened up a new field." Joshua Coffin of the Philadelphia Vigilance Committee in late 1861 began raising money for the association, which, he said, "must be sustained & its efficiency increased." Gerrit Smith, a stalwart antislavery leader whose home in Peterboro, New York, was a haven for black refugees, sent $500 in 1862. He sent an additional $1,000 in 1863 and again in 1864, saying he was happy to contribute to the AMA because of its expenditures for the freedmen's welfare. J. P. Williston, a former association vice-president from Massachusetts, sent checks totaling $2,500, and Ichabod Washburn, a wire manufacturer from Worcester, Massachusetts, contributed $5,000.[19]

Smith, Washburn, and Williston could afford to give thousands, but most supporters gave sums ranging from twenty-five cents to a few dollars. An elderly New Yorker sent a deathbed contribution. "I begin to raise some blood," he wrote, "I expect to be called soon. . . . I want to be ready to go so please to find two dollars. Please use it where most needed at this time." R. W. Lyman, who said he "loved" the AMA work, sent fifty cents "out of my scanty means." Another New Yorker, ninety-two-year-old Anna Parmele, who had been supporting the association since 1849, contributed fifteen dollars, all she "could well spare now," and B. B. Curry of Wisconsin, who previously had been limited to "offering feeble prayers for success of this glorious work," donated one dollar in appreciation of what the AMA had done for "our race."[20]

Sarah Jane Nason of Freeport, Maine, who lived "by her needle," was able to do more. She contributed fifty dollars and drew up a will designating the association as her beneficiary. The AMA "conscience" in Litchfield Corner, Maine, David Thurston, had little money so he became a self-appointed collection agent. Thurston, who mourned that so many New England ministers "should be so blinded to the real character of slaveholding," was an example of a Christian abolitionist. He rejoiced that the war might end slavery, but said emancipation was merely the beginning of Christian work. Christians had a duty not only to minister to freedmen but also to destroy the "vile spirit of caste." There yet remained "very much to be done to remove that unnatural, mean, proud, hateful, cruel, exceedingly wicked prejudice. . . . It is as contrary to the principles of & spirit of Christianity as hatred is to love" he said. He feared that "more prayerful & prolonged efforts" would be required to destroy the deep-rooted, "shamefully wrong & wicked" hatred of blacks than for the removal of slavery since the former was so "extensively tolerated even in church." Thurston tirelessly collected clothing and money for freedmen until he died in 1865 at the age of eighty-six.[21]

Many devoted followers such as Nason and Thurston willed the association parts or all of their property. Most of the legacies were small, ranging from $30 to $700, and sometimes they seemed more trouble than they were worth. When a woman who had lived alone without known relatives for twenty-five years willed the AMA property amounting to approximately $600, nine relatives suddenly appeared to contest the bequest. Mrs. Sally Giddings of Jamestown, New York, deeded one-half of a farm to the association. Shortly after the papers were executed Mrs. Giddings began to demand small favors from the secretaries. Once she asked them to shop for two pairs of shoes and some blue calico. Later she mailed them an old shoe and asked them to have a similar pair made for her. A busy secretary found a shoemaker to make the shoes. When they reached Mrs. Giddings she decided they were too narrow and so returned them, asking that still another pair be made. Soon afterwards Mrs. Giddings burned two of her husband's barns containing sixty tons of hay and considerable oats. When she was carted off to an asylum, her husband asked the AMA to return the portion of the farm it owned as his losses would make it difficult for him to prosper on only half a farm. The secretaries, usually hard-headed businessmen, apparently returned the property.[22] The early legacies generally were too small to appreciably benefit the association.

Many contributors sent donations after reading the *American Missionary*, the association's most important propaganda tool. Indeed, AMA officials attributed 50 percent of the association's annual income to funds received in response to the *Missionary*'s appeals. The *American Missionary* was influential in enlarging and sustaining the special constituency that supported freedmen. Its pages were filled with stories of freedmen's sufferings, hopes, and fears and the association's struggles and successes. Teachers were urged—sometimes virtually compelled—to write moving articles about their work. Jocelyn instructed a Virginia teacher to write for the journal, saying, "We must have things spicy and good." On another occasion Whipple asked a Georgia agent to send some "notable instances of progress in learning—cases of terrible suffering—hopeful conversions to Christ—deeds of hatred and violence on the part of the whites toward the colored. Such individual instances arrest the attention and start the emotions much quicker than any general statement, however correct they may be." An eleven-year-old sent his "first charity money" of fifty cents to aid freedmen after learning about their problems in the magazine. "An aged mother" who had "been greatly moved" by reading of "the poor contrabands" contributed five dollars. A New York man who mailed two dollars for the freedmen wrote that "the reports in your last Missionary has moved me to tears." The *American Missionary* probably contained more information about freedmen than any other source.[23]

Unfortunately the magazine had a limited readership and collections for 1861–62 were disappointingly small. Receipts were actually slightly less than for the previous year. Despite its best efforts, the association had been unable to arouse much enthusiasm for assisting freedmen. The members of a Winnebago County, Wisconsin, church who were Republican in politics but did not care "deeply for the poor slaves" perhaps reflected the general northern apathy. AMA officers decided upon several approaches to stimulate concern and secure support for blacks. First they urged the federal government to take greater responsibilities. Simeon Jocelyn informed President Lincoln of AMA activities in Virginia and asked for an interview. In a subsequent meeting Jocelyn persuaded Lincoln to assign an army surgeon to the contrabands. Whipple, with letters of introduction from Senators Charles Sumner and Henry Wilson, also met with Secretary of the Treasury Salmon P. Chase to seek his assistance.[24] Association officers exerted all their limited political influence to encourage the government to care for contrabands.

Government protection of contrabands was, of course, not expected to fill the AMA's depleted treasury. Something must be done to awaken the northern public to the freedmen's needs for relief and education. The association decided to follow the earlier example of abolitionist societies and use ex-slave speakers. In early 1862 William Davis of Hampton, Virginia, was contracted to make a northern lecture tour. Davis, the son of a slave woman and a white sailor who had raped his mother while she was on a slave ship bound for Virginia from Madagascar, had been taught to read and write and had grown into an articulate, religious man. For several years before the war he had hired his own time as the operator of a pleasure boat and was obviously a good choice to assist in fund raising. William L. Coan, an AMA agent from Chelsea, Massachusetts, who traveled with him, thought Davis "is now doing and can do a work such as *no* man who has before appeared before the public can do. You would be surprised to hear him on some occasions." But in many ways Davis's tour proved more painful than rewarding. Davis was welcomed at Leonard Grimes's black Baptist church in Boston but was too ill to speak, and at another church Coan was hit with an egg. A well-advertised public meeting in Boston was sparsely attended. Coan was disappointed, but Tappan was not surprised. He had warned that Bostonians would not attend a missionary meeting. He reminded associates of the time years earlier in Boston when a lecture on astronomy had few listeners while the same hall was crowded a few weeks later for the exhibition of a trained pig. "Moral reform . . . is a poor thing to live by, as far as this world's goods are concerned," he said.[25]

Davis continued to speak primarily at Baptist and Congregational churches, but "the sin of *caste,* the hate of the colored skin" showed itself at Coan's church in Chelsea. Davis's attendance at a church social provoked an attack upon Coan, who was accused of disgracing the community. Coan tried to shelter Davis from the controversy, but "an unprincipled scamp" attacked Davis and "abused him so far as words would go abominably calling him a God damned nigger repeatedly and everything else abusive." Moreover, some Massachusetts Baptists became concerned about whether the association would tamper with black Baptists in Virginia and sometimes refused to open their church to Coan and Davis. The North was not yet sympathetic to the AMA work. Coan, when later touring New York, wrote of "Hunkerism, proslavery, caste, Negro hating and Secesh sympathy" which impeded collections.[26]

Despite Davis and Coan's experience, churches remained the association's best source of income and it continued to "work" them, trying to excite interest in black education. Other contrabands and freedmen teachers were sent on tour and Tappan, Whipple, and Jocelyn traveled constantly. At first the results were discouraging. Michael Strieby was surprised by a meeting with Boston clergymen. "If Boston ministers are representative men then God help the black and the AMA," he wrote. But the constant soliciting began to produce results—more, it appeared, from the country and small churches. The Quakers, Baptists, New School Presbyterians, Reformed Dutch, and Wesleyan churches began to take collections for the association. Donations were usually small. In August 1864 fourteen Methodist Episcopal churches gave sums ranging from $4.30 to $21.15 for a total of $131.64. The Free-Will Baptists, Wesleyan Methodists, and the Dutch Reformed church designated the AMA as their agent for southern missions. Receipts more than doubled between 1862 and 1864, and the churches donated thousands of dollars worth of clothing for freedmen as well as cash.[27]

Although most northern blacks were poor, they generously contributed to the AMA. Children gave their pennies and nickels in Sunday school classes, and black organizations sent money and clothing. In 1861 Ithaca, New York, blacks were "getting up another box of articles for a Christmas present to their sable brethren" in Virginia. A Yonkers maid sent two dollars, a blanket, and a shawl. The Colored Ladies Freedmen and Soldiers Aid Society of Geneva, New York, contributed fifty dollars, and the Society of Colored Ladies of Syracuse donated $200 in clothing. Black teacher Sallie L. Daffin collected clothing in Wilmington, Delaware, and Edmonia Highgate canvassed upstate New York in 1864–65. In October 1864 Highgate forwarded $110 and seven boxes and three barrels of clothing.[28]

By mid-1864 the public was more amenable to AMA pleas. There were still "copperhead areas" where collection was impossible, but most observers perceived an improvement. The Reverend Mansfield French concluded that God had "wrought a wonderful change in public sentiment" in Saratoga, New York. He spoke to a large audience in a Presbyterian church where two years before, French said, his remarks would "have scattered half the congregation, but their nerves bore up well under my abolition utterances." The widow's mites and larger donations began to arrive with increasing frequency. A Cook County, Illinois, couple sent their life savings of $300. Treasurer Tappan credited $200 to receipts and $100 to them in case they might need it. Of course, not all contributors were motivated by compassion. Some were concerned with preserving the New England–Puritan tradition, which they believed could be done only by "civilizing" the freedmen. Religion and education could be used to stem the "black threat." A correspondent to the *American Missionary* proclaimed that blacks had been brutalized by slavery. "The problem of our national salvation is to be wrought out upon their minds, after war and battle are done; and we have not a moment to lose," he wrote. Whatever the motivation of the supporters—fear of blacks, guilt stemming from the nation's role in slavery, or compassion—receipts increased for 1864–65 to $134,181, almost triple the 1861–62 income. Still, receipts did not keep up with need. Strieby wrote prospective teachers in November 1864 that new teachers could not be commissioned unless their salaries were "wholly or nearly secured" elsewhere.[29]

The greatest expansion of AMA activity came between 1865 and 1870. As already seen, growth was made possible in part by the Freedmen's Bureau, but another event of great importance for the association occurred in June 1864 when the National Council of Congregational Churches met to discuss what Congregationalists should do concerning southern missionary work. Association officials hoped that the National Council would channel its funds through the AMA, but such a decision was not certain. Although many Congregationalists, especially in the Northwest, supported the association, relations with Congregationalists were strained. The AMA had denounced the American Home Missionary Society (a Congregational agency) because it sustained churches that accepted slaveholders and slavery. Conservative Congregationalists feared the AMA's abolitionism. When the war began, a majority of Congregational churches had not fully accepted the AMA.[30]

During the war New England Congregational churches had given limited support to the association. An agent found that a Bristol, Rhode Island, church, "under a conservative Congregational pastorate, did not furnish me a field for gleaning—the 'Am. Missionary' had sown no seed there." Jocelyn determined that in Massachusetts those who gave the most for freedmen were not Congregationalists. A prominent minister confidentially informed Strieby in 1864 that he doubted the Congregationalists of New England would "lay hold of the Association" as long as Tappan directed it. Nevertheless, after considerable and sometimes heated debate the National Council resolved to endorse the AMA and recommended that its churches raise $250,000 for the association.[31] The National Council's endorsement brought greater financial stability to the AMA and an increasingly close relationship with Congregationalism. As other denominations began to open their own freedmen's schools, leaving the association more dependent upon Congregational churches for revenue, Congregational leaders began to pressure the AMA to abandon its policy of nonsectarianism.[32]

Endorsement by the National Council did not bring immediate funds. It remained for the AMA to make the collections. The present soliciting staff of two corresponding secretaries, the treasurer, and a few peripatetic agents was inadequate for the task at hand.[33] Three district secretaries were appointed: Jacob R. Shipherd was located in Chicago, Edward P. Smith in Cincinnati, and Charles L. Woodworth in Boston. Agents were also assigned to England and Scotland. Even though the association captured the support of such prominent ministers as Henry Ward Beecher, early collections from the Congregational churches were scanty. Eleven months after the National Council's recommendation, only about $100,000 had been raised. Samuel Hunt wrote of "the ominous silence of the large majority of 'the congregational churches of America.'" The pastor of a Donaldsonville, Connecticut, church told his congregation of the council's decision without speaking in favor of it. A subsequent collection netted only fifteen dollars, one-third of which was given by an AMA agent. There were 213 Congregational churches in New England, but by July 1866 only about 75 had made contributions to the association. Whipple decided that nothing would reach the "neglectful" Congregational churches except visitation by district secretaries or agents. He sought a way to enlist pastors without compromising the association's nonsectarian stance. As late as 1869 the association arranged for General O. O. Howard to speak to a Hartford, Connecticut, Congregational church to persuade its members that the AMA was worthy of support.[34]

The association was canvassing England almost as vigorously as the United States. Since the AMA had contributed more than $100,000 for educating emancipated slaves in Jamaica, Tappan assumed that English friends would now reciprocate to aid American freedmen. The Congregational Union of England and Wales had recommended that its members contribute to the association, and Tappan hoped that if fully informed of AMA aims the evangelical Quakers, Independents, Baptists, and other English churchmen would also lend support. Because he feared that friends of William Lloyd Garrison were inciting opposition to the association, J. Sella Martin, a black minister and member of the AMA executive committee, was sent to England to counter Garrison's influence.[35] Approximately $40,000 was received from England in 1866, but English collections virtually collapsed the following year.[36]

The association's energetic solicitation campaign in 1865–66 brought in $253,046, plus $105,441 in donated clothing. Although this was approximately $157,000 more than in 1863–64, it was not enough to cover expenses. Expenditures for freedmen had increased by a like amount, and the new staff had to be paid. The association was therefore compelled to borrow money to meet its obligations.[37] The next two years were even more difficult ones. In 1866 receipts declined while expenditures and the debt increased. Teachers, already underpaid, were asked to loan or donate part of their salaries. When Strieby, exhausted from constant work among New York Presbyterians, asked for a one-week vacation, Whipple refused, saying the financial situation had never been worse and that all were needed to collect funds. The association, Whipple said, was receiving "scarcely half enough to meet daily wants, and tens of thousands of borrowed money was falling due." Strieby continued to court church people, but with growing irritation. "Oh this miserable business of dancing attendance on religious bodies," he wrote, "one almost loses ones sense of self-respect."

Other freedmen's educational societies were in similar straits. The *Freedmen's Record* complained that "friends and well-wishers" had grown "rather lukewarm." Lyman Abbott of the American Freedmen's Union Commission blamed "hard times, the slow process of reconstruction," and "the decadence of the enthusiasm enkindled by the war." There was a business depression and some people objected to being taxed twice for freedmen—once by government for appropriations for the Freedmen's Bureau and again through "begging agents." Others believed that blacks should be able to care for themselves by now, and that the sooner they became self-reliant the better. Northern zeal for assisting freedmen, always limited, was already waning. As a result the AMA operated with a deficit from 1866 to 1878. It constantly borrowed from banks, supporters, and its own officers and teachers. The association temporarily chose debt rather than forfeit the opportunity to establish schools and purchase school property. The AMA finally cancelled its debt in 1879, but only by understaffing its schools, underpaying personnel, and contracting its work.[38]

One fairly effective money-gathering scheme used by the association was to seek large donations from prominent or wealthy individuals, then name a school for them, hoping that the honoree and his friends would support the school. General Clinton B. Fisk gave approximately $30,000 to Fisk University and solicited additional funds from his friends. Seymour Straight was the principal benefactor of Straight University for years. LeMoyne Institute in Memphis began with a gift from Washington, Pennsylvania, abolitionist Julius LeMoyne, and Jabez Burrell of Oberlin, Ohio, gave the first $10,000 for Burrell School in Selma. Beach Institute in Savannah was named after Alfred E. Beach, editor of the *Scientific American*.[39]

Only a few people could be honored by naming schools for them, but there were other ways to cause contributors to feel personally involved. The association quickly learned that if a teacher corresponded regularly with a particular church the congregation seemed to take a greater interest. Letters recounting student nakedness and hunger brought barrels of clothing and food. This experience showed the AMA an even better method of involving supporters. It began to urge churches and aid societies to select their own teachers, who would be commissioned and supervised by the association but who would be paid by and report to the sponsoring agency. This plan worked well during the mid-sixties. Dozens of churches and aid societies participated. For example, the Andover Freedmen's Aid Society supported Harriet Billings. In Westminister, Massachusetts, no agency could afford to pay a teacher so the Baptist and Congregationalists combined to employ Martha Boutelle.[40] Some of the money so used would have gone to the association anyway, but it stimulated greater interest.

Although the AMA was financed primarily by northern evangelical Christians, the association assiduously and unblushingly sought public funds. It took every possible advantage of Bureau assistance and attempted to place its agents on the government payroll when possible. Several men worked for the AMA and the Bureau simultaneously, with the latter paying their salaries. In 1869 Edward P. Smith urged Whipple to use his influence to secure appointment as collector at Hampton, Virginia, for Samuel Chapman Armstrong. "If he can get it," Smith wrote, "it will be $2,000 per annum for A.M.A. It will not take the time of the Genl. so but that with an assistant he can attend to all our work." The Freedmen's Bureau often matched funds and constructed school buildings on property purchased for freedmen's education. The AMA fearfully accepted an $87,726 deficit in 1868 in order to take advantage of Bureau funds. The gamble paid off because the association owned $200,000 worth of southern school property by June 1869. As previously seen, the association also arranged for its teachers to be paid with city or state funds if this could be done without violating the AMA's educational aims. Indeed, association handling of state funds at times bordered on the unethical. The association contracted teachers for a fixed sum, and when the state salary was higher than that promised the teacher, it pocketed the difference and used it for expenses. Edward C. Silsby, principal of the Selma school, was paid $125 per month by the local school board. The association allowed him $80, applying the other $45 toward his board.[41] Since the AMA ordinarily furnished board for teachers and kept its schools open for eight months while the state paid salaries for only three, the association could perhaps justify retaining part of the stipend if the teachers agreed, but there is evidence that on at least one occasion it profited from the arrangement, much to its workers' dismay.[42] Even Whipple was willing to sanction sharp practices to support freedmen's education. State school funds, however, were never more than a very minor part of the AMA income.

The association began the 1870s with a $78,000 debt and a declining field for collections. The Bureau ended in 1870, and northwestern charitable giving was concentrated on Chicago after the great fire of 1871.[43] Moreover, by this time most of the major denominations had established their own southern schools and churches, and this left the association more dependent on Congregationalists, who had two other missionary societies to support. The panic of 1873 further affected receipts. The association's regular income declined by 41 percent between 1869 and 1875. More important than the Chicago fire and a turbulent economy, however, was declining northern interest in freedmen's problems. Most northern whites considered blacks innately inferior. Their humanitarian instincts had been temporarily kindled by the freedmen's plight, but by 1870 they began to believe that Bureau aid and Congressional Reconstruction had been more than enough assistance. As early as 1867 E. L. Godkin, editor of the *Nation*, suggested that blacks were safe. The country should not be ruined, he said, in order to set them up in business. Increasingly convinced that blacks could never be successfully integrated into American society, most northerners were easily able to ignore pleas for still more money for freedmen. Teacher Carrie M. Blood, who had become expert in loosening the purse strings of friends and churches, wrote from Tennessee in 1875 that she could no longer get money from northern friends. They had tired of giving. Trying to explain its fund-raising difficulties in 1876, the association intimated that its major source had been abolitionists and many old abolitionists were dead and others had lost their zeal. A distinguished New England clergyman was quoted as saying: "The truth is, sir, the negro is not popular. If a man has a dollar to give, he would rather give it to a white than a black man." The black cause simply no longer enlisted the same sentiment as it had during the early postwar years. The North had developed "a calm and cool—somewhat too cool—consideration of Christian duty."[44]

Certainly the fervor for assisting blacks had declined, but hundreds of northerners were persistent in their support. In 1876 a donor who signed himself a "Life long Friend" sent five dollars as "a centennial offering for the Freedmen from an invalid who feels a great interest in them & would gladly send them an armful of money if it was possible to do so." Calvin Ely first sent money to the association in 1861. He continued to send twenty to fifty dollars each year.[45] Mary Thomas of Union Springs, New York, is an example of the many who continued to finance black education. Thomas, a member of the orthodox Society of Friends, was a "life member" of the association and had contributed for blacks through both the Friends and the AMA. She especially approved the latter's "evangelical doctrine." When collections decreased in 1871, an association secretary wrote asking her if she could suggest someone in Union Springs who would solicit for the AMA. She replied that twenty years earlier she would have been the one, but that now her health was too poor. She tried to interest others, including a former freedmen's teacher, but could "light no fires." However, she contributed twenty dollars. A few months later Thomas suggested that if she and her friends concentrated their donations on one school and received correspondence from there it might "stir up the torpid energies" of those who ought to contribute. If people knew details of suffering in a more personal way, they might be more sympathetic. "A small fire in our village would bring out more compassion for the sufferers than all the desolations of Paris, and all the needs of the millions of freedmen."

Thomas asked the AMA to select "an industrious, self-sacrificing man" who could both teach and conduct religious services as she wished her money to be spent on mental culture and spiritual elevation. In October 1871 she sent $300 which was applied to Talladega, which disappointed her. She and her friends had at great sacrifice collected the money, and it seemed to them that they were doing little if their money paid a teacher who was already being supported. She preferred a new teacher and location. The following year the association pleased Mary Thomas by sending Edward Bull to Woodbridge, North Carolina. Bull wrote regularly to Thomas and her friends, who in turn provided his salary and occasionally sent him a "box of comforts." By late 1872 most of Thomas's collaborators had abandoned her and she was sustaining Bull almost by herself. She wrote that she had observed great impatience with blacks. They had been emancipated, inadequately helped, yet the North wanted to turn them adrift. The North had combined with the South to oppress blacks, Thomas said, "and it is high time we undertook in good earnest to make amends. Although we are not the individuals that oppressed them, yet slavery was our nation's sin."

When the AMA fired Bull, whom Mary Thomas admired and had become fond of, she protested, but she agreed to pay the salary of his successor, Alicia Blood.[46] She continued to provide for the Woodbridge teacher, and additionally began to increase her donations to AMA colleges. She claimed that if everyone gave in proportion to their means, as she had done, the association would be able to "educate the poor colored people. O what has become of the abolitionists of ten or twenty years ago," she lamented. In 1878 Thomas complained that she could ill afford her annual contribution as her income had been much reduced, but she retained her "undying interest in the freedmen" and continued to aid the AMA.[47]

As fund raising became more arduous the association reluctantly permitted the colleges to begin their own collection campaigns. It endorsed the Fisk University Jubilee Singers and provided them with an advance agent. Joseph W. Healy of Straight University managed to collect several thousand dollars in 1870–71 after the association gave him a list of prospective donors. Unfortunately the colleges collected from the AMA's usual constituency. Association agents found themselves competing for funds with their own colleges, and total revenues increased little.[48]

There was a small flurry of renewed church interest in AMA work in the early 1870s when the association began to emphasize the colleges' training of ministers for freedmen and missionaries for Africa. The Freedmen's Aid Society of Great Britain was perfected in 1872, and its president, the Earl of Shaftesbury, was an ardent advocate of African missions. Who, association officials asked, was more suitable to "Christianize" Africa than black Americans trained in evangelical AMA schools? An urgent call from Straight for assistance in training young men as missionaries brought pledges of more than $30,000 from Great Britain in 1872–73. Fisk, Talladega, and Atlanta University also received some British donations for training ministers.[49]

By 1875 the association was dependent upon a few score faithful supporters and the Congregational churches. It continued to receive small legacies and occasionally large donations. The association's first large gift was the Charles Avery trust fund of $100,000 in 1865, but Avery stipulated that the income be used for African missions only. In 1879 a $150,000 bequest from Mrs. Daniel P. Stone of Malden, Massachusetts, enabled the AMA to complete building projects at several of its institutions. But it remained for Daniel Hand of Guilford County, Connecticut, to place the association finally upon a stable financial basis. In 1888 Hand's attorney walked into the association office and transferred securities amounting to $1,000,894 to be designated the Daniel Hand Educational Fund for Colored People. It was a permanent fund with only the income to be used. When Hand died in 1891, the AMA received another half million dollars as his residuary legatee.[50] Fund raising would continue to be a major AMA activity, but for the first time in its history the association had a dependable permanent income. In the meantime, the AMA had contributed approximately one-third of the $20 million the numerous benevolent societies and government agencies spent helping ex-slaves between 1861 and 1890.[51]

Public Schools
and Teacher Training

ALTHOUGH the AMA aggressively founded common schools in the South, its leaders had always believed that education was a public responsibility, and the need for tax-supported training was painfully obvious by the end of the war. Even with Bureau support, northern societies could not reach all needy youth. Moreover, many students had progressed sufficiently to warrant graded and secondary schools. Such institutions required more teachers and greater expenditures. The association hoped public funds would support at least primary education so that northern benevolence could be concentrated on secondary schools and teacher training. In 1865 the AMA issued a call for a national system of education to include recently liberated slaves and southern whites. Ignorance, said the AMA, was the parent of crime, pauperism, wretchedness, and even disunion. Since it was the government's duty to protect its citizens from these vices, the government should establish a system of schools which would "reach every child born within the Union." A system of education that embraced both black and white children would be especially fitting at the moment, the association added. It would "solve many questions now under discussion [the black's role in American society], promote the union and loyalty of the states, prevent future rebellions, and tend to consolidate and bless the country."[1]

Association leaders realized that a national system of schools was unlikely, but state-supported education was a distinct possibility, especially after passage of the Congressional Reconstruction acts. The AMA continued to expand its own schools while at the same time strongly encouraging "the result for which we have all been laboring— not simply the immediate education for a few pupils, but the establishment of a permanent public school system." The AMA, more than other northern Protestant evangelical missionary societies, adhered to the principle of working with states in building up common schools. It, more than others, avoided the practice of grafting primary parochial schools onto its churches.[2]

In some southern states association agents were instrumental in the enactment of public school legislation. John Silsby was the most prominent member of the committee which wrote the educational article for the Alabama Constitution of 1867. Francis L. Cardozo drafted the South Carolina public school law while he was superintendent of Avery Institute of Charleston. The association's superintendent at Macon, Georgia, John A. Rockwell, helped write the school bill submitted to the Georgia legislature in 1867 and served on the state board of education. C. Thurston Chase in Florida and Samuel S. Ashley in North Carolina, both AMA agents, became superintendents of public instruction. Several agents became county superintendents of schools. The association further supported the budding public schools by withdrawing from the field when public funds were available, by giving, renting, or selling its property to local school authorities, and by sharing school expenses with state and local boards.[3] The AMA knew that founding public schools would be difficult and would require constant vigilance and support. At its 1869 annual meeting it resolved "that a system of common public school education is essential to the welfare of the people of the south; that the disposition manifested at the South to repudiate that system calls for continued efforts on the part of friends of education and humanity to sustain public schools, and especially normal schools, open to all persons, without respect to previous condition or color."[4]

The AMA claim that in many places its teachers "laid the foundations of a common school system for their districts or states" may be exaggerated, but the association, together with the Freedmen's Bureau and the AFUC, played a prominent role.[5] As early as 1865 the association transferred its Baltimore schools to the Baltimore Association for the Moral and Educational Improvement of Colored People, saying: "If the main object is accomplished, it hardly matters by whom it is done."[6] It withdrew its support from the District of Columbia schools in 1867 when it learned they could be sustained by public funds. Association schools were turned over to the city officials in Lexington and Louisville, Kentucky, in 1867. Soon afterwards, Chattanooga schools were incorporated into the city system. The Reverend Ewing O. Tade, AMA agent, was placed in charge of both white and black schools. In Memphis the Lincoln Chapel School, with seven grades and ten teachers and two small schools, was transferred to the city. The Lincoln principal became the assistant superintendent of education. Schools established by the AMA and the Freedmen's Bureau in Louisiana were conveyed to state and local authorities in the early 1870s. When the Georgia system achieved some credibility in 1871–72, the AMA began transferring its schools to the public and "quickly launched a concerted campaign to pry from the clenched fists of Democrats as much money as possible for black education."[7]

That the AMA advocated public schools and cooperated with state and local school officials did not mean it willingly gave up all influence on southern education. An ideal situation, in its view, was publicly funded schools staffed by association teachers. The AMA strongly believed that southern white teachers could not be trusted with black interests. It favored black teachers, but assumed there were still too few competent ones available. As a result the association placed as many northern teachers as possible in southern public schools while blacks were being trained, and sometimes rented its property to local systems only with the stipulation that its teachers be kept. Local boards wanted association buildings but often disdained its teachers. Association success in placing teachers varied according to local prejudice and politics. In 1868 the Macon, Georgia, board refused to administer the teachers' examination to AMA personnel until forced to do so. Later the board requested the use of Lewis High School, but wished to supply it with local white teachers. Tough negotiations resulted in the board employing both southern and northern instructors, with the latter abandoning the teacher's home where they often entertained blacks. The following year the board president recommended that Lewis High be dropped if the AMA insisted upon selecting half of the teachers. "This arrangement," the president said, "compels us to employ and pay teachers from distant states having no sympathy with us, and who render themselves obnoxious to our people by attempting to introduce ideas of social equality among whites and blacks opposed to the best interests of both races." When the building was later set on fire, local blacks suspected school board members. They further objected to southern white teachers. A local black committee urged the AMA to withdraw from the public system and reopen the school with northern teachers and Atlanta University students.[8]

After a similar confrontation over Beach Institute in Savannah in

1874, the school board outmaneuvered the association by persuading local blacks to support it in opposing northern white instructors so that they could be replaced with teachers of their own color. The following year Beach became a public school without northern teachers. The board president taunted the AMA principal, telling him that his sole object had been "to get rid of yankee teachers" and their influence on Savannah blacks.[9] The Reverend Henry M. Turner, the fiery African Methodist Episcopal minister and black leader, reputedly said there would have been no public schools for Georgia blacks except for the AMA, and that if it withdrew, public schools for blacks "would be of little value." Turner was partially correct for two reasons. The association constantly badgered state officials to create schools for blacks, and local boards sometimes organized public schools with black teachers in order to rid the locality of AMA influence.[10]

The AMA's relationship with local and state officials was not always so strained. In 1869 North Carolina Superintendent of Public Instruction Samuel S. Ashley proposed that the association transfer its schools to the state. As one of its former missionaries, Ashley cherished the "warmest" regards for the AMA and agreed to employ its teachers. "You may know," he wrote George Whipple, "that I prefer turning the state patronage to your favor than to that of any other organization." Association schools became the public schools in several cities and smaller communities. Howard Primary and Grammar School in Fayetteville, under the leadership of black AMA teachers Robert and Cicero Harris, evolved into one of the best secondary schools in the state.[11]

The Alabama board of education employed northern teachers when the benevolent societies agreed to pay their way to and from the state. Under this arrangement the AMA not only supplied scores of teachers but also improved upon the state system. Public schools were ordinarily open for blacks for only three months each year. In several areas the association supplemented state salaries to keep them open longer. At other times it sustained teachers while they waited months for their tardy salaries. In 1873 Alabama public schools were seriously embarrassed by lack of funds, but according to the U.S. commissioner of education, AMA and Peabody Fund aid kept schools in successful operation in the larger towns.[12] Except for Montgomery, where local boards feuded with AMA teachers, the state and the association managed to cooperate sufficiently, despite constant tension, to keep schools open until the Democrats redeemed the state.[13] After Democrats regained control they freely hired black students from association schools, but rarely employed northern teachers. In the meantime, Alabama had paid out approximately $60,000 to AMA personnel.[14] The association was most actively involved with public schools in Alabama, Georgia, Tennessee, Mississippi, and North Carolina, but it worked with officials in all southern states.

Southern school systems were so weak that the AMA was not disposed to withdraw completely from its elementary work. It continued some schools and occasionally established new ones in areas where no other educational opportunities were available. Nevertheless, greater emphasis was placed on secondary and normal training. In 1870 the association had 157 common schools. That number declined to 70 in 1871 and to 13 in 1874.[15] In the meantime, graded schools, high schools, and normal schools were increased from 5 in 1867 to 29 in 1872 with the primary objective of training black youth as teachers.[16]

Even during the Civil War the association became convinced that its major task was "to teach the teachers." In 1863 Louisa A. Woodbury wrote from Virginia: "I am very sure that our great work just now is to teach these freedmen, & women & children to teach each other—& thus hasten their mental growth & development." When in 1866 a skeptic advised Superintendent of Education Samuel Hunt that it was too soon to experiment with training black teachers, Hunt asked how freedmen were to be educated. Could a sufficient number of northern teachers and their support be found? The AMA estimated that 20,000 teachers would be needed. Most of them must come from black ranks. Freedmen were eager to become teachers, and their progress proved their capability for the work. From the beginning a few advanced students had been used as monitors and assistants. In early 1866 Francis L. Cardozo already had prepared a Charleston class of one hundred to become primary teachers. Moreover, at least some AMA officials believed that no group or race should be permanently dependent upon another for its ultimate development. Thenceforth, teacher training became perhaps the association's most valuable educational gift to the freedmen because it enabled them to become their own educators. The AMA planned to establish a "school of high grade" or a normal school in each major population center of the South.[17]

Although the association recognized the need for training black teachers, its decision was expedited by the knowledge that many blacks had a strong preference for teachers of their own color. Professor William H. Woodbury wrote from Virginia in 1862: "These people though, clanish,—commendably so, & partial to their own race, have . . . the discernment to perceive that white people have had the best opportunity to learn, & hence are supposed to know more than their own race. But let a colored man . . . like Bishop [Daniel A.] Payne . . . come before them & he has a power in his race & color, which no white person with the same talents can command."[18] S. W. Magill found a "spirit of exclusiveness" among Savannah blacks toward all whites, northern or southern. Certainly freedmen were not motivated simply by clannishness or prejudice. They enthusiastically welcomed northern teachers and constantly demonstrated their gratitude. Nevertheless, many freedmen had visions of schools taught and run by blacks. Parents wanted black role models for their children, teachers who understood their culture and needs. Despite their appreciation of white efforts, many blacks believed that it was impossible for whites, given their education and background, "to enter into the feelings" of black pupils as black teachers could.[19] Freedmen responded positively to the decision to train black teachers.

The AMA never managed to place secondary or normal schools in every principal population center, but by late 1867 it offered normal training at Nashville, Hampton, Charleston, Talladega, and Atlanta. By October 1871 it was operating twenty-one normal and secondary schools with 110 teachers and 6,477 students. Indeed, the AMA may have expanded its schools too rapidly. When in 1868 it asked the Freedmen's Bureau for aid in establishing a normal institution at Beaufort, South Carolina, the usually cooperative Commissioner O. O. Howard declined. Howard had recently toured association schools, several of which were doing well, but others were disappointing. They especially lacked good principals, he said. They required "men who know what a good school is, and who have the ability to organize and control. Such men must be paid and you cannot pay them if you attempt to employ too many." Howard accurately pinpointed a weakness of association schools. The AMA had expanded beyond its means, and in an attempt to economize it sometimes selected inexperienced principals. Despite such shortcomings, these schools were often the best, or only, ones available to black youth.[20]

Some of the twenty-one schools mentioned above were normal institutions, while others were little more than graded schools with a few advanced students, but the latter sometimes made a remarkable impact on the community and since a normal diploma was not generally a prerequisite for teachers, furnished teachers as well.[21] Trinity School in Athens, Alabama, was organized in 1865 by Mary F. Wells, a Mount Holyoke graduate, Civil War army nurse, and former Michigan schoolteacher. Wells bravely faced social ostracism, personal threats, insults, and numerous annoyances, thereby winning the affection of blacks and the grudging toleration of whites. For thirty years she and her assistants effectively taught students from the ABC's to high school. According to a white observer, her pupils "were far in advance of local whites of the same age." Scores of her students became teachers and virtually monopolized black schools in the region. The black editor of the Huntsville *Gazette* proclaimed in 1882 that Wells had "done more toward elevating the Colored people in North Alabama than any other teacher in it, and should have a place in all our hearts."[22]

Lincoln School in Marion, Alabama, was probably even more influential than Trinity. When Dr. William Childs Curtis was asked in 1962 to account for his academic success, he credited the "fine AMA school in Marion" that both of his parents had attended. The family tradition of attending Lincoln began with Patsey Childs, who was born a slave in 1856. After completing Lincoln in 1874 under thorough northern teachers, Childs went to Talladega College, where she earned a normal diploma. She became a "well educated woman with an excellent command of the language" and with an intense desire to educate her family. An answer similar to Curtis's was given by several other black scholars whose parents had attended Lincoln. Horace Mann Bond, in his study of black scholars, concluded that the nature of the family was of first importance in producing scholars. The nature of the secondary school was next. On that basis Bond judged Lincoln School "to have been the best predominantly Negro secondary school this country has ever known." No doubt motivation and intelligence would have enabled many of those successful families to excel, even without Lincoln, but sound secondary training helped provide essential tools. Other secondary institutions such as the Storrs School in Atlanta; Williston School in Wilmington, North Carolina; Lewis High School in Macon, Georgia; Beach Institute in Savannah; and the Howard School in Chattanooga did yeoman work in training black community leaders and teachers.[23]

The AMA hoped that secondary education would soon be supported by public funds, but it assumed that some of its normal schools would have to be continued indefinitely. It saw both the need and the opportunity to train black teachers for the southern public schools. By providing teachers it could encourage public efforts and at the same time affect the type of education offered. As other benevolent societies and states began normal training, the association relegated some of its normal institutions to graded and secondary schools, but in 1878 it still operated nine with almost two thousand pupils. As late as 1890 it was training approximately one-third of the southern black normal students.[24] Much of the normal teaching was being done at association colleges, but some normal institutions were retained. Avery Normal Institute in Charleston and Emerson Institute in Mobile are examples of the latter.

In August 1865 a tall, elegantly tailored young black man returned to Charleston to help educate his recently emancipated brethren. Born 1 January 1837 of a Jewish businessman father and a free black mother, Francis L. Cardozo received his early education in Charleston schools for free blacks and as an apprentice carpenter. When he was twenty-one he renounced the carpenter's trade and sailed for Glasgow, Scotland, to study for the ministry. Although working part-time as a carpenter to support his studies, Cardozo graduated from the University of Glasgow with honors, winning prizes in Latin and Greek. He did additional study at seminaries in London and Edinburgh before returning to the United States in 1864 to become pastor of the Temple Street Congregational Church in New Haven, Connecticut.[25] Quickly deciding that he would be of more service to his race as principal of a normal school than as a minister, Cardozo offered his services to the AMA.

When he arrived in Charleston he planned to become a professional educator. He had no intention of entering politics, and though he remained devoted to religion he abandoned the occupation for which he had been trained. Firmly convinced of the importance of training black youth, he had forsaken "the *exclusive* duties of the ministry" to become an educational leader. Although the AMA apparently made no promises, Cardozo emphasized that his objective was to establish a normal school. By November 1865 he had a thousand students divided into nineteen classes taught by twenty-one teachers. His school immediately attracted attention both because of its size and his excellent management. Reuben Tomlinson, Bureau superintendent of schools for South Carolina, doubted that a northern school could be found that was "conducted with more system and intelligence than Cardozo's."[26]

Cardozo's first concern was securing and retaining effective teachers. He had little anxiety about color. Competency was more important than race. Ordinarily he preferred northern teachers because generally they were better trained, but he insisted on having some black teachers and recruited several talented ones from the Charleston free black community.[27] Of the northern teachers sent him, only two, Amanda Wall and J. L. Alexander, were black. Since most of the local blacks were qualified to teach only primary education, Cardozo asked the AMA to employ his sister, Mrs. C. L. McKinney, and her husband to assist him. The McKinneys, who had lived and taught in Flushing, New York, for several years, were proposed by Cardozo as excellent examples of blacks who had proved themselves "intellectually fitted." They arrived in January 1866.[28] As long as Cardozo was principal there were comparable numbers of black and white teachers. Cardozo's actions wedded the black community to his institution. It became and remained their school.

Cardozo's first year was filled with both frustrations and rewards. White opposition, the usual economic problems suffered by black schools, and a feud with Samuel Hunt, AMA superintendent of schools from 1864 to 1866, had been troublesome.[29] Despite problems Cardozo had collected a racially mixed and efficient faculty who worked together harmoniously in leading students to remarkable advancement. Even local whites were impressed. Avery was widely acclaimed as the outstanding school for black youth in South Carolina and one of the superior schools in the South.[30] However, the Charleston *Daily News* referred to Avery students as "an aristocracy of color" (about 25 percent of the students came from free Charleston families who had enjoyed some educational advantages before the war) and warned that the school was not a fair representation of black education in the city.[31]

Although proud of his accomplishments, Cardozo was unhappy. He reminded AMA officials that he had gone to Charleston to establish a normal school. "It is the object for which I left the superior advantages of the North and came South," he wrote. "It is the object for which I have labored during the past year and for which I am willing to *remain* here and make this place my home." Because they had been free and had enjoyed some previous education, approximately two hundred of his students were now ready for normal training, Cardozo said. AMA officials were convinced, and in the fall of 1866 Avery became a normal school.[32]

Unfortunately for Avery, Cardozo was persuaded by friends to become a candidate for the South Carolina Constitutional Convention of 1868. Whether or not he realized it at the time, his election to the Constitutional Convention marked the close of his career as a South Carolina educator. The same characteristics that made him an excellent principal resulted in his becoming an effective politician. He continued to supervise the school until mid-1868. In the meantime, he had laid a firm foundation for Avery Institute.[33] Not until 1915 would Avery have another black principal.

Avery continued to teach some primary students, but it became the premier black teacher training school in South Carolina. By 1881 it had graduated 125 thoroughly trained normal students, most of whom became teachers.[34] Hundreds of other Avery students were teaching without having received their diplomas. Probably no normal school was better supported by the AMA than Avery, which remained under association control until 1947, when it became a public school.[35]

A comparison of Avery and Emerson Institute demonstrates how fortunate the former was to have an able administrator initially, a pool of already partially trained students, and strong support from the black community. Emerson was organized in 1868 as what a wildly optimistic principal called a college. Unfortunately the school was located away from the concentrated black city population and suffered considerable white hostility. Moreover, the school administration and faculty changed constantly. A normal department was organized in 1869, but it was several years before many normal students were trained. Emerson became primarily a public school for elementary pupils.[36]

Finally, in 1873, the AMA determined to transform Emerson into an adequate normal school. The energetic Edward P. Lord, the new prin-

An abolitionist and an ardent advocate of equality, Lewis Tappan was the driving force behind the AMA until his retirement in 1866. *Amistad Research Center*

George Whipple, corresponding secretary of the AMA from 1847 to 1876. After Lewis Tappan's retirement Whipple became the most influential figure in the AMA. *Amistad Research Center*

Cover of *The American Missionary*, the AMA's most efficient propaganda tool. Although the association's major focus was on blacks, it also had missions among the Chinese, Indians, and mountain whites.

Noon recess at a school for blacks at Vicksburg, Mississippi. *From a drawing in* Harper's Weekly, *1866*

Lewis Normal Institute, Macon, Georgia. Lewis Institute trained teachers and prepared students for Atlanta University and the AMA's other colleges. *Amistad Research Center*

During the Civil War, Contraband Jackson became Drummer Jackson of the 79th United States Colored Troops. *USAMHI*

Women and children in a contraband camp at Baton Rouge, Louisiana, 1863. *Charles East Collection*

THE FREEDMAN'S

SPELLING-BOOK.

PUBLISHED BY THE

AMERICAN TRACT SOCIETY,

NO. 28 CORNHILL, BOSTON.

Title page from *The Freedman's Spelling-Book*,
1866. The Freedman's Speller was widely used in
AMA schools.

Wartime view of Slabtown, a contraband village near Hampton, Virginia. The AMA sent teachers, farm superintendents, seeds, and plows to Slabtown residents. *USAMHI*

Midway Congregational Church, in Liberty County, Georgia, was one of the few antebellum Congregational churches in the South. After the war former slave members of Midway formed a black Congregational church and took over the building. *Amistad Research Center*

cipal, observed that the school had many obstacles to overcome, especially black lack of confidence created by earlier administrators. Lord's hard work and enthusiasm resulted in a normal department of one hundred with four graduates in 1876. Unfortunately the school was burned by an incendiary the same year.[37] A new building was constructed and in 1878 the school was training 117 normal students. Still, all was not well at Emerson. Frequent faculty changes continued, as did confused relations with the black community. Blacks were puzzled by the absence of black faculty. A black minister wrote that there was a prejudice against the AMA which an intelligent black teacher could do much to alleviate. Despite problems Emerson trained many teachers for Alabama, and in 1889 an educational historian could write of the school: "Among the private educational enterprises undertaken for the benefit of the colored people of Alabama this institute, whether considered with regard to age, excellence or achievement, is entitled to a place of first rank."[38]

Other AMA normal schools were as important in teacher training in their states as Avery and Emerson. In 1870 a majority of normal students in Tennessee and Kentucky were in AMA schools. In 1888 there were an estimated 15,000 black teachers in the South. Of this number, at least 7,000 had been trained in association schools and several of them had become influential educators. These statistics give credence to the AMA's claim to have played a significant role in southern public education.[39]

8

The AMA Colleges

TLANTA UNIVERSITY? Atlanta University?" Ralph Waldo Emerson responded querulously when Thomas N. Chase handed him an Atlanta catalog. "There is no institution in this country that comes anywhere near being a university except Harvard and that does not really deserve the title."[1] If Emerson's view is accepted, black institutions of higher education did not exist during Reconstruction. Nevertheless, a system of colleges and universities was established soon after the Civil War that became the black American's major assurance of advanced training. A pioneer in black higher education in the South was the American Missionary Association, which between 1866 and 1869 chartered seven "colleges" and assisted in founding Howard University.[2]

The AMA concept of "equality" led it from the beginning to assume that its task would be incomplete until blacks had access to all levels of education. Although the AMA advocated equality, most of its officers believed that blacks were "an absolutely undeveloped race with a long heredity of ignorance, superstition and degradation" that would require generations to erase. Their "civilizing mission" demanded permanent institutions where exceptional black youth could be educated to uplift their brethren. The AMA officers believed that education was a state and local responsibility. Their elementary work was to be pursued only until it could be turned over to the states. The association believed the same about secondary education, but public black high schools developed so slowly that the AMA was required to continue them longer. Black colleges, on the other hand, were to be permanent.[3]

The establishment of colleges for blacks was, of course, a long-range plan. Association officers did not naively think that adequate colleges could be immediately founded. Capital, students with sufficient training, able and sacrificing faculty, and especially hard work would be required. But they dreamed of a time when black youth would have the same opportunity for higher education as whites. The association denied that it ever chartered a college solely for blacks; students of all races were welcome. Such colleges were necessary because white colleges were not readily available to freedmen. The association officers realized that few whites would attend AMA schools, but as Edward P. Smith said when proposing a college in Atlanta, "I would, by all means open the school to all without distinction of color. Practically, the whites will exclude themselves for a while—not long—for I am confident we can make it such a school as will attract them over the high wall of prejudice, and, in the course of years, will grow to the character and power of a school like Oberlin." Smith was too optimistic. The only whites in most early AMA colleges (except Berea and Straight) were faculty children.[4]

A description of Fisk, Talladega, and Straight (now Dillard) will illustrate problems encountered and the range of quality of the seven colleges the AMA had chartered by 1869.[5] Among the scores who went South to teach freedmen were John Ogden, Erastus M. Cravath, and Smith, all of whom became the prime movers in founding Fisk University, one of the outstanding black schools in the United States. Ogden, a former Union officer who had been a Confederate prisoner, was Bureau superintendent of education in Tennessee. Cravath, an underground railroad worker, Oberlin graduate, and Union Army chaplain, was field secretary for the AMA. Smith was district secretary of the association's Middle West Department at Cincinnati. In the fall of 1865 the AMA directed Smith and Cravath to establish a freedmen's school in Nashville. With Ogden's assistance they secured an abandoned Union hospital complex and opened Fisk on 9 January 1866 with Ogden as principal. The aims of Fisk School were commendable and lofty— some thought impractical. The founders proposed a free graded school based upon a "broad Christian foundation." Initially the school was designed to supply desperately needed black teachers, but the founders had more grandiose plans: they intended that Fisk become a first-class college.[6]

When Fisk opened, students came by the hundreds. Almost two hundred enrolled immediately and by the year's end there was an average daily attendance of one thousand ranging in age from seven to seventy. Naturally, most of the students were in primary work, learning the alphabet or struggling to master the words in the *First Reader*. But the dream of a normal school and college was not lost. Ogden argued that Fisk should be in the "business of making teachers," leaving elementary education to others. In keeping with his desire, the school was incorporated on 22 August 1867 as Fisk University. Trustees were authorized to confer all such degrees and honors as were granted by universities in the United States. This was a masterly statement of human expectation and optimism since Fisk did not yet have students even of normal grade.[7]

College work could not be offered immediately, but normal classes began in 1867. Two years later Dr. Barnas Sears of the Peabody Fund declared that Fisk was the best normal school he had seen in the South. The college department, including a three-year preparatory course, was fully organized in 1869, but there were no students until four were accepted in 1871. The number increased to nine in 1873. For years the college was the smallest department at Fisk. The secondary and normal schools were continued not only to train teachers but to provide students for the college.[8]

The college curriculum was similar to that in a majority of contemporary liberal arts schools. Freshmen studied Latin, Greek, and mathematics. Greek, Latin, French, mathematics, and natural science were taught to the sophomores. Juniors labored over the same courses with additional work in German, natural philosophy, history, English, and astronomy. Mental and moral science and political science were added for the seniors. In conjunction with regular studies, essays, debates, declamations, and original addresses were required at stated times.[9]

Bible and ethics were sometimes taught in the classroom, and religion was always emphasized in and out of class. The organization of the college was accompanied by the creation of a boarding department or "home" where students lived with the faculty. Such an arrangement, the faculty believed, would provide "general Christian training" that could be received in no other way. Rigid regulations were uncompromisingly enforced. Boarders rose promptly at the ringing of the first bell and studied from 5:30 to 7:00 A.M.; lights were extinguished at 10:00 P.M. Each student was compelled to attend chapel every morning and Wednesday afternoon, and regular services on Sunday. Men and women were not allowed to visit each other in their rooms.

All interviews had to be public and in a teacher's presence. Tobacco, alcohol, and gambling were strictly forbidden. These regulations seem even more severe when it is realized that not all students were children. Although many "boarders" were young and perhaps needed supervision, the average age of Fisk students in 1883 was twenty-six. Religion remained a major part of the Fisk experience for several years.[10]

College training at Fisk received a boost in 1870 when Ogden resigned to accept a similar post at the Ohio State Normal School. He had been an excellent principal who won the respect, if not the affection, of blacks and whites alike, but his emphasis had been normal education. He was replaced by Adam K. Spence, professor of Greek at the University of Michigan, who was recruited specifically to build up the college department. The scholarly, deeply religious Spence is properly credited with the initiation and development of collegiate work. At first he was uncertain whether blacks and whites were equal in ability, but he believed in equal opportunity. If blacks were inferior to whites, he said, they should have superior training; if superior, inferior training would suffice; but if equal, they should enjoy the same. A strong advocate of civil rights, Spence sometimes sat in the galleries in Nashville theaters because the management refused to seat Fisk students elsewhere. He was assisted by a faculty of fifteen, two of whom left their imprint on the school. Helen C. Morgan, an 1866 Oberlin graduate, remained for thirty-eight years as professor of Latin. Frederick A. Chase, who resigned the presidency of the Lyons Collegiate Institute in Lyons (now Clinton), Iowa, to join the Fisk faculty, is remembered best for establishing the science department.[11]

Just as Fisk began to admit college students and secured an adequate faculty, it seemed that the school might collapse. Spence, an excellent teacher, was less effective in leading a bickering faculty. Even more significant was the school's precarious finances. From the beginning the school courted bankruptcy. Tuition, which was supposed to defray part of the expenses, was difficult to collect from poverty-stricken students. Often there was inadequate food. Teachers were pressed into service to preserve fruit and vegetables during the summers to feed boarders through the year. Not even local debts for food and fuel could be paid. On one occasion Spence was compelled to go through the school dunning students for tuition to collect enough money to buy produce for the evening meal. The good name of the institution was at stake. Even the most optimistic faculty were seeking employment elsewhere. At this juncture began one of the dramatic stories in the history of education—a trial tour of the Fisk Jubilee Singers to secure funds for the university.[12]

A group of untried student singers led by an untrained musical director, George L. White, took most of the remaining money at Fisk and traveled North in October 1871 to try to earn money for their school. They attracted only passing interest and limited support until they began to sing spirituals. Initially they sang what the troupe called "white man's music," but they soon recognized the intense effect of "slave songs," even upon musically enlightened audiences. Their superlative renderings of the spirituals brought respect, attention for their school, and money. They sang their way into the consciousness of both the United States and Europe, and charmed the world with the beauty of black music. In the process they gave Fisk $150,000 and made it the best known black university in the world.[13]

While the Jubilee Singers were gaining recognition and funds for Fisk, the school continued to progress. In 1873 the cornerstone of Fisk University was laid on a new campus. Perhaps more important, in 1875 the strong-willed Erastus M. Cravath became president of the school. Of large vision, of great faith, with positive convictions, Cravath moved Fisk toward becoming a good college. In the same year the first college class was graduated—James Dallas Burrus, John H. Burrus, Virginia E. Walker, and America W. Robinson. If a school can be judged by the success of its alumni, the first graduates were excellent recommendations for Fisk.[14] The college department grew slowly but steadily, and fifteen Bachelor of Arts degrees were conferred in 1885. Scholarship at Fisk during these years was not equal to that at a first-class college, but it was better than that at many American colleges and it was improving. W. E. B. DuBois, who entered Fisk in 1885, found his contacts with faculty "inspiring and beneficial." After studying at Fisk and Harvard and in Germany, DuBois claimed that Spence was "a great Greek scholar by any comparison." The other faculty, he thought, were good. DuBois's evaluation of Fisk was accurate. "Fisk was a good college; I liked it; but, it was small, it was limited in equipment, in laboratories, in books, it was not a university." The school was not yet what it would become—a center of scholarship and culture that would have a special appeal for the black talented tenth, but it was on its way.[15]

A comparison of Fisk and Talladega shows the advantage of being in a population center, having vigorous leadership, and strong support from the AMA. The rural-based Talladega progressed much more slowly than some of its sister institutions. In late 1866 the AMA opened a small school in Talladega, the only black school in a ten-county area. Although local teachers were concerned about the lack of educational opportunity, it was William Savery, a former slave, who provided the leadership in establishing Talladega College. He convinced the commissioner of the Freedmen's Bureau in Alabama of the desirability of a college at Talladega. The Bureau then joined the AMA in buying the unoccupied Baptist College building. Talladega faculty later proudly proclaimed that Savery, who as a slave carpenter had "sawed the first plank and chipped the first shaving" for the original building, became a college trustee and saw three of his children receive diplomas at Talladega.[16]

Classes opened on the campus in November 1867 with 140 students and four teachers under the leadership of the Reverend Henry E. Brown. All of the students were elementary, but Brown planned to develop a normal school. In his travels in surrounding counties he was constantly asked for teachers he could not provide. He began to urge churches to select their best potential teachers, send all the bacon and corn they could collect for the students' support, and Brown would train them a teacher. Young men and women chosen by their churches walked up to thirty miles to Talladega with sacks of corn and bacon on their backs. Unfortunately there was no campus housing for such students, so the AMA began a campaign for funds to build a dormitory. In 1869 the cornerstone was laid for Foster Hall for girls and Talladega was chartered as a college.[17] Despite the charter, however, there was little thought of doing more than normal work in the near future. The Talladega experience refutes the charge that black colleges offered their students higher education before they were ready. Officials did not begin planning college work until 1878, and no such courses were outlined in the catalog until 1890. The first bachelor's degree was not granted until 1895. Talladega's immediate thrust continued to be preparation of students for successful and thorough teaching.[18]

To enter the normal department a student had to be fifteen or had to have passed satisfactory exams in reading, writing, spelling, elements of English grammar, general geography, and arithmetic through general fractions. Good moral character was also required. Prospective students were warned that "those who have not a fixed purpose to improve their time, and an earnest desire to fit themselves for usefulness, should not seek admission as presence of such is not tolerated." The course of study for normal students included a thorough review of algebra, geometry, natural science, mental and moral philosophy, history, and theory and practice of teaching.[19] Naturally the normal department remained small since Talladega was isolated and local blacks had little opportunity for education, but by 1874 there were thirty-seven students in lower normal, nine in higher normal, and fifteen in college preparatory. The first normal class was graduated in 1876. In the meantime, scores of students had gone out as teachers without benefit of diploma.[20]

During the 1870s the Talladega faculty worried and fretted about the school's direction. Some wished to develop a college, but they correctly believed that the AMA favored Fisk and Atlanta University at their expense. When the association had to retrench, as it did in 1876, Talladega seemed to suffer most. The school never had adequate financial support or faculty. Even more damaging was unstable leadership. The first principal, Henry E. Brown, steered the school from elementary to normal training. In 1871 Brown was supplanted by Albert A. Safford, who further graded the normal school and increased the faculty from eight to twelve.[21] The Reverend George W. Andrews was sent to Talladega in 1875 to take charge of the church and theological department. Andrews, a courageous but petty and spiteful man, believed that religious instruction should take precedence over academic work and began a backbiting campaign against Safford, whom he claimed had been "inimical" to theological studies. Safford was relieved.[22] Andrews, now in charge, determined to make Talladega a theological school. However, his inefficient management led the association to send G. Stanley Pope to assist him. Pope, although a minister, believed that Talladega's main task should remain normal education. Another whispering campaign by Andrews, assisted by a new teacher, Edward P. Lord, resulted in Pope's ouster in 1877. Lord was then placed in charge of the school, a move that proved almost ruinous.[23]

Perhaps assuming that the association had no intention of making Talladega a college, Lord decided to transform the institution into an agricultural and mechanical school. The idea of industrial training was not new to the faculty. Since 1870 students and faculty had raised meat and vegetables on college land, but the object had been to provide food for students, not to teach agriculture. In 1876–77 Lord established an agriculture and industrial department. He began training young men at printing and convinced Connecticut donors to purchase a 160-acre farm. Lord wrote that the great mass of blacks were and must remain farm workers. What blacks needed, he said, were "more enterprise and more intelligent methods" of farming. Students spent more and more time on the farm and less in the classroom. Local whites seemed pleased by the new trend at Talladega, but most of the students and faculty were not.[24]

Even more injurious to Talladega than Andrews and Lord's indifference toward academics were their racial views. The school had not always been fortunate enough to have completely unprejudiced teachers, but prejudice had been openly faced and essential racial equality proclaimed. Andrews was a courageous missionary. Because of white hostility it had been his custom to preach to blacks with a loaded revolver on the pulpit, yet at the same time he had a low opinion of his flock and refused to stay or eat with them while traveling in the country. He seldom publicly discussed his views of the "*dreadful immorality,* and the *momentous, unrecognized and unsettled* problems" of blacks, but Talladega's constituency could hardly have failed to sense his attitude. Both he and Lord, especially the latter, catered to local whites in an attempt to gain their support.[25]

Lord's willingness to compromise principle became evident when he publicly humiliated a prominent black man, James F. Childs, at the 1877 commencement exercises. When Childs and a female companion arrived at a concert, only a few seats were unoccupied. As they started to sit down an usher warned them that the seats were reserved for whites. Childs sat down and sent the usher to fetch Lord. Lord, without speaking to the visitor, mounted the stage and, according to Childs, "drove us from the building not as you would drive a good dog, but as you would drive the meanest and lowest brute." Lord announced that there were some who refused to conform to the segregated seating pattern and asked them to leave at once.[26] Childs, accompanied by his brother Stephen, a member of the Talladega board of trustees, walked out. Childs angrily condemned Lord's actions and chided the association for inflicting such a man upon blacks. Unfortunately AMA secretary Michael E. Strieby, though obviously distressed at Lord's blunder, upheld him. He reminded Childs that the AMA had benefited many blacks, Childs included, as he had attended Fisk. Strieby's response made it appear that the association had abandoned its long-standing policy of racial equality.[27]

The Childs incident greatly offended Alabama blacks who had accepted Talladega as their college. Blacks from every major Alabama city were present at the 1877 commencement. Excursion trains had taken large groups from Montgomery and Selma. The following year there were no excursion trains, and there were no leading black men present from outside the county. During its first decade Talladega had been beset by white prejudice, Ku Klux Klan threats, poverty, inadequate financing, AMA neglect, and poor leadership. Despite these difficulties it had survived, if not prospered. Talladega students had taught thousands of Alabamians. Still others had become attorneys, businessmen, physicians, ministers, and community leaders. Black Alabamians were proud of "their college." Lord's leadership threatened to end all that. In 1878 it appeared that the dream of Talladega becoming a major college might be destroyed by a pandering to white prejudice.[28]

Fortunately AMA officials recognized and partially rectified their error by firing Lord. An 1879 decision to elevate Talladega to a college was followed by the auspicious appointment of Henry S. DeForest as president. DeForest, Yale graduate, former Union Army chaplain, minister, and professor of mathematics, moved quickly to stabilize and upgrade the institution.[29] Within two years a black newspaper could claim that "Talladega College is an Institution of which every Alabamian should be proud." Under DeForest's exceptional leadership Talladega slowly and steadily, against great obstacles, progressed toward becoming a fine small college. Talladega would reflect the masthead motto of its school paper, the *Southern Sentinel:* "The Noblest Act of Man: To Help a Brother On."[30]

Straight University, organized in 1869 in New Orleans, differed from Fisk and Talladega in that it had law and medical as well as normal and college departments.[31] Within five years of its founding,

Straight had fifteen students studying law, ten in medicine, twenty in normal training, eighteen in college preparatory, and six in college. The law department was the most productive in the university. Between 1876 and 1886 it had 115 students and 81 graduates. Most of the law faculty were prominent New Orleans attorneys, and a degree from Straight admitted its holder to the Louisiana bar without taking the bar examination. As with other AMA schools, Straight was open to all races. Three of the first law graduates were whites. However, the law department was the only one that consistently breached racial barriers.[32]

Although it had fewer graduates than law, the medical department for a short time may have been one of the best in the state. The medical program was initially funded by a $35,000 grant from the state legislature, and its initial faculty was composed of local white physicians. The first dean of the medical faculty, C. B. White, was a member of the state board of health, as was S. C. Russell, professor of materia medica and therapeutics. Students and faculty practiced at New Orleans Charity Hospital. In 1871 a well-trained black physician, Dr. James T. Newman, became dean of the faculty and professor of surgery. Dr. Newman unsuccessfully urged the AMA to create a genuine medical school in New Orleans. All university departments suffered from lack of funds, but poverty was probably most damaging to the medical department.[33]

Straight was fortunate in that New Orleans had an able, prosperous black community, and it wisely urged local blacks to play a large role in the school.[34] In the early years Straight also had a better record for employing black teachers than Fisk or Talladega. John Turner, the black secretary of the board of trustees, was the first teacher hired. P. M. Williams, a Dartmouth graduate, became principal of the normal department. Dr. Charles H. Thompson of Oberlin directed the theology department, and Louis A. Bell directed the law school. Louis A. Martinet, linguist, lawyer and politician, was a popular language teacher. Dr. Newman supervised the medical school, and other blacks taught elementary students.[35] Straight further pleased the community by providing needed services. It offered night classes in business, bookkeeping, accounting, and commercial law, and for a time it operated a free infirmary at Hathaway Home for the poor. In 1872 Dr. Newman prescribed for almost three thousand people at the infirmary.

The university furnished an "audience room" on Sunday and week-nights for those who sought "intelligent preaching and interesting discussion." Dr. Newman, J. Sella Martin, and P. B. S. Pinchback were among those giving lectures in 1871–72. The most influential blacks patronized Straight. The Antoines, Lewises, Pinchbacks, Dumases, and other distinguished families enrolled their children. It was not a school merely for the upper class, however. More poor than wealthy students attended. Enrollment usually declined in the spring when students left to work on plantations.[36]

Straight temporarily lost favor in the black community under the administration of James A. Adams. Adams, a keen satirical writer of strong will and considerable ability, was a devoted leader of the school. It was largely his adept financial management that enabled Straight to succeed between 1873 and 1876. But he was also cold and unbending. "His face, his words and his conduct are like those of a confirmed dyspeptic," wrote a colleague. More important were his views of blacks and politics. He concluded that "in spite of all our fine spun notions and even of our aspirations colored students as a body do not grasp with ability more advanced studies." He further angered blacks by blaming the state Republicans for "grinding poverty, corruption, fraud, turmoil & strife." A Republican defeat would be desirable, he said, because it would weaken black "arrogance, pomposity & strong color feeling" which were so prejudicial to their interests. Lieutenant Governor C. C. Antoine complained to the AMA that any man hostile to the Republican Party was unfit to teach black youth. The association recemented its ties to New Orleans blacks in 1877 by firing Adams.[37]

The successful law and medical departments gave the impression that Straight was thriving, but that was a misleading picture. Many of the more able black faculty left for better positions. The school had too few faculty and too many poverty-stricken students. As with most other black colleges, it had too little money to support proper growth. Then in 1877 an arsonist destroyed the campus. Within a few years the law department became independent and the medical school ceased to exist. The university was rebuilt, but during the 1880s it concentrated on normal education and collegiate work languished. Still, it was the strongest black college in Louisiana. It had sent out hundreds of teachers and would dispatch hundreds more. As a local black newspaper said, "It is a beacon light and a benefactor to this community."[38]

Of the other colleges founded by the American Missionary Association, Atlanta University was probably the best. The school was chartered in 1867 and the first normal and academic classes began in 1869. By 1872 fifteen students had graduated from the preparatory classes and were to commence college work the following fall. They had not read quite as much Greek and Latin as was required for admission to New England colleges, the faculty thought, but they had had more than was required in southern and western schools. For a time the Georgia legislature made an annual appropriation to Atlanta, but the grant was withdrawn because the faculty mixed socially with their students and the black community. Under Edmund A. Ware's wise leadership, Atlanta University trained many teachers and moved in the direction of collegiate work.[39]

Though it was founded as a college, Hampton Institute in Hampton, Virginia, was a normal and industrial school and made no pretense of offering college work for several decades. Moreover, its early history is more closely associated with its leader, Samuel Chapman Armstrong, than with the AMA. As one association officer wrote: "It is a sorry caricature of the original impulse of Hampton to define it in the terms of a pedagogical idea. It was rather a man incarnate—Armstrong himself, multiplied and in action." The AMA continued to assist the school financially, but by the 1870s it played a limited decision-making role.[40]

Tougaloo was organized in 1869 and incorporated as a university in 1871. It contributed importantly to Mississippi by training superior teachers (its first normal class graduated in 1879), but did not grant a bachelor's degree until 1901. From the beginning Tougaloo offered industrial and manual training. No other school controlled by the AMA so thoroughly coordinated manual training with its academic program.[41]

Berea, the only AMA college not founded specifically for blacks,[42] was organized in 1859 by abolitionist and AMA missionary John G. Fee and a recent Oberlin graduate, John A. R. Rogers. Its bylaws prohibited discrimination because of race. The school was almost immediately broken up by slavery sympathizers. Berea was incorporated soon after the war and added its first black students in 1866. The school was unique in that it not only denounced discrimination but provided "a *practicable* demonstration of impartial education."[43] By the 1870s it was almost equally divided by race, with students living and studying together harmoniously.[44]

As can be seen from a brief description of its colleges, the AMA did not advocate a particular type of education to the exclusion of others. Fisk, Atlanta University, and Straight emphasized teacher training and a classical education, while Hampton became one of the most outstanding industrial schools. Relatively ambitious programs of industrial education were also inaugurated at Tougaloo and Talladega. That the association found industrial training and the liberal arts compatible was not surprising. Both were popular in mid-nineteenth-century America. George Whipple, the AMA's principal leader from 1865 to 1876, had received his first training at Oneida Institute, a manual labor school, but he had also been principal of the preparatory department and professor of mathematics at Oberlin. Whipple strongly supported Fisk and Atlanta and at the same time championed Armstrong and Hampton Institute. The debate on the merits of a liberal or industrial education for blacks was active on AMA campuses well before Booker T. Washington became a spokesman for the latter. Spence and Cravath of Fisk, Ware of Atlanta University, and DeForest of Talladega staunchly defended classical studies.[45] Armstrong was a national spokesman for industrial education. The association fostered both. It believed that blacks should have access to all levels of education— from elementary to industrial and technical, professional, teacher training, and the classical. It supported industrial education but vigorously opposed concentrating on it alone. Its concept of equality of education for blacks allowed no such limitations.[46]

Whatever their location, stage of progress, or type of training offered, the AMA colleges experienced similar problems. All suffered from frequently changing faculty. Fisk was fortunate to have Spence, Chase, and Morgan until their retirement, but such stability was uncommon during the early years. Most of the first teachers were northerners who considered themselves missionaries. Occasionally their commitment was long-term, but more often it was one to three years. Even when teachers remained for long periods, they might be shifted from school to school. More damaging to some colleges was changing leadership. Only Hampton, Atlanta, and Berea had consistent early leadership. Fisk had been founded nine years before Erastus M. Cravath became president. DeForest, appointed in 1879, was the first director of Talladega who understood what a college should be. Leadership was erratic even longer at Tougaloo and Straight.[47]

If a school was fortunate enough to have a vigorous, competent leader, he was hampered by his dependence on the association. Decisions relating to salaries, repairs, personnel, and even curriculum were made at AMA headquarters in New York. Almost every action had to be cleared with New York, and frequently it was months before answers were received. A. A. Safford of Talladega had to badger association officers before finally getting reluctant permission to build a privy for female boarders. Permission was required for making even small expenditures, and mail communication was slow and uncertain. The most able men were sometimes given more power, but seldom did the AMA delegate authority to its administrators commensurate with their responsibilities. Such a centralized system, which required submitting even inconsequential problems to New York to be decided by men unacquainted with local details, proved impractical. E. M. Cravath, who had previously been one of the most inflexible and difficult AMA officials, refused to accept the Fisk presidency until authority was vested in the university trustees.[48]

One reason why the AMA retained financial control was because funds were so scarce. In its haste to provide education for freedmen, the association established more schools than it could comfortably support. Frequently bills could not be paid in the South until further collections were made in the North. After the association expended $25,000 more than it had collected in the summer of 1874, Secretary Michael E. Strieby recommended that Straight and Tougaloo be placed on the "most limited basis consistent with preservation" and that Talladega's college and theological departments be transferred to Atlanta University. Strieby's recommendation was rejected, but the colleges continued to suffer. Salaries were often in arrears, and even minor repairs had to be postponed. Equipment, supplies, and libraries were inadequate. Since the AMA's constituency was so poor, assistance from tuition was minimal.[49] Annual begging campaigns became the norm for the struggling black colleges.

Lack of well-prepared students also inhibited college growth. Since education had generally been forbidden during slavery, there were few freedmen prepared for even normal training. Moreover, secondary schools for blacks remained scarce for several decades, with the result

that the institutions had to educate their own students up to college
level. And while there was no lack of able, ambitious black youth, it
was a rare student who could afford to remain in school for several
years. Staying in school was a desperate struggle for most. In 1873
almost one-half of the Fisk student body taught in country schools six
months of the year to finance their education during the remainder.
Andrew Gleaden of Talladega taught school to pay his college expenses. During one three-year period he was able to attend classes for
only three months. James F. Childs dropped out of school to work as a
carpenter for fifteen cents an hour to save for tuition. At the end of
twelve months he had a balance of only ten cents. A few fortunate
students such as the daughter of a white man, a former Confederate
colonel, were able to pay tuition easily, but for most, simply to clothe
and feed themselves was a strain. In 1871 the Talladega principal
asked for several pairs of shoes or "some of the young men will have to
go *barefoot* ere long." Sterling Brown's case was not unique. Brown
was born a slave at Post Oak Springs, Tennessee. After emancipation
he worked on a farm until 1867, when he attended Fisk for a short
time, then dropped out to earn enough money to return. A decade
after his first enrollment he was still a student. In the ten years he had
managed to be in school only about twenty-six months.[50]

As if poverty and hesitant leadership were not enough, the AMA
colleges had to contend with white hostility. When W. E. B. DuBois
enrolled at Fisk he was astonished to learn that some of his fellow
students carried firearms for protection. Klan activity and violence in
Nashville affected attendance at Fisk in 1869 and again in 1874. In
1870 Talladega was debilitated by fear. Two schools taught by Talladega students had been destroyed, and there were threats of burning
the college. The principal ordered weapons from New York to defend
the school. On one occasion approximately fifty Klansmen marching
toward the campus were dissuaded by local citizens, who perhaps took
seriously the promise of local blacks to burn the town if Talladega were
destroyed. In August 1871 male faculty and students stood guard
nightly. As has already been mentioned, Straight fell victim to an arsonist in 1877. Buildings were also burned at Hampton, Talladega, and
Tougaloo. After Straight was burned, the Continental Insurance Company of New York canceled AMA policies on the grounds that its work
was hazardous.[51]

How significant were the AMA colleges? Were they valuable institutions encouraging black progress or were they simply inferior pseudo-colleges giving their students false hope? The AMA itself had doubts. In 1881 association and college representatives met at Fisk to discuss the future of black higher education. Only Atlanta University and Fisk, they concluded, had justified their existence as colleges. Opinion was divided about Talladega, in part because of its location, and there were even more reservations about Tougaloo, which had offered almost no collegiate work. Straight University, although in the midst of a large, progressive black population, had not recovered from the earlier fire. Hampton was no more than a normal school, and Tillotson, chartered in 1875, had just that year begun normal classes. After much wrangling the association approved Fisk, Atlanta, Straight, Talladega, and Tougaloo as colleges. Association delegates were not under the delusion that they had five strong institutions. They knew that even the best of them were marginal, but they determined to continue their quest to provide blacks with the best education the country had to offer.[52]

Not only were the colleges limited in libraries and laboratories, but they were understaffed. The faculty was predominantly white, and they were often cultural imperialists, unable to recognize many of the positive aspects of black culture. Indeed, some were tainted with racism, and almost all believed their ways superior to those of southerners, black or white. One reason why all the colleges had boarding departments where students lived, ate, and worked with the faculty was to infuse students with a reputed superior northern Christian culture. Yet most of them assumed that it was Christianity, religious training, and experience, not whiteness, that gave them superiority. Blacks had been degraded by slavery and perhaps were not their equals, but at worst freedmen could be improved and at best they were potentially equal. Moreover, the association assumed that the more quickly blacks conformed to white standards the sooner artificial racial barriers would be dismantled. Teachers were often paternalistic and sometimes arrogant in their assumptions of cultural superiority, but their intent was egalitarian.[53]

Despite their shortcomings, these fledgling colleges founded after the war represented the best opportunity to most freedmen for higher education and they had a profound and lasting impact on black Americans. They were not comparable to major universities, but neither were scores of white colleges. Limited faculties and scarce equipment were not peculiar to black or even southern schools. If the AMA had accomplished nothing more than training teachers, the expense and effort would have been justified. In 1873, 710 teachers from association schools and colleges were instructing approximately 64,000 pupils. By 1890 AMA institutions had trained thousands of teachers whose influence had penetrated virtually every southern black community.[54]

John H. Burrus, who became president of Alcorn Agricultural and Mechanical College in Mississippi in 1882, was only the first of several Fisk graduates to head colleges. In 1900 at least forty-six graduates of the school were principals. Fisk-educated W. E. Mollison served as superintendent of schools of Issaquena County, Mississippi, in the 1880s. The other colleges produced their share of administrators and furnished competent teachers for their regions. A Pennsylvania traveler found a flourishing black school on the banks of the Oconee River in Georgia. The correctness with which the eighty students answered the visitor's questions convinced him of the extraordinary ability of the eighteen-year-old teacher from Atlanta University. Tougaloo and Talladega could barely meet state requests for their graduates, and Straight students were in demand throughout the Southwest. Traveling through Texas in 1879, field secretary Joseph E. Roy came upon a country school with half a dozen ponies picketed nearby. Some of the students had ridden five miles to school. The excellent teacher was a Straight graduate. She also taught a night and Sabbath school and, Roy observed, was "really the mistress of the community. And so one educated girl is lifting the whole neighborhood." These black teachers are forgotten heroes and heroines in the battle against illiteracy.[55]

Association colleges did more than educate teachers. More than one-third of the blacks who graduated from southern and border-state colleges by 1890 were from AMA schools. They became not only teachers but also ministers, physicians, attorneys, editors, bookkeepers, businessmen, government employees, politicians, housewives, farmers, druggists, and community leaders. But the graduates themselves may not have been the colleges' most important contribution during the late nineteenth century. For each student who graduated, the colleges provided a thorough elementary and secondary education to hundreds of others who in turn passed on their knowledge and acquired habits to family and friends. Their children and grandchildren were not compelled to begin their education in illiterate homes and wretched schools.[56]

The early colleges dramatically demonstrated to a skeptical nation that blacks were as capable of higher education as any other people. The schools continued to grow and mature, eventually acquiring black faculty and presidents. They trained twentieth-century black leaders in every field of endeavor. The AMA dared to dream of equality and holds a prominent place among the people and agencies that organized and developed schools which became outstanding black institutions of higher education.[57]

The AMA and
the Black Church

A LTHOUGH intimately involved in black education, the American Missionary Association was equally concerned about the freedmen's spiritual welfare. Duty "imperatively called" upon the AMA to furnish former slaves "with the Gospel of impartial love and with such instruction, as could enable them to read the precepts and understand its provisions of salvation." The association was determined not only to sunder the bonds of slavery but to free blacks from the fetters of superstition and sin and bring them "into the glorious liberty of the gospel."[1]

The possibilities for influencing black religion seemed limitless. Long desiring religious freedom and repelled by discrimination in white churches, blacks after emancipation quickly began to renounce their old religious connections and form churches of their own. With few exceptions, association personnel perceived black ministers as ignorant and immoral and their congregations as loud, emotional, and sinful. "The people are a *religious* people," one teacher wrote, "they love to sing and pray and have their shouts, but practical religion they know little of." Teachers spoke disparagingly of the freedmen's emotional fervor, their dancing and rolling on the floor. A northern black teacher declared that meetings were "generally demonstrative, and often boisterous, as they seem to worship on the principle that the Kingdom of heaven suffereth violence and the violent take it by force." Or as an elderly slave said, "It don't seem as if we poor ignorant Africans can come to the Savior as you educated folks do. We have to worry it out." Most AMA workers never fathomed the slave's religion, which emphasized joy and collective hope rather than personal guilt and self-denial.[2]

Black ministers and services did not offend all AMA observers, however. Mary Burdick, a teacher in Norfolk, Virginia, was charmed by "a genuine African 'down South' Methodist prayer meeting—a kind of national opera of feeling it was—the soul forgetful of worldly restraint . . . a wild wail of the human spirit—unrestrained . . . it was so impressive their rocking to and fro—their melodious response 'Oh Yes!' 'Oh Us!' to their speakers as they told them of the sorrows of the lost or the joys of the blessed." The service "affected me strangely," Burdick added. A Mississippi teacher heard "a rough uncultivated" but effective preacher. Another described a sermon as "simple, and part of it mere rant perhaps, but much of it seemed to me like genuine eloquence." Unfortunately more were appalled than charmed by black religion. They viewed services as "painful exhibitions of . . . barbarism" and unfairly branded black ministers as licentious, lazy clowns, forgetting "the many who toiled with stern morality and unremitting industry." The AMA concluded that a "serious religious reconstruction was in order."[3]

The association undertook to "raise" the level of southern black religion, to introduce a "pure" religion which imposed New Testament ethics on everyday life. Despite the tendency to condemn religious fervor, emotionalism was not at fault. Perhaps whites should take some lessons on that point. The danger of black religion was, in the association's view, that it was without morality and that it had a "magical system of salvation divorced from ethical imperatives." The freedmen needed not more religious enthusiasm or preaching but more accurate ideals of Christian character. The association was confident that it knew what those ideals should be. American religious groups are commonly influenced by class and provincial considerations and so was the AMA. Its officers confused "pure" religion with the "social, economic and intellectual style" to which they subscribed, and it was with the greatest difficulty that they avoided regarding their "way" as the correct one. Uplifting black religion therefore meant bringing freedmen "to that level of intelligence, character, Christian personhood, emotional sobriety, and economical social self-sufficiency" in keeping with the AMA's ideal and image.[4]

The decision to reconstruct black religion did not at first include establishing denominational churches. Reconstruction required an extensive program of acculturation and education to modify the freedmen's "peculiar" culture, religion, and past. Therefore, schools were temporarily more important than new churches. In 1865 the association announced measures "looking to a more thorough and systematic prosecution of our distinctively *religious* efforts." The plan embraced three classes of workers: the pious teacher, female family missionaries, and male missionaries. The teachers were to educate their pupils "into Christ," to rid them of their superstitious notions, and to teach morality. The women missionaries would visit homes, reading the Bible and giving practical instruction in personal, domestic, and social religion. The men were to supervise Sabbath schools, distribute Bibles, preach the gospel, serve as pastors for the teachers and schools, provide theological and academic instruction to black ministers, and organize churches when practical. When churches were organized, they were not to interfere with existing black churches, and they should be nondenominational. The association was heeding the advice of one of its agents who in 1864 had written: "The colored people have preachers of their own color . . . & though many of them are very ignorant & unsuited . . . there must be no manifest opposition to them, & no violent efforts to supersede them."[5]

The AMA's early religious work was nondenominational. It had cooperated with the African Methodist Episcopal and the African Methodist Episcopal Zion churches, even supporting some of their ministers, and it had commissioned missionaries and teachers from all evangelical Protestant denominations. Treasurer Lewis Tappan, who had been a Unitarian, a Presbyterian, and a Congregationalist, was especially adamant about the association's nondenominational stance. His antislavery struggles had led him to associate with Christians of all denominations, he said, and thus "cured" him of all sectarianism. Nevertheless, the AMA became more closely linked to Congregationalism in 1865 when it was endorsed by the National Council of Congregationalists. At the same time, other denominations that had supported the AMA began to establish their own freedmen's aid societies, and this left the association more dependent upon Congregational churches for its collections. Congregationalists then began to urge the association to plant Congregational churches in the South. For the next decade the AMA had to solicit and retain Congregational support while resisting becoming a denominational agency for church extension.[6]

When in 1866 some supporters urged the AMA to abandon its schools and concentrate on church buildings, it energetically resisted. Without being faithless to God and the freedmen, the association said, it could not relinquish education to secular societies. Although some critics believed that no society could adequately educate and at the same time propagate the gospel, the association claimed the two were inextricably linked. It bid godspeed to others who wished to plant churches. Despite the AMA's clearly stated position, the controversy over church extension continued to fester and worsen, with the greatest pressure coming from Congregational supporters.[7]

In response to renewed Congregational criticism in 1867, the AMA admitted that it had established few churches, but for good reasons. The Puritan element in the South was weak. Yankee sentiment among blacks pertained more to civil liberty than to ecclesiastical affairs. Moreover, freedmen were traditionally and heartily devoted to other denominations. The "sentiment and ability" for Congregationalism was yet to be created. But, more important, the association was nondenominational. "Its proffers are made with equal sincerity to all evangelical churches." The association, in the face of criticism of those who pledged much of its support, courageously and explicitly stated "its commitment to interdenominational evangelicalism." It would not actively proselytize for the Congregationalists.[8]

The stand was not easily made. There was dissension even among association officials. As early as February 1865 Michael E. Strieby considered turning education over to the Freedmen's Bureau and state systems and emphasizing church expansion. Strieby, only recently pastor of a Congregational church, was sympathetic to denominational proselytizing and was susceptible to pressure to do so. District secretaries Erastus M. Cravath and Jacob R. Shipherd were eager to establish Congregational churches. Tappan, although a confirmed nonsectarian, was now retired, and this left George Whipple the only officer genuinely opposed to the association's becoming a Congregational church-planting agency.[9] Whipple was concerned about Congregational pressure, but he also feared that becoming blatantly denominational might diminish the flow of funds from the Freedmen's Bureau and check contributions from other churches. Moreover, he was deeply committed to the AMA's long-standing policy of nonsectarianism. Whipple resisted Congregational demands while at the same time hinting that more would be done. In 1868 the association announced that the "auspicious time for the formation of churches" among freedmen "on the basis of intelligence and active piety . . . has come," but it became only slightly more active in church building than previously.[10]

Although the AMA did not advocate vigorous church building, it boasted of the ones founded by local agents. In mid-1868 it had ten "promising churches" among freedmen; of the ten, three in Kentucky and the Union church at Fisk University in Nashville were non-denominational. The others were struggling Congregational churches whose memberships included primarily teachers and a few students from the schools. Much more significant to the AMA were its scores of nondenominational Sabbath schools with thousands of pupils. If possible, each day school was accompanied by Sunday schools. Higher institutions not only had Sunday schools but their teachers and students organized them in outlying areas. In 1864 "a monstrous mission" Sunday school in New Orleans had approximately nine hundred scholars "made up of white, red, yellow, black and indeed every shade ever known in the human family." In 1868 teachers in Wilmington and Beaufort, North Carolina, organized seven Sabbath schools with an attendance of two thousand. These schools were aimed as much at reading as at religion. Thousands who could not attend day school attended Sunday school.[11]

In 1869, in response to Congregational criticism that it had moved too slowly in establishing churches, the AMA called a conference of representatives of its southern churches to discuss strategy for church expansion. Convinced that the South badly needed the Pilgrims' "faith and church polity," and believing that such polity was based upon intelligence, the conference recommended placing churches "side by side" with good schools. One AMA minister argued that it was useless to found a church without a school. "Without an intellectual foundation it is a suspension bridge without abutments or piers," he said. Thus began the association's "church beside school" policy that it pursued for several years.[12]

By the 1870s the AMA had become more openly denominational. Most of its officers had always been Congregationalist, and now funds from other denominations were limited. Furthermore, with the end of the Freedmen's Bureau Whipple no longer feared that denominationalism would limit government largess. Still, the association did not rush heedlessly into church building. It was never industrious enough to please Congregationalists, who were always disappointed in the number of new members. The association continued to stress religious training for preparation of membership. In 1871 Whipple and Strieby said they made no attempt to proselytize; they intended to prepare

freedmen through Christian schools "to appreciate and demand an educated ministry and a pure church." The church would be given increased attention, "not by abandoning but by pushing forward the
work of Christian education."[13]

As late as 1874 the AMA, now admittedly sectarian, defiantly told
disgruntled Congregationalists that it had carried out church work in
the proper way by "planting the pure church, the Christian school, and
thus laying the foundation for the cultured home, the useful citizen and
the intelligent Christian." It added that it had not met Congregational
expectations in church expansion because the AMA had directed most
of its money and energy toward the greater need for education.
"Evangelization through education and acculturation" rather than establishment of churches remained its major thrust. The association
was still determined to export a "way of life" to freedmen. It refused
to sacrifice religious schools for churches.[14]

Even when churches were founded, they were sometimes nondenominational. In 1874 Atlanta University organized an independent
church which had Baptist, African Methodist, Methodist Episcopal,
Congregational, Presbyterian, Lutheran, and Episcopal members.
The church at Athens, Alabama, was union though the local association teacher and church leader was a Methodist with Presbyterian pre-
dilections. J. K. Nutting, Tougaloo College president, complained in
1873 that he had been "notified to keep my Congregationalism in
abeyance down here," which operated "as a kind of dead-lock on all the
religious part of our work. Judging from results," Nutting added, "I
am sure it operates so all over the field." Nutting lamented that he was
"manufacturing a ministry for every denomination except for the one I
love best."[15]

The history of southern Congregationalism proved that the association policy of deliberate church expansion was justified. In the 1870s
none of the churches was self-supporting. The association paid the pastors and often were compelled to maintain the building as well. The
stronger churches were associated with schools and colleges, and when
these churches withdrew from college fellowship, as happened in
Nashville and Talladega, they tended to decline. In 1869–70 Joseph W.
Healy, an energetic Congregational minister, established thirteen mission churches in Louisiana. Within a year most of them were struggling for survival. Some were Congregational in name only, and ser-

vices were sometimes a mixture of several denominational practices. When the association demanded that the churches become "full-fledged Congregationalists," many members left and joined the Baptists and Methodists. Even the church at Straight University, Central Congregational, which boasted some of New Orleans's black elite as members, languished. Not only did members neglect to pay the pastor but they ignored the gas bill so long that the gas was turned off. The Straight principal charged that the wealthier parishioners would rather spend $1,000 on politics than $100 on religion.[16]

Numerous AMA missionaries concluded that one reason for church frailty was black discontent with white ministers. Although Healy had placed black preachers in mission churches in Louisiana and there were a few freedmen ministers in other rural areas, most Congregational pastors were white. Missionaries had quickly noted that "as to preaching they seem to prefer their own colored ministers to us." In 1869 C. W. Sharp asked that the Reverend Robert Carter be assigned to the Savannah church because he "can influence these old leaders, in a manner that no *white* man can." The "old preachers stand between us & the people," Sharp continued, "& the people are declining into a sort of heathenism." In Macon, Georgia, the Reverend E. E. Rogers requested a black replacement. The interest of the church demanded it, Rogers said, adding that "there is a prejudice on the part of this community against a *white face* which only those on the ground can feel."[17]

The association began to employ more black ministers, but the results were not always gratifying. Carter proved to be more a Presbyterian than a Congregationalist. He borrowed money from the church that he refused to repay, and he had an alarming fondness for alcohol. After he was dismissed, two young men from nearby missions were sent to Savannah. Their character, sincerity, and energy were commendable, but they were judged too uneducated for city service. The subsequent white pastor was replaced by black James Porter after other blacks sneered that it was the only church with a white minister. Porter was unable to "get hold of the people . . . and like a man handed in his resignation." He was replaced by Leonadus A. Rutherford, a black medical doctor as well as minister. Rutherford seemed popular until his congregation learned that his sister had once been a prostitute and was now a Roman Catholic. Although Rutherford was "an excellent spirited man [of] good judgment, fair ability, tolerable education," his sister's reputation and the response to his wife, who was so fair that few knew whether she was white or black, resulted in his leaving Savannah for another Congregational church in Bryan, Georgia.[18]

The Reverend W. A. L. Campbell's experience at Macon was no more pleasant than Rutherford's at Savannah. At first Campbell, a Jamaican, was favorably received. He preached well, expounded the scriptures wisely, and showed "himself in every way so much a man." But soon he quarreled with Secretary E. M. Cravath, whom he accused of paying him less because of his color. By the time Campbell resolved his differences with Cravath he had become disillusioned with the freedmen's "semifetishism" and low morals. His congregation soon petitioned for his removal on the grounds that his manner repelled the people, that there had been no recent revival, and that his wife was a Catholic.[19]

The St. Paul Congregational Church in New Iberia, Louisiana, illustrated the futility of establishing churches simply to appease northern Congregationalists. St. Paul was organized in 1871. Its congregation was drawn more by the promise of financial aid than by creed, and within two years church members had driven off two ministers who were trying to train them in New England ways. The AMA then decided to send the patient and puritanical Hardy Mobley to take charge. Born a slave in Georgia, Mobley had managed to free himself and his family and migrate to Brooklyn, New York. Mobley had returned South at the war's end, and he and his daughter Laura had proven to be able, patient, hardworking friends of freedmen. The Mobleys cheerfully and optimistically began work in New Iberia, even though upon their arrival a member said the church wanted no "Congregationers" who were a nuisance and in fact wanted no "foreign teachers nohow." The ever hopeful Mobley thought the situation was as pleasant as could be expected, given the fact that many of the members were Baptists.[20]

After a year of relative success with both the school they taught and the church, the Mobleys' position rapidly deteriorated. An attempt to collect money to replace the shabby, unheated church building failed. The already poor congregation was damaged first by flood, then by drought, and political turmoil and violence caused further economic distress. Mobley alienated two of the most powerful members of his congregation by refusing to support their campaign for political office.

He irritated even more members in a quarrel over baptism. They preferred immersion and Mobley refused "to go into the water." After the pastor severely reproached church youth for their frivolity, his daughters were attacked on the streets. In early 1875 a majority of the congregation voted to withdraw from the AMA "now & forever" in view of the fact that there had been nothing but trouble since the church came under the association. Although some of the members were devoted to Mobley, the association fired him in order to appease the majority, who reluctantly agreed to remain in the church but chased away the subsequent pastor within a few months.[21]

The weakness of the several churches hastily organized between 1869 and 1871 reinforced the AMA's view that gathering nondescript congregations into the fold to please the Congregationalists' desire for new members was unwise. It determined to exercise greater care in planting churches and to emphasize the training of ministers who could then create a closer union between religion and morals in the community. By the 1870s the association despaired of educating older ministers as "their age, the necessity of toil and their prejudice are all in the way." It now saw "more and more clearly that the effort must be to *train a race of young ministers.*"[22]

In order to meet the need for trained ministers, theological departments were begun at Straight, Talladega, Tougaloo, Fisk, Atlanta, and Howard.[23] The last was not an AMA school, but the association supported and selected the theological faculty. There was no intent to train only Congregational ministers. The theological departments were nondenominational. The dean of the Howard department was a black Presbyterian minister, John Bunyan Reeve. In 1872 Howard had eighteen students of different denominations as well as four Methodist preachers from the city who attended when they could. Since the number of theological students was always small—sixty-nine in 1874— the association developed an auxiliary plan to provide more "enlightened" preaching.[24] Beginning in 1873 some of the more pious and promising college students were sent out during the vacation to preach. Students had traditionally taught in rural areas during summers. These men would preach and be paid by the AMA equal to what they would make teaching. The money would be well spent, the association claimed, because it would at the same time be educating a potential preacher and the "ignorant people" who heard him, and the pay would enable the student to continue his education. During the next several years college and theological students did much of the association's rural mission work.[25]

Association students and teachers were responsible for what little success the AMA experienced in spreading Congregationalism during the 1870s and 1880s. There were clusters of mission churches surrounding the colleges and Beach Institute in Savannah, and these mission churches were usually pastored by AMA students or former students. Dozens of able black men devoted their lives to directing infirm Congregational churches and teaching in rural schools. Floyd Snelson is an example of such a laborer. Snelson, a former slave, enrolled in an AMA school in Andersonville, Georgia, in 1868. Family responsibilities caused irregular attendance, but with hard work and further study at Atlanta University Snelson achieved a fair common-school education. After being ordained for the ministry in 1871, he pastored churches at both Bryan and Andersonville. Although extremely poor, he boarded several rural children to enable them to attend school. In 1874 the AMA sent Snelson to Golding Grove, Georgia, where he and his family lived in an open corncrib until he managed to rent a small three-room house. After moving into the house, the Snelsons boarded the local schoolteacher without charge.

Snelson soon became preacher, friend, advisor, and political counselor to a large and devoted flock. When in 1877 the association determined to send him to Africa as a missionary, his congregation objected. The AMA sent Field Secretary Thomas N. Chase to persuade them that Snelson's departure was God's will. After Chase spoke to the church an elderly member went to the podium, fell upon his knees, and threw his arms around his pastor. "This fired the tinder and such a pandemonium I never saw," Chase wrote. One man announced, "If you take him away put fire to the house, congregation dead." Another said, "He is the Shepherd. When he speaks we hear. When he weeps we groan." Still another protested, "We haint got no sight. We jest blind till this brother come here." Despite protests Snelson went to Africa in late 1877. When he returned a year later due to his wife's delicate health, more than a thousand people gathered to hear him speak.[26]

Other ministers labored no less diligently than Snelson. Lindsey Roberts pastored an Athens, Alabama, church for several years. A three-week revival in March 1876 resulted in thirty-seven conversions and twenty-three additions to the church, which increased total membership to only forty-one. Constant effort was required to keep the church alive. John McLean was studying for the ministry at Talladega when passion overcame circumspection and he was expelled from school. He decided to continue his ministry, and the association, showing unexpected compassion, gave him the pastorate of a small church in Ogeechee, Georgia. McLean's meager salary forced him to live in the church house. When the building proved too small for services, he himself built an addition. Poorly educated, but an eloquent speaker and a fine singer, McLean was a good pastor. He had more than ordinary ability, was deeply concerned for his people, and was devoutly pious. He studied hard to compensate for his lack of formal education.[27]

With the aid of McLean and other black preachers—there were sixty-nine missionaries in the field in 1878—the association increased the membership in churches under its care from 2,757 in 1871 to 4,189 in 1878. A majority of the new members supposedly were Congregationalists. In 1878 the AMA placed new emphasis on church expansion by appointing the Reverend Joseph E. Roy as field secretary. Roy, who was the first field secretary to be more concerned with churches than with schools, moved to the South and gave the first genuine direction to southern Congregationalism. A few of the churches became self-supporting during this period. In 1880 a young black Oberlin graduate, the Reverend Benjamin Albert Imes, went to the Second Congregational Church in Memphis, which in twelve years had never become financially independent under white pastors. Imes was able to transform his mission church into a self-reliant congregation. Henry Hugh Proctor, Fisk and Yale University Seminary graduate, did the same for the Atlanta Congregational Church.[28]

Despite the indefatigable labor of Roy and dozens of missionaries, Congregationalism grew slowly in the South.[29] Without the many AMA schools it would hardly have grown at all. A large percentage of southern Congregationalists were association teachers, students, or former students. In 1876 A. N. Niles, a longtime AMA representative, advised about church work in Savannah. "The conclusion is obvious and at hand. If you are going to carry on your church work here—*hold on to your school work. If you are going to give up school work let go of your churches.* It certainly would be spilling water on the ground,"

Niles counseled, "to spend money to establish churches which at best are *exotic* here and will not in half a doz. generations rise into the atmosphere of self-support without the aid of schools." Congregational churches seldom flourished without an AMA school nearby.[30]

Thirty years of AMA prayers, work, and money made only a feeble impression on black religion. The reasons why the association failed in church expansion were numerous, not the least of which was Niles's claim that Congregationalism was exotic in the South. It had never been a national church. Even though they had separated from southern whites, blacks tended to remain in familiar denominations. One of the few successful black Congregational churches away from a major school was the Midway Congregational Church in Liberty County, Georgia. Established in the 1750s, it had a number of slave members who continued to worship there after emancipation, including black patriarch William A. Golding, a delegate to the Georgia Constitutional Convention in 1867–68 and a member of the legislature. Golding had been a member of Midway Church since 1839 and a selectman since 1843. His grandfather had been a Congregational minister. When these black Congregationalists decided to organize a church of their own after the war, there were 103 charter members of the New Midway Congregational Church. Had there been more such churches before the war, the AMA would have had greater success. Its zeal and money could not overcome unfamiliarity.[31]

Congregational services were as unfamiliar to many blacks as the name itself. Association missionaries quickly learned that freedmen were not always responsive to their methods of worship. In 1865 E. P. Smith warned that "our preachers must be wide awake men who will not only allow *fervor* of worship in both expression and form, but will heartily enjoy it." As late as 1870 the AMA cautioned against going too far in repressing freedmen's religious emotions. "While the feelings are not all of religion," an *American Missionary* editorial noted, "there is no full-orbed religion without them. The defect of the piety of the white race is that it has so little emotion." Indeed, the editorial continued, "One of the beautiful and blessed effects of a real Christian culture for the negro would be the reflex influence of his emotive religion upon the unimaginative and unemotional white people who are now benefitting him."[32]

These warnings went largely unheeded by association missionaries.

Congregationalism was noted for its soberness, its simplicity, and its
leaning toward intellectualism. Such services simply did not appeal to
many former slaves, whose religion was "fiery glad." According to the-
ologian Joseph R. Washington, Jr., black folk religion was experien-
tial. It began and ended in the black folk experience. It was a religion
of dramatizing or acting out "the experience of the people through
uninhibited feelings expressed in powerful tones." Black religion,
Washington added, was one "of ritual, drama, and 'didactical cathar-
sis.'" African Methodist Episcopal Bishop W. J. Gaines claimed that
fervency and emotion were among the most admirable characteristics
of black religion. Blacks, he said, loved "the moving stirring appeal"
and reveled "in the full tide of emotional feeling." They had no tolerance "for the coldly intellectual discourse, and the quiet formal worship." They wished "to be moved to tears," to be deeply touched, to be
swept away "by the thrilling, the pathetic, the awe-inspiring."[33]

Naturally, not all freedmen demanded emotional services, but the
black preacher was often judged by the "rousement" of his sermons.
Congregationalism not only failed to arouse but its ministers denounced demonstrativeness in black churches. They mistook a genuine
folk religion for superstition and ignorance, fervency of worship for
mere noise. To many freedmen Congregational services were "a cold,
icy, formal mode of worship, which so deadens all religious life and
delight." When an AMA teacher chided a black minister for being a
"shouter" and asked him to prove by the Bible that such practices
were holy, the minister replied haughtily that blacks did not want
"book religion," they wanted "heart felt religion." Despite warnings
from association agents that the work was "suffering . . . from our
lack of sympathy with what is good in the old churches," the AMA
gave freedmen book religion. Freedmen would not easily be persuaded
to abandon the religious fervor and practices that had served them so
well. As Leon Litwack observed, it was not that blacks refused to
consider new methods of worship, "but only that they often found
these new ways too far removed from God's presence."[34]

Another weakness of association churches was the tendency to provide northern pastors for urban congregations. Few of the churches
prospered under white leadership. Black preachers and congregations
better understood each other. Moreover, most white ministers were
"unable to intone the spirituals or invoke the traditional ritual neces-

sary for stirring the unconscious, the soul of the black believer," nor could they preach in the freedmen's vernacular. Black congregations were also sensitive about derisive comments that they had "a white master over them." Northern-trained black preachers were usually more acceptable than whites, but even then cultural and educational differences often separated them from their flocks. As a rule no minister seemed as successful among the freedmen as one who "had arisen among them."[35]

Many churchgoers also resented their lack of power. Since Congregational churches were often missions, many decisions were made for them. The St. Paul Congregational Church in New Iberia, Louisiana, selected neither Hardy Mobley nor his successor. Members of the Congregational Church in Montgomery, Alabama, indignantly complained that as Congregationalists they should have the right to choose their pastor and control their own affairs. In a sense the early churches were schools of democracy, with former slaves becoming trustees, deacons, Sabbath school superintendents, and church secretaries, but ultimate authority rested with New York officials. Freedmen were willing to accept association aid in locating church buildings or even pastors, but they resented the control that accompanied church organization. When AMA ministers sought to alter their methods of conducting church business and styles of worship, they believed that their independence was being compromised.[36] Or perhaps it was not the authority itself but the source and how it was applied that was resented. Congregationalists advocated eventual local autonomy, while the A.M.E. church was rigidly episcopal in nature. But A.M.E. ministers were black and they made fewer radical changes in methods of worship.

Closely connected with northern control was AMA paternalism. The association had denounced caste, advocated black suffrage, and recognized no racial distinction in its churches and schools. In 1874 the AMA reiterated its stand on segregation. It said that it opposed "now as it did in the days of slavery, all class distinctions—none of its schools or churches will tolerate it, nor will it assist in . . . sustaining teachers or missionaries who make these distinctions." The association stood almost alone in the United States when in 1878 it declared "that all men shall be regarded as equal *before God and the law*" and that no racial distinctions should be made in "churches of Christ."[37]

Nevertheless, even those who defied southern white racial mores often suffered from racial prejudice themselves. A majority of the most flagrantly bigoted were quickly culled out. Most missionaries saw equality as an ideal even if they sometimes failed to practice it, but nearly all AMA personnel were severely afflicted with a feeling of cultural superiority that could be as annoying and destructive as racial prejudice. They were determined to direct and control. Armed with the arrogant belief that their culture and faith were superior, they were often impatient with and intolerant of those upon whom they were trying to impose their views. Most northern missionaries were never able to appreciate or fully comprehend other life-styles. That may have been their greatest weakness.[38]

The AMA believed that black sectarianism limited the spread of Congregationalism, and although the common view that sectarianism was more pronounced among blacks than whites is not demonstrable, it was a factor. A Congregational revival in Childersburg, Alabama, in 1878 resulted in eleven youths uniting with the church. Parents and guardians forbade nine others to join. The pastor regretfully observed that as soon as the church showed "signs of unusual life" great opposition developed. The irate pastor of a black Baptist church declared that he would rather see the children go to hell than join the Congregationalists. A Missouri preacher thought that black ministers so feared the AMA school's religious influence over pupils that they would crush it if they could. In Cuthbert, Georgia, the Baptist minister encouraged students to attend a private school that charged tuition rather than the association school, which was free.[39]

Far more important than sectarianism in inhibiting Congregationalism was blacks' enthusiasm for their own religion. Black religion sprang from the slaves' creative response to the reality of slavery. Blacks developed a folk religion and a spirit that tended to unite them "in a brotherhood" which took "precedence over their individual patterns for the worship of God, or the lack thereof."[40]

W. E. B. DuBois claimed that the church was "the first distinctively" American black social institution. After emancipation it "represented both the institutionalization" of black "community life and defiance to white authority." It became the freedmen's sanctuary. They turned to the church for cultural, social, and recreational as well as spiritual needs. Black ministers gave them messages of hope, political advice, and even news of the price of cotton. As Leon Litwack said, "Far more than any newspaper, convention, or political organization, the minister communicated directly and regularly with his constituents and helped to shape their lives in freedom." The church represented to blacks not only their religion but also their independence. Only in church did they have autonomy. Only in church did they meet with no white interference.[41]

The AMA early recognized that the black church was unique, that freedmen preferred their own services and preachers. After touring the South in 1865, E. P. Smith predicted that black denominations would attract a majority of the freedmen. Northern white churches, he added, could not stand "against the tide toward Africa. The ebony preacher who promises perfect independence from white control & direction carries the cold. heart at once." Missionaries had witnessed what happened when the Reverend Alexander W. Wayman of the African Methodist Episcopal church visited them in Norfolk, Virginia, in 1863. Wayman's short stay had resulted in eight hundred members and nine ministers joining the A.M.E. church. The Reverend Amos G. Beman, a black AMA missionary, correctly claimed that blacks needed and wanted their ministers to be "of them 'bone of their bone flesh of their flesh.'" Still, the association underestimated the strength of the black church. Its schools were overcrowded; surely numerous freedmen could be brought into their churches.[42]

Not surprisingly, black denominations sometimes encouraged the black tendency toward separation. The African Methodist Episcopal church proclaimed that it was "the church for all colored Methodists of this country." A northern Methodist lamented that "the . . . wholly colored churches" were as intensely prejudiced against whites as southern whites were against blacks. Black ministers argued that blacks could never have their rights in a white-dominated denomination, and in most cases they were correct. The African Methodist Episcopal Zion church in Texas advocated separation on a scriptural basis, asserting that the Bible instructed: "Come out from among them, and be ye separate." In 1870 the black-edited *New Era* charged that the "keeping up of distinctions in the churches 'rests with us.'"[43]

The AMA was destined to fail in its sometimes hesitant attempts to convert blacks to Congregationalism. Congregationalism "encompassed a social and religious orientation" that was foreign to freedmen, who responded to it with more trepidation than enthusiasm. Only a few stable churches were formed. There were too many obstacles. The missionaries did not understand black religion, were sometimes insensitive to black needs, and were too often white. The church was too unfamiliar and its services too alien. But if all these weaknesses had been absent, the association still would have failed. The attraction of the black church was too great. Congregationalists grappled unsuccessfully with "the already profoundly entrenched" black church, which "could be neither easily flouted nor broken through." Two forceful church movements, created and nurtured by widely dissimilar religious, social, and racial traditions and with divergent views of what society and the church should be, contended for the freedmen, and the black church won easily. The AMA's failure to establish Congregationalism among blacks cannot be understood except by recognizing the black church "which—going back even to its far-off African past—met and resisted it with remarkable strength."[44]

10

Yankee Schoolteachers

THE NORTHERNERS who came South to teach the freedmen have been variously viewed as courageous heroes or meddlesome fanatics, idealistic egalitarians or hypocrites who taught blacks for ulterior motives.[1] According to southern reports, legions of "slab-sided old maids" assisted by an occasional "Dr. Malgamation" flocked to the South to teach former slaves "to lie and steal." A Louisianian branded them as "miserable wretches, imported scalawags, pale faced renegades and pensioned pimps," while a Georgia editor claimed they were mostly women, "all either fanatics or knaves" with the "sole mission" to "stir up strife and sow the tares of hate and evil in the minds of their pupils." Their supporters, on the other hand, portrayed these teachers as angels in the midst of devils and neglected their human attributes. W. E. B. DuBois concluded that these "saintly souls" were New England's gift to freedmen. They brought "not alms, but a friend; not cash, but character." The education crusade, DuBois added, was the "finest thing in American history, and one of the few things untainted by sordid greed and cheap vainglory."[2] Neither detractors nor supporters gave a true picture of Yankee teachers. They were much the same as other people: selfish and selfless, cowardly, courageous, understanding, and arrogant. But whatever their human failings, they were as a group far more sympathetic to blacks than was the country at large.

Most teachers were motivated to go South by a genuine desire to assist blacks; some had been abolitionists for years. John G. Fee had risked his life fighting slavery in Kentucky, and B. C. Church, who joined the antislavery movement in the 1830s, had once been pelted with rotten eggs in Ohio for his views. Adam K. Spence had hated slavery from the time he learned of Elijah Lovejoy's death. The first president of Atlanta University, Edmund A. Ware, had been con-

163

verted to abolitionism by Wendell Phillips and by Harriet Beecher Stowe's *Uncle Tom's Cabin*. He was succeeded by Horace Bumstead, an abolitionist who had been an officer in a black regiment. Mrs. R. M. Bigelow volunteered as a teacher because she wished to devote her time to the cause so dear to her late abolitionist husband, Jacob. However, a majority of the teachers had not been abolitionists before the war. Of 138 teachers who submitted applications to the AMA in 1866, only 15 could be clearly identified as active abolitionists by their letters and testimonials.[3]

Although not abolitionists, most of the teachers were antislavery. John Lowrey was "firm & radical" against slavery, but was "averse to war" and did not wish to enter the army. He became a teacher to make himself useful in the cause. James F. Sisson had worked with blacks for several years in a New Bedford, Massachusetts, mission school. Antislavery sentiment had led Rebecca Veazie to teach Jamaican blacks before going South in 1864, and Harriet Arnold had taught fugitives in Canada at her own expense. Several male teachers became concerned about the freedmen's plight while in the military, and others viewed the AMA's work as a continuation of the struggle. Lieutenant John Silsby concluded that "a great moral warfare yet remains to be endured" as "slavery is not yet fully dead much less is the Negro enfranchised" and "conservatism is far from being rooted out of the church even." Silsby worked for the AMA for several years in Alabama.[4]

Closely connected with sympathy for blacks was a religious motivation. H. S. Beals, a public school principal who had drawn "my love for freedom from my mother's breast," viewed the Civil War as a great battle between good and evil. He had given his two sons to the war, and joined the AMA because he loved "God & *Humanity*" and because, he said, if the country did not make amends for the terrible wrongs of slavery "we shall see darker days & surer judgments than those just past." Beals's wife and daughter also became teachers. Annie R. Wilkins became a freedmen's teacher because she loved "to work for Christ," and Mary E. Hilliard wished to spend the rest of her life in active service to God. Many teachers had been former missionaries or children of missionaries. Frederick Ayers and Marcia Colton had been missionaries to the Indians. Samuel Chapman Armstrong and John and Mary Green were children of missionaries to Hawaii. Susan Drummond was ever ready to minister to the poor and suffer-

ing, including blacks. Others simply wished to "do good." Hattie Foote
was adopted, and since her adoptive parents had "done so much" for
her, she longed "to repay their kindness by helping the needy."[5]

William S. McFeely has suggested that the Civil War provided an
outlet for emotional energy and an opportunity for fulfillment for thousands of men. The black educational movement did the same for both
men and women. John A. Rockwell was a college graduate of independent means from a well-known Connecticut family. After returning
from a two-and-a-half-year voyage for his health, he supervised the
family business and attended lectures at Yale, neither of which provided the fulfillment he sought. Rockwell went to Georgia as a teacher
without a salary in order, he said, to feel "useful." Opportunities for
gratifying work were even more limited for women. Mary J. Conkling,
a childless twenty-four-year-old widow who was financially comfortable, offered her services to the AMA gratis because she needed a
cause in her life. Indeed, freedmen's education was an ideal outlet for
antislavery women who, according to Jacqueline Jones, believed "that
they as individuals had both the duty and the ability to rectify certain
moral and institutional evils" and who at the same time wished "to
liberate themselves from the comforts and complacency of a middle
class existence." Harriet Haskell of Massachusetts was only one of
many who had lived a life of ease and desired a more productive existence. Scores of women taught without pay, "asking no reward but the
pleasure of being allowed to do the work."[6]

That these teachers sought self-fulfillment did not necessarily mean
they had no commitment to freedmen. Most applicants listed multiple
reasons why they wished to go South. Frances Goodell sympathized
with blacks, had long wanted to do missionary work, but also admitted
that she was motivated in part by the desire for adventure. Many were
thrilled with the thought of venturing into enemy territory and defy-
ing the Rebels. Many women who worked in army hospitals shifted
their attention to education after the slaughter stopped. Others taught
blacks as a tribute to husbands and brothers killed in the war. Mary N.
and Parthena Barber volunteered to teach in Louisiana because they
had lost a brother at New Orleans and a cousin at Baton Rouge. Mrs.
Caroline A. R. Briggs began teaching after both her husband and
brother were killed. All three of Lydia A. Montague's sons were in the
Union Army. After two of them were wounded, her husband also en-

listed. Both of her daughters were teachers of freedmen. Mrs. Montague decided that she also should do something for the cause, and consequently accepted an AMA commission to teach in St. Louis. Still others went South hoping to improve their health or because they needed a job.[7]

The AMA established relatively rigid requirements for its personnel. Foremost they must "furnish credentials of Christian standing" and be of impeccable character. Although evangelical Christians were preferred, the association appointed teachers from almost every Protestant denomination, but it unashamedly discriminated against Roman Catholics and Unitarians. Teachers should be committed to aid freedmen. George Whipple once vetoed the appointment of three experienced teachers because he doubted "very much whether they have the views of the importance of the work that we have, and whether their hearts are in it." Energy, ability to endure hardship, and good health were further prerequisites. The association warned that it was "not a hygenic association to help invalids try for a change of air." The service demanded not only vigorous classroom work but "a disposition and ability to find something beyond these prescribed duties—to set oneself to work—to seek to do good for Christ and his poor." Again Whipple rejected a prospective teacher for Hampton Institute, saying: "I feel sorry for him, but our enterprise there is not a hospital for invalids . . . and his health is such as not to promise much efficiency."

Culture, common sense, good personal habits, and the ability to get along with colleagues were also desirable. Idiosyncracies of character, marked singularities, moroseness, petulance, "frivolity or undue fondness for society" were considered "incompatible with the benevolence, gravity, and earnestness of our work." No one was knowingly commissioned who used opium or intoxicating drinks, and only rarely was a tobacco smoker employed. In short, the AMA wanted healthy, experienced, evangelical Christians with culture, commitment, personality, and common sense. A teacher, the association said, must not only instruct but also be "a Leader—a Social center—a Founder, and a believer that there is no better sphere." The AMA advised none to apply who were influenced "by either romantic or mercenary motives; who go for the poetry or the pay; who wish to go South because they have failed at the North."[8] Naturally, not all teachers met the AMA's strict standards. The secretaries occasionally misjudged ability and character. When local churches and freedmen's aid societies provided the salaries, they chose the teachers. The AMA could veto the choice; still, it lost some control over the selection process. Moreover, there is evidence that the secretaries were sometimes inclined to examine less closely the credentials of teachers who went out at their own expense or who were recommended by those in a position to aid the AMA financially.

Association teachers ranged in age from eighty-year-old Charles Tappan to fifteen-year-old Eugene Upton. Most often, however, they were young single women from farm or professional families. The many comments about old maids and spinsters was not really indicative of old age. When A. N. Niles, principal at Savannah, said that "Dames so *ancient* and honorable ought not to go so far from home in midwinter," he was speaking of the forty-two-year-old Eliza Ann Ward. Though a few women listed their age as "of mature years" or "middle life," most were in their twenties.[9] Women were in a majority among freedmen's teachers for several reasons. They could be employed more cheaply, few men were available during the war, men had greater occupational opportunities, and women already dominated northern common schools. Perhaps making a virtue of necessity, the association argued that women were especially fitted for southern work. Their gentleness and kindness uniquely qualified them to aid the aged, poor, and suffering and to assist the black woman whom the AMA thought would be the key to black moral elevation. Finally, the association assumed that women were safer in the South. They could reputedly go anywhere without being physically molested. Not so with men, who were "fair game for the work of midnight bands." In 1866 men made up only 17 percent of the association's southern personnel. The proportion gradually increased to around 37 percent in 1872, but many of them were either ministers or principals or in the colleges. Few men taught in common schools.[10]

Most of the women teachers had the proper credentials for their work. A majority had attended normal schools, female academies, or colleges. Etta Payne had additional training in medical schools in Boston and Philadelphia. Mt. Holyoke Seminary and Oberlin College especially seemed to provide a large number of workers for the AMA. Of the 105 women employed in 1866 and whose applications were available, at least 89 had prior teaching experience. Anna C. Parks had taught for twenty years in girls' high schools. Laura Stebbins was a teacher and former preceptress and proprietor of the English Classical Institute at Springfield, Massachusetts. Elizabeth James had seventeen years' experience as an instructor and principal of a grammar school, and Mary F. Adams had been principal for five years of a primary department at the Central Graded School in Scranton, Pennsylvania. On the other hand, Ella Fenton believed that her informal instruction to several black children who had lived with her family qualified her to teach freedmen. More typical than the above was Eliza A. Summers, who was sent to a plantation school outside Hilton Head, South Carolina. She had taught in the Woodbury, Connecticut, public schools for four years with "marked success."[11]

Many of those lacking teaching experience served as matrons and missionaries. Grace H. Clemons of Northboro, Massachusetts, was neither well educated nor an experienced teacher, but she had successfully conducted the "domestic affairs" of a large boarding school. On this basis she was hired as matron of the orphanage at Wilmington, North Carolina. Although Maxine Jones and Jacqueline Jones in their respective studies of North Carolina and Georgia determined that a majority of northern teachers were from New England, this was not true for the association throughout the South. The AMA "schoolmarm" was more likely to be from Ohio than from Massachusetts. The Midwest and New York were fertile association recruiting grounds. Illinois, infamous for its antebellum laws governing free blacks, provided as many AMA teachers as Connecticut. Michigan furnished more than Vermont and New Hampshire combined.[12]

Association officials frequently lamented their inability to secure enough *"competent, moral men, white or black"* for their work, but those they managed to employ were generally able. The men tended to be slightly older than the women and were more likely to be married. Many of them were college graduates. At least half were clergymen. Some were unusually well qualified as teachers and principals. H. S. Beals had been a teacher and principal in New York and Massachusetts public schools for twenty-two years, and R. M. Manly was president of a New Hampshire women's college when he resigned to become chaplain of a black regiment. John Ogden, Ebenezer Tucker, Adam K. Spence, and Frederick Chase had been college professors. Others had had considerable experience in education. The Reverend Ira Pettibone had been proprietor and principal of a Litchfield, Connecticut, boarding school for fifteen years, and Joseph Kimball had taught for seven years at Phillips Academy at Andover, Massachusetts, and had superintended a large school in Ohio. Joseph Evans supervised the "Colored Department" of the Westchester, Pennsylvania, public schools, and George Andrews had been principal of an academy in Illinois and of Bloomfield Seminary in Ohio.[13]

These men were generally not the type inclined to flinch in the face of difficulty and white hostility. John G. Fee had stood up to southern wrath for two decades. Willard W. Wheeler and John Ogden had both been in Confederate prisons, and the Reverend James Brand, a Yale graduate and Andover Theological Seminary student, had won a medal for bravery as a color-bearer. Enoch K. Miller, who became AMA superintendent of Arkansas, had been wounded at Gettysburg. After his recovery he was licensed to preach by the Presbyterians and became chaplain for the Twenty-fifth Regiment, U.S. Colored Troops. The Indian raids that Frederick Ayer faced in Minnesota in 1863 were more frightening than any danger he encountered in Atlanta.[14]

The AMA sought not only educated but also practical, energetic men who could "take hold" whenever work needed to be done. The Reverend A. Scofield was such a man. An abolitionist, graduate of Union College and Auburn Theological Seminary, Scofield had taught in academies, high schools, and select common schools and was a preacher, farmer, and mechanic. He was eminently successful in Kentucky. He communicated well with freedmen, defended them against Union troops, taught them, and built houses for them. John G. Fee praised Scofield as a man who "can do something of almost all kinds of business." Thomas N. Chase was hired in part because of his business talent. The association recruited W. W. Mallory even though he refused to pledge never to use tobacco. Mallory was a carpenter and handyman as well as a minister and teacher.[15]

Not all male agents were experienced. Many were hired directly out of college, some of them apparently never having held a job. Despite their inexperience these young men often were assigned to supervise efficient women who had taught for years, much to the latter's dismay. Mary F. Wells at Trinity School in Athens, Alabama, and Amy Williams at Storrs School in Atlanta were two of the very few women principals in AMA schools. Many women accepted the injustice of being supervised by immature males as a given in American society, but a sizable minority did not. They were quick to apprise the AMA secretaries of male weaknesses, and some of them refused to be governed. They also resented discrimination in pay between men and women. One who made such a complaint claimed that she had become "strong minded under the fostering influences of the AMA." Amy Williams, principal of Storrs, which was jointly operated by the AMA and the state, was furious when she learned in 1876 that salaries of all teachers were to be reduced except those of male principals. "I am indignant!" she wrote, "more indignant than I can possibly tell! Indeed I would not have promised to return if I had known that such an injustice was being committed. I thought all were suffering alike." The male principals were paid $1,500 while Williams received only $575. Jennie Spencer wrote from Atlanta in 1872 asking for a higher position. "You spoke about engaging some men as new professors at Atlanta," she said. "Why not a woman as well as a man? And if, upon inquiry, you find that I am worthy, why not me?"[16]

It was these sometimes hardworking, devoted, competent women who were often characterized by male principals as "maiden ladies of . . . uncertain age . . . usually old enough to have asperities and positive opinions and without those softening and mollifying influences which are a condition precedent and requisite to the easy and right discharge of life's duties *anywhere* and especially *here*." Independent-minded women were liable to be judged as difficult by even able men and supervisors. Although the AMA vigorously championed education of women and acclaimed their special role in black education, many of its agents could not overcome a tendency to patronize them. Some had a "special horror" of "old maids." No doubt some of the teachers, both old and young, were difficult, but eccentricities seemed more acceptable in men than in women. The head of a Virginia mission house informed headquarters that "we do not wish any old maiden ladies, or those of confirmed old maid habits sent to this point." Mortimer A. Warren, principal at Avery Institute, asked that none of those "shrewd managing old maids" be sent to Charleston. Thomas N. Chase even suggested that women should not be allowed to vote in Straight University faculty meetings. Naturally, many principals worked comfortably with women and some women advanced in association schools. A few became principals, but, as in the country at large, women generally had to be content to be hardworking, efficient subordinates in the AMA.[17]

Between 1866 and 1880 the AMA employed more than two thousand agents in the South, and of this number some were certain to be unfit for the work. The Savannah superintendent advised the secretaries to scrutinize future candidates more closely and "send out none that cannot 'lap water.'" In 1875 George W. Andrews privately admitted that AMA work in Montgomery, Alabama, "has been *retarded & injured* more by *incompetent & unworthy* workers than by *all other causes combined.*" An Arkansas agent asked for fewer "young *fops* or *flirts*" and more experienced teachers with good education. These criticisms were unduly harsh, but a small minority of teachers were failures. One was so "very peculiar" that some thought her mentally deranged. The Reverend George N. Greene in North Carolina was reputedly lazy, quarrelsome, and was "fast lapsing into utter imbecility and chronic nothingness." The state superintendent was reluctant to fire him because he was a Baptist and the Baptists might "raise a cry." Others were guilty of abuse of alcohol and opium and of moral turpitude.[18]

More common than the mentally and morally unfit were those simply unprepared for conditions under which they were to live and work. Good intentions did not guarantee success. One teacher arrived in New Bern, North Carolina, frightened and homesick. Wartime uncertainty so unsettled her that she returned home. When Timothy and Helen Lyman were sent to Hatteras Inlet, North Carolina, they found it "too crude." Mrs. Lyman had no idea "people could live as they do here, so few comforts." A colleague sarcastically remarked that the Lymans probably "expected to be met by a welcoming delegation and escorted publicly by a band . . . to elegantly furnished quarters within the fort." John Taylor was satisfied with his housing at a contraband settlement in Virginia, but he left saying that he could not live anyplace where the land was so level. His supervisor "thought rather singular of it." Fortunately the fainthearted and peculiar were few in number.[19] Others sent South were of sound mind and hardy spirit but were inexperienced or simply poor teachers. Yet the surprise is not that some were unsuitable but that so many did well. Despite its rigid requirements the AMA obviously made some unfortunate choices. Moreover, it provided limited orientation and no training for the tasks it wished performed. Nevertheless, for every teacher who failed there were scores who succeeded to some degree, and many were truly outstanding.

Whatever their abilities, teachers faced a life far different from the one they left. The AMA warned its agents that southern work was demanding and life often difficult. Teachers were expected to instruct in day, night, and Sabbath schools and attend Sunday worship services. In spare time they might issue clothing to the needy, visit the sick, write and read letters for freedmen, and do mission work. In Carondelet, Missouri, Alma Baker, in addition to schoolwork, assisted in the church, instructed parents in their responsibilities to their children, sought out the needy, and waged war against liquor and tobacco. In rural areas where there were no Bureau agents, freedmen often went to teachers for protection. In Newton, Georgia, a woman with blood streaming down her face fled to Miss S. H. Champney's boarding place. After she had refused to plow in the field, claiming weakness, the overseer had knocked her down and kicked her in the face and head. Champney, who feared that one of the victim's eyes had been destroyed, treated her wounds but could provide no redress.[20]

Esther Douglass was teacher, church advisor, community leader, missionary, and nurse in McLeansville, North Carolina. On different occasions she was roused from bed by the worried wife of a seriously ill man and walked nine miles to confer with a church deacon. In boarding schools the teachers not only met day and night classes but supervised boarders twenty-four hours a day, held study hall at night, tutored weaker students, preserved food in season, cooked, cleaned, and acted as parents. Frequently they were compelled to sit up all night with ill students. At Fisk even the women teachers took turns splitting kindling and carrying coal to build fires in public sitting rooms. When teachers were sick, healthy colleagues took over their classes. Julia Shearman, an energetic, well-educated, widely traveled Englishwoman with a good sense of humor, taught at Augusta, Georgia. She was an ideal teacher-missionary, but even she sometimes faltered under her heavy burden. When a co-worker became ill she said with a hint of resentment: "How do you think I like the prospect of managing 230 wild asses colts tomorrow without her?" Shearman began to complain of being exhausted and having a poor appetite. Although a "very strong temperance person," she began to take a little ale to help her swallow the bread which "otherwise I could not touch." Bureau agents sometimes warned the AMA that it demanded too much of its laborers. Overwork and too little leisure impaired the effectiveness of some teachers.[21]

Most teachers who went South expected to give up the comforts and luxuries of home, but few were prepared for their initial living conditions. Fannie Campbell lived and cooked in a tent in Vicksburg, Mississippi, and two Brunswick, Georgia, teachers resided in a rude shack without shelf, table, box, or closet. A teacher on a Lowndes County, Georgia, plantation was not only uncomfortably lodged in the former slave quarters but was frightened as well. Two men, including one of her night students, were murdered within a few yards of her schoolhouse. "I have almost come to the conclusion," she sadly wrote, "that I am not adaptable to the work." Since whites often refused to rent to freedmen's teachers, they sometimes boarded with blacks who freely shared their frequently wretched accommodations. James Lyman and Kate Tenney lived with a family of four in a "small rough shanty" in Pine Bluff, Arkansas. Another Arkansas teacher went to her tiny room one February night and found her bed and floor covered with snow. Two Thomasville, Georgia, teachers grew fond of the black family they stayed with, but were slightly disgruntled that "swine flesh in some form is never once absent from the table, while pies, cake, milk and preserves are never seen, and butter scarcely ever." Minnie C. Owen slept in a pantry and George Greene, who shared a 14 × 19-foot cabin with a dozen others, laid his pallet in the attic. Not all teachers who lived with blacks did so because they had no choice, and accommodations were not always primitive. Stephen W. Laidler boarded with blacks to lower expenses, and two Milledgeville, Georgia, teachers moved from a white boardinghouse to the home of a black Baptist preacher for greater comfort. Alma Baker enjoyed good food and a comfortable bed in the home of a black Missouri widow.[22]

Teacher housing tended to be better in urban areas. The military and Freedmen's Bureau sometimes provided houses for teachers, and the AMA quickly began to rent or buy mission homes. Even the homes, however, were often cold and poorly furnished. The Savannah residence was so cold that most teachers were ill in January 1868. Samuel S. Ashley complained about the cold and uncomfortable mission house in Wilmington with its broken furniture, old washstands, cracked mirrors, dilapidated bedsteads, and pine packing boxes. Julia

Shearman was so enraged when she received no response to her complaints about her hard husk mattress that she ripped it to pieces, removed some hard objects, and sent them to New York with a request that the secretaries try sleeping on them. The matron at Augusta urged that no teacher be sent there without silverware, since there was too little of it with which to feed the family. The local superintendent suggested that she contact the notorious General Benjamin Butler "as he is said to be so rich in spoons." Josephine Pierce cleverly solved the problem of cold floors at Talladega by tying a string to a square of carpet and dragging it with her from bed to washstand to writing table. "It was a new sensation in Alabama," she said, "to hop out of bed in the morning and have the feet touch a carpet." Association housing gradually improved, but as a rule teachers continued to live spartanly.[23]

Teachers complained even more about food than housing. At the colleges and mission homes teachers ate at a common mess. The matron or the unfortunate wife of the principal was usually in charge of food preparation, and she probably had the most thankless task of any association worker. The AMA provided board and it demanded a strict accounting and economy. Some teachers complained about lack of variety—"For some months nine-tenths of my food has been batter-cakes sometimes meal—sometimes buckwheat, sometimes flour," the Reverend David Peebles wrote. But more often they were concerned about quantity. Francis L. Cardozo, Charleston principal, warned the secretaries that it was "mistaken economy" to give teachers too little to eat. When Charles L. Woodworth toured AMA schools in 1866, he found "more dissatisfaction among our teachers in regard to the matter of board than anything else." The AMA limitation on the amount spent for food had an "unhappy influence," Woodworth wrote. "Some of the teachers feel as if they are grudged their food, and are humiliated with the thought that they should be watched and scolded, and allowanced like the inmates of a workshop or a poor house." He advised the association to dissipate the notion that it was governed by a "penurious policy" inconsistent with the great Christian work it had assigned the teachers.[24]

General Charles H. Howard on a Freedmen's Bureau tour in 1869 found AMA teachers "suffering without a word of complaint *from a lack of proper food.*" Whether there was sufficient food depended on the cost of local produce and the balance in the association treasury. Although stingy with food allowances, the association did not deliberately starve its teachers. Sometimes no money could be sent South until more was collected. J. K. Warner, Augusta principal, had eleven people to feed and only twenty cents in his treasury in December 1867. The previous month's rent was unpaid. He had already borrowed all the money the teachers had and owed the local grocer five dollars for flour. "Our dinner is purchased for today," he said, "beyond that we know not." Many teachers planted gardens, picked blackberries, preserved and dried fruit, canned vegetables, and supplemented the table with their own meager salaries, not only to save money for the association but also to improve their diets. In some areas students aided their teachers. They furnished Eliza Summers at Hilton Head, South Carolina, with eggs, sweet potatoes, and all the oysters she could eat.[25] Probably most teachers suffered more from a lack of tasty food and variety than from a nutritionally deficient diet.

Generally, teachers thought the overwork, improper housing, inadequate diet, and the oppressively hot southern climate weakened their health. Certainly living in the South was not without hazards for Yankee teachers. Far more lost their lives to disease than to white violence. Northerners believed they were especially susceptible to hot weather maladies, but southern black workers were as sickly as northern ones.[26] Despite the AMA's attempt to choose healthy laborers, some were ill when they went South. One of the best teachers in Georgia was Miss A. E. Allender, "a consumptive little creature who will cough and spit blood half the night and then walk her mile & teach with all the vigor and brightness imaginable." Allender attended the closing school exercises in 1867, though she was in danger of fainting, and was then immediately sent home for fear she would die in the field. However, most teachers were relatively healthy when selected. Still, they suffered greatly from the almost inescapable malaria and other ailments.[27]

Various types of "fever" and debilitating diarrhea were the most common problems. In 1862 Charles B. Wilder wrote plaintively from Virginia: "My bowels are closing better but my appetite is quite poor." Elizabeth James was so weakened with chronic diarrhea in 1864 that she was unable to walk. Influenza or malaria sooner or later seemed to strike a majority of the teachers. Descriptions of symptoms—chills and fever, lassitude, nausea, delirium, loss of appetite, headache, and general pain—suggest that malaria was common. Since many teachers had lived in malaria-free regions, they were susceptible to all strains of the disease. Annie R. Wilkins contracted a fever in South Carolina that was unknown to her—"broken bone" fever. She probably had an especially painful type of malaria. That illness seriously interfered with AMA work can be illustrated by events at the mission home, Tyler House, in Hampton, Virginia. There were only five or six people living there in November 1863. Mrs. James P. Stone, the matron, was confined to her room with "the fever." Charles P. Day was so ill that his school had been suspended. His co-teacher, Lucy Martindale, fell headlong down the stairs and was disabled. The next fall Day's infant daughter died suddenly. His wife became so ill he took her home to New York to recover. When Day returned to Hampton his sister, also a teacher, was fatally ill with typhoid fever. Less than a week after her death another teacher died. Soon thereafter Joseph A. Shaw became the third typhoid victim at Tyler House.[28]

The AMA thought of its agents as Christian soldiers waging a battle against illiteracy, ignorance, and sin in the South, and scores of them lost their lives in the line of duty. At the same time typhoid struck Hampton, two workers died in Norfolk. Three teachers died at Beaufort, South Carolina, during the summer of 1864 and in Beaufort, North Carolina, Carrie M. Getchell suffocated from inflammation of the glottis. She had caught a cold crossing the sound daily in an open boat to her school in Morehead City. The Reverend Aaron Rowe succumbed to cholera morbus in Savannah in 1875. Martha Johnson died of "bilious fever" during her "seventh year of self denying labor" in South Carolina. The mortality rate was especially high among the workers' children. "I buried my baby yesterday," Mortimer A. Warren wrote in 1871. "There is a great vacant space made. I didn't know that one little baby took up so much room." Almost every year one or more association workers died from disease or accident. More dreaded than the usual diseases were the terrible epidemics of yellow fever that periodically scourged the South. Yellow fever raged in New Bern and Beaufort, North Carolina, in 1864. When a New Bern teacher died she was hurriedly buried by moonlight the same evening. People were so frightened of the disease that the Reverend Timothy Lyman had to secure a provost marshal's order to get help burying the corpse. When yellow fever ravaged Memphis in 1876, it infected all six teachers at LeMoyne Normal and Commercial School, who had refused to flee the city. Three, including principal D. Elliott Cottle and his wife, died.[29]

The conditions under which teachers lived and worked, combined with white ostracism and threats of violence, took a toll on both the weak of body and of spirit. There was a high turnover among association personnel. Some of them remained only a short time. Illness, family death, or inability to adjust to living in a hostile environment sent them home. A few had the desire but lacked the stamina. Many apparently never intended to make a career of teaching freedmen. A year or two in the South helped to expiate their guilt and they returned North. Others planned to spend their lives in the work, but a winter in the South altered their plans. Some simply were not missionary material. Helen Dodd arrived in Virginia in November and departed in December. The Reverend C. M. Southgate of Vermont, who arrived in Atlanta late in the year, immediately became ill and hardly left his room for four weeks. By spring he was ready to give up the work permanently. The services of neither Dodd nor Southgate were worth traveling expenses South. Lack of continuity seriously impaired the AMA's educational efforts in some areas. Half the teaching staff at a particular location might change from year to year. Occasionally this was because association officers for some reason decided to shift teachers, but more often it was because personnel decided not to return or requested transfers in order to be with friends. Samuel S. Ashley, a North Carolina superintendent, warned that "a healthy, permanent school system" was impossible if teacher migration continued. "We must have teachers who *identify* themselves with the schools not only, but with the people. Our teachers must be willing to be life missionaries."[30]

Although a sizable minority of teachers were unhealthy, uncommitted, or fainthearted, many remained in the South for years. Just as some who intended to make teaching freedmen their life's work gave up after a year or two, some who viewed their involvement as temporary became so interested that they remained for several years. Eliza Ann Ward, who taught in Savannah, Hilton Head, South Carolina, and the small community of Golding Grove, Georgia, was probably representative of the teachers. When she first went to Georgia she had no clear idea of how long she would stay. After five years of hard work, poor health forced her retirement, but she continued to collect clothing for and corresponded with black friends at Golding Grove. Hundreds of teachers worked in the South for five to ten years. Others became "life missionaries" and dedicated themselves to black education. Spence, Chase, Morgan, and Cravath remained at Fisk until death or retirement. George W. Andrews was at Talladega from 1874 to 1908. Edmund A. Ware died on the job at Atlanta. Black educator and Atlanta University graduate William Henry Crogman told blacks of Ware: "Whether you have realized it or not, God gave us for twenty years a character resplendent with virtues and graces to move in and out among us that we might see how men are made—yes he fell going up hill. God grant that I may so fall." It was not only the colleges that inspired such loyalty. Esther W. Douglass taught, cajoled, and loved black children for thirty years in four different states. She finally quit teaching only when compelled to do so by blindness. Rachael Crane Mather became an AMA teacher in 1867. She established a school in Beaufort, South Carolina, the following year and remained there for thirty-six years. In 1885 Mary F. Wells celebrated her twentieth anniversary at Trinity School in Athens, Alabama, and continued teaching with vigor and enthusiasm. She occasionally spent a few summer weeks in the North visiting friends and relatives, but Athens was her home. The Wellses, Wares, and Spences had an important and positive impact on black education.[31]

Those teachers who remained in the South certainly did not do so for mercenary reasons. Association salaries were typically small and often in arrears. During the war women were paid nine to ten dollars a month and room and board, but food was so dear that teachers frequently had to use their own funds to supplement the table.[32] From their small salaries teachers paid incidental expenses, purchased clothing, and saved for the summer months since housing, food, and pay were received only during the school year. The Reverend E. H. Alden, AMA agent in Louisiana, scolded association officers for their treatment of women. "If you knew how much the lady teachers denied themselves to live here & not get in debt you would do more," he wrote. "Certainly you would no longer withhold money due them to enable them to meet their board bills." Many teachers had to borrow money to pay rent. Alden suggested that their salaries be doubled.[33]

By 1866 salaries had generally increased to fifteen dollars a month, but nearly all teachers except the financially independent complained of poverty.[34] Jonathan Cory wrote from South Carolina that he was less destitute than usual since joining the AMA. "I have ten cents, two postage stamps, 2 lbs of pork, 12 lbs of wheat flour, ½ lb of coffee and 2 oz of tea," he said, but he owed money and asked for his last month's pay. Helen M. Leonard sent the following cryptic message from the Montgomery mission house in 1875: "Please send something to take away appetites or else money to buy food. Cash on hand seventy cents minus sixty-five dollars." Salaries were not paid on a regular schedule. Usually they were sent only upon request and then were sometimes delayed for months. In 1864 Mary D. Williams reminded Assistant Treasurer William E. Whiting that she had received no compensation for seven months. "If it is convenient I should like whatever is now due," she added. In 1868 the association asked teachers to contribute a portion of their salary to the AMA and to delay asking for the remainder for as long as possible. They were made to feel guilty if they demanded their salaries when due. In May 1868 Mary Withington, who had received no money since arriving in Augusta the previous fall, apologetically asked for thirty dollars if convenient—or, if not, less. If it was inconvenient to send any, she said, she would try to secure funds elsewhere. Her shoes were worn out and she was certain the AMA did not want her to miss church for lack of shoes. S. S. Straight, an AMA benefactor in New Orleans, urged the association to correct "the great delay in paying teachers." Most were poor, he added, and could hardly wait until the end of the month for their wages. "Being compelled to wait and suffering two or three months created great dissatisfaction which leads to public reproaches of a great and good society and sometimes ripens into open hostility." Association tardiness was earning it and its workers censure from creditors. Straight suggested that it would be preferable for the AMA to borrow at 10 percent rather than force its agents to wait months for their pay.[35]

Although men ordinarily were paid substantially more than women, there was no uniform pay scale. In 1867 in North Carolina S. S. Ashley received $100 per month, the Reverend Fisk P. Brewer $75, H. S. Beals and the Reverend Alfred A. Ellsworth $50, Alva Hurd $35, and John Scott $25. Those paid the higher salaries furnished their own lodging and food. The few men who taught in common schools with no supervisory duties sometimes earned no more than women. The AMA policy was to hire the best men available at the cheapest rates. As a result, male agents tended to be ministers, inexperienced, incompetent, or truly devoted to AMA work. Many fitted the latter category. G. Stanley Pope, one of the most able workers in Alabama, was paid $1,500 per year and he furnished his own house and board. When in 1877 Secretary Strieby offered to increase his salary, Pope declined on the grounds that his labor and responsibilities were no greater than previously. Low pay caused the AMA to lose good workers, both male and female. Mary McAssey received $120 and board for teaching eight months at Talladega in 1876. There was no summer salary. She wisely concluded that she could not pay the $700 debt incurred while in college on such a salary and terminated her relationship with Talladega.[36]

Most AMA teachers apparently accepted poverty, hardship, and white hostility with equanimity. They expected mission life to be difficult and drew strength from their religious beliefs and their devotion to freedmen and to each other. Mission homes were havens where teachers did not feel as keenly as they otherwise might "the lack of social courtesy from without." But on occasion mission homes produced negative results. Usually teachers had no outside social life. They were forced to associate with each other day after day. They did not have their own homes in which to escape and did not always have separate rooms in the mission house. Such constant proximity created short tempers and sensitive nerves. Underpaid, overworked, and sometimes unappreciated, the teachers often succumbed to petty bickering. Even their earnestness may have been partially responsible for intramural strife. As Clarice T. Campbell said, "With so much at stake it was difficult to condone imperfection—especially in others." Hattie W. Andrews, who was more guilty than most, made an acute observation about AMA workers. When they discovered a fault in a co-worker, she said, rather than attempting to correct or mollify it they exaggerated it and criticized each other. Mrs. Andrews could have added that they were quick to inform the secretaries in New York. Irritating self-righteousness was in plentiful supply among Yankee teachers. Sometimes quarrels arose over food, a perceived slight, authority, or, most often, personality conflicts. Ellen Pierce was so provoked by quarreling and backbiting (she was adept at both) that she suggested the AMA "employ a practical phrenologist to determine . . . who possessed the most fitting characteristics for this peculiar work." One association official comforted himself with the thought that even "the Master had in his college a poor treasurer, & those who contended which of them should be the greatest. Even Paul & Barnabas went apart."[37]

A few teachers were simply obnoxious. Sisters Addie and Emma Warren, assigned to a school in Mississippi, were capable teachers, but they were always dissatisfied and were in "a perpetual wrangle with each other when . . . together and faultfinding, disagreeable associates when with others." They shamed their principal, John P. Bardwell, by their public contentiousness. Bardwell believed Addie "has never been quite satisfied . . . that she was not made a *man*." The sisters were so fractious that the AMA fired them despite their good teaching records. Thoroughly disagreeable teachers were rare, however. A more explosive issue was religion. Nearly all personnel were religious, yet some found a lack of proper piety in others. John Ogden at Fisk celebrated student conversions, yet a portion of the faculty tried to force him out on the grounds that he was uninterested in church building. The Reverend Cyrus W. Francis thought that Ware regarded the religious interests of Atlanta University too lightly. A Charleston teacher objected to principal Mortimer A. Warren because he never prayed publicly except for repeating the Lord's Prayer and during the entire school year had read no scripture to students other than the Sermon on the Mount. The local AMA minister admitted that Warren "has a reputation for school management in this city which no other could acquire in a moment," yet hinted that he should be fired because he was not evangelical enough. Such "decided hostility" developed at Charleston "as to lead to practical non intercourse."[38]

Some of the faculty at Beach Institute in Savannah complained to headquarters that the principal, the Reverend C. W. Sharp, held too few prayer meetings at the mission home. Sharp responded that he led lengthy morning and evening devotions after meals, a regular Wednesday night prayer service at the church, and a weekly social prayer meeting at the school. Moreover, he had just completed a two-week revival. He had discontinued the Saturday evening prayer meeting, Sharp said, because he was tired by the week's end and needed that night to prepare for his Bible class and preaching on Sunday. The Reverend Sharp, obviously annoyed at having his religiosity questioned, informed Secretary E. P. Smith that if the "family" demanded more "*public prayers* & devotions . . . than is already supplied, then I judge there must be some deficiency in the *private* devotions, or else a conventional view of the matter with which I have no sympathy." Sharp, a New Yorker, added that there was "a type of piety" in New England which was not particularly genuine. "It *professes* more than it does; it speaks what *ought* to be said or felt, but not what overflows from the inward life. It requires a Jewish legality & exactitude in the *machinery* of religion; and its conscience is thrown into spasms when the machinery stops." Such people, Sharp suggested, were "not the most devoted or useful, when real spiritual and moral force is required." The Savannah faculty became so factionalized that opposing prayer meetings were held. Sharp was not retained the following year. A quarrel at Tyler House that ended with the firing of Charles P. Day began, in part, when Day objected to attending prayer meeting on Saturday evening, the only recreational night of the week.[39]

At least one teacher thought regional and cultural differences were divisive. The Reverend George W. Walker found the milieu at Atlanta University uncongenial. He wrote E. M. Cravath that he and his wife were "decidedly *western*. We are Oberlinites. The powers that be are decidely *eastern*." His friendly interaction with students apparently offended the stern, undemonstrative members of the faculty. One teacher told Walker that her mother had never kissed her. He likened the atmosphere at Atlanta to "that of the *severe faithfulness* that might be found in such a New England mother. The government is one of authority & of severity, rather than fraternal & of principle instilled in the heart." This austere environment, combined with "the 'Boston is the hub' feeling" on the part of some teachers, depressed the warm, lighthearted young Oberlin graduate. A difference in perception of proper behavior also damaged John Ogden at Fisk. Many of the faculty believed the principal was too flippant for his position. He joked and laughed with students. One censorious teacher informed headquarters of Ogden's behavior, saying, "Is it right for a Supt. to *chuck* young ladies under the chin—and especially for a man who wooed and won his present wife while a school girl." There was little tolerance of frivolity or even a sense of humor at Fisk. Apparently the faculty felt more comfortable with Ogden's successor, the somber Adam K. Spence, of whom student America Robinson said: "Deliver me from such as he. I do not want to be afraid to laugh."[40] With some teachers

Trinity School, Athens, Alabama. For thirty years at Trinity, Mary F. Wells trained the black teachers who taught in many of the black public schools in North Alabama. *Amistad Research Center*

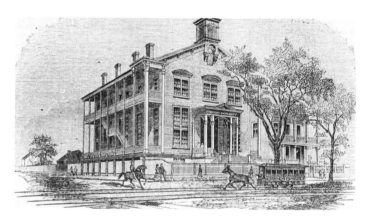

Above, Straight University in New Orleans, 1876. For several years Straight, now Dillard, was the major college for blacks in the Southwest. *Amistad Research Center*

Right, Avery Institute, Charleston, the premier black teacher-training institution in South Carolina. *Amistad Research Center*

Fisk University Jubilee Singers. The Jubilee Singers popularized slave songs and made Fisk University known throughout the United States and Europe. *Fisk University Special Collections*

Fisk College students, 1888–89. W. E. B. Du Bois found his contact with Fisk faculty and students in the 1880s beneficial and inspiring. *Fisk University Special Collections*

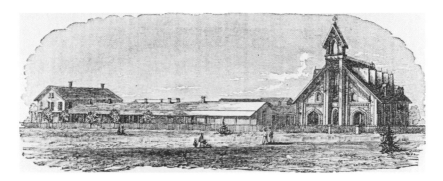

Fisk University, Nashville. Fisk was the AMA's prize school. It graduated its first college class in 1875. *Amistad Research Center*

Overleaf: Atlanta University. Under Edmund A. Ware's wise leadership Atlanta University became one of the AMA's finest schools. *Amistad Research Center*

Top, Chemistry class at Atlanta University, 1886. *Bottom*, Grammar class at Atlanta University, 1886. *Photograph Collection, Atlanta University Center Woodruff Library*

Top, Talladega College Normal Class, 1890. At this time Talladega still emphasized its normal and theological departments more than its college. *Bottom*, Talladega College Normal graduates, 1890. *Talladega College Archives*

The Freedmen's School at Beaufort, South Carolina, was typical of the AMA's common schools. *USAMHI*

Children ready for school at New Bern, North Carolina. *USAMHI*

being so rigid and intolerant of their co-workers' religious and cultural differences, it is not surprising that they sometimes clashed with freedmen on the same issues.

Although interpersonal strife damaged association efforts in a few places, teachers generally managed to prevent it from obstructing their work. Most laborers were "disposed to be kind and pleasant to all," and laughter and warmth were not unknown in the mission house. Teachers found mates, made lifelong friendships, and sustained each other during crises. More important than how teachers responded to each other was how they viewed the people with whom they had elected to labor. Teachers generally professed to believe in equality, but contrary to their professions many of them had not freed themselves of the taint of racism which afflicted most nineteenth-century Americans. After a western minister told Lewis Tappan in 1867 that his friends believed the AMA was "not up to the mark" on the question of caste, the association reiterated its stand on color prejudice. At its annual meeting the AMA condemned color prejudice as both wicked and a barrier to black elevation and resolved "that no person who yields to it, or sutters himself to be influenced thereby, ought to be appointed or sustained among its officers, teachers or agents." But the AMA found it easier to proclaim racial egalitarianism than to match rhetoric with deeds. It was unrealistic even to assume that thousands of teachers could be employed, none of whom had preconceived negative perceptions of blacks.[41]

Probably most teachers were prejudiced to some degree, and a few were overtly so. As will be seen, some refused to share rooms and tables with black colleagues. The Reverend Henry S. Kelsey, principal of Emerson Institute in 1869, reportedly had "but little faith" in blacks and was all too eager to express his views. Others adopted the theory of equality but found practice difficult. A Savannah agent acknowledged the correctness of the association's racial views. "I am of the old abolitionist stamp," he proclaimed, yet he admittedly avoided boarding with blacks. A Charleston teacher worked happily under the supervision of mulatto Thomas W. Cardozo, but when a very dark man came to live in the mission home she was uncomfortable. Casual remarks frequently revealed negative views. The matron at Talladega who had recently hired a student assistant reported: "We all consider her as *near perfection* as a daughter of Ham could get."[42]

Numerous teachers who honestly admitted initial reservations about freedmen grew in tolerance and understanding. William T. Briggs began his work in North Carolina "with no very exalted" view of black ability for improvement, but a year among blacks inspired him "with unbounded hope." Notwithstanding sympathy for blacks since childhood, Annie Winsor had lingering doubts about their capacity. She was delighted to discover "good and noble traits" and greater intellectual ability than she had suspected. Mary Chase, who at the outset had doubted she could love black children as she did whites, believed after a time that God had "taken all the wicked prejudice" from her heart and left her "perfectly color blind." "I had some feeling about *color*," G. W. Walker confessed a year after going to Atlanta University. "I feared it would be unpleasant to teach colored people. But it is a *pleasure*. I love them as much as I ever did any pupils. They are as *smart* as any. I have marched with them through the streets of Atlanta without feeling one particle of shrinking uneasiness. I had thought that impossible." These people may not have banished all their prejudices, but at least they showed capacity for growth.[43]

Other teachers had little or no color prejudice, or else carefully guarded against revealing it in their correspondence. Dozens of teachers lived with black families, and at least one married a black colleague. They entertained black friends in the mission house, visited in their homes, and attended church with them. In 1871 James F. Sisson was ordained an elder in the African Methodist Episcopal church and continued that association until his death. The Storrs School principal, Amy Williams, rejected a competent teacher because she had heard "she would have nothing to do with the colored people only as far as actual school work was concerned." When the AMA considered closing the Macon, Georgia, mission home in 1873 as an economy measure, Mary E. Sands vigorously protested because, she said, "the Home affords us the privilege of meeting the colored people as we could no where else. I should not wish to live where the people could not call on us, and they could not do so if we board in a Southern family." Of course, living and associating with blacks did not prove an absence of racial prejudice. Samuel Chapman Armstrong organized a church at Hampton, Virginia, because his scholars were unwelcome at the nearby Presbyterian church. He refused to attend services where he could not go with his students if he desired. Armstrong went to

Hampton as "the champion and protector of the freedmen," but he took with him conservative views of black potential and of their place in society. He was almost as paternalistic as southern whites.[44]

Although white AMA teachers and agents were rarely free of all racial bias, most did not fit a dictionary definition of racist. Many believed blacks were inherently equal. They were environmentalists or culturalists who explained racial differences by pointing at slavery and blocked opportunities. They measured their students by white, northern, middle-class standards, but unlike the majority of their contemporaries they believed that blacks were capable of attaining those standards. Others subscribed, even if unknowingly, to the theory that George M. Frederickson has labeled romantic racialism. They acknowledged that whites and blacks were different and would perhaps remain so, but they unequivocally denied that black peculiarities made them inferior. Indeed, they believed blacks might be superior in some ways. A South Carolina teacher reflected this view when she claimed that freedmen had "preserved so much genuine heart, notwithstanding the iron bondage to which they have been subjected—so much capacity for love, hope, gratitude, confidence, and all the genialities of the soul." Teachers admired what they perceived as blacks' warmth, emotion, trustfulness, musical ability, and especially their "Christian nature."[45]

Unfortunately a comparatively benign romantic racialism could be productive of evil. It could easily, as Frederickson suggested, "be transmuted into an overt doctrine of Negro inferiority, distinguished from harsher forms of racism only by a certain flavor of humanitarian paternalism." This was done by a few teachers who went South with exalted views of blacks and were quickly disillusioned and sometimes embittered. S. K. Hyde reported from Virginia in 1862 that some "who came here with great expectations—looking for that on earth which can only be found in Heaven—they did not think this people would steal or break the Sabbath—and when they see them so much like white people—say 'well modified slavery is best for them.'" Such a reaction was extreme and rare, but disillusionment occurred and became more prevalent as the years passed. Whether they were racists, environmentalists, romantic racialists, or a combination of these, many teachers could not escape being paternalistic. Even the most devoted and enlightened teachers sometimes saw themselves as heroic figures leading a benighted people out of the darkness of ignorance and sin. At their worst, paternalistic teachers gave black youth an opportunity to gain literacy while assuring them by word and deed that they were inferior. At their best, they provided a good education and became members of the black community, forming warm relationships with students, parents, and friends that were "egalitarian in their impact."[46]

11

Black Teachers and Missionaries

"I MYSELF am a Colored woman, bound to that ignorant, degraded, long enslaved race, by ties of love and consanguinity: they are socially and politically 'my people'" was Sara G. Stanley's stated reason for joining the AMA as a freedmen's teacher. The twenty-five-year-old Stanley was only one of many northern blacks who rushed to aid their recently freed fellows. It has too frequently been assumed that the crusade to educate former slaves was a white movement. Blacks were intimately involved in freedmen's education as teachers, often as pioneers in opening schools in areas where whites could not or would not go. Mary Peake, the association's vanguard instructor in the South, was black and she was already teaching when Lewis C. Lockwood secured permission for her to operate her school openly. The first white teachers usually were aided in the classroom by local freed people. Mary Green assisted Charles P. Day at Fortress Monroe, Virginia, in 1862 until she became ill. Her place was taken by Lucinda Spivery, who had been freed by her white father and given "a fair English education" by her aunt. Day believed her "considerable teaching ability" qualified Spivery to become a full-time instructor. At least fifteen advanced students had served as assistants or monitors at Norfolk by November 1863. Six of them had been paid small amounts, while the others had received only rations as compensation. After the monitors went on strike for higher wages, William H. Woodbury, Norfolk superintendent, agreed to pay them one dollar a week and rations.[1]

The monitors and assistants had been employed by teachers in the field because they badly needed help, but from the beginning the AMA sought eligible blacks who desired to become teachers and missionaries. As well-educated, available black teachers were necessarily scarce, the association operated under the tacit principle that blacks would be given positions when possible, even though they might be less well prepared than white candidates. Black friends encouraged the association in its hiring policy. When the Reverend Leonard A. Grimes visited Union-occupied areas in the South in 1863, he pronounced himself "delighted and highly pleased with the noble work" the AMA was doing "for the salvation and the education and elevation" of freedmen, but added pointedly that he wished to see among its appointments "some good faithful colored preachers and teachers."[2]

The first northern black agent the AMA sent South was Boston carpenter John Oliver. After hearing contraband William Davis speak of the condition of fugitives fleeing to Virginia, Oliver unsuccessfully applied to the recently formed Boston Educational Commission for a position as contraband teacher. Association agent William L. Coan charged that the commission objected to hiring blacks. Oliver then wrote the AMA of his desire to teach and assist fugitives. "With my knowledge of both slavery and the slave and the condition in which the former has left the latter," he stated, "I believe that I would be of great service to that people." Oliver arrived in Virginia in May 1862 and was sent to Newport News. He soon was operating two schools on alternate days and a night school. From Newport News he went to Portsmouth, where he taught school, organized a benevolent society, and tried to protect contrabands from Union soldiers. Secretary Whipple commended Oliver for his "moral and christian character" and his devotion to the work, but suggested that he had weakened his usefulness by trying to do too much. Unfortunately Oliver enraged military officials by his constant criticism of their treatment of contrabands. When he offered to resign as a result, the association accepted, Whipple said, because it was paying him more than some much better educated white teachers who were preaching as well as teaching.[3]

Oliver was soon followed to Virginia by a small corps of better prepared and more efficient teachers. By late 1862 Thomas DeS. Tucker was living and teaching with Charles P. Day at Fortress Monroe. William D. Harris, Clara C. Duncan, Sara G. Stanley, Blanche V. Harris, and Mary Watson, all quite able, arrived shortly afterwards. In early 1864 Secretary Whipple visited the Norfolk schools. All were "good," he reported, but the best was taught by Blanche V. Harris. Generally black and white teachers worked together, but in Norfolk Woodbury decided to establish a school run completely by blacks as an example of their ability. Blanche Harris, an Oberlin graduate, was principal. Sallie L. Daffin, Clara C. Duncan, and Edmonia G. Highgate were the other teachers. However, the plan was interrupted by illness. Daffin had to replace a sick white teacher in another school, and Harris became ill. The white woman who replaced Harris as principal judged her black colleagues to be extremely competent, but thought the all-black school unwise because it caused whispers that black and white teachers could not work together. Before the war ended, the AMA had sent black teachers to Virginia, South Carolina, Kentucky, Louisiana, and Mississippi.[4]

By 1865 the AMA had concluded that black teachers and missionaries were essential to its work. As mentioned earlier, it believed blacks should eventually supply most of their own educators. Of more immediate importance, however, freedmen demanded at least some teachers of their own race. Even those white teachers who assumed that most blacks were ill prepared thought it expedient to employ a few. In 1865 the white Beaufort, South Carolina, superintendent requested that half of his teaching force be black. "This I think will suit the people and show them you are willing to support their own color," he wrote. Others agreed with John G. Fee, who strongly urged using black teachers so that "these people may *see* what they *can* be" and because "the *example* may put down the spirit of cast[e]." By 1870 the association admitted that the most effective teachers of freedmen came from among themselves. "They have the readiest access to their own race, and can do a work for them no teachers sent from the North can accomplish."[5]

At times the AMA seemed needlessly slow in adding blacks to its teaching corps, but internal correspondence reveals the frustration of recruiting blacks whom the secretaries considered competent.[6] Nevertheless, the number of black association agents gradually increased. During the 1866–67 school year there were only 28. The number increased to 100 in 1868–69 and to 105 in 1869–70. In the latter school year blacks made up about one-fifth of the AMA's southern personnel. The association's black agents came primarily from three sources: northern blacks, free blacks from the South who had some education, and those trained in AMA schools. Since well-trained free blacks were scarce and it took years to train teachers, the most important initial source was the North.[7]

Most of the black men and women who were engaged by the AMA to teach freedmen were obviously motivated by a strong wish to aid their race. Twenty-six-year-old George C. Booth had enrolled in the Connecticut Normal School for the "sole purpose of qualifying myself to benefit my race. . . . More than I desire my own life I desire to elevate these, my people," he wrote. New Yorker Nathan T. Condol said he would have no peace of mind if he selfishly stayed at home. William Jones, born and reared in the North, said that "as I am a Coloured man I feel it my duty [to go South] and take up my cross there among my people." "Since the dawn of Emancipation," Mary E. Watson wrote, "I feel that God calls me to work for them, to devote my time to those who have so long been trodden under foot . . . so long been denied the privilege of being taught." Watson's letter of application surely caught the association secretaries' attention when she added, "Perhaps while teaching them the things pertaining to this life I might persuade some to seek an interest in that life which is eternal and fadeth not away." William D. Harris believed it his duty "to do all I can for the elevation and salvation of my people, in this auspicious and momentous hour as they have just begun to struggle up from chattelism to manhood, from bruised and mangled slaves to good citizens."[8]

Some black teachers clearly believed and bluntly stated that they could do more for freedmen than could whites. Hezekiah H. Hunter said, "I believe *we* best can instruct our own people, knowing our own peculiarities—needs—necessities." Sallie Daffin wrote that she fully appreciated "every effort" whites were making for blacks, yet "how much soever those of other races may sympathize with them, yet none can so fully experience the strength of their needs, nor understand the means necessary to relieve them as we who are identified with them." Daffin unhesitatingly affirmed that "if we have the same advantages afforded us, as the whites, we will convince those who deny the fact that we are inferior to none." And as a teacher and worker Daffin proved superior to most. In a normal month for her in Virginia she taught day and night school, visited more than forty families, and during her spare moments went to local hospitals to write letters for the sick and wounded. Desire for ease and money were not strong motives for black teachers. They viewed their journey southward as a serious and significant undertaking. They were thrilled with emancipation and the prospect of aiding freedmen, but their excitement surely was tempered by fear and anxiety. Some knew the South and slavery from experience, and all were aware that they would likely encounter white hostility.[9]

Although the AMA and other educational societies grumbled about the difficulty of finding competent black teachers, most of those the association eventually selected were well qualified for their chosen tasks. Clara Duncan, an orphan, had worked her way through Oberlin by teaching and doing housework. Sara G. Stanley, described as a "lady of color of high intellectual culture and personal accomplishments," had attended Oberlin for three years and was an experienced teacher. Louisa L. Alexander and Blanche V. Harris were two of several Oberlin graduates who successfully taught in the South. Samuel M. Coles graduated from Lincoln University and the Yale Divinity School.[10]

Two black teachers dispatched from the North were African-born, and one had been a missionary to Africa. Barnabas Root, the son of an African chief whose ability attracted the attention of teachers at the Mendi Mission in West Africa, was sent to the United States, where he graduated with honors from Knox College. Root later earned a Bachelor of Divinity degree from the Chicago Theological Seminary. He taught Hebrew at Straight University and directed the AMA church at Montgomery, Alabama, before sailing back to Africa in 1874. Thomas DeSaliere Tucker also came from the Mendi Mission and was trained at Oberlin. Association officials knew him well, since they sponsored his education and initially had misgivings about employing him, apparently doubting both his physical and intellectual energy. Tucker taught for a time, graduated from the Straight University Law School, edited several newspapers, and became president of the Florida State Normal College for blacks. Mrs. Mary Miles was a black American who went to Africa as an AMA missionary, where she married white fellow missionary Richard Miles. When he died she returned to the United States and became a freedmen's teacher. The Reverend Francis Frederick was not well educated, but his experience made him a good choice. Born a slave in Kentucky, Francis escaped to the North, joined the antislavery movement, and spent several years on the English lecture circuit. Many other teachers had normal and college training. Several northern black teachers were as well educated as their white colleagues.[11]

Occasionally blacks charged that the AMA kept its black agents in subordinate positions. This accusation had some merit when considering southern workers, but several northern men were placed in supervisory positions. Louis A. Bell directed the Straight University law program, Charles H. Thompson was dean of Straight's theological department, and Dr. J. T. Newman was dean of its medical department. Thomas W. Cardozo was a proficient and trusted principal of the AMA's Charleston school until officials learned that he was being blackmailed by the mother of a student he reputedly had seduced in Flushing, New York. Although Cardozo protested that it was he who had been seduced and although his brother testified that the experience had "humbled him in the sight of God," the AMA fired him. Cardozo was replaced by his brother Francis, who became one of the most efficient principals and teachers in the South. The Reverend C. L. Woodworth, a white association agent, toured Dixie in 1866. He was generally impressed with the AMA's efforts, but Cardozo's Charleston school, he said, "stands at the head of all the Colored schools of the South. We have other schools which are a credit to the association, but his is the 'bright consummate flower' of them all—it should be carefully cherished and guarded." John Mifflin Brown, later an A.M.E. church bishop, and his wife headed a mission home in Norfolk.[12]

Although the Harris brothers, William, Robert, and Cicero, had not enjoyed the educational advantages of Cardozo, Bell, Thompson, and Newman, their intelligence and energy made them trusted AMA agents. They were born in Fayetteville, North Carolina, and moved to Ohio where Cicero, the youngest, attended Cleveland High School. Thirty-seven-year-old William was a plasterer with a limited education when he went to Virginia in 1864, but he proved to be an unusually able teacher, organizer, and preacher for the AMA until he became the minister of an A.M.E. church and was transferred to Washington, D.C.[13] Robert was twenty-four and also a plasterer by trade. His only teaching experience was secretly instructing slaves in North Carolina. He taught for the association for two years in Virginia before being transferred to Fayetteville, North Carolina, where he became principal of the AMA school there. Cicero labored alongside Robert at Fayetteville and together they developed an excellent school and became prominent educational leaders. In 1870 the state assistant superintendent of education pronounced their school the best in the state. With tact and good judgment they won and held the goodwill of all classes of the community. Writer Charles Waddell Chesnutt credited Robert with keeping him in school and encouraging his aspirations. Robert taught in Fayetteville until his death in 1879. Cicero was one of the founders of Livingstone College and later became an A.M.E. Zion bishop.[14]

Most northern black AMA teachers were not as prominent as educators as those discussed, but they were generally able and many made significant contributions. Jonathan J. Wright was sent to Beaufort, South Carolina, to teach soldiers of the 128th Regiment of United States Colored Troops. In his spare time he taught a Sabbath school and opened a law practice to defend impoverished blacks. When Samuel Hunt charged him with spending more time as an attorney than as a teacher, Wright denied it and added that his duties included serving all the freedmen's needs. "I came here for the express purpose of working among this people," he told Hunt, "and while I am here if anybody stops me from so doing they will have to put me in jail." In one case Wright secured child support for a black woman who had had a child by a white man. His efforts on behalf of freedmen resulted in his being shot at "by some enemy of my race." Wright claimed he knew no person "by color": he judged them by their intrinsic value. He advised the AMA that it was not enough to send teachers of good moral character—they should also be "of good Christian character, feeling and showing by their acts that of one flesh and blood God has created all persons." He had little patience with racial prejudice from any source. "Wherever ignorance, prejudice, oppression & the devil come in contact with me there will be a fuss & people will hear from me," he wrote. Wright was impressed with how rapidly his soldier-students learned, and he believed that with the knowledge they now possessed there was not "power enough on earth to hold them again in slavery." Since law and politics were Wright's main interests, he resigned his association position and became a successful politician and judge. Yet he remained interested in black education and continued to cooperate with the AMA.[15]

In 1864 Edmonia G. Highgate, "an unusually talented and efficient young woman," left the principalship of a Binghampton, New York, black school to join the AMA at half her former salary to labor "for my newly free brethren." In Virginia she was ecstatic "to get so near to so many of my people who have spent most of manhood's and wom-

anhood's freshness in slavery." Several months of frenetic and ex-
hausting work left her seriously ill and so "deranged" a colleague had
to take her home. A few days' rest restored her strength and "a moderation, a calm prudence . . . which many friends feared I never
would possess." Still too ill to return South, Highgate in December
1864 began a successful lecture tour of New York for the AMA. By
February 1865 she was impatient to be doing "pioneer work" with
freedmen again. Reluctantly the association sent her to Darlington,
Maryland, a "very miserably poor country place" with few blacks and
many "ignorant" whites. Highgate was unhappy at Darlington. She
did not think it her "duty to stay here in the woods and teach thirty-
four pupils when I have . . . an opportunity to teach hundreds. . . .
Colored teachers when *imbued* with the right *spirit and properly
qualified* [should be] *in the front ranks of this work.*" Highgate persuaded the association to assign her mother to take her Darlington
school, and after going home to attend the funeral of a brother fatally
wounded at Petersburg, went to New Orleans to become principal of
the Frederick Douglass School.[16]

In New Orleans Highgate was depressed to learn that some of the
wealthy free blacks "do not feel in the least identified with the freedmen or their interests. Nor need we wonder," she said bitterly, "when
we remember that many of them were formerly slaveholders." After
the New Orleans Riot of 1866 Highgate decided to seek a new field in
Lafayette Parish, where her "little knowledge of French" was put to
constant use in instructing "French Creoles." Blacks liked her, but
whites were no friendlier than in New Orleans. They threatened to
burn her school and boarding place and twice she was shot at in her
room. The next year she returned to New Orleans, where she opposed
the "old rebel School Board" that proposed the "perpetuation of a cruel
caste" by opening separate city schools for blacks. She would rather
starve, she proclaimed, than "stoop one inch" to teach in such schools.
In a public speech protesting segregated education she announced that
if her school was transferred to the old board's control, "all I have to
say is that Edmonia G. Highgate will then resign her situation as its
teacher." She would go teach again in the country where she had faced
Rebel bullets before. When the board opened separate schools, Highgate went to Enterprise, Mississippi. In January 1868 she was teaching in a freezing, unheated, windowless church. The following year she

again became a collection agent for the AMA. Her experiences, combined with her intelligence and rousing stories, made her an effective agent. She continued to work for the association and freedmen until 1871.[17]

Nellie A. Ramsey of Ohio, who taught several years at Amite City, Louisiana, was less frantic than Highgate, but was effective. A local Catholic priest wrote that when she arrived whites and blacks were armed and "ready to fight to the death at the least provocation." Ramsey became the "Head Pacificator" in the town. Both races "could not but applaud . . . her integrity, fairness, courage & love of order & harmony among the citizens." Moreover, she was an excellent teacher. A "very competent judge" who attended public examinations of both black and white schools reported that Ramsey's "children beat the others all to pieces." Mary E. Watson, a twenty-three-year-old graduate of the Rhode Island Normal School, overcame fear of Confederate raids to go to Virginia in 1864. She despaired at the suffering and disease among the fugitives, but was inspired by her first close contact with slavery. "As I grasped the hand of each and bade them goodbye," she wrote at the end of her first year in Norfolk, "tears started to my eyes, and I felt that I had been taught by those aged ones." In 1865 she was sent to Darlington, Maryland, where she quietly and confidently took the lead in building a new schoolhouse, taught day, night, and Sabbath school, and lectured on good citizenship. She founded an active educational society "for the moral and intellectual promotion" of its members and as an auxiliary in supporting the school. When President Johnson's vetoes cast gloom over the community, she called a meeting at the church and urged members of the society "to be patient and hopeful that the loyal heart North is on the side of justice and liberty." She told them that if blacks strove to have more morality, education, wealth, and untiring industry it would be difficult to keep them from elevation if not equality, and "Every hour that fleets so slowly, / Has its task to do and bear."[18]

Watson apparently successfully instilled her views in her students. One year they begged to attend school on July 4 rather than have a holiday. "Thinking of their history . . . I could not but yield to their entreaties, and a happy Fourth . . . they spent over their lessons." They saw Christmas vacation as "an unwelcome summons," fearing the week "could not be profitably spent." She organized "an interesting" adult debating society and a Lincoln Temperance Society for children. Little wonder that the local black school committee wrote the AMA in 1868 that Watson was "a light shining in a dark place and many cross or flock toward it." After four years of sometimes impatient and painstaking supervision, the new stone school building was completed. It was the finest schoolhouse in Darlington and excited "not a little jealousy among the whites." Unfortunately Watson never taught in the new school. Blacks at Port Deposit, Maryland, were dissatisfied with their teacher. The AMA considered Port Deposit a larger, more significant field and, judging Watson to be one of its more efficient teachers and community leaders, transferred her there in late 1869. The Darlington school committee sorrowfully thanked her for "her labours in the diffusion of knowledge" and informed the AMA that "the impression she has made will as long as life lasts remain in her scholars. They love and respect her." Watson perhaps best summarized her work at Darlington when she said, "We are advancing step by step, slowly, but surely."[19]

Although the proportion of AMA northern black teachers and missionaries to whites was always small—the largest number during any one year was fifty-one in 1868–69—their impact was considerable. Most were effective teachers, leaders, and role models. Even southern whites could hardly deny their ability. According to a Texas Bureau superintendent, William A. Jones and James H. Washington, both Oberlin products, had been "wonders" to white Texans. "Under the molding of their skillful hands the most obdurate of the unreconstructed . . . have surrendered the idea the 'Negro can't learn.'" Unfortunately many of the more able northern teachers, including Francis Cardozo, Jonathan Wright, William Steward, and Charles H. Thompson, left the association for politics, Bureau appointments, promotions at other schools, or better paying positions. Lewis Tappan's claim that "we give small *salaries* choosing that the teachers realize their largest compensation in the pleasure of doing good" was no more appealing to some blacks than it was to whites.

Being black did not necessarily guarantee success or acceptance by freedmen. William Henry Morris, trained at Ashmun Institute (later Lincoln University) in Pennsylvania, was sent to a rural area near Norfolk, Virginia. He liked the city better and often left his work in the hands of an untrained monitor, whose salary he charged to the

AMA without authorization, in order to go there. He quarreled with everyone in authority, including black John Mifflin Brown. An Arkansas correspondent wrote a black newspaper: "We are much disappointed [with northern black teachers]. . . . They do not seem to have any kindred feelings with the natives, but hold themselves up as superior, and soon come out as politicians caring nothing for the educational interests, but all for the votes." Macon, Georgia, blacks denounced Jamaican-born William A. L. Campbell because his manner repelled the people and because his wife was Catholic. Campbell admitted that he had not yet "become quite acquainted with the modus operandi of the American mind." John W. A. Shaw, not understanding the freedmen "as children of slavery," collided with blacks in Charleston. Floyd Snelson, a black minister, said Shaw refused to yield "to the weakness of our people." He expected much of them and when they failed he bitterly reproved them. A local church deacon wrote that Shaw hated whites and mulattoes and constantly quarreled with and threatened to attack people physically when they disagreed with him. A group of Port Deposit, Maryland, blacks demanded Mrs. E. Garrison Jackson's resignation when she became too closely identified with an opposing denomination.[20]

Some northern blacks were unable to escape the feeling of cultural superiority that afflicted many white teachers. Like their white counterparts, they talked of ignorance and superstition and sometimes referred to adult freedmen as "these untutored children." Many northern-born or northern-trained agents were especially critical of the freedmen's religious practices. William D. Harris objected to loud, emotional services. Thomas W. Cardozo asked the association to send a minister to Charleston because he could not "worship intelligently with the colored people." Some local blacks who were Episcopalians worshiped "intelligently," he said, but they were segregated and their pastor was a "known rebel." Cardozo refused to "put my foot into such a church." There was a black AMA minister in Charleston, "but he preaches for the class with whom I cannot worship for want of intelligence." Francis Cardozo criticized "ignorant and fanatical" black Methodists and claimed there were few southern blacks morally and intellectually fitted for AMA work. Nevertheless, most northern blacks worked comfortably and effectively with the freedmen.[21]

Southern black teachers had less formal education than their north-

ern counterparts, but they were no less important. Of the approximately five hundred black agents the AMA employed during the Civil
War and Reconstruction, well over half were southern. Mary Peake
was only one of the many natives the association found capable of becoming a teacher. When Thomas Cardozo arrived in Charleston to
organize a school in early 1865, he immediately hired six teachers from
the local free community. All had received some classroom instruction.
William O. Weston had been a bookkeeper for a tailoring firm, Mary
Weston had taught a school for free blacks for several years, and
Frances Rollins had been trained at the Philadelphia Institute for Colored Youth. Although Cardozo was satisfied, he commented that most
were unfamiliar with "our system of teaching." One experienced
northern teacher, he said, could accomplish as much as two southern
ones. When Francis Cardozo succeeded his brother, he retained the
southern teachers but diligently sought northern-trained blacks because he thought they were more competent.[22]

Association Superintendent W. T. Richardson employed several local teachers in Savannah in 1865. In Natchez, Mississippi, J. P. Bardwell observed a small school operated by Josephine Nicks. "I have
visited no school room that was kept in better order & no school that
appeared to be under better discipline," he reported, and he immediately hired her. The AMA commissioned Mrs. Lily Granderson, whose
prior experience consisted of stealthily teaching fellow slaves at night.
Gabriel Burdett, whom the Reverend A. Scofield said "blows the Gospel trump with rare eloquence and power," was an AMA minister and
teacher for more than a decade at Camp Nelson, Kentucky. Mary Day,
a native of North Carolina who boasted, "I am proud to say that I am a
daughter of the south with no taint of yankeeism in my veins," was one
of the first association teachers in Wilmington. After about six weeks a
new superintendent summarily replaced her with a northern white
teacher. She later taught for the AMA again, but disdainfully rejected
a formal commission since "a burnt child dreads the fire." In many
cases the association relieved southern teachers as quickly as northern
ones could be secured, in so doing alienating the teachers and their
friends.[23]

Most southern agents had enjoyed little opportunity for schooling,
but some were adequate teachers and many, including John H. H.
Sengstacke, were good. Sengstacke was born in Savannah in 1848 of a

black mother and a German father. After his mother died his father took him and his sister to Germany, where young Sengstacke was given intense instruction. He later traveled extensively as a seaman. Upon their father's death, the Sengstackes sailed to Savannah to claim their inheritance. The sister returned to Germany because "she could not endure the pressure of prejudice against her," but Sengstacke remained, feeling it his duty to labor for freedmen. When hired by the AMA he was a licensed public schoolteacher and minister. He became a hardworking, dedicated association teacher and minister in Woodville, Georgia, serving the Plymouth Congregational Church there for thirty years. The AMA commissioned dozens of other native teachers throughout the South, some of whom had little more education than their students. Such teachers usually were placed in rural areas where no educational opportunity would otherwise have been available.[24]

Many of the best AMA teachers and ministers were educated in the association's own schools. But training teachers took time, and there were many factors which prevented bright youth from attaining more than a common-school education. Poverty made staying in school for lengthy periods impossible for most. Moreover, the need for teachers meant that they could get jobs in the country with inferior training. The association encouraged northern benefactors to provide scholarships to keep able students in normal schools and colleges, though only a small minority received such grants. As a result, for several years most association-trained teachers taught mainly in primary departments. Gradually, however, the association began to place them in its own and other secondary and normal schools. William Scarborough, who attended Lewis High School in Macon, Georgia, Atlanta University, and Oberlin, returned to Lewis High as an instructor. He later became president of Wilberforce University. At Avery Institute in 1875 all of the four lower grades were taught by Avery graduates. The principal reported that their classes were as well taught as those with northern teachers. The next year Ella Cooper, the valedictorian of her class, was also employed. Usually Avery graduates taught in the lower departments, but in 1877 Cornelius C. Scott, an 1872 graduate who had just completed college work at the University of South Carolina, was hired to teach advanced students. Nearly all of the AMA normal schools and colleges used their outstanding graduates to teach beginning pupils. Eventually most of the AMA elementary schools were staffed by association-trained teachers. The AMA colleges also employed a few of their graduates. James Dallas Burrus joined the Fisk faculty as a mathematics instructor, and Louis A. Martinet, "a fine classical scholar" and a graduate of the Straight University law department, taught at Straight. AMA-educated ministers eventually pastored most of the association's churches.[25]

Black teachers faced the same hardships as whites. They too endured poor housing, inadequate food, poorly constructed school buildings, and white hostility. As has already been seen, some black teachers were whipped and threatened by the Klan. E. Garrison Jackson taught night school at Port Deposit, Maryland, but only reluctantly, for at night blacks were "stoned and driven about at the pleasure of rowdies." Jackson had been beaten and stoned in the streets by boys until she began fighting back. They then kept a safe distance and shouted insults. Once she was walking with a friend when a man behind her stepped on her dress and belligerently demanded that she not "take up" the sidewalk. When she stepped aside for him to pass, he called her a "nigger," saying he would not tolerate her "sass" and would slap her mouth. She told him "in a very decided manner he would not do it." Jackson said she had learned by experience that if whites attacked, it was better "to stand your ground" than run. On the other hand, William Steward wrote from Americus, Georgia, in 1869: "The whites use me very kindly and in no case among them have I been treated as a colored man— always with the utmost equality . . . and when speaking to my own color about me they invariably use the highest term of commendation."[26]

Black teachers were subjected to additional indignities not suffered by whites. When Thomas Tucker tried to purchase a cabin berth ticket on a steamboat in Baltimore, he was refused. A white colleague who defended Tucker was verbally abused and told it was "a pretty business to be doing with niggers." Two young women who traveled to Mississippi by steamboat from St. Louis were excluded from the dining cabin and ejected from their staterooms. Mary Watson was "jim crowed" before she reached the South. She accompanied H. S. Beals and two white teachers from New York to Virginia. At Jersey City she was told she could not sit in a first-class car. Beals unsuccessfully appealed to the conductor and a "higher" train official. He angrily claimed that in the first-class car there were "women of Irish and

Dutch descent, unmistakenly ill bred uneducated, and one, who had a late acquaintance with a whiskey bottle." Beals and the white teachers left the clean, roomy car and accompanied Watson to one filled "with men, profanity and tobacco smoke." When the party reached Baltimore, they once again encountered the "shame of America." Beals ordered breakfast for four, but when the three women arrived, the black teacher was informed she must eat in the kitchen. After Beals said that all or none would eat in the dining room, Watson was allowed to remain.

Clara Duncan accompanied white teacher Samuel A. Walker to supper on a boat en route to Virginia. The captain's assistant called her "a negro wench," rebuked Walker, and forbade Duncan coming to breakfast the next morning. Walker complained to General Butler, who, after a hearing, fired the man responsible for the incident and ordered that all passengers be served, regardless of color. Francis L. Cardozo refused to send two northern women home on the cheapest available steamship line because blacks rode only as steerage passengers. In order to avoid "pandering to southern prejudice," Cardozo paid twice as much for tickets on a line which took them first class. When two Alabama teachers, a black woman and a white man, entered a first-class railroad car, the black woman was ordered to the smoking car filled with drunken, swearing men, even though several blacks holding white children remained. The male colleague explained that she was a teacher and friend and asked that she be permitted to stay. When the request was denied, they both "went, amid sneers and hisses," into the other car. "The threats and avowals to kill us, were not a few, and it required not only much faith in the Lord, but also much coolness and steadiness of nerves to face down such a crowd of drinking restless men. We arrived at last . . . at Talladega, and stopped off amid threats and oaths."[27]

Most teachers refused to submit to such insults without protest. After a fire destroyed all her clothing at Port Deposit in 1866, E. Garrison Jackson went to Baltimore to replenish her wardrobe. At the conclusion of a day's shopping she and a friend went to the Philadelphia, Baltimore and Wilmington Railroad depot, where they were "outrageously abused and insulted." We took "our seat in the ladies room *from which we were thrown out literally thrown*," Jackson wrote. She indignantly complained to the Bureau commander and took the railroad to court. More than her injured feelings were involved, she said: it was the principle. Only the importance of the question justified her making a "public spectacle" of herself by going to trial. "Our soldiers went forth with sword and bayonet to contend for right and justice," she added. "We could not do that. But we contend against outrage and oppression wherever we find it."

When the Reverend W. A. L. Campbell was ejected from a Georgia "white" railroad car in 1875, he debated whether to bring action against the railroad or suffer the indignity quietly "for the sake of the gospel." He decided on the former, and as a consequence was threatened by railroad authorities. However, Campbell wrote, "I am not afraid of their threats and am willing if necessary to suffer for what is right."[28]

More demoralizing to black teachers than southern white insults were affronts from their white colleagues. Obviously many white teachers worked comfortably with and respected blacks, but others were uneasy living with them. Friction developed in Norfolk, Virginia, in 1864 when black and white teachers shared a mission home. Mary Reed privately said she was willing to teach freedmen but did not wish to eat and sleep with them, including teachers. Blacks outnumbered whites at the home, Reed wrote, and at the table they "assumed so much that I have *almost thought* the persons who said 'Give them the opportunity and they will take advantage of your very kindness' were right." She assumed she reflected the majority view among the white women teachers. Her sentiments were not shared by Samuel Walker, who charged that there was considerable "copperheadism" among the teachers and asked that he be fired if he ever had reservations about eating "with our colored friends," since he would then not be "a fit laborer for that race." The tension was exacerbated when a black and a white woman teacher chose to sleep in the same bed. The local superintendent, W. L. Coan, objected, which outraged some of the teachers, who accused him of advocating social distinctions.

Ostensibly because the Norfolk mission home was too crowded, another one was opened. All the black teachers moved there except Sara Stanley, who angrily claimed that Coan's "peculiar secession, proslavery . . . negro hating principles, and malign prejudices" were responsible for the arrangement. Coan, who had previously traveled the lecture circuit with blacks and who had advocated the hiring of black teachers and publicly decried "caste," denied Stanley's accusation. He said he would appoint as many blacks as could be fitted for the work. Any teacher or superintendent who showed partiality on account of color should be fired. At the same time he advised avoiding, if possible, blacks and whites sharing the same rooms and beds, kissing each other unless in private, and mixed members of opposite sexes walking arm-in-arm. The latter, Coan thought, unnecessarily provoked already hostile whites. He admitted that although some black workers agreed with his views, some did not. Much conflicting testimony came out of Norfolk. Coan's behavior prior and subsequent to the incident shows that he was not a rabid racist, as Stanley suggested. Neither was Stanley a white-hating black woman inclined to manufacture ridiculous charges. She respected and felt affection for many white teachers, including Samuel Walker, with whom she had an affair. There is no doubt that some white teachers were uneasy about mingling with blacks. Apparently the teacher who chose a black bedmate was not, and Clara Duncan reported that Frances Littlefield, with whom she worked and lived, treated her wonderfully. Emotional, confusing reports about prejudice were common. One Norfolk black teacher said Superintendent William H. Woodbury acted "upon the decision of Chief Justice Taney that a negro has no rights that a white man is bound to respect." Another wrote glowingly: "Since I have been under the charge of Prof. Woodbury I have received nothing but kindness and encouragement at his hands."[29]

Who would live in the mission home was a most sensitive issue in the South, and the association seemed to have no consistent policy. In many areas it courageously defied local custom, while in others it was more accommodative. In Natchez, Mississippi, in 1865 Superintendent S. G. Wright advised new black teachers Blanche V. Harris and Pauline Freeman that he could not treat them as he had in Oberlin and that they must not board in the mission house for fear whites would mob it. In a number of small ways Wright made them feel they were less worthy than white teachers. He had earlier lived with and hired black teachers, but under the circumstances thought it prudent to avoid social contact. Harris and Freeman, convinced they were being discriminated against because of their color, became insubordinate and took their complaint to the local black community. The association sent J. P. Bardwell to investigate. He concluded that although Harris and

Freeman could legitimately be fired for insubordination they should be retained because they were "quite as much *sinned against* as sinning." Bardwell, who had known Wright for two decades, said Wright hated slavery and was dedicated to freedmen, yet there had been "a little too much yielding to the spirit of *caste* . . . a little too much anxiety for the favor & society of military officers." The AMA reprimanded Wright, but retained him.[30]

A similar incident occurred in North Carolina when Samuel S. Ashley decided it would be better if Sallie Daffin boarded with a black family. Daffin, Ashley said, was "an excellent teacher and a faithful Christian" whom he admired as "a lady and a friend." She had previously lived in the mission home, and this, he believed, had created unnecessary tension. Black teachers must come South, Ashley insisted, but it was unwise to send them to board with whites. There were few places in the North where such an arrangement was judicious, and in the South it placed teachers "in such sharp contact" with local prejudices as to make their situation almost intolerable. Whites had already charged the AMA with promoting social equality, and mixed mission homes proved their assertion. Ashley was quite fond of Daffin and was sensitive to her feelings, yet he was clearly more concerned about white teachers and the response of white southerners. Daffin believed that as a commissioned AMA teacher she should live as well as work with her white colleagues, and she refused to return to North Carolina. The association approved Ashley's decision, thereby consenting to unequal treatment of its teachers. Such housing controversies posed a dilemma for the association. Local agents' reluctance to fuel southern anger by housing AMA teachers together is understandable, if not admirable. Some sincerely believed they could do more for freedmen by appeasing local whites. However, by accommodating itself to southern custom—and sometimes to the prejudices of its white agents—the AMA wronged its black teachers, violated its own stated principles, and weakened its credibility among blacks.[31]

Some mission homes housed black and white teachers together throughout Reconstruction, but not always without conflict. In 1877 the Reverend R. F. Markham, his wife, and three teachers boarded in the Savannah home when the Reverend L. A. Rutherford was assigned there. The teachers taught for the city board of education, whose superintendent informed Markham that "for white people to eat and associate with niggers on an equality outraged society and ought not to be tolerated." Markham feared that if Rutherford lived in the house the teachers would be fired. On the other hand, he said, if he were not boarded with the teachers, blacks would charge prejudice. Assuming that black goodwill was the more important, he took Rutherford into the home. A young Atlanta University graduate politely declined Markham's invitation to live in the home, not only because it would displease the city superintendent but also because, she said, blacks thought that anyone who boarded with whites was "stuck up" and such a teacher would have little influence in the community. In Charleston, teachers as well as white southerners opposed mixed living. Blacks had previously boarded at the mission home, but it was white-only when Mrs. M. E. Shaw was sent there in 1875. Principal James T. Ford reported that "none of our ladies had . . . been wholly satisfied to receive a colored sister to our house," but that they had "swallowed their feelings" until Mrs. Shaw arrived with a nursing baby who "raised quite a commotion." They then petitioned Ford "to decide that we could not keep them in our house & pleading also that a woman with a nursing baby could not be relied" on to take charge of a class. Ford replied that Mrs. Shaw would stay. A few weeks after her arrival she wrote: "Although my welcome here was not the most cordial, yet I am now getting on very nicely. Mr. Ford is a perfect gentleman and a most efficient principal. The ladies treat me with uniform kindness, in fact I scarcely remember that I am of a different race." In Atlanta, Amy Williams did not object to one of Storrs' Oberlin-educated black teachers living in the mission home, but thought she should not be matron, in a sense head of the family: it would give southerners new provocation.[32]

Association agents also sometimes catered to what they perceived to be black prejudice against black teachers. Generally freedmen were pleased to have black teachers, indeed often demanded them, but occasionally they expressed a preference for whites. Some simply assumed that white teachers were better trained. Others were biased against people whose skin was darker than theirs. Mortimer A. Warren, who preceded James T. Ford as principal of Avery Institute, resisted adding more black teachers in 1870 because it "would damage the school's reputation." Avery was the favored school among Charleston's prewar free population, many of whom were light, and there was some dissatisfaction when the dark-skinned Mrs. Shaw arrived later, even though she was an excellent teacher. Ford had not anticipated problems when informed she was arriving because he assumed she was "a light-colored woman like most of our school." Had he known of her darkness, the principal said, he would have advised the AMA of the inexpediency of dispatching her to Avery. In 1878 Amos W. Farnham, Ford's successor, praised Cornelius C. Scott as "a good teacher, a pleasant companion, an earnest moral Christian . . . a warm friend of the school, in fact he is all I wish, but he is colored, and his color hinders his popularity." Avery traditionally had black teachers in the primary departments, which was acceptable, a former Avery student told Farnham, but northern whites should instruct the higher grades. One young man dropped out before graduating, claiming he did not want a "nigger" signing his diploma. Farnham suggested that if the AMA could find Scott a better position he should go "for the sake of giving" Avery "*character.*"[33] For white AMA personnel who had reservations about black teachers and ministers, the claims that freedmen preferred whites, that white northern teachers were necessary to give "character" to or "build up" schools, that mixing teachers would increase southern opposition, and that blacks had too little training were good excuses and were widely used.

In 1877 the AMA found itself in the strange position of resisting a white Democratic board of education's demand that it appoint more black teachers at Tougaloo. One had been recommended and rejected as unfit. The board's motives could be questioned since it preferred black to northern white teachers. Perhaps the candidate suggested was a poor choice, but there is evidence that some Tougaloo personnel, for whatever reasons, wanted no more black teachers, regardless of ability. A few outstanding blacks such as Francis Cardozo, Henry Hugh Proctor, and James Dallas Burrus were widely admired, respected, and promoted. J. A. Adams, Straight principal, whom New Orleans blacks denounced for his racial views, made a strong, eloquent, and successful plea for hiring Louis A. Martinet, but too many whites assumed without question that blacks were inferior teachers. Under the circumstances there were few experienced blacks with advanced training during Reconstruction, but even the rare college graduates were sometimes compelled to prove their worth.[34]

Even the most open-minded white teachers presumed blacks must remain in subordinate positions for the foreseeable future. A case in point was Mary Wells, one of the AMA's most sensitive and devoted teachers. Wells became a part of the Athens, Alabama, black community. She adopted, loved, and raised a black son, yet in 1876 she too believed that few blacks were capable of leading their people. Lindsey A. Roberts, a pious young man who had lost his right arm as a Union soldier at the Battle of Nashville and who was a student of the Fisk theological department, was sent to Athens to pastor the AMA church. However, there was some dissatisfaction with him: he was not a dynamic preacher and lost his temper too easily. Wells confided in a letter that a "thousand" times she had been ready to report that he was unfit to be a minister and should be removed. She was restrained only by the thought that he was as good a black man as she knew, and more exemplary than most. If blacks were to be redeemed by their own race, men of moral power must be developed. This was not possible without experience, and so she had said nothing. Many AMA agents were less charitable than Mary Wells. At the turn of the century, except for its elementary schools which were staffed mainly by blacks, association faculty and principals were still primarily white.[35]

Although blacks generally occupied the least important positions and many from the South were undertrained, their contributions were invaluable. They faltered, stumbled, made mistakes, and became discouraged. They also became community, church, and educational leaders. Perhaps they were no more devoted than many white teachers, but as a rule they better understood freedmen, more easily fitted into the community, and could live with fellow blacks without provoking southern white fears of social equality. More important, they went into areas whites feared to enter. The AMA without apology located blacks where it assumed whites would be unsafe and could not find suitable places to live. Hundreds of black men and women either trained or employed by the association labored in obscurity and often in poverty in outlying areas that otherwise would have lacked schools. In the crusade to educate former slaves, blacks were heroes and heroines quite as much as the more famous Yankee teachers.

12

The AMA and
the White Community

ONFLICT between northern teachers and southern whites was inevitable in the postwar South. Hatred, fueled by years of sectional discord and the war, was intense. Augusta J. Evans of Mobile reflected the views of many southerners. In late 1865 she accompanied her brother to consult a New York physician, and while there "freely expressed her abhorence of the principles and people of the North. Nothing but the desire to save my brothers' life," she confided to a friend, "would have induced me to visit a section, which . . . I cordially detest." An AMA teacher stationed in Louisiana during the war concluded in November 1865 that hatred of northerners was actually increasing. Yankees generally were not widely admired in the South and freedmen's teachers were even less so. Those who fought so determinedly for slavery could hardly be expected to welcome "abolitionist emissaries" among their former chattels. When an association agent visited a fellow Presbyterian, an Atlanta pastor, in December 1865, social relations were pleasant but the minister stated "fully & frankly" that the southern cause was just and that he was "only sorry" it did not succeed. "And in all the efforts of our church to help the Freedmen or in his elevation," the agent reported, "he can not wish us success."[1]

Initially, black education found little favor among southern whites. A Kentucky Bureau agent's claim of white "malignant hostility" was confirmed by southern testimony. A Louisiana physician and planter confessed that there was "a bitter prejudice" against freedmen's schools, and a former Mississippi slaveholder agreed that "unfortunate though deep seated" opposition to educating former slaves would frustrate any attempts in that direction. An American Missionary Association agent in Missouri concluded that "the bushwhacking miscreants and unrepentant rebels" there could "be civilized in no way so well as to furnish and sustain colored schools among them; but they swear vengeance on the attempt."

A few prominent whites cautiously supported black education. Howell Cobb privately admitted that freed people should have some learning, as did Ben Yancey, brother of the famous fire-eater William L. Yancey. A former master purchased books for an Atlanta student and helped him with his studies. The master's daughter was teaching the youth's mother and sister to read. But a Mississippi Bureau agent's evaluation of white attitudes applied generally to all of the former Confederate states. There was a small minority, he said, who saw the propriety of educating blacks, yet opposition by enemies was "so virulent, and hatred is so much more active a principle than faint and uninterested approval" that implementation of an educational system would be hazardous. An AMA supporter in Louisiana, who directed that the *American Missionary* be sent to four men in the interior, requested that it be wrapped in order "to guard the receivers . . . from the abuse of those who hate the principles you advocate."[2]

Whites opposed black education for reasons that seemed logical to them. It had been forbidden to slaves, and most saw no need to change that policy with emancipation. Moreover, states which had "looked with criminal indifference" upon the education of the white masses were not likely to be enthusiastic about training freedmen. A more obvious reason for resisting black schools involved the issue of control. Blacks wished to assert their independence, while whites were just as determined to retain economic and social domination over former slaves. The school was discerned as a direct threat to white supremacy. Still others agreed with a former Confederate colonel from Virginia that the idea of freedmen's schools was not so much repugnant as it was "absurd and ridiculous." Whites chuckled at talk of educating blacks, the editor of *De Bow's Review* said, because they "have been accustomed to the idea that the negroes are pretty stupid."

Some "well meaning" women informed a young Arkansas teacher that she was wasting northern money and her own energy on those "poor creatures," since God's curse on blacks made efforts to improve them fruitless—she could better spend her time with poor whites who were capable of advancement. The following sarcastic comment in the Richmond *Times* was typical of, though less bitter than, many newspaper responses to black education. "White cravatted gentlemen from

Andover with a nasal twang, and pretty Yankee girls with the smallest
of hands and feet, have flocked to the South as a missionary ground;
and are communicating a healthy moral tone to the 'colored folks,' beside instructing them in chemistry, botany, and natural philosophy,
teaching them to speak French, sing Italian and walk Spanish, so that
in time we are bound to have intelligent, and probably, intellectual,
labor."[3] Some whites felt personally threatened by black education.
Several AMA teachers concluded that considerable opposition to training freedmen arose from whites who realized their own deficiencies
and who were mortified to see blacks receiving advantages which they
and their children had never enjoyed. A Kentucky woman, lamenting
her own lack of training, said, "Since its got so fashionable to teach the
niggers I feel as if I'd like to know a little something myself."[4]

The southern view of AMA teachers as self-righteous fanatics, intent upon teaching social and political equality and distrust of whites,
exacerbated their rancor. When Yankee teachers reputedly committed
to black equality were combined with the belief that the school was an
instrument of social control and the black-white struggle for direction
of black destiny, the stage was set for an explosive drama that, in the
words of Jacqueline Jones, "made the neighborhood school a political
and cultural battlefield." Many southerners felt that black schools
were as significant a force for social change as black voters. AMA
teachers, with their talk of "constructing Christian civilization" in the
South, did little to mitigate southern hostility. Caroline Briggs wrote
from Warrensburg, Missouri, in 1864 that she had just arrived in
"Dixie Land which I have found by sad experience is not yet the land
of the Free or the Home of the Brave." Local citizens were, she said,
"mostly Sesch and oh, so ignorant." M. W. Martin described Pine
Bluff, Arkansas, as "this Sodom of the South," and added, "Sin verily
cries out."

Writing after the turn of the century, Myrta L. Avary could not
suppress her indignation at the Yankee schoolmarms who "overran the
country" with their "holier than thou" expressions and who, she said,
were bent upon instructing native whites in what they ought to be
doing as much as upon "teaching the negroes to struggle indecorously
for the semblance of a non-existent equality." More circumspect teachers were not well liked either. An Athens, Georgia, Bureau agent who
wrote that AMA teachers were unpopular there added, "From a long

experience I say it not in a profane sense that our *Lord* and *Saviour* could not please or be respected by these rebellious individuals if he were to assume control of a cold. school."[5]

The South demonstrated its animosity toward black education and northern teachers in numerous ways. There was a fairly widespread effort around Brookhaven, Mississippi, in 1865 to refuse employment to black parents whose children attended school. As late as 1871 an AMA teacher discovered "a secret compact" made by Newton, Georgia, planters to keep money out of black hands in order to "starve out schools" and thus deprive freedmen of an education. A more common ploy was to refuse to rent to or board teachers. Board with a private family was "utterly out of the question" in Gainesville, Florida, in 1865. Board for association teachers was almost impossible to secure in Texas except among "loyal Germans" throughout the state. Mrs. Lizzie S. Dickinson rented a room with a white family in Hempstead until a Rebel son returned home and ordered her out of the house. The only place Maggie Farrar could live in Van Buren, Arkansas, was in a "bitter rebel hotel." The Georgia Bureau superintendent of education despaired of organizing schools in some of the smaller towns in 1868 because it was almost impossible to get boarding places. Fred A. Sawlett found a house in Athens, but was ousted after the attempted murder of a Bureau agent. The owner feared damage to his property. Sawlett was unable to find another place. "They tell us that they will burn their houses before 'nigger' teachers shall live in them," he wrote. When teachers were unable to rent from whites, they lived with blacks and then, a Kentucky Bureau agent reported, "the old hue and cry of miscegenation" was raised and schools were broken up.[6]

In Missouri, teachers were driven from their schools, thrown in the river, and otherwise abused, and "noble women assailed with the vilest slanders." Maligning the teachers' character and motives was a favored method of discrediting them. When some dead infants were reportedly found in a Florida river, a resident wrote that it was "probably the spawn of some . . . who have come here, under their pretended sanctimoniousness & philanthropy to teach negroes and to practice their infamy, where they are not known." When a prominent Mississippian announced in a public speech that, of seventy female teachers sent to South Carolina the previous year, more than sixty had borne illegitimate black children, the remark was greeted with considerable glee by his audience. Northern women migrating South, presumably as teachers, an Alabama editor charged, were in fact seeking black husbands. If "the buck niggers will welcome them with ebony arms, to African couches," he added, then the next generation of southern radicals would "smell only half as bad" as the present one. "I suppose you have no teachers in those colored schools who are *really virtuous*," an Arkansas minister coolly remarked to a male supervisor. Association teachers were so conscious of these widespread accusations that they sometimes made great exertions to avoid giving credence to them. Sarah W. Stansbury moved her night school in Cuthbert, Georgia, to her home, even though it was crowded and uncomfortable, because she feared going home after school in the dark without an escort. Previously she had been walked home by older male students. "I have always aimed to give these Southerners not so much of a shadow of a chance to say aught truthfully against me," she said.[7]

Association personnel were frequently and publicly subjected to sneers, taunts, and insults. "Nigger teacher" was a common epithet. Emma Engleman and a colleague were strolling along an Augusta, Georgia, street when a "splendid barouche" passed transporting four women, one of whom rose, shook her fist, and screamed, "See those yankees! Oh you ____ ____ , using words too profane and vile to write." Petty annoyances sometimes accompanied verbal assaults. An interior Georgia town had no public conveyances except an express wagon which the teachers were not allowed to use. In Augusta, a man spat upon an association instructor as he met her on the street. The Newton, Georgia, postmaster opened the teachers' letters and packages before delivery to check for "incendiary material." Local merchants occasionally harried association teachers by refusing to extend credit, a great hardship since AMA salaries were so often late. Apparently, however, the need for trade usually overcame the traders' loathing of Yankees. Other whites were less easily persuaded. When two women arrived in Fayette, Mississippi, in 1865, "a number of lewd fellows" gathered, shouted unpleasant remarks, and became so noisy that the mayor ordered them to disperse with the promise that the offending women would leave the next morning. One local newspaper suggested that white teachers of black schools be hanged without benefit of judge or jury.[8]

Usually the schoolmarms accepted insults and threats with remarkable fortitude, as illustrated by Mary Close, who went to Brandon, Mississippi, in early 1866. Since whites refused to acknowledge or board her, she found housing with a mulatto woman and her daughters and proceeded to open both a day and a night school. When white boys from a nearby school disrupted her classes by throwing rocks through the windows, a note to the wrongdoers' teacher brought no action. Close then complained to the mayor, who stopped the stone throwing, though this only increased community anger. The local newspaper editor wrote her, warning that if she continued her night school the consequences would be upon her head. Not one to be easily intimidated, Close vowed to continue her school, bidding the editor to "bring on his consequences." He then informed her that if she were a "person of any refinement" she would not remain in a community where everyone looked upon her "with loathing and disgust." He reminded the young woman that when she went to church children vacated adjacent pews. Close replied that children of "well bred Christian parents" never left when she entered that or any other church. The editor retorted that he could hardly restrain one child's father from going "right up to see her about that." Send that "Christian parent," she answered. Close exchanged three letters with the editor and made no concessions, apparently even hinting that there were Union troops in Jackson who might be detailed to Brandon in case of trouble. Threats frightened most teachers, but they also strengthened the resolve of others.[9]

Ostracism of Yankee teachers was almost universal during the years after the war in small towns and rural areas. Caroline Briggs was "persecuted and treated with utmost contempt" in Missouri. Women seldom noticed her. Teachers at Bainbridge, Georgia, sometimes attended a white church, but no one ever spoke to them or acknowledged their presence. One teacher commented on the strangeness of never being greeted by a white person. In McLeansville, North Carolina, no white woman had dared visit Esther Douglass over a period of three years for "fear of losing caste." Another North Carolina teacher learned after a few months "to retreat into a shell of unconcern toward local whites and to avoid going into white sections of town." As a rule, men were more likely to speak courteously to teachers than were women.[10]

Maggie Farrar thought Van Buren, Arkansas, whites treated her with more contempt than they did blacks. She was lonely and isolated.

"I will not deny," she wrote, "but what at times a feeling comes over me as though I could not endure this life much longer." Naturally, this stifling social atmosphere was less oppressive to teachers in cities where there were others from the North. In rural areas and villages some could not bear the isolation and requested transfers to be near friends, or gave up mission work after a year or two. Others maintained a satisfactory social life in the black community despite awkward cultural and educational differences. Most attended black churches. A black Virginian remembered that when missionary teachers were ostracized and threatened they were undeterred. Rather, it seemed to stimulate them. They went into the slaves' huts and treated them as equals, or at least as capable of becoming equals. But even the most steadfast and those the most comfortable with blacks sometimes found such a life dispiriting. Mary Wells, preparing to visit Boston after eleven years in Alabama, was anxious to "*be* recognized by Christians of my own race—feel that I am no longer a leper."[11]

More serious than threats and ostracism was violence aimed at students, teachers, and schools. Students were intimidated, stoned, and had their books stolen. John Ogden angrily complained in early 1866 that Fisk pupils were "almost daily assailed on their way to and from school, and frequently cut and bruised to an alarming extent." In Norfolk a fifteen-year-old white boy struck ten-year-old Carolina Swan with a brick and kicked her "in the belly so severely that she bled from her lower regions." White youths in Warrensburg, Missouri, encouraged by adults, regularly beat black students and injured one so badly he missed several days of classes.[12] School buildings were vandalized and occasionally burned. During the Memphis riot of 1866 the AMA's Lincoln Chapel and other schoolhouses were destroyed. When some of the teachers fled the city, the Memphis *Avalanche* editorialized: "Another lesson has been taught the white fanatics. It is that we want none of their 'school-marms' among any of our population. . . . It is said they have all left in a great fright. A happy riddance."[13]

Threats were more common than assaults upon teachers, but the latter occurred often enough to make them cautious about traveling at night. Edmonia G. Highgate was shot at twice in her room at Vermillionville, Louisiana. A Florida teacher left after six shots were fired into her home late one night. Attempts were made to assassinate Charles B. Wilder and other missionary workers near Hampton, Virginia. Shots were fired into Butler School, barely missing an instructor. In early 1867 an agent in North Carolina was forcibly taken from his home by an armed gang of mounted men, robbed, taken to a nearby woods, severely beaten, and threatened with death if he remained. A mob of armed Kentuckians broke up the Reverend A. Scofield's school at Camp Nelson and drove him and his family from their home. Soon after the Reverend Edwin H. Freeman was threatened in Franklin, Tennessee, his son was shot and seriously wounded. In Grenada, Mississippi, Tom Sherman—backed by a mob—choked, struck, and then viciously beat AMA emissary J. P. Bardwell with a cane. The Freedmen's Bureau agent who assisted Bardwell was soon afterwards fatally wounded. While the agent lay dying, a citizens committee called upon another Bureau officer and demanded that all teachers leave town.[14]

The AMA was determined to avoid initiating incidents and to give as little provocation for violence as possible. Its agents were advised to let the military, the Bureau, or civil officials deal with cases of attack against person or property, but it was not a pacifist organization. Its teachers sometimes armed themselves, most often with weapons sent from New York headquarters. A fellow teacher advised Bardwell to provide himself with a good revolver and be ready "to send any Rebs who shall in the future assault you to the place prepared for them from the foundations of the world." Arming in self-defense occasionally had its comic aspects. In Columbus, Kentucky, Linda Slaughter was persuaded to conceal a loaded pistol in her dress pocket for protection during a session of night school. Once there and finding no cause for alarm, she became so terrified that the gun would explode in her pocket "even a rebel would have been a relief." More often, in areas away from Bureau agents or Union soldiers, teachers depended upon their black friends for protection.[15]

Despite continued attacks on black schools and teachers, the southern attitude seemed to be slowly changing by late 1866. At an 1867 meeting of Georgia teachers Edmund A. Ware learned that some favored educating freedmen, although they were apprehensive that blacks who received early training from advocates of equality would soon be *thundering* at the gates of the State University." A few leaders began to speak out for limited black schooling, but their support was qualified. Training should be rudimentary. Schools should be funded primarily by taxes paid by blacks, and teachers should be from the South. When it became clear that blacks were determined to have their youth educated, whites resolved to try to keep such training in their hands. The southern position, at least that of the small minority who publicly advocated teaching blacks, was that whites were not absolutely hostile to freedmen's education; they were simply opposed to the type provided by Yankees.[16]

An Alabama minister voiced the above argument when he claimed that blacks would be educated and that the only question was who would teach them. Northern teachers, he declared, sprang from the lowest class of society, believed that southerners were the "sum of all villanies," and advocated social equality, black suffrage, miscegenation, agrarianism, "and every mischievous outgrowth" of northern fanaticism. The preacher warned that if "we do not mean to suffer the distinction of races to be destroyed and permit equality in every respect we must keep these men from among us. We can keep them out only by ourselves giving to these people the instruction they need." Ten years later Gustavus J. Orr, Georgia school commissioner, made a similar observation in his annual report. Southern whites who taught blacks benefited themselves, he said, by "having the inferior race" under their control "at the only time which gives promise of so moulding them as to form them into peaceable, virtuous and useful citizens."[17]

Even the minority who accepted black education distrusted AMA and other northern agents. One teacher said, "Many times the first feeling we find in Southerners is that we are enemies, come to spy out, to censure, to subdue." Yankee instructors were viewed as political envoys who had come South to foster social equality, black suffrage, Republicanism, and hatred of southern customs, and even though that was not their paramount purpose they sometimes did do all those things. The charge that teachers taught blacks to distrust southern whites was patently false, however. Freedmen had learned that lesson well through experience, but some teachers were bluntly critical of the South and its institutions. The AMA's teachings of the utter sinfulness of slavery and the slaveholder were not reassuring to former slave masters. Neither were comments about southern traitors and equality of all men. Lincoln "the Emancipator" was held up to students as a man to revere. Blacks were even encouraged to discard habits of slavery. Males at Tougaloo were drilled in the "common facing positions" and marching "simply to cure them of their cringing manners, slouchy postures and shuffling gait inherited from the plantation." What teachers saw as indications of manhood and dignity, southern whites often considered insolence.[18]

Teachers frequently, and sometimes unknowingly, violated southern custom. In April 1866 Augusta, Georgia, women paid tribute to Confederate dead by placing flowers on their graves. Graves of Union soldiers in the same cemetery were left unadorned. Some AMA teachers then decided to decorate the resting places of the Union dead. They formed a procession of students and marched to the cemetery, where they were barred by the mayor and a group of armed men. Finally the mayor agreed to let the women enter with only enough students to carry the flowers, thus acting as servants rather than citizens: a city ordinance prohibited blacks from going into the cemetery except as servants. The women refused to enter under these conditions and complained to a Freedmen's Bureau agent, who refused to assist them. Teachers and students returned home amid jeers. The northern women were angered by the experience, and local whites were irate at the flouting of local custom. The assistant commissioner of the Bureau, who believed these women made his job more difficult, reputedly denounced them as "damned whores" and complained to AMA officials that after being insulted they retaliated and exhibited independence, which needlessly excited white suspicion. Caroline Briggs, who advised Missouri blacks to stand up for their rights, was accused by a prominent white of having "Negro on the brain" and of putting blacks *"above the whites."* Freedmen were respectful before Briggs arrived, he wrote bitterly, but now daily insulted citizens.[19]

Aware of southern sensitivity on the issue, the AMA was cautious on the question of social equality. As has already been seen, some teachers were frankly prejudiced. Others who believed in equality and the right of public contact were hesitant to further antagonize the South and acted accordingly. They suggested that ostentatious violations of local racial etiquette was self-indulgence rather than an indication of commitment to equality and was useful to neither blacks nor the teachers. Nevertheless, the association consistently challenged the southern racial code. Black men were appointed to boards of trustees; teachers lived with black families, attended church with them, entertained them in mission homes, and operated integrated schools when whites could be persuaded to attend; and black and white teachers lived together.

In Charleston, Francis L. Cardozo lived in and ran a mission home which housed a corps of white women teachers. The AMA published and endorsed a resolution of Macon, Georgia, blacks protesting segregated railroad cars. Erastus M. Cravath, president of Fisk, reacted swiftly and angrily when a Nashville ticket agent refused to sell Pullman berths to the Fisk Jubilee Singers. He telegraphed George Pullman himself, who overturned the local agent's decision. Tougaloo faculty mingled and danced with students at social gatherings. The white South generally condemned these activities, and even acts of courtesy were sometimes interpreted as social equality. John A. Bassett was walking to the store one morning in Alabama when he overtook a black woman just as it was beginning to rain. He shared his umbrella and they hurried on to the store. He considered it a simple act of civility and thought nothing more of it until he was attacked in the local newspaper under the headline "Social Equality; A white man escorting a negro woman." The paper asked readers to observe that "such people ought not to thrust themselves upon the white people of Eufaula" and that such behavior was "not indigenous to the soil."[20]

Some association personnel made little attempt to avoid perturbing whites. Berea College issued a resolution on interracial dating which assured students that becoming engaged to marry a person of a different race would not jeopardize their standing in the school. Missionary teachers William D. Harris, black, and Elizabeth P. Worthington, white, were married in Virginia and continued good relations with AMA officials. Teachers and students ate and lived together in the colleges and boarding schools. In 1874 several Georgia newspapers attacked the AMA "based solely on the fact that our workers recognize respectable colored men & women *socially*. We open our parlors to them; we invite them to our tables; we eat with them in our homes." Since a majority of white Georgians denied the blacks' right to be recognized and treated "according to their manhood," Macon Superintendent Frank Haley concluded, "This, therefore, is just where, for a long time to come, we are to be of most benefit to the colored people at large—*as pioneers in securing to them their social rights*." A group of Macon blacks protested that local whites were trying to drive away teachers who "*dare to* and do recognize us as *men* and women." The

Georgia state superintendent of instruction admitted that the Atlanta University faculty was well qualified and had furnished "a considerable supply of the best teachers that have entered the public colored schools," but grumbled that "although social equality between the races is not taught formally at the college, it is taught by example, in the most effective way."[21]

The association's political stance further enraged southern whites. The AMA said it had no partisan mission, but its leaders believed Republican rule was essential and they freely used their considerable lobbying power to promote legislation favorable to freedmen. They also actively supported black suffrage. Tappan's view on the subject was publicly accepted in 1865 when in its annual report the AMA said there was nothing in their nature or disposition that should bar blacks from suffrage. Rather, their "unswerving and universal loyalty entitles them to the first privilege of this kind in the States lately in rebellion." At first Tappan assumed that President Andrew Johnson would not "spare the execrable" southern system, but Johnson's placing civil and judicial powers in the hands of the original seccessionists distressed association officers, who condemned his liberal pardoning policy and the consequent restoration of confiscated lands. In the *American Missionary* they heatedly censured the president for returning freedmen-occupied, abandoned, and confiscated lands to "treason-plotters and murderers," thereby saying to blacks that "the nation has no land for them, and therefore they must go back to their masters or shift for themselves."[22]

Whipple defended the Freedmen's Bureau against "the President in his madness" and denounced Johnson's vetoes, saying there was a higher power that might veto the vetoes. Michael E. Strieby spoke for the association when he said during the 1868 impeachment proceedings: "Hope Andy's head will come off today." The AMA-supported Congressional Reconstruction was "mainly right," Strieby said, but he warned that the "old aristocracy are bent on regaining their lost supremacy over the blacks." The freedmen's "mental acuteness and moral stamina" would be severely tested; therefore, "teachers and schools" must provide moral support. The association modestly claimed some credit for blacks voting Republican in the 1868 Mississippi election. Many had been coerced into voting Democratic, but in places where schools had been kept and preaching had been available freedmen had held "fast in their principles." The AMA was very much interested in the 1868 presidential contest, "not merely for the triumph of a party, but of those principles of liberty, which are essential to the prosperity of our whole country, the South not less than the North, the blacks as well as the whites." Although the AMA clearly favored the Republican Party, its direct political participation in the South was limited. Yet, not surprisingly, white southerners saw it as a partisan society.[23]

The AMA did not encourage party proselytizing in the classroom, but as Robert C. Morris said, "The distinction between civics instruction and political indoctrination was not always clear." Lincoln was glorified as the martyred emancipator, Union soldiers were acclaimed, and students were taught that life, liberty, and the pursuit of happiness were rights of all American citizens. Andrew Johnson was occasionally branded as a traitor. In North Carolina, Elizabeth James asked: "What think you of President Johnson's pardoning all these wicked, *wicked* rebels and restoring them to position and power? What have we been fighting for if the right is not to prevail?" Students might be assigned to read selections from the Emancipation Proclamation and speeches by prominent Republicans or abolitionists. An Andersonville, Georgia, class debated whether the state legislature had the authority to expel its black members.

A few teachers directly involved their students in politics. Ellen E. Adlington helped form a "Grant Club" in Berne, Georgia, and planned to travel and form others. Minnie B. Hanson became embroiled in the 1870 Newton, Georgia, election. Election tickets were "interrupted" before reaching Newton, and when they were distributed two names had been marked through with a pencil. Upon discovering the sabotage, Hanson hurried to school, organized her students to erase the marks. Still, whites asked black voters for their tickets and marked through or tore off names of those they did not wish elected. At some polling places, Hanson learned, those with Republican tickets were banned. She finally closed her school during the election because "I could not have school and attend to election matters too and it seemed absolutely necessary to attend to the latter." In 1872 a teacher wrote from Emerson Institute in Mobile: "Political combatants are now acting on the aggressive plan of warfare & the combat deepens. A political meeting in the chapel tonight—turbulent times are expected here until after the president is elected." A great Independence Day celebration was held at Talladega in 1870, and prominent Republicans made speeches. The crowd included about three thousand Republicans and a dozen Democrats.[24]

A majority of teachers did not become embroiled in political contests. A. A. Safford believed teachers should avoid politics except to vote, but even politically inactive teachers sometimes instructed blacks about their voting rights and made little secret of their views. "I am a Republican and believe it as much a duty to vote right as pray right," wrote R. F. Markham in 1877. Although Ira Pettibone knew that Georgia "Rebs" despised Congressional Reconstruction, he thanked God it was going "steadily forward." Teachers prayed for Senate conviction of President Johnson and celebrated when Grant was elected to the presidency in 1868. When passage of the Fifteenth Amendment was celebrated in Macon, Georgia, the AMA chapel bell rang "a merry peal." A nighttime parade went by Lewis High School, "which was handsomely illuminated, [and] cheers rent the air." Emma B. Eveleth voiced the fears of many teachers during the 1872 election when she said: "We tremble when we think what it *will* be, if the democrats get into power, which I hope the Lord will prevent." An Atlanta University teacher confessed shame and prayed for forgiveness for having once been guilty of being a Democrat. Certainly there were few Democrats among AMA personnel. An association minister visited Straight University in 1877 and learned something that gave him "considerable pain." What he learned was that J. A. Adams of Straight was a Republican but sympathized with the Democrats.[25]

A few association agents were elected to office or were given patronage positions. Three black AMA teachers achieved considerable prominence. Francis L. Cardozo was an early Republican organizer in South Carolina, a delegate to the 1868 Constitutional Convention, and was elected secretary of state and secretary of the treasury respectively. His brother Thomas became superintendent of education in Mississippi. Jonathan J. Wright was sent to the South Carolina Constitutional Convention and sat on the state supreme court for several years. White agents were not as conspicuously successful as the Cardozos and Wright, but Samuel S. Ashley was a delegate to the North Carolina Constitutional Convention and superintendent of instruction in that state. Thomas C. Steward served in both the House and Senate in Alabama. John Silsby became a register of voters in Alabama in

1867 while teaching for the AMA. Silsby saw his additional job as consistent with his mission to freedmen. He was elected to the Alabama Constitutional Convention and later became Dallas County circuit court clerk. Ashley, Steward, and Silsby continued to cooperate with the AMA while in office and rejoined the association after their political careers ended. At least four agents became county superintendents of schools and a few, including Ellen Adlington, were appointed postmasters or postmistresses. Of the thousands of AMA personnel in the South, only a few were working politicians, but they were sufficiently active to lend credence to southern charges that the association was teaching Republicanism as well as reading and writing.[26]

Hostility toward teacher-politicians clearly did not cause southern opposition to freedmen's education. After all, schools were destroyed and teachers were molested before blacks received voting rights. Nevertheless, Congressional Reconstruction and attendant black political participation signaled a renewed and more extensive attack upon freedmen and their schools.[27] Several AMA properties were burned and its teachers were threatened by the Ku Klux Klan (called Thugs of America by the association) and White Leaguers. Armed men burst into Sarah A. Allen's room around midnight and warned her to be gone from Monroe County, Mississippi, within three days.[28] Disguised men seized two Fisk students teaching in Dresden, Tennessee, placed ropes around their necks, dragged them outside, and "cruelly lacerated" their backs with whips. R. H. Gladding was insulted and threatened by the Georgia Klan. His landlord was abused and a black supporter, legislator Abram Colby, was beaten almost to death. A Virginia teacher wrote in 1868: "Five men disguised in a Satanic garb . . . dragged me from my bed, and bore me roughly in double quick time . . . to a thicket, whipped me unmercifully, and left me to die. They demanded of me that I should cease teaching niggers and leave in ten days or be treated worse." W. W. Wheeler of Berea College was dragged from his room and stretched out on a log, where he was given "a terrible scourging with hickory withes." Alonzo B. Corliss was stripped and whipped in North Carolina. Corliss had four of his tormentors, whom he recognized, arrested. Although three admitted the deed, they were released without trial. A Klan beating with a bullwhip left inch-deep wounds "of a fearful nature" on the shoulders, back, and side of C. W. Washburn near Seguin, Texas, and William Luke was murdered in Alabama. The Marion *Commonwealth* approved the Luke killing, saying he "was one of the most rabid negro equality fanatics that ever came into this section."[29] The AMA responded to these and numerous other atrocities by petitioning Congress for protection of freedmen and its agents, lobbying for the Force Acts of 1870 and 1871, making greater efforts to avoid provoking its southern opponents, and arming some of its workers. After the Klan threatened to assassinate Thomas C. Steward and either expel or starve out all association teachers in Marion, Alabama, the AMA sent Steward rifles and "a stock of Bibles" with a note expressing the hope he would have more use for the latter than the former. Caution and circumspection were more to the AMA's liking than armed defense.[30]

Throughout the South scores of black schools were destroyed and many teachers were exiled. Although a few association agents were frightened away, most remained. Esther Douglass defied a Klan suggestion that she leave McLeansville, North Carolina, but at night she was careful to sit so that her shadow would not reveal her location. Once the Klan lined up around Mary Wells's house in Athens, Alabama, fired volleys of shot through the window, and later burned her schoolhouse. Twenty years later Wells was still in Athens. Even though most association teachers defied white violence and remained at their posts, terrorism in the early 1870s seemed to have altered the AMA's stance. The association did not suggest that Douglass, Wells, and other teachers violate their principles to accommodate whites, but it did advise them to try to make friends, to avoid provocation, and to maintain a low profile. James H. Simonson, who received a letter telling him to leave Georgetown, South Carolina, or he "would be sent home in a wooden box" and who was constantly insulted on the streets, sometimes felt "like resenting the affronts," but adhered to the counsel that "discretion is the better part of valor." When, after being captured, roughly treated, and released by fourteen armed men in Columbus, Mississippi, Joseph N. Bishop continued to stand firm, do what was just, and act discreetly, he was following AMA admonitions. Teachers were discouraged from making disparaging remarks about their enemies. When a newspaper quoted George L. White as saying unkind things about the South, the association chastised him. It fired "a good man and faithful worker" in Alabama in 1873 because of inexperience, which meant he was indiscreet when he talked to and about white southerners. As will be seen, the association made so great an effort to blunt southern hostility that it sometimes made blacks suspicious of its motives.[31]

Even during the worst of the terror some teachers were able to form uneasy truces with their white neighbors, and a few evoked praise. In 1870 an ex-Confederate colonel visited Mrs. J. E. Beigle's school in Russell County, Alabama, and agreed that she was "doing a good work & the school would prove a blessing & not a curse as was feared" at first. In late 1871 Mary Wells reported that the native white county superintendent of education "who 'came in like a lion' seems quite lamb-like." He appeared delighted with teachers Wells had trained for black country schools. The more teachers were willing to accommodate themselves to southern views, the more acceptable they became. Still, white support remained spotty and limited. In 1875 the AMA invited its most experienced teachers and missionaries to a two-day conference in Atlanta. Included on the agenda was a discussion of white southern attitudes toward black education. The conference concluded that few whites had "accepted our Northern view" that blacks "should be educated just as white people are. Such an opinion is exotic in the South, and will be a plant of slow growth." Many whites for various reasons were willing to offer blacks "some" training, but the mass of native whites remained indifferent; "perhaps we ought to say hostile."[32]

The Democratic overthrow of southern Republicans relieved some of the pressure on black schools, but still anger and violence frequently surfaced. At least ten association schools were burned after Democrats redeemed the South.[33] Suspicion of Yankee teachers and northern-supported schools continued. In 1877 a Savannah teacher bought pictures, including those of Lincoln and Charles Sumner, as prizes for students. The native white superintendent of city schools forbade her to distribute them, saying that he would rather have a picture of Lincoln's assassin in his home than one of the martyred president or Sumner. Jabez L. M. Curry, a former Confederate congressman and now a proponent of training former slaves, admitted in 1881 that on the question of black education the South had made some progress but still had far to go.[34]

If white southerners were far from accepting black education, they were even more distant from the AMA's ideal of all youth going to school together. The association's primary thrust was black relief and education, but its agents quickly learned that many whites were as destitute and ignorant as freedmen. George N. Greene thought many whites around New Bern, North Carolina, "were more abject than the contrabands are themselves and need more teaching." Missionaries provided food, clothing, and occasionally medical assistance to whites. H. S. Beals said freedmen had been his first care, but poor whites had not been forgotten. "They are poor & weak & ignorant," Beals wrote. "They have not as many friends . . . as the poor col. child. They too are Jesus' poor."[35]

The AMA concluded that poor whites needed preaching and teaching as much as relief. Alma Baker suggested that missionaries be sent to laboring whites in Missouri. "They are so very wicked. Much lower than blacks in morals," she reported. She sometimes dropped "a word of warning," hoping that God would "trouble them" to repent. The association instructed missionaries and teachers to invite whites to their religious services and classrooms. George Greene wrote: "In accordance with your instructions I have been doing what I could to get the poor whites to come into the school arrangements." A few whites accepted the AMA's invitation. At least a dozen association schools had white pupils during the war. At Portsmouth, Virginia, black teacher William D. Harris had one white student. Trustees of a white Portsmouth church asked the AMA to publish a notice in a local newspaper that whites might attend its schools. The Norfolk school had two whites, one "noble boy," a former drummer in the Confederate Army. At Port Hudson, Louisiana, Thomas A. McMasters taught a mixed class of fifty. White children enrolled in a Raleigh, North Carolina, school, but all soon dropped out. They went without schooling, the teacher claimed, rather than bear the ridicule meted out to them for attending with freedmen. In Smithfield, North Carolina, several parents petitioned to send their children to an association school. "One old gentleman . . . with tears in his eyes" asked the teacher to take his offspring. The instructor readily agreed. One man sent five children. The white youths seemed to enjoy school and the teachers as much as the freedmen did. Some of the black pupils who objected to this "spotting the school," as they termed it, were satisfied when the teacher explained it would break down racial barriers.[36]

Unfortunately the AMA's attempt to teach whites in Beaufort,

North Carolina, may have strengthened rather than weakened racial barriers. Beaufort whites pleaded so earnestly with H. S. Beals that he admitted them to the freedmen's school. The *American Missionary* reported that whites, ages nine to forty-five, were "sitting side by side with colored children, without seeming to know or care what is the complexion of their fellow students." However, the whites were soon tormented, abused, and "ultimately driven away by the prevailing sentiment of white people." Beals concluded that a white school was needed. He successfully negotiated with the county commission to furnish a building if the AMA would supply a teacher. Beals believed this joint effort was "a great breaking down of the walls of separation." The school opened in December 1866 and operated smoothly until black enrollment threatened to close it the following February. Although blacks had a superior school and more teachers, they were concerned that the association directed a white school and demanded a public declaration that it was open to black children. They complained to the AMA that Beals was "building up a wall of separation between the two races" and that the school created "harsh feelings" among blacks.[37]

Local AMA teachers were divided on the issue. Beals approved of integrated education in theory, but under the circumstances thought "moulding these hundred white children to the genuine New England type" was more important than principle. John Scott argued against opening the school to blacks. The white school was full. The black one was not. If opened to blacks, some whites would be forced out. "This would be making *a distinction on account of color strongly in favor of blacks.*" Samuel J. Whiton, on the other hand, charged the association with violating its stated principle that its schools were open to all, and he encouraged blacks to seek enrollment in the white school. The association faced a serious dilemma. It knew that if blacks enrolled in the white school most white students would leave. It believed that whites badly needed educating and that it could thereby reduce white prejudice. Yet it might alienate its major constituency in the process. The school was transferred to the county commission.[38]

The association made a few other hesitant and temporary efforts to train whites. When C. B. Whitcomb lost his black school to the Louisiana military system, he began another for white refugees in Baton Rouge. He soon had 140 students. Mrs. M. C. Milligan opened a school for whites in Morgan County, Alabama, in June 1866 with thirty-five pupils. But since the AMA opened its schools to all, prejudice prevented its playing a large role in educating whites. A Bainbridge, Georgia, teacher discussed the problem in 1869. The association was teaching five hundred black youths and only two whites in the county. Many whites could not afford private seminaries and institutes and consequently received no education rather than attend with freedmen. "They went with the negro to draw rations; they go to the polls together. Many, *alas!* Drink together," a teacher reported, "but all our efforts to have them attend the same school, thus far have failed." White parents at the Black Creek Road community near Jacksonville, Florida, petitioned for a teacher. When asked if they would admit black children from an adjoining community, one parent answered: "Admit them! Of course we would. I've got three children. I'd have no objections . . . Why," he continued, "should I keep a child away from his dinner when he is hungry and there's enough for him and us too." Apparently he did not speak for a majority of parents. Arrangements were made to board a teacher and build a schoolhouse. Emma B. Eveleth was dispatched to Black Creek Road. A local family agreed to board her in their one-room cabin, but she eventually left when it became clear that no schoolhouse would be provided.[39]

The only truly successful integrated AMA school during Reconstruction was Berea College, and for it John G. Fee deserved much of the credit. Fee strongly believed in mixed education. In 1865 he warned the AMA: "We should avoid making a *'nigger school'*—avoid the idea that there must be a separation. I believe we ought to make a school for humanity—make efforts to have in here a due measure of white faces." His determination to make Berea a model was successful until a state law in 1904 prohibited interracial education. In 1867 Berea had 96 black and 91 white students. In 1881 there were 249 blacks to 120 whites. But Berea was an exception.[40] The association's ideal of integrated schools was generally quickly abandoned in the face of the South's demand that they be separate. It continued to invite whites into its schools and advocate universal public education. It believed that education and elevation of both races was "the demand of the hour, the duty of the nation and the requirement of God," but its efforts were concentrated on blacks. Association officials assumed that educating freedmen would stimulate whites to seek the same for themselves, and there is evidence that they were correct. "Having rested on their fancied superiority," H. S. Beals wrote in 1868, poor whites were being awakened from "their sluggish dreams by the rapidly advancing throng of freedmen passing them. They are now pleading for the advantages of a common school."[41] The AMA's halting efforts in the area of white education and its accommodation to white views won few southern friends. When it began a new emphasis on work with mountain whites in the late 1880s, its relationship with the white South was still uneasy at best.

13

The AMA and
the Black Community

FREEDMEN were contributing partners in the AMA's southern work from the beginning. When the Reverend W T. Richardson went to Savannah in early 1865 to determine the feasibility of starting schools, he discovered that freedmen had formed the Savannah Educational Association, had collected $730, and had employed several local teachers. After passing a resolution of confidence in the AMA, the SEA invited its cooperation. In several instances the association sent teachers only after blacks had furnished a school building or promised to board the teachers. Dozens of communities struggled to provide board and more if possible. Beaufort, North Carolina, blacks fitted up the schoolroom and bought furniture at great sacrifice. "I assure you there is a willingness to do all they can," George N. Greene wrote. In Carondelet, Missouri, Alma Baker had only thirty students, but parents regularly paid her board bill and rent on the schoolhouse. Before classes started in 1865 they had raised a fund of $400. When Baker tried to secure local white charity, some parents objected. They had been "niggers" long enough, one said; now they wished to be men. In 1869 Thomasville, Georgia, blacks willingly paid ten dollars a week to board two teachers, plus tuition for their children. In addition to paying board and rent, freedmen made direct donations to the association. In 1866–67 they gave $7,756 to the AMA. The amount increased to $13,056 in 1867 and to $21,500 in 1868–69.[1]

Montgomery, Alabama, blacks asked the AMA for teachers only after they had collected money and arranged to construct a school building. In Marion, Alabama, freedmen led by former slave barber Alexander H. Curtis formed a school corporation and elected a board which secured a school lot. In 1867 the board deeded the property to the AMA. In some outlying areas the AMA sent teachers only if the community agreed to pay tuition to assure their salaries. Newton,

Georgia, parents gladly paid the fee, elected a committee of twelve to canvass the neighborhood to discern the number of school-age children, and formed a benevolent association to pay tuition for orphans. Several Milledgeville, Georgia, parents lost their jobs after voting Republican in 1868 and were borrowing money to pay tuition and the teacher's board. They were "willing to make any sacrifice, that the school may continue," their teacher said. Freedmen assisted and showed their gratitude in numerous other ways. When the teachers arrived in Macon in 1865, they were greeted by members of a welcoming committee who had "swept, scoured and garnished" the mission home. While Carrie Semple was on vacation from her small Florida school, freedmen led by their minister dug trenches to drain the water-filled school lot, cleaned and refurbished the house, and planted trees in the yard. The AMA, other societies, and the Freedmen's Bureau made invaluable contributions to black education. They stimulated the freedmen's desire for schooling, encouraged black self-help, and established hundreds of schools, but they in turn were prompted to make greater efforts by enthusiastic freedmen who were disposed to make great sacrifices to educate their children.[2]

The AMA also joined freedmen in their attempt to secure land. Initially the association wished to settle contrabands on land to prove their industry and capability and to relieve physical suffering and dislocation. If they could persuade the government to allow blacks to cultivate abandoned plantations in South Carolina and Virginia, AMA officials thought, "all our educational and missionary aspirations generally will go forward and our efforts will, under the providence of God abundantly satisfy the incredulous as well as friends." George Whipple spent several days in Washington in March 1862 trying to effect such an arrangement. Eventually U.S. officials agreed to the association's plan, and Charles B. Wilder, the AMA's choice, was appointed to supervise an agricultural system in eastern Virginia. The AMA strongly advocated the distribution of confiscated and abandoned lands to freedmen and vigorously protested President Johnson's later return of such land to owners. The government, the association claimed, was obligated to guarantee to freedmen "all the rights implied in the use of lands already granted them of lands abandoned by rebel owners, including the produce of the cultivation of the crops." But the AMA wanted more than temporary custody of land for freedmen. It wanted permanent ownership.[3]

Association officials envisioned a South filled with small, independent landholders who would be happier, more ambitious, and more stable than landless laborers. Some agreed with Samuel S. Ashley, who said in 1868 that "everyday's experience increases with me the conviction that the next step to be taken in reconstruction is to break up the immense landed estates, and secure homesteads to the landless." But there is no evidence that they believed this should be done by wholesale government confiscation. Rather, they appealed to northern benevolence. In late 1864 Tappan cooperated in circulating a flyer throughout the North notifying the public that sale of confiscated lands in eastern Virginia would begin 30 January 1865. The flyer was designed to appeal to patriotism, greed, and benevolence. Northerners were urged to buy the land in order to make the area loyal. Moreover, it might be a "profitable investment for the owner, and yet be held for the ultimate benefit of landless whites and blacks at the South." Tappan's idea that wealthy northerners should buy land and sell to blacks on credit provided land for only a small number. Since all of the AMA's income was being expended for relief and education, the association was in no position to implement any large-scale plan to provide land for freedmen, but it made some small efforts in that direction. It consistently advised freedmen to work hard, to be frugal, and to invest in property. In 1865 an AMA agent in Providence, Virginia, formed freedmen into an association to purchase homesteads. Members vowed to deposit their savings in a bank until they had accumulated a sum sufficient to buy land.[4]

In 1867 more concrete steps were taken when the AMA bought a tract of 175 acres near Hampton, Virginia, which was divided and sold to more than forty families. In 1869 it bought 615 acres in Cateret County, North Carolina, and several hundred acres at Dudley and Haverlock, North Carolina. The tracts were divided and sold to freedmen on five-year terms, and the money received as payment was invested in more land. At each settlement the association began a school and church, hoping to make permanent communities. The plan met with some success. By 1871 several families had purchased plots in Dudley and neatly painted cottages were rising. Eighty acres acquired in Marion, Alabama, became an "enterprising colony" with houses, fences, yards, thriving gardens, and fruit trees. But often black poverty and natural disasters prevented success. In 1870 the AMA bought a 220-acre plantation in Jefferson County, Florida, on which it intended to establish a model village. The plantation was carved into five 40-acre tracts and one tract of 20 acres, each of which was quickly sold for ten dollars down with the remainder to be paid within three years. There was a crop failure the first growing season, and the next year a cotton surplus reduced prices by half. At the end of two years only one man had made an additional payment of three dollars. The association had received a $63 return on its $1,320 investment. Some AMA workers used their own money to buy land for resale to blacks, the association encouraged freedmen to take advantage of the southern Homestead Act of 1866, and it sent teachers to several black established colonies, but its land policy benefited only a few dozen families. The AMA also occasionally helped black businessmen. In 1869 teacher Sarah W. Stansbury informed the association that Ruben Richards, a Cuthbert, Georgia, farmer, wished to open a store to sell to fellow blacks at a reasonable price since white merchants exploited them. Association secretaries shipped produce to Richards from New York on credit, often shopping for seeds, molasses, lard, syrup, crackers, flour, and other goods for him themselves. The AMA thus assisted in establishing a black-owned business, which was rare in Reconstruction Georgia.[5]

The AMA–black community relationship extended beyond cooperating in establishing schools and buying land. Though association teachers worked primarily with youth, education was not confined to the classroom. The teachers tried to influence the entire black community. Not only should freedmen be taught the rudiments of citizenship, but vices created and perpetuated by slavery must be eradicated. In their place northern teachers wished to instill their values of industry, economy, thrift, temperance, and sexual purity. One of the areas on which the AMA missionary-teachers first concentrated was the institution of marriage. Slave marriages had not been sanctioned by law, and the association energetically urged slave partners to legalize their relationships. Smart and Venus Campbell, who had been married forty-five years according to slave custom, were remarried in 1863 at the urging of an AMA missionary. Great mass weddings were often performed. David Todd married fourteen "old couples" on Christmas Day 1864 at Pine Bluff, Arkansas. He united fifty-six more couples the following March. Most association teachers constantly lectured on the sanctity of marriage. They were shocked that even some preachers openly indulged in "concubinage with a plurality of women." Teaching a puritan sexual code remained a major AMA goal.[6]

The association also attacked snuff, tobacco, and alcohol. Tobacco was widely used by all classes in the South. Teachers succeeded in virtually banishing its use in day schools, but had difficulty with adults in the community. Emma B. Eveleth, a Gainesville, Florida, teacher, feared that they were so addicted they would rather give up food. Alcohol was attacked even more vigorously. The AMA viewed it as a major cause of poverty, idleness, and licentiousness. Blacks were poor, and according to the association, spending for liquor and tobacco helped keep them impoverished. Eveleth reported that "those who use it think they *must* have it at all hazards even if their families suffer for the necessities of life." Teachers and ministers denounced alcohol and drunkenness at school, in the churches, and at public meetings. John Silsby warned Alabama blacks not to drink, adding, "You don't find such men as General Howard . . . or the martyred Lincoln, whiskey drinkers." In cooperation with the Freedmen's Bureau, the AMA established scores of temperance societies (the Lincoln Temperance Society being the most common) with thousands of members. Old and young alike were pressured to take a pledge not to use liquor.[7]

Most teachers organized temperance societies at school and used their students as missionaries to help spread the message to their elders. Eveleth's students acted as spies to report on those who broke the pledge, so that she could visit backsliders and bring them back to sobriety if possible. As with tobacco, the association had greater success in making teetotalers of students than of adults. The AMA failed to end drinking even among its church members. When the Reverend Aaron Rowe was sent to Savannah in 1874 to supervise AMA churches, he reported: "My bro. you have no idea what a terrible work liquor drinking was doing in all these churches before I came here." Several members sold liquor, and others were habitually drunk. Some of the deacons were "dram drinkers," and the Reverend Robert Carter, an AMA black minister, drank with members in their homes. Not only were older freedmen less receptive than students to the teachers' influence, they often resented their self-righteous interference with their personal lives. As a result the AMA's dry crusade often met black opposition. John Scott was alarmed and angered when a North Carolina minister told his students that Scott was in error, that there was nothing wrong or immoral about drinking whiskey. Many AMA teachers piously agreed with D. T. Allen, who concluded in 1872 that blacks had little "moral tone" and resisted every effort to "reform the abuses."[8]

Not content to battle against the vices of tobacco and liquor, AMA personnel became involved in almost every aspect of the freedmen's lives. They gave instruction in domestic arts with emphasis on order, housekeeping, sewing, and maintenance of a proper home environment. Men were told of their responsibility to work and to care for their families. Parents were advised how to raise their children, how to use their earnings, and how to treat each other. Missionaries told freedmen how to worship, and occasionally how to vote. A few agents worried about this paternalism. John G. Fee, who sought AMA and government assistance in helping blacks secure land, said: "There is a danger just here—that after all we are attempting to treat the black man as a 'nigger' not as other men. To get the right use of his bones and muscles he must stand as other men—not too much nursing." Others complained that blacks relied on them for counsel on "questions ranging from the cut of a baby's apron, to the validity of the title deeds securing to them their little homes." But all too often teachers took pride in black dependence. An Alabama teacher boasted that he and his colleagues exerted an influence for good on freedmen such as no race had previously had an opportunity to do because blacks, "regarding us as their deliverers from the horrors of slavery, look upon us as the very messenger of God, sent to answer their secret prayers, offered up through long years of suffering." He added that he was "surprised every day at the readiness which is manifest in complying with my advice even when it is most against their natural feelings."[9]

Most teachers advocated black independence, but their actions sometimes inspired the opposite. In some ways they were similar to paternalistic masters. David Peebles referred to Dudley, North Carolina, blacks as "my people." Although many of the teachers were sincere in their desire for black progress, their attitudes strongly suggested a fundamental belief in white superiority. While rendering valuable assistance to freedmen, the AMA and other aid societies ignored an important problem. Or, as Maxine D. Jones concluded in a study of North Carolina, teachers and missionaries often became so consumed with freedmen affairs, so certain of their superior knowledge and wisdom, so intent upon elevating them and "aiding them in their first steps of freedom that they neglected to allow them to walk or even stand on their own."[10]

Certainly some freedmen did look upon northern whites as their protectors and leaders. H. S. Beals left Virginia in August 1865 "with painful anxieties, and depressed spirits. I left many of the Freedmen in tears," Beals said. "They were sorely tried & frightened with the intense hatred & cruel violence of the returned rebel soldiers." A Fisk student wrote: "Our good teacher is kind and good to us. Mr. John Ogden is our Gen. in school. He takes a great pride in looking in the chapel every morning at us. We have a good God above us at all times." In 1869 blacks at a public meeting in Milledgeville, Georgia, resolved "that we tender our sincere thanks to the American Missionary Association and all other Benevolent Societies which in the past have aided us in the moral and mental culture of our race, as well as to those noble teachers who have sacrificed the comforts of home and society to come here and teach our children." Esther Douglass thought some of her North Carolina students "loved" her too much. Jennie, a "smart" older student, lived five miles from Douglass, but would walk that distance at any time to do her a favor. Other students were as devoted. Butler Wilson, a black leader and attorney in Boston, said in 1882 that blacks "felt toward the AMA 'as a man should toward his mother.'" Others seemed to believe they had exchanged one master for a more benevolent and distant one. An elderly man, speaking to members of the Marion, Alabama, church, said, "That association man [E. M. Cravath] way up yonder who we all belong to says he'll send" us a pastor soon.[11]

Although some freedmen accepted northern teachers and missionaries' advice and leadership without question, many did not. They appreciated the aid the AMA and other societies gave them and looked to northern whites for protection from the military and from former masters. Northern white teachers obviously were different from southern whites. They lived with freedmen, advocated full citizenship, taught their children, and reminded them that they were free and must learn the ways of freedmen. The teachers' evident sympathy and concern compelled blacks to view whites in a different light. Yet lifelong habits and suspicions were not easily changed. Despite their gratitude, blacks still saw the missionary-teachers as whites and scrutinized them closely for signs of prejudice and desire to dominate. A black delegation told Chief Justice Salmon P. Chase that freedmen would more likely trust blacks than whites, no matter what the origin of the latter. A northern observer concluded that freedmen had "a general suspicion" of whites that lay "deeper than trust in this or that individual. Accustomed to kindness only in the form of an owner's interested protection, they cannot appreciate disinterested effort in their behalf." The freedmen took umbrage at the superior air of some teachers and at being treated as if they had no minds of their own. A Norfolk missionary had little success in his Sabbath school in 1863 because, a colleague said, he was not elected by the church and because of his dictatorial manner. "He does not understand the colored people," the colleague added. "They are *sick* of slavery & very sensitive to anything like usurpation—greatly desiring free election." Earlier Charles Wilder had expelled an AMA teacher because his "bad temper & domineering policy" had alienated freedmen. Another Virginia teacher was distrusted because he sold groceries to blacks after school. Even though he sold items at reduced prices, freedmen suspected he was just another exploitative white.[12]

Freedmen especially resented any hint of color discrimination. Teachers quickly learned that serious disagreements or quarrels with blacks could bring charges of racial bias. When the AMA superintendent at Natchez, Mississippi, treated Blanche Harris and Pauline Freeman differently from white teachers, freedmen immediately came to their support and discussed the issue in their churches. The association's influence in the black community was badly damaged. Julia Shearman warned from Georgia that there was a "very general distrust of everything white" among the freedmen, and that if they saw "even white missionaries cannot brook to eat with them—then we shall lose influence." Cuthbert, Georgia, blacks were cordial to teacher S. W. Stansbury and were anxious to have a school, but they disapproved of her boarding with a white family. Attempts to appease southern whites by avoiding social contact with blacks often resulted in the loss of black trust. In 1876 a majority of male Tougaloo students petitioned for S. C. Osborn's dismissal on the grounds that he was incompetent and lacked sympathy for blacks. After the president's investigation found many of the charges "either *false* or *frivolous*," the students prepared another petition to send to New York. As has already been seen, community opposition forced the removal of leaders at Talladega and Straight for making racial distinctions, and blacks frequently and publicly charged that Samuel C. Armstrong at Hampton believed in and observed the color line.[13]

Apparent absence of racial prejudice among teachers did not guarantee that freedmen would unquestioningly accept their guidance. When Alma Baker read a temperance tract to a black Missouri congregation, they strongly denounced it. After she informed them that it had been written by a St. Louis black man, however, they retracted some of their earlier statements and listened to her with greater interest. Numerous white missionaries noted that many freedmen were racially exclusive. This did not necessarily mean that white assistance or even direction was unwelcome but, rather, that blacks were suspicious of whites and desired to retain some control over their own destiny. And the longer they were free the more determined they became to define their own goals and the methods of achieving them. Freedmen were adept at accepting aid and advice they wanted and rejecting the undesirable. They gladly sent their children to missionary schools while resisting the teachers' interference in their personal lives. They permitted the AMA to build church houses and pay pastors but continued to worship according to their own lights. Association work was usually most prosperous in areas where the AMA formed coalitions with black leaders, and when it did not "an unhealthful" and "ugly disposition" sometimes arose. The New Orleans community warmly supported the AMA as long as it "kept in view the development of a capacity for self government" among them and made them an integral part of its work. When the association began to ignore black leaders, it lost support. Failure to consider freedmen's wishes could lead to violent confrontations. In 1875 Swayne School principal J. M. McPherron barely escaped being attacked by a black mob in Montgomery, Alabama. The mob's stated reason for wishing to punish McPherron was that he had been intimate with a female student. The rumor of intimacy was false and evidence suggests that the vigilantes were motivated more by resentment.[14] McPherron's habit of ignoring blacks and their plans had created dislike so intense that they were ready to seize upon any pretext to get revenge.[15]

As already seen, the freedmen's resolve to retain religious independence caused the AMA's church planting programs to fail. Although blacks were more amenable to the association's educational plans because such assistance was more badly needed and schools were perceived as a less direct threat to black customs, a similar yearning for some control was visible. Freedmen welcomed aid society schools, yet many of them dreamed of schools taught and directed by blacks. From the beginning some freedmen had requested black teachers. Whites noted with dismay that parents sometimes sent their children to pay schools taught by poorly educated blacks in preference to free schools with well-trained teachers. Bainbridge, Georgia, freedmen bluntly told AMA teacher Lizzie Parsons that they did not want northern teachers and preachers, "for we don't teach right." This attitude, she said, made her work "a constant warfare." Black Amos G. Beman declared that seeing educated blacks conducting schools would be an inspiration to freedmen "such as no words could describe." Black minister Richard H. Cain said: "We must take into our hands the education of our race. Honest, dignified whites may teach ever so well, it has not the effect to exalt the black man's opinion of his own race."[16]

Although the AMA understood and sympathized with the freedmen's longings to have teachers of their own color, it apparently never fully appreciated their aspirations to achieve as much control over their lives and institutions as possible. Its officers blamed black attempts to gain ascendancy over schools on ignorant black ministers afraid of losing their congregations and thereby their power, and on black teachers "fearing for bread and butter." Or they viewed it as a laudable but premature ambition. Sometimes the association was correct. Black ministers and teachers often felt threatened by AMA schools, and some blacks wanted to run the schools without either the necessary money or expertise. Nevertheless, the AMA's superior attitude, its insistence on Yankee efficiency, and its impatience with black leaders while they were learning through trial and error created serious tensions.[17]

In late 1863 St. Louis blacks at a mass meeting organized a school board to raise funds and conduct free schools in the city. George Candee, an AMA agent, was appointed corresponding secretary and general superintendent. Association schools and teachers became part of the system, and the AMA continued to pay its teachers' salaries. Candee soon became disillusioned with the board. He had thought the board could be persuaded to accept superior teachers regardless of color, he wrote, but they were more concerned with securing positions for blacks. In order to avoid bruising sensitive feelings, "superior" white AMA teachers were forced to teach primary pupils while blacks instructed advanced classes. By April 1864 Candee had decided "the colored people are exceedingly jealous of the whites—they hate them." Perhaps Candee revealed his true sentiments when he added, "The real interests of the colored people are in the hands of the whites, but the hearts of the former class are shut to the benefit of the latter." In June he recommended that the AMA withdraw its St. Louis teachers, since it appeared they would be unable to work with the black board of education. Candee was no doubt influenced by the knowledge that the board was trying to replace him with a black superintendent. The board obviously wanted to retain authority while the AMA furnished the money. It was equally clear that Candee assumed the board could not possibly succeed without white leadership.[18]

The association was no more diplomatic in dealing with the black-dominated Savannah Educational Association. As in St. Louis, Savannah blacks hoped to operate schools "by their own wit & will" and, in the AMA's view, admit "their white friends only to inferior places & as assistants in carrying out their duties & wishes." The AMA was to provide the funds. Association agent S. W. Magill convinced AMA officers that the SEA was "a radically defective organization." The ensuing struggle between the AMA and the SEA over who should teach Savannah's freed children created a rift that never quite healed. The AMA's perception of the seriousness of the task to be done and its views of efficiency prevented it, with rare exceptions, from financially supporting black-administered and black-taught schools.[19]

In St. Louis and Savannah, blacks wanted the AMA to support schools established by them, but in some instances blacks attempted to take over institutions already established by the association. A battle for control resulted in the association's Selma, Alabama, school being closed for a year, and Montgomery blacks contested the AMA for direction of Swayne School for years. In 1875 Macon, Georgia, blacks, dissatisfied that Lewis High had so few black teachers, appointed a "Board of Responsible Managers" and suggested to the AMA that the board direct the school and appoint a black principal and half of the teachers. In return the board would collect money to help pay teachers and keep the building in repair.[20] College officials at Atlanta University and at Tougaloo were dismayed to learn that some of the strongest opposition to giving them state aid came from black legislators who wanted colleges managed and instructed by blacks. Atlanta University in 1870 appointed additional black trustees, hoping to lessen the demand for a separate black college. The AMA resisted Mississippi Governor James L. Alcorn's suggestion that it appoint all black administrators and teachers at Tougaloo. "We should hardly care to be *connected* even with such an Institution under such management as this will be sure to get at so raw hands," E. P. Smith wrote. Smith doubted that a state black-run college could succeed. "The state will vote the money and the colored trustees will use [it], but it will go principally for the aggrandizement of some Dinah & Sambo, until they have floundered through two or three years—perhaps five—experience of incompetency and then new foundations will be laid and a good Institution set up."[21]

Most blacks probably did not wish to seize all AMA schools, but many wanted a greater decision-making role and more black teachers. Indeed, some wanted all instructors to be black. Several association teachers lost their positions in public schools in response to black demands for blacks. Dora Ford returned to Fayetteville, Arkansas, from vacation in 1873, only to learn that the board had appointed a black principal for her school who had immediately fired her and hired one of his students. Freedmen at Washington, Arkansas, prevented Mary Stuart's AMA school from joining the public system. "The 'color line' has been drawn at Pensacola," an association teacher reported from Florida, "and those fanatical colored men who belong to the so-called Equal Rights Club, oppose, by every means in their power, the employment of Northern teachers in public schools." M. W. Martin, a six-year AMA veteran at Pine Bluff, Arkansas, said black leaders drew "the color line strictly." They told him in 1876: "We can take care of ourselves. We are in the majority in the county. We don't want any Carpet Bagger among us." That same year blacks in St. Augustine, Florida, gained control of the school board and forced all white teachers out of their schools. In Atlanta, the board of education, already hostile to the AMA, was "emboldened" in its attacks "by the effort that many of the colored people of the city are making to have colored teachers substituted for white." Ironically, the blacks' demand for teachers of their own color aligned them with southern whites who also sought to oust northern white instructors.[22]

The AMA could have muted black criticism of its schools if it had been more willing to share control and less reluctant to place blacks in supervisory positions and advanced classes. Many freedmen would have been satisfied if the association had shown them it was ready to advance blacks as soon as they were prepared. Unfortunately it often failed to demonstrate such readiness, and it too seldom allowed substantial black involvement in running its institutions. As has already been seen, there were blacks who preferred white teachers, and color for many others was not a dominant factor. At an 1865 black convention in Raleigh, North Carolina, a resolution advocating black teachers was defeated by those who argued that it would place still another barrier between the races. In 1874 the trustees of Lincoln Institute in Missouri asked the AMA for a black woman music teacher, but added, "Color is not indispensable." During the time Storrs School in Atlanta was operated jointly with the city board, the board annually received two sets of petitions from blacks, one requesting black teachers and one asking for northern whites. When in 1875 Frederick Douglass declared that blacks wished to be free of white, "so-called" benevolent societies with their wandering teachers and their second-rate men soliciting funds in the name of blacks, the Philadelphia *Christian Recorder*, organ of the African Methodist Episcopal church, firmly replied: "We are not prepared to have the American Missionary Association recall its 'second-rate' men and close its seven chartered institutions, its seventeen normal schools and its thirteen other schools." The AMA was appreciated and admired by large numbers of blacks, and the good-will would have been even greater if the association could have understood the black desire to share control of schools and to have black teachers. Freedmen could attain practical knowledge from white teachers. With black teachers, administrators, and trustees, they could also foster race pride and gain practical power. All too often the AMA saw these desires as ingratitude, ludicrous ambition, or racial hostility. In theory the AMA favored black-operated and black-supported schools, but it rarely relinquished control of its own. In its view, blacks were not yet capable of assuming that responsibility. Some blacks began to wonder if the paternalistic AMA would ever perceive them as competent.[23]

Association agents and freedmen were further separated by a cultural gulf that was seldom completely bridged. Abbie Howe spoke for many teachers when she said of freedmen in 1868: "What a study these people are! Ever pleasing, disappointing and puzzling us." As the years passed, some teachers seemed disappointed and puzzled more often than pleased. Alma Baker claimed that the longer she worked with freedmen the less she understood them. Even the most devoted and compassionate teachers suffered periods of discouragement over the cultural barrier which inhibited their work. The encounter between former slaves and northern whites was one of "a rational nineteenth-century, middle class culture and a premodern one" with beliefs in ghosts, spirits, and conjuring. Teachers taught piety, self-control, industriousness, and individualism. Blacks, on the other hand, had created their own system of emotional support through the extended family and friends and, as Lawrence N. Powell said, "having by stealth and genius created a folk culture that was expressively rich and essentially communitarian . . . felt no burning need to sacrifice in freedom what had served them so well in slavery." They seized upon emancipation as an opportunity to consolidate their customs and institutions and secure them from outside interference. They cooperated with and accepted northern assistance, yet they wished to work out their own destiny. The AMA, however, was determined to impose its customs and values.[24]

When freedmen placated the missionary-teachers' cultural biases, they paid a price in damaged sensitivities and infringements upon their freedom. When they refused to appease northerners, the result was often disillusionment and even bitterness. The cultural chasm was not as great between teachers and many urban blacks. Free blacks in Charleston, Savannah, New Orleans, and other cities were more familiar with middle-class white culture. The values and ideals of William O. Weston, Catherine Winslow, and Amelia Ann Shrewsbury, free black teachers at Charleston's Avery Institute, probably were not so different from those of the northern white teachers there. A few such people preferred whites to their former slave brethren.[25] But for many, greater familiarity did not mean they appreciated white paternalism and supervision. Savannah had an intelligent, resourceful group of blacks with a tradition of freedom. It was this same group that had told Chase they were distrustful of whites, and the constitution of a local ministerial association specifically prohibited white members.

The freedmen's personal habits alienated northern teachers more than "racial exclusivity." Antislavery literature had taught them that slaves were indolent, immoral, and adept at deception and thievery, but many missionaries were able to see beyond such broad generalizations. A South Carolina teacher claimed observers judged black traits too quickly. Blacks, like any other group, he said, were "made up of a variety of tempers and dispositions as numerous as the colors of Joseph's coat; they are *men*, moral and intellectual beings, and in almost every stage of development." Prolonged contact enhanced H. S. Beals's evaluation of freedmen. He concluded that some freedmen were beggars and dependent while others showed great intellectual and physical vigor. "I am sure," he wrote, "that if we give them all the advantages of education many . . . will come up among the nation's noblemen and mark the age in which they live." After three decades of teaching freedmen, Esther Douglass responded to the question "Are all colored people thieves?" by saying: "I always trusted them and I never found them so." Unfortunately some teachers were so overwhelmed by what they perceived as negative characteristics that they tended to see and speak of blacks in stereotypical terms.[76]

Many of the negative views of freedmen related to the missionary teachers' attitude toward religion and their rigid code of conduct. They found card playing, smoking, drinking, dancing, and recreational activity on the Sabbath repugnant. To many blacks these seemed reasonable methods of relaxation and unconnected with morality. "Lust and liquor are eagerly consuming these miserable remnants of sin and slavery", D. N. Walcott reported from South Carolina. "They [freedmen] love idleness, they love whiskey, they love sin." Walcott added that he was speaking of prominent black deacons and church members. After eleven years in Athens, Alabama, Mary Wells was temporarily disheartened with the "whole" southern work. Blacks, she said, were gossipy and, "having all their lives been accustomed to an atmosphere of moral impurity, their ideas are so radically different from ours, that were we to judge them by our standards who shall be able to stand." Blacks had a clear concept of what was right and wrong to them, and their notions did not always coincide with those of puritanical teachers. Many of the teachers' codes of behavior were too arbitrary to tolerate aberrant conduct by freedmen. The AMA's response to black religion and morals seriously colored its entire attitude toward the freedmen, and its attitude further alienated them. In 1875 the AMA attempted to galvanize northern churches into making greater contributions by publishing a pamphlet, *The Nation Still in Danger*, which depicted blacks and their churches as disgracefully immoral and degraded. John Mercer Langston, black lawyer and longtime friend of the association, accused it of circulating "cruel slanders of an inoffensive and confiding, struggling and comparatively helpless people." An A.M.E. church spokesman branded the AMA's portrait of black churches as an "outrageous lie."[27]

Few teachers became disillusioned with black youth. It was the adults they despaired of changing, and many never lost their faith in blacks at all. Teachers and missionaries worked, lived, and suffered with blacks in numerous communities. They exulted at black victories and resented white prejudice and abuse. Nevertheless, disillusionment, "ungrateful" freedmen, a changing leadership, and a desire to accommodate southern whites changed the AMA's stance. Black suffrage is an example. The association had enthusiastically supported black suffrage and then used black voting as an appeal for funds for its educational work. Ignorant, inexperienced blacks must be taught how to use the ballot intelligently. Despite laments about black ignorance, the AMA had consistently advocated black political rights. However, there was a change in tone in the early 1870s reflective of the general northern attitude. An 1873 *American Missionary* editorial confessed that "the success of the freedmen as legislators and politicians had not been very marked." They still were subject to white hatred and contempt. Moreover, the "ignorance of the colored man is not removed by election to office; nor is honesty promoted amid the temptation of lobbyists and demagogues." But, the editorial asked, what could have been expected after generations of slavery? In 1874 the AMA pointed out the presumed failure of freedmen in South Carolina and Louisiana where they had the most power. "These colored people are ignorant and depraved and easily made the tools of worse men than themselves." It was no satisfaction to know that northern legislators were also corrupt, "nor is it any relief to know that we must blame slavery as the remote cause." The Republican Party, the AMA added, was "beginning to be awake to the injury it will suffer if this state of affairs is allowed to continue." The editorial was patently unfair. Little notice was given to the many honest, able black politicians.[28]

The association continued to decry southern violence and fraud designed to neutralize black voting strength, but in 1875 it admitted that Reconstruction measures had been badly planned. The country had been busily reconstructing the superstructure while the foundation went untouched. The problem, according to the AMA, lay with black ignorance, white prejudice, and racial antagonism, which could be solved only by education. If blacks and poor whites were "cultured and fitted for private prosperity and public duty," they would come to respect each other, and if the North earnestly and successfully engaged in this Christian and unselfish work, then perhaps educated southern whites, despite their prejudices and past hatreds, would follow. While admitting the existence of white hatred, fraud, and terror and the fact that slavery was responsible for presumed black shortcomings, the AMA seemed to be blaming the victims for their problems. In 1876 another editorial contended that if a million voters unable to read the ballot were unleashed upon New England it would cause consternation. "But that million of illiterate voters were suddenly thrown into the South, and nobody at the North seems troubled about it." All of these statements were accompanied by pleas for money to educate blacks. In its fund-raising efforts the AMA had consistently exaggerated both the good and bad aspects of freedmen. Yet this was not mere propaganda. The AMA officials obviously considered black suffrage a failure. They accepted the prevailing view that freedmen legislators "with reckless rascality" had squandered public funds. In spite of their low opinion of black politicians, association personnel fretted over the 1876 election, abuse of black voters, and what a Democratic victory would mean for freedmen. They celebrated Hayes's eventual election and mourned the loss of the last Republican regimes in the South. Walter S. Alexander wrote from Straight University that "the restoration of Bourbon Democracy brings with it impoverishment, distress, persecution and the denial of the most sacred rights of the black race."[29]

In 1879 Michael E. Strieby rhetorically asked if the country had been wise to give the ballot to ex-slaves in 1867. Yes, Strieby said, because it had saved blacks from being reduced to slavery again, it had given them a sense of self-respect and sustained them during the early years of freedom, and black power had given the South a free school system. But now, Strieby added, blacks were politically conquered and the only thing that could be done was to try to protect them in their political rights and enlighten them as to the use, not abuse, of these rights. Only bayonets, he said, could sustain black political power at the moment, and "a far better thing" would "be speedily, steadily and efficiently" training the black voter "for an intelligent and responsible manhood and citizenship." Again Strieby seemed to be faulting blacks for their loss of voting power. If blacks became educated property owners and acquired "a weight of character," soldiers would not be needed to take them to the polls. When freedmen reached such a position, caste prejudice could be conquered and the color line obliterated in politics. The AMA was always naive about the power of black education and property acquisition to destroy prejudice.[30]

Although the AMA conceded that white voters temporarily had everything their own way and that there was little it could do, the association continued to advocate black civil rights. An 1876 editorial in the *American Missionary* proclaimed that one of the great achievements awaiting the country's second century was caste emancipation. Three years later, after carefully claiming that it was making no appeal for interracial marriages, the AMA condemned a Virginia law which prohibited such unions. The law was especially repugnant because it permitted illicit black-white extramarital relations. If whites were really concerned about miscegenation, the association said, they should punish illicit relations and allow racial mixing only when couples were legally married. The AMA further complained that granting civil rights by formal enactment was "of small importance unless the rights themselves" were honestly allowed and faithfully accepted. It also continued to oppose segregation laws and admit whites to its schools. But the AMA's former staunch egalitarianism faltered in the face of combined southern and northern white opposition and indifference. In 1878 it announced that it did not "affirm that races any more than individuals, are equal in physical and moral fibre and development." At the same time it stubbornly adhered to its claim that blacks were not inherently inferior and that all people should be "regarded as equal before God and the Law." What blacks needed, the AMA said, was a change in environment and opportunity. Hundreds of black youth who had gone through missionary schools were morally pure, worshiped intelligently, spoke grammatically, and had refined manners. They could achieve "positions of honor, profit and power" equal to whites if only given the same chance. Moreover, such men and women became a "leaven" in their communities which improved the mass. It was clear, however, that to the AMA, blacks improved to the degree that they became more like Christian, middle-class northern whites.[31]

By 1880 the AMA obviously was not the same vigorous advocate for blacks that it had been in 1865. It was more cautious—officials probably assumed more realistic—more infected by racial prejudice, even more paternalistic, and increasingly inclined to pacify white southerners by avoiding social contact with blacks, except in schools and churches. It retained great faith in black youth, but was badly disillusioned with adults. The unenviable position of blacks in American society is poignantly pointed up by the recognition that, for all its shortcomings, the AMA was still among the most concerned and progressive white friends the blacks had.[32]

Afterword

THE AMERICAN MISSIONARY ASSOCIATION obviously was imperfect. It was too paternalistic, too enamored with northern white middle-class culture, and, at first, too naive about the strength of racial prejudice. It only belatedly recognized that entrenched southern tradition and national racial discrimination allowed even educated blacks few of the opportunities granted to most other Americans. Moreover, northern weariness with "black problems," increasing difficulty in fund collecting, and political compromise caused the association to become more circumspect in its dealings with white southerners. By 1880 "the great crusade" for the full integration of blacks into American society had apparently lost its momentum.[1]

Despite its shortcomings, the AMA was the most significant of the many missionary societies engaged in training blacks, and it made notable contributions. It helped convince the North that blacks should be freed and assisted in their transition to freedom. It protected freedmen from the military, saved hundreds of lives with relief, and tried to help the freedmen acquire land. It organized scores of schools and colleges in which it trained thousands of teachers who taught many thousands more. These mission schools were often derided as unrealistic in curriculum and in appraisal of the freedmen's needs, yet many of them were eminently successful. They became a significant force in acculturation and in training black teachers, ministers, attorneys, physicians, businessmen and women, and community leaders. These leaders guided their people through the trying years of lynching, poverty, discrimination, and disfranchisement, and in later years were instrumental in changing the pattern of American race relations. W. E. B. DuBois believed that without black schools and colleges freedmen "to all intents and purposes" would "have been driven back to slavery."[2]

The AMA's concern for blacks did not cause it to ignore other needy members of society. It established schools for mountain whites in Kentucky, Tennessee, and Georgia, and for the Chinese and Japanese in California. When 1920s immigration laws excluded Orientals, the AMA was one of the few voices of protest. During World War I the association concluded that Mexican-Americans were largely neglected by American benevolence. It established schools in New Mexico and Utah. It began schools for Eskimos in Alaska after futile attempts to persuade the government to do so. Soon after the Spanish-American War the AMA sent teachers to Puerto Rico, where it maintained schools until public education was provided.[3]

The association's major service was to blacks, however, and its contributions to blacks did not end in 1890. Although the momentum for full integration had been slowed, the AMA never abandoned its original goals. Despite occasional attempts to cooperate with the white South, it remained one of the most progressive organizations working with southern blacks well into the twentieth century. The AMA continued to support schools and colleges, gradually allowing them greater self-government. It retained integrated faculties and taught equality by example, even though the rhetoric had been muted. It never lost sight of the black need for land and during the 1930s renewed its efforts to improve conditions for southern tenant farmers. In 1934 the AMA began the Brick Rural Life School in North Carolina where tenant farmers lived for five years and learned improved farming methods and management. At the end of their tenure the farmer-students were to have good credit ratings and enough money for down payments for their own land. A cooperative credit union and store were created to assist local residents. By 1946 there were five hundred people in the Brick Community Cooperative.[4]

The AMA opposed disfranchisement, white primaries, and segregation. The latter was condemned as "a dangerous, short-sighted policy." In 1896 the AMA successfully contested a Florida law that prohibited educating black and white youth in the same school. It advocated "securing the full rights and privileges of citizenship of Negro Americans and their complete integration in American life." Long before the Brown decision, the AMA claimed that separate could never be equal, that segregation was "a false social distinction, a self-defeating economic goal, and an undemocratic practice." When it created the department of race relations at Fisk University in 1942, it acted on the long-held conviction that "segregation is as incompatible to the American democratic ideal as was 'taxation without representation' and equally as offensive and unjust. Prejudicial law and customs which uphold caste make a mockery of Christianity." Hoping that education would promote better understanding between the races, the department in 1946 began an annual Race Relations Institute, which brought together politicians, ministers, labor leaders, social workers, and staff members for intensive study and discussion of human relations.[5]

For a century AMA colleges provided much of the best education available to southern blacks. The Civil Rights Movement, significantly assisted by AMA graduates and faculties, opened formerly white colleges to black youth, thereby giving them greater educational options. Ironically desegregation, by providing more opportunities for blacks, seriously damaged the already financially precarious AMA colleges. Desegregation, however, did not mean that the association's work was complete. Its initial dream of equal justice and opportunity for all is not yet a reality. The AMA and its colleges are still striving toward that goal.

Notes

Preface

1. The Union Missionary Society grew out of the Amistad Committee, which had been formed in 1839 to collect funds to instruct and engage counsel for forty-two Africans charged with mutiny aboard the slaver *Amistad*. John Quincy Adams and Roger S. Baldwin successfully argued the captives' case before the United States Supreme Court. When the Africans set sail for their homeland, they were accompanied by Amistad missionaries. The missionaries were soon transferred to the Union Missionary Society. Under its aegis a mission was formed at Kaw Mendi, West Africa. The Committee for West Indian Missions was organized in 1837 to assist recently freed Jamaican slaves. The Western Evangelical Missionary Society was organized in 1843 with the primary object of carrying on mission work among western Indians. For a detailed study of the organization and prewar activities of the AMA, see Clifton H. Johnson, "The American Missionary Association, 1846–1861: A Study of Christian Abolitionism" (Ph.D. diss., University of North Carolina, 1958).

2. *History of the American Missionary Association with Facts and Anecdotes Illustrating Its Work in the South*, 2d ed. (New York, 1874), 3–5; Maxine D. Jones, "'A Glorious Work': The American Missionary Association and Black North Carolinians, 1863–1880" (Ph.D. diss., Florida State University, 1982), v–vi; Clara M. De Boer, "The Role of Afro-Americans in the Origins and Work of the American Missionary Association, 1839–1877" (Ph.D. diss., Rutgers University, 1973), 12.

3. Robin W. Winks, *The Blacks in Canada* (New Haven, 1971), 224–27; *History of the American Missionary Association*, 9–10; Jones, "'A Glorious Work,'" vi; Fred L. Brownlee, *New Day Ascending* (Boston, 1946), 53–54; S. S. Adair to S. S. Jocelyn, 21 October, 16 November 1854, S. Blanchard to S. S. Jocelyn, 23 April, 6 June 1860, American Missionary Association Archives, Amistad Research Center, New Orleans, Louisiana (cited hereafter as AMAA); *American Missionary* 17 (November 1873): 241.

Chapter 1. A Grand Field for Missionary Labor

1. Augustus Field Beard, *A Crusade of Brotherhood: A History of the American Missionary Association* (Boston, 1909), 117–18; *American Missionary* 5 (July 1861): 163; *American Missionary* 6 (January 1862): 14.

2. Butler had declared men working on Confederate fortifications contrabands of war. Women and children did not fit that category, but were permitted to stay. Finally, on July 6, recognizing what Butler had already done, Congress enacted a law providing that slaveholders who allowed slaves to be used in any military capacity against the United States forfeited their claim to the labor of those slaves.

3. *The War of the Rebellion: A Compilation of the Official Records of the Union and Confederate Armies*, 128 vols. (Washington, D.C., 1880–1901), series 1, vol. 2, pp. 649–51; Edward Pierce, "The Contrabands of Fortress Monroe," *Atlantic Monthly* 8 (November 1861): 627–30; Richard S. West, *Lincoln's Scapegoat General: A Life of Benjamin F. Butler, 1818–1893* (Boston, 1965), 84; B. F. Butler to S. Cameron, 30 July 1861, Simon Cameron Papers, Library of Congress, Washington, D.C.

4. Many of the contrabands were working on entrenchments at nearby Hampton, Virginia. The women were washing and sewing for soldiers. But in early August an impending Confederate attack forced Butler to move the contrabands to Fortress Monroe. M. Weber to B. F. Butler, 8 August 1861, Benjamin F. Butler Papers, Library of Congress; *Harper's Weekly* 5 (24 August 1861): 531.

5. L. Tappan to B. Butler, 8 August 1861, B. Butler to L. Tappan, 10 August 1861, L. Tappan to B. Butler, 14, 17 August 1861, Benjamin F. Butler Papers.

6. Mrs. Peake was paid $1.50 per week by the AMA. *American Missionary* (Supplement) 5 (1 October 1861): 242–45; *American Missionary* 5 (November 1861): 256; L. C. Lockwood to Dear Brethren, 15 March 1862, AMAA; Robert F. Engs, *Freedom's First Generation: Black Hampton, Virginia, 1861–1890* (Philadelphia, 1979), xvii, 47; Samuel L. Horst, "Education for Manhood: The Education of Blacks in Virginia During the Civil War" (Ph.D. diss., University of Virginia, 1979), 117–19.

7. Lewis C. Lockwood, *Mary S. Peake: The Colored Teacher at Fortress Monroe* (New York, 1969), 5–15; Horst, "Education for Manhood," 12–13; L. C. Lockwood to G. Cheever, 29 January 1862, George B. Cheever Papers, American Antiquarian Society, Worcester, Mass.; L. C. Lockwood statement, 2 September 1862, AMAA.

8. Lockwood, *Mary S. Peake*, 32–39; *American Missionary* 5 (December 1861): 289; M. S. Peake to S. S. Jocelyn, n.d. January 1862, L. C. Lockwood to

Dear Brethren, 4 January 1862, W. L. Coan quoted in L. C. Lockwood to Dear Brethren, 9 March 1862, AMAA.

9. *American Missionary* 6 (January 1862): 83; R. K. Browne quoted in L. C. Lockwood to Dear Brethren, 8 March 1862, AMAA; De Boer, "Role of Afro-Americans," 242–3; Horst, "Education for Manhood," 1.

10. *American Missionary* 5 (November 1861): 256–57; Horst, "Education for Manhood," 58; *Harper's Weekly* 7 (31 January 1863): 78; J. Oliver to S. S. Jocelyn, 6 July 1862, C. P. Day to S. S. Jocelyn, 30 September 1862, AMAA.

11. Lincoln did not order a surgeon to be assigned. He wrote on the back of Jocelyn's letter to him and suggested that Jocelyn send it to General Wool, who had replaced Butler. Lincoln wrote: "If Genl. Wool is of the opinion that the services of a surgeon are needed for the colored persons under his charge, and will select a suitable person and put him to the service, I will advise Congress that he be paid." Copy of S. S. Jocelyn to A. Lincoln, 26 November 1861, L. C. Lockwood to Dear Brethren, 23 December 1861, AMAA; Engs, *Freedom's First Generation*, 25.

12. For in-depth studies of military treatment of blacks during the war, see Louis S. Gerteis, *From Contraband to Freedman: Federal Policy Toward Southern Blacks, 1861–1865* (Westport, Conn. 1973), and C. Peter Ripley, *Slaves and Freedmen in Civil War Louisiana* (Baton Rouge, 1976).

13. L. C. Lockwood to Dear Brethren, 6 January 1862, AMAA; L. C. Lockwood to G. Cheever, 29 January 1862, Cheever Papers.

14. S. S. Jocelyn to G. Whipple, 13 March 1862, G. Whipple to S. S. Jocelyn, 10 March 1862, AMAA; Engs, *Freedom's First Generation*, 31–32; Horst, "Education for Manhood," 48; W. D. Whipple to G. Tallmadge, 26 March 1862, U.S. Army Continental Commands, Department of Virginia, National Archives, Washington, D.C.; Oliver Otis Howard, *Autobiography of Oliver Otis Howard*, 2 vols. (New York, 1907), 2: 175.

15. Engs, *Freedom's First Generation*, 32–33; C. B. Wilder to Gentlemen, 6 January 1862, C. B. Wilder to A.M.A., 29 April 1862, L. Tappan to G. Whipple, 15 March 1862, AMAA; *American Missionary* 7 (January 1864): 12.

16. Gerteis, *From Contraband to Freedman*, 21–25; L. Tappan to W. G. Kephart, 27 February 1862, AMAA.

17. L. Tappan to G. Whipple, 17, 18 June 1862, S. S. Jocelyn to G. Whipple, 20, 23 June 1862, G. Whipple to J. A. Dix, 11 October 1862, C. P. Day to S. S. Jocelyn, 11 August 1862, C. P. Day to W. E. Whiting, 24 August 1862, AMAA; J. A. Dix to E. M. Stanton, 13 December 1862, U.S. Army Continental Commands, Department of Virginia.

18. C. B. Wilder to J. A. Dix, 27 June, 1 November 1862, U.S. Army Continental Commands, Department of Virginia; G. Whipple to S. S. Jocelyn, 18 July, 1 August 1862, S. S. Jocelyn to G. Whipple, 5, 7 August 1862, J. Oliver to

S. S. Jocelyn, 5 August, n.d. September 1862, AMAA; *American Missionary* 7 (June 1863): 137.

19. L. Tappan to S. S. Jocelyn, 11 August 1862, O. Brown to S. S. Jocelyn, 11 July 1863, AMAA; Bertram Wyatt-Brown, *Lewis Tappan and the Evangelical War Against Slavery* (New York, 1971), 337–38.

20. S. S. Jocelyn to J. G. Fee, 11 September 1862, AMAA; *American Missionary* 7 (March 1863): 58, (August 1863): 180.

21. Wilder said of Butler: "No other living man has been found who has the sagacity to perceive, the practical knowledge to apply, & the courage to execute both the Civil and Military laws of the land, so as to strike rebels with terror and the friends of freedom with hope & admiration at every step he takes, or blow he strikes. He ought to be in genl. Halleck's place *now* & in the *presidential chair next term*." C. B. Wilder to G. Whipple, 31 December 1863, AMAA.

22. C. P. Day to S. S. Jocelyn, 8 December 1863, S. S. Jocelyn to Dear Brethren, 3 September 1864, AMAA; *American Missionary* 8 (May 1864): 125; Gerteis, *From Contraband to Freedman*, 37–39.

23. Horst, "Education for Manhood," 59–61; L. C. Lockwood to Dear Brethren, 3 May 1862, AMAA.

24. C. P. Day to S. S. Jocelyn, 7 April 1862, A. Seymour to S. S. Jocelyn, 11 April 1862, C. Barstow to S. S. Jocelyn, 4 February 1862, AMAA; *American Missionary* 8 (April 1864): 83.

25. L. C. Lockwood to Dear Brethren, 3 May, 9 June 1862, C. P. Day to S. S. Jocelyn, 11 August, 30 September 1862, J. Oliver to S. S. Jocelyn, 27 July 1862, AMAA; L. C. Lockwood to Bro. Weaver, n.d. 1862, in *Christian Recorder* 2 (22 November 1862): 185.

26. C. P. Day to S. S. Jocelyn, 11 August, 30 September 1862, J. Oliver to S. S. Jocelyn, 26 January 1863, AMAA; *American Missionary* 7 (July 1863): 147–48.

27. G. N. Greene to S. S. Jocelyn, 18 April 1863, W. O. King to S. S. Jocelyn, 28 April 1863, J. F. Sisson to Dear Bro., 16 July 1863, AMAA; Beard, *A Crusade of Brotherhood*, 124; Stephen B. Oates, *With Malice Toward None: The Life of Abraham Lincoln* (New York, 1977), 294.

28. *American Missionary* 7 (June 1863): 135; J. F. Sisson to G. Whipple, 7 March 1864, AMAA.

29. The women were prisoners, but had never been convicted. They were arrested and arbitrarily sentenced without trial or military court.

30. M. Colton to G. Whipple, 14 June, 9 July, 1 September, 7 October, 1 November 1864, AMAA.

31. W. L. Coan to S. S. Jocelyn, 12 May 1863, 1 March 1864, C. P. Day to S. S. Jocelyn, 2 January 1864, AMAA; *American Missionary* 8 (March 1864): 64.

32. *American Missionary* 8 (July 1864): 173; H. M. Dodd to G. Whipple, 3 August 1864, E. F. Jencks to G. Whipple, 2 December 1864, W. O. King to S. S. Jocelyn, 7 January 1863, J. B. Lowrey to S. S. Jocelyn, 11 June 1863, AMAA.

33. Beals quoted in *American Missionary* 8 (September 1864): 211; C. Duncan to G. Whipple, 1 July 1864, C. P. Day to S. S. Jocelyn, 2 Janaury 1864, AMAA.

34. General Orders No. 262, 23 September 1864, printed copy in AMAA; G. F. Shepley to E. W. Smith, 1 February 1865, U.S. Army Continental Commands, Department of Virginia.

35. Engs, *Freedom's First Generation*, 64–65, 77–78.

Chapter 2. Wartime Expansion

1. Tappan and Whipple probably sent French to South Carolina, in part in response to a letter from Chaplain W. P. Strickland, who had written Tappan asking for his help in securing books and blackboards. W. P. Strickland to L. Tappan, 20 Janaury 1862, AMAA; Willie Lee Rose, *Rehearsal for Reconstruction: The Port Royal Experiment* (New York, 1964), 26–27, 41; M. French to S. P. Chase, 16 February 1862, Port Royal Correspondence, Records of the Civil War Special Agencies of the Treasury Department, 5th Agency, vol. 19, National Archives.

2. M. French to S. P. Chase, 28 February 1862, Port Royal Correspondence; Sarah Forbes Hughes (ed.), *Letters and Recollections of John Murray Forbes*, 2 vols. (Boston, 1899), 1:296; Rose, *Rehearsal for Reconstruction*, 44–45.

3. The Boston Educational Commission had selected twenty-nine men and six women. Edward L. Pierce, leader of the Boston group, had not wanted women, so he assigned them to Mansfield French. Since French was the one who suggested taking women, he said, "I think its success should be specially confided to him." E. L. Pierce to S. P. Chase, 21 February 1862, Port Royal Correspondence.

4. Henry N. Sherwood (ed.), "Journal of Miss Susan Walker, March 3 to June 6, 1862," *Quarterly Publication of the Historical and Philosophical Society of Ohio* 6 (January–March 1912): 16, 18; Rose, *Rehearsal for Reconstruction*, 52.

5. Rose, *Rehearsal for Reconstruction*, 50, 55, 217–18; *History of the American Missionary Association*, 14; Luther P. Jackson, "The Educational Efforts of the Freedmen's Bureau and Freedmen's Aid Societies in South Carolina, 1862–1872," *Journal of Negro History* 8 (January 1923): 7, 17.

6. *American Missionary* 7 (February 1863): 39, (July 1863): 161; *Eighteenth*

Annual Report of the American Missionary Association and the Proceedings at the Annual Meeting . . . October 26 and 27, 1864 (New York, 1864), 16; J. M. McKim to B. Butler, 24 February 1863, Benjamin F. Butler Papers.

7. *American Missionary* 5 (August 1861): 178–79; S. S. Jocelyn to G. Whipple, 20 June 1862, AMAA; Horst, "Education for Manhood," 143; A. Knighton Stanley, *The Children Is Crying: Congregationalism Among Black People* (New York, 1979), 45; L. Tappan to H. W. Williams, 12 September 1863, Lewis Tappan Papers, Library of Congress.

8. *American Missionary* 5 (August 1861): 178–79; L. Tappan to W. Armistead, 17 May 1865, L. Tappan to M. White, 18 June 1864, L. Tappan to A. Pearson, 28 September 1863, L. Tappan to T. DeS. Tucker, 27 October 1863, L. Tappan to F. E. G. Stoddard, 20 November 1863, L. Tappan to M. Hamlin, 10 March 1864, Lewis Tappan Papers; Beard, *A Crusade of Brotherhood*, 13.

9. Tappan quoted in De Boer, "Role of Afro-Americans," 222–23, 588.

10. L. Tappan to D. Baldwin, 3 June 1865, L. Tappan to C. Sumner, 13 February 1865, Lewis Tappan Papers; *American Missionary* 9 (July 1865): 155, (December 1865): 268.

11. L. Tappan to M. B. Lowry, 1 February 1865, Lewis Tappan Papers; De Boer, "Role of Afro-Americans," 107–8, 138, 153, 211; Jacqueline Jones, *Soldiers of Light and Love: Northern Teachers and Georgia Blacks, 1865–1873* (Chapel Hill, 1980), 20.

12. L. Tappan to J. P. Warren, 23 December 1864, L. Tappan to M. Hamlin, 10 March 1864, Lewis Tappan Papers; W. H. Woodbury to G. Whipple, 28 January 1865, AMAA; Dwight O. W. Holmes, *The Evolution of the Negro College* (New York, 1934), 69; Jones, *Soldiers of Light and Love*, 4.

13. *American Missionary* 7 (January 1863): 12–13, (July 1863): 147.

14. Horst, "Education for Manhood," 229, 237–38, 278–79; *American Missionary* 7 (July 1863): 159.

15. Penelope L. Bullock, *The Afro-American Periodical Press* (Baton Rouge, 1981), 61–62; De Boer, "Role of Afro-Americans," 304–5; W. J. Wilson to Rev. & Dear Sir, 6 June 1864, W. J. Wilson to S. S. Jocelyn, 28 April 1864, 19 June 1864, W. J. Wilson to G. Whipple, 30 August 1864, J. Landre to G. Whipple, 4 May 1865, AMAA.

16. W. J. Wilson to G. E. Baker, 12 October 1864, G. F. Needham to G. Whipple, 4 October 1864, W. J. Wilson to G. Whipple, 24 October 1864, W. J. Wilson to W. E. Whiting, 17 November 1864, W. J. Wilson to G. Whipple, 28 November, 7 December 1864, 22 January, 4 May 1865, W. S. Tilden to S. Hunt, 17 June 1865, W. J. Wilson to G. Whipple, 25 October, 8 November 1865, W. J. Wilson to W. E. Whiting, 8 November 1865, W. J. Wilson to G. Whipple, 16 November, 23 December 1865, J. A. Nichols to S. Hunt, 13 January 1866,

W. S. Tilden to G. Whipple, 31 January, 5 February 1866, J. A. Nichols to G. Whipple, 7 February 1866, M. E. Strieby to G. Whipple, 12 April 1865, AMAA.

17. *Freedmen's Advocate* 1 (June 1864): 21; *American Missionary* 7 (June 1863): 140; General D. Ullman to E. M. Stanton, 1 January 1864, C. Strong to S. S. Jocelyn, 18 March 1864. T. A. McMasters to G. Whipple, 20 May 1864, C. B. Whitcomb to G. Whipple, 21 June 1864, AMAA; L. Tappan to H. Wilson, 12 December 1864, Lewis Tappan Papers.

18. *American Missionary* 9 (August 1865): 177, (September 1865): 200; M. E. Reeves to S. Hunt, 2 April 1866, J. P. Bardwell to G. Whipple, 11 April 1866, F. J. Scott to C. H. Fowler, 1 February 1864, AMAA.

19. J. G. Fee to S. S. Jocelyn, 8 August 1864, AMAA; Victor B. Howard, *Black Liberation in Kentucky: Emancipation and Freedom, 1862–1884* (Lexington, Ky., 1983), 112, 161.

20. John G. Fee, *Autobiography of John G. Fee, Berea, Kentucky* (Chicago, 1891), 174; J. G. Fee to S. S. Jocelyn, 6, 30 June 1864, 12, 18 July 1864, 8, 25 February 1865, AMAA; S. S. Jocelyn to J. G. Fee, 6 June 1864, John G. Fee Papers, Hutchins Library, Berea College, Berea, Ky.; Isabella Black, "Berea College," *Phylon* 18 (Spring 1957): 275–76.

21. J. G. Fee to S. S. Jocelyn, 12, 18 July, 8 August 1864, A. Scofield to W. Goddell, 30 November 1864, AMAA; *American Missionary* 8 (November 1864): 263; Robert K. Loesch, "Kentucky Abolitionist: John G. Fee" (Ph.D. diss., Hartford Seminary, 1969), 173.

22. J. G. Fee to G. Whipple, 21 February, 7 March 1865, E. Davis to M. E. Strieby, 14 April 1865, AMAA; *American Missionary* 7 (October 1863): 236; Howard *Black Liberation in Kentucky*, 116.

23. A. D. Olds to S. S. Jocelyn, 16, 21 May 1863, E. R. Pierce to S. S. Jocelyn, 9, 29 April 1863, AMAA; *American Missionary* 7 (May 1863): 111, (November 1863): 242–43.

24. *American Missionary* 8 (January 1864): 101; J. R. Locky statement about Mrs. S. F. Venatta, 5 January 1864, E. Austin to G. Whipple, 10 May 1864, D. Todd to G. Whipple, 4 July 1864, E. A. Lane to G. Whipple, 8 December 1864, W. T. Richardson to S. S. Jocelyn, 21 July 1863, AMAA; Joseph E. Roy, *Pilgrim's Letters: Bits of Current History* (Boston, 1888), 37–38.

25. Jones, "'A Glorious Work,'" 47–51; G. N. Greene to G. Whipple, 5 February 1864, H. James to G. Whipple, 22 April 1864, W. T. Briggs to G. Whipple, 18 March, 24, 27 April, 7 May 1864, E. Gill to S. S. Jocelyn, 24 February 1864, S. A. Hosmer to G. Whipple, 5 May 1864, E. James to G. Whipple, 20 May 1864, AMAA.

26. *American Missionary* 9 (October 1865): 221; H. James to G. Whipple,

20 January 1864, W. T. Briggs to G. Whipple, 9 June 1864, J. L. Richardson to
S. S. Jocelyn, 30 April, 12, 16, 22 May, 5 June, 4 July, 17, 28 November, 18
December 1863, AMAA.

27. C. A. Briggs to Miss Dodge, 4 January 1864, H. J. Ward to G. Whipple,
17 March 1864, C. A. Briggs to Dear Friend, 4 March 1865, W. Baker to G.
Whipple, 25 February, 9 March 1865, L. A. Montague to M. E. Strieby, 20
June 1864, W. Porter to M. E. Strieby, 14 October 1865, L. A. Montague to
S. S. Jocelyn, 28 July 1864, AMAA.

28. Ripley, *Slaves and Freedmen*, 139–40; New Orleans *Tribune*, 13 September 1864; Charles Kassel, "Educating the Slave—A Forgotten Chapter of
Civil War History," *Open Court* 31 (April 1927): 251–52; E. M. Wheelock to
N. P. Banks, 9 August 1864, E. M. Wheelock to T. E. Chickerrag, 9 August
1864, N. P. Banks Papers, Library of Congress.

29. *American Missionary* 8 (November 1864): 261; E. Gill to S. S. Jocelyn,
24 February 1864, AMAA; *Eighteenth Annual Report of the American Missionary Association*, 21; Bell I. Wiley, *Southern Negroes, 1861–1865* (New
Haven, 1965), 275; *Liberator* 34 (13 May 1864): 77; Natchez *Courier*, n.d.
March 1864.

30. At least one Union officer agreed with Wright. He said that Natchez
commanders "not only have no sympathy with the colored people,
but . . . harbor a prejudice and a hatred toward them far more intolerable and
wicked than their predecessor, the rebels." Statement of "an officer of the
U.S.A." (anonymous), 4 April 1864, AMAA.

31. S. G. Wright to G. Whipple, 9 March, 1 April, 20 June 1864, S. G.
Wright and four others to J. M. Tuttle, 1 April 1866, copy in AMAA.

32. S. G. Wright to G. Whipple, 9 March 1864, AMAA; *American Missionary* 7 (June 1863): 140, (July 1863): 160–61.

33. Ripley, *Slaves and Freedmen*, 128–29; W. B. Stickney to N. P. Banks,
13, 19 October 1863, G. Hanks to N. P. Banks, 26 September 1863, N. P.
Banks Papers; G. Whipple and S. S. Jocelyn to N. P. Banks, 12 December
1863, S. S. Jocelyn to G. Whipple, 25 January 1864, AMAA.

34. I. Hubbs to S. S. Jocelyn and G. Whipple, 14 January 1864, C. Strong to
S. S. Jocelyn, 8, 23 January, 19 February 1864, D. M. Knowles to G. Whipple,
30 May 1864, Teachers Monthly School Reports, May, June 1864, AMAA;
Freedmen 1 (July 1864): 28; Joe M. Richardson, "The American Missionary
Association and Black Education in Louisiana, 1862–1878," in Robert R. Mac-
donald, John R. Kemp, and Edward F. Haas (eds.), *Louisiana's Black Heritage* (New Orleans, 1979), 148–49; *American Missionary* 8 (December 1864):
285.

35. For more detailed treatments of the conflict between the AMA and the
military, see Ripley, *Slaves and Freedmen*, 126–45, and William M. Messer,

"Black Education in Louisiana, 1863–1865," *Civil War History* 22 (March 1976): 51– 52.

36. Ripley, *Slaves and Freedmen*, 130; I. Hubbs to S. S. Jocelyn and G. Whipple, 8 January, 6 February, 4 March 1864, AMAA.

37. Chaplain E. M. Wheelock wrote the AMA that General Banks "has informed us that sound policy demands that we should employ mainly Southern teachers." E. M. Wheelock to G. Whipple, 12 September 1864, AMAA.

38. Messer, "Black Education in Louisiana," 51–52; Ripley, *Slaves and Freedmen*, 131; C. Strong to S. S. Jocelyn, 7, 18 March 1864, I. G. Hubbs to S. S. Jocelyn, 5 March 1864, G. Hanks to N. P. Banks, 24 February 1864, AMAA; *Freedmen's Advocate* 1 (April 1864): 14; New Orleans *Times*, 2 September 1864 in *Liberator* 34 (30 September 1864): 160.

39. Plumly and Wheelock not only succeeded in gaining control of AMA schools but they also managed to expel Hubbs. On 16 October 1864 General Order No. 280 ordered Hubbs to leave the Department of the Gulf. He was accused of selling books for profit, keeping faulty accounts, demanding money of some teachers as a condition of their employment, making false charges against other board members, and unbecoming conduct with a female teacher. The latter charge was almost certainly false. The other charges are more difficult to refute. Naturally, Hubbs denied them, pointing out that the board was unfriendly to the AMA and that its hostility was "culminating in a vigorous persecution of *us and all our interests.*" Whatever the truth of the charges— and Hubbs at best was inefficient—they did not necessitate ousting the association. General Order No. 280, Department of the Gulf, 16 October 1864, copy in AMAA; I. G. Hubbs to W. E. Whiting, 24 September 1864, F. H. Bartlett to G. Whipple, 25 September 1864, T. A. McMasters to G. Whipple, 28 September 1864, C. Strong to G. Whipple, 7 May 1864, E. M. Wheelock to S. S. Jocelyn, 3 May 1864, I. Hubbs to G. Whipple, 17 June 1864, AMAA.

40. E. M. Wheelock to G. Whipple, 12 September 1864, AMAA; *Liberator* 34 (30 September 1864): 160; *Liberator* 35 (21 April 1865): 62.

41. *American Missionary* 8 (June 1864): 148, (July 1864): 163, (December 1864): 284–86; J. N. Coan to M. E. Strieby, 30 April 1865, C. A. Drake to M. E. Strieby, 6 April 1865, C. B. Wilder to W. E. Whiting, 7 April 1865, L. A. Woodbury to G. Whipple, 10 April 1865, AMAA; *American Missionary* 9 (December 1865): 270.

Chapter 3. AMA Common Schools After the War

1. Between October 1866 and June 1867 the AMA sent 508 teachers and missionaries to teach freedmen in nineteen different states and the District of

Columbia. Of that number, 250 were in Virginia, North Carolina, Georgia, and Alabama. *American Missionary* 11 (July 1867): 157.

2. *American Missionary* 9 (July 1865): 146; *American Missionary* 10 (December 1866): 269; *American Missionary* 11 (June 1867): 124, (November 1867): 242; *American Missionary* 12 (December 1868): 269; G. L. Eberhart, Georgia School Report, 30 July 1867, Bureau of Refugees, Freedmen and Abandoned Lands, Educational Division, National Archives, hereafter cited as Bureau Records, Ed. Div.

3. Howard N. Myer, *Colonel of the Black Regiment: The Life of Thomas Wentworth Higginson* (New York, 1967), 213; Charlotte L. Forten, "Life on the Sea Islands," *Atlantic Monthly* 13 (May 1864); 591; *American Missionary* 7 (June 1863): 137; *American Missionary* 16 (October 1872): 216; U.S. Congress, *Senate Executive Documents*, 39th Cong., 2d Sess., No. 6, p. 13.

4. Harriet Beecher Stowe, *Palmetto Leaves* (Boston, 1873), 296–97; Henry L. Swint (ed.), *Dear Ones at Home: Letters from Contraband Camps* (Nashville, 1966), 41; R. M. Manly, Virginia School Report, 31 October 1866, Bureau Records, Ed. Div.

5. H. B. Greely to G. Whipple, 23 January 1865, M. J. Gonsalves to S. S. Jocelyn, 31 December 1863, Anne C. Canedy, Monthly School Report, May 1864, E. A. Easter to ?, 12 February 1866, AMAA; *American Missionary* 9 (May 1865): 104.

6. Richard Foster Petition, 14 February 1865, U.S. Senate Records, 1789–1944, 38th Cong., 1st Sess., RG 46, Sen. 38A–H2O, Box 97, National Archives; H. B. Greely to E. M. Cravath, 9 May 1867, A. W. Johnson to E. M. Cravath, 28 November 1870, N. B. James to E. M. Cravath, 12 December 1873, AMAA; *American Missionary* 13 (October 1869): 221; *American Missionary* 14 (March 1870): 54; S. L. Smith to J. V. Richardson, 29 January 1873, Miscellaneous Collection, P. K. Younge Library, University of Florida, Gainesville.

7. Harriet Beecher Stowe, "Our Florida Plantation," *Atlantic Monthly* 43 (May 1879): 648; E. A. Young to C. H. Fowler, 4 February 1864, AMAA; De Boer, "Role of Afro-Americans," 532; Tennessee, *Senate Journal*, 2d Sess., 1866–67, p. 200; Richard B. Westin, "The State and Segregated Schools: Negro Public Education in North Carolina, 1863–1923" (Ph.D. diss., Duke University, 1966), 6.

8. S. Allen to O. O. Howard, 8 February 1866, O. O. Howard Papers; C. McKowen to My Dear Tommy, 18 October 1866, John Clay McKowen Papers, Department of Archives and Manuscripts, Louisiana State University, Baton Rouge; Edwin Beecher, Alabama School Report, 13 July 1869, Bureau Records, Ed. Div.; U.S. Congress, *House Reports*, 39th Cong., 1st Sess. No. 30, pt. 3:161.

9. Cape Girardeau *Weekly News*, 16 June 1869; *Louisiana Sugar Bowl* (New Iberia), 8 May 1873.

10. Leon F. Litwack, *Been in the Storm So Long* (New York, 1978), 472; U.S. Commissioner of Education, *Report for the Year 1871* (Washington, 1872), 5–6; W. T. Briggs, Annual Report of the Colored Schools in North Carolina, July 1865, AMAA; W. E. B. DuBois, *Black Reconstruction* (Philadelphia, 1935), 641; Jones, *Soldiers of Light and Love*, 3, 58–59, 76.

11. Jones, *Soldiers of Light and Love*, 26; Horst, "Education for Manhood," 55; J. L. Richardson to S. S. Jocelyn, 7 November 1863, AMAA; Litwack, *Been in the Storm So Long*, 452; L. Tappan to M. A. Burnap, 25 January 1865, Lewis Tappan Papers; G. Whipple to J. R. Blake, 8 June 1864, E. Whipple to E. P. Smith, 18 July 1867, AMAA; James M. McPherson, *The Abolitionist Legacy: From Reconstruction to the NAACP* (Princeton, 1975), 163.

12. *American Missionary* 11 (April 1867): 82, (May 1867): 108; Ronald E. Butchart, *Northern Schools, Southern Blacks, and Reconstruction: Freedmen's Education, 1862–1875* (Westport, Conn., 1980), 25, 34–35; William Channing Gannett and Edward Everett Hale, "The Education of the Freedmen," *North American Review* 101 (October 1865): 529–30.

13. For detailed studies of texts used in freedmen's schools, see Butchart, *Northern Schools, Southern Blacks, and Reconstruction*, chap. 8, and Robert Charles Morris, *Reading, 'Riting, and Reconstruction: The Education of Freedmen in the South* (Chicago, 1981), chap. 6.

14. Jones, "'A Glorious Work,'" 103–4; Butchart, *Northern Schools, Southern Blacks, and Reconstruction*, 135–39; Morris, *Reading, 'Riting, and Reconstruction*, 195, 197, 200, 205–7; L. Tappan to I. P. Warren, 10, 27 December 1864, L. Tappan to G. Whipple, 25 January 1865, Lewis Tappan Papers.

15. Although AMA teachers sometimes used Child's *The Freedmen's Book*, association officers, according to Mrs. Child, refused to assist her in circulating the book "unless they could be allowed to cut out several articles, and in lieu thereof insert orthodox tracts about 'redeeming blood & c.'" Child quoted in Morris, *Reading, 'Riting, and Reconstruction*, 207.

16. Jones, *Soldiers of Light and Love*, 109; McPherson, *Abolitionist Legacy*, 80; Washington, D.C., *New Era*, 24 February 1870; L. D. Rurchard to Union Sabbath School, n.d. 1864, AMAA.

17. C. P. Day to S. S. Jocelyn, 12 February 1863, F. L. Cardozo to G. Whipple, 27 July 1866, AMAA; Whitelaw Reid Diary, 20 May 1865, Whitelaw Reid Papers, Library of Congress; Augusta *Loyal Georgian*, 10 March 1866; Morris, *Reading, 'Riting, and Reconstruction*, 178–79.

18. Nearly all teachers were distressed by what they considered a casualness toward time among blacks. Maria L. Root asked for a bell for her school at Andersonville, Georgia, for "we are so troubled to 'collect our faces' in time;

the colored people having no time pieces and no guide but the sun are often, yes *usually* behind times especially on the Sabbath." M. L. Root to E. P. Smith, 1 November 1869, AMAA.

19. "Rules and Regulations of Fisk University" (flyer, 1868); T. N. Chase to M. E. Strieby, 19 September 1877, H. E. Townsend to M. E. Strieby, 20 July 1864, C. A. Drake to G. Whipple, 13 March 1866, F. Gleason to G. Whipple, 8 March 1864, S. Drummond to G. Whipple, 1 May, 1 July 1864, Teachers Monthly School Report, November 1872, St. Augustine, Florida, J. N. Coan to G. Whipple, n.d. April 1863, AMAA; *American Missionary* 11 (September 1867): 197.

20. *American Missionary* 9 (September 1867): 203; *American Missionary* 8 (April 1864): 96; *American Missionary* 12 (August 1868): 180; G. N. Carruthers to S. S. Jocelyn, 12 June 1863, A. G. Marment to E. M. Cravath, 1 November 1873, B. V. Harris to G. Whipple, 28 February 1867, J. Ogden to G. Whipple, 29 February 1868, AMAA.

21. C. L. Tambling to S. S. Jocelyn, 22 April 1864, E. Stuart to G. Whipple, 2 February 1865, AMAA; *American Missionary* 7 (March 1863): 62–63; *American Missionary* 10 (June 1866): 147–48; *American Missionary* 11 (July 1867): 158; *American Missionary* 19 (July 1875): 159; *American Missionary* 24 (April 1880): 104.

22. J. W. Alvord to O. O. Howard, 28 January 1870, Bureau Records; Fayetteville, Arkansas, Monthly School Report, February 1871, E. C. Stickel to E. M. Cravath, 18 February 1871, M. F. Wells to E. M. Cravath, 16 January 1873, AMAA; *American Missionary* 11 (June 1867): 123.

23. Walter White, *A Man Called White: The Autobiography of Walter White* (New York, 1948), 16; *American Missionary* 11 (June 1868): 138; *American Missionary* 15 (April 1871): 77; C. M. Blood to E. P. Smith, 30 November 1869, 28 January 1870, H. E. Brown to E. P. Smith, 12 March 1869, E. B. Eveleth to E. P. Smith, 28 May 1870, A. G. Marment to E. M. Cravath, 22 November 1873, AMAA; *Southern Sentinel* 2 (September 1878): 5.

24. Butchart, *Northern Schools, Southern Blacks, and Reconstruction*, 119–22; J. Scott to S. Hunt, 30 November 1866, B. F. Jackson to G. Whipple, 18 February 1868, W. Hamilton to S. S. Jocelyn, 25 January 1864, AMAA; Jones, "'A Glorious Work,'" 92–97.

25. Jones, "'A Glorious Work,'" 95, 97; *Liberator* 34 (30 September 1864): 160; Minutes of the General Faculty of Fisk University, Fisk University Library, Nashville; *Southern Sentinel* 1 (December 1877): 4.

26. A. L. Etheridge to W. T. Briggs, 6 June 1864, C. Spees to S. Hunt, 3 January 1866, L. S. Dickinson to J. R. Shipherd, 30 March 1867, J. McNeil to E. P. Smith, n.d. December 1869, AMAA; Jones, "'A Glorious Work,'" 96.

27. F. E. Ganse to E. M. Cravath, 15 August 1871, E. Gill to S. S. Jocelyn,

11 January 1864, D. Todd to G. Whipple, 13 May 1865, H. S. Billings to E. P. Smith, 27 December 1868, E. G. Highgate to M. E. Strieby, 30 January 1868, AMAA; *American Missionary* 14 (March 1870): 55; A. K. Pierce to Bro. [E. K.] Miller, 3 May 1867, Enoch K. Miller Papers, Arkansas Historical Commission, Little Rock; H. Paul Douglass, *Christian Reconstruction in the South* (New York, 1909), 216.

28. Jones "A Glorious Work,'" 100; *American Missionary* 8 (March 1864): 65; E. A. Summers to My Dear Sister, 21 February 1867, Eliza A. Summers Papers, South Caroliniana Library, University of South Carolina, Columbia; E. B. Eveleth to S. S. Jocelyn, 4 February 1865, AMAA.

29. A. A. Carter to S. S. Jocelyn, 22 January 1863, A. G. Marment to E. M. Cravath, 31 January 1874, W. S. Bell to G. Whipple, 31 October 1864, H. B. Greely to G. Whipple, 1 March 1865, H. E. Stryker to J. R. Shipherd, 4 February 1868, AMAA; *Freedmen's Advocate* 1 (November 1864): 37.

30. *American Missionary* 10 (March 1866): 49; *American Missionary* 12 (March 1868): 52; *American Missionary* 18 (January 1874): 9; *American Missionary* 12 (August 1868): 174; E. A. Summers to My Dear Sister, 23 May 1867, Eliza A. Summers Papers.

31. *American Missionary* 7 (July 1863): 161; H. B. Greely to G. Whipple, 29 April 1865, E. M. Wright to E. P. Smith, 1 April 1869, A. S. Blood to E. M. Cravath, 8 November 1871, F. Snelson to E. M. Cravath, 24 March 1875, E. B. Eveleth to E. M. Cravath, 31 January 1873, AMAA; E. W. Wheelock to J. W. Alvord, 29 December 1866, Bureau Records, Ed. Div.

32. L. Welsh to G. Whipple, 25 January 1864, C. Blood to E. P. Smith, 30 November 1869, N. B. Carleton to E. P. Smith, 8 June 1869, M. C. Owen to E. P. Smith, 7 March 1870, M. F. Wells to M. E. Strieby, 26 January 1878, AMAA; *American Missionary* 16 (October 1872): 221.

33. Jones, "'A Glorious Work,'" 101–3; Teachers Monthly School Reports, Georgia, February 1866, AMAA.

34. McPherson, *Struggle for Equality*, 173; J. G. Fee to S. S. Jocelyn, 18 July 1864, J. Beardsley to G. Whipple, 27 June 1864, F. H. Greene to G. Whipple, 12 August 1866, AMAA; E. K. Miller to F. M. Jeffreys, 10 February 1867, Enoch K. Miller Papers; *American Missionary* 11 (September 1867): 200.

35. *Freedmen's Record* 1 (April 1865): 53; F. H. Greene to G. Whipple, 23 September 1864, H. C. Foote to S. Hunt, 1 February 1866, S. K. Hyde to W. E. Whiting, 28 February 1862, C. P. Day to S. S. Jocelyn, 11 March 1863, AMAA; A. C. Pierce to E. K. Miller, 3 May 1867, Enoch K. Miller Papers.

36. L. A. Hess to S. Hunt, 28 May 1866, E. W. Douglass to E. P. Smith, 26 May 1870, J. K. Nutting to E. M. Cravath, 4 December 1873, A. A. Safford to E. M. Cravath, 29 October 1874, AMAA.

37. Some white southerners disagreed with the AMA assumption that there

was no difference between mulattoes and blacks. The editor of the Charleston *Daily News* warned his readers against assuming that Avery Institute represented "a fair advantage" of black education in the city. In some advanced classes "scarcely a pure black is seen," he added. Avery students constituted an "aristocracy of color." Charleston *Daily News*, n.d. June 1866, quoted in *Twentieth Annual Report of the American Missionary Association and the Proceedings at the Annual Meeting . . . October 31st and November 1st, 1866* (New York, 1866), 27; M. L. Kellogg to S. S. Jocelyn, 30 January 1864, AMAA; Cardozo quoted in *Twenty-first Annual Report of the American Missionary Association and the Proceedings at the Annual Meeting . . . October 17th and 18th, 1867* (New York, 1867), 33.

38. Jones, "'A Glorious Work,'" 87; *American Missionary* 15 (July 1871): 148; M. F. Wells to E. M. Cravath, 15 July 1872, AMAA; E. P. Smith to J. W. Alvord, 18 February 1870, Bureau Records, Ed. Div.; R. R. Wright to O. O. Howard, 10 November 1869, O. O. Howard Papers.

Chapter 4. Freedmen's Relief

1. H. S. Beals to S. S. Jocelyn, 7 September 1863, W. T. Briggs to G. Whipple, 14 May 1864, AMAA.

2. W. Perkins to S. S. Jocelyn, 19 January 1863, S. G. Wright to S. S. Jocelyn, 20 January 1863, E. James to G. Whipple, 19 December 1863, J. L. Richardson to S. S. Jocelyn, 18 April 1863, W. T. Richardson to G. Whipple, 30 December 1864, AMAA; F. L. Olmsted Journal, 1 April 1863, Frederick Law Olmsted Papers, Library of Congress; *American Missionary* 7 (August 1863): 185, (October 1863): 233–34; Jones, "'A Glorious Work,'" 3.

3. J. A. Dix to E. M. Stanton, 12 September 1862, E. D. Keys to J. A. Dix, 15 September 1862, D. T. Van Buren to E. Ludlow, 12 October 1862, J. A. Andrews to J. A. Bolles, 16 October 1862, J. A. Dix to J. A. Andrews, 5 November 1862, U.S. Army Continental Commands, Department of Virginia.

4. *American Missionary* 7 (January 1863): 13–14, (July 1863): 154; John Eaton, *Grant, Lincoln and the Freedmen: Reminiscences of the Civil War with Special Reference to the Work for the Contrabands and Freedmen of the Mississippi Valley* (New York, 1907), 222–23.

5. *American Missionary* 6 (July 1862): 147; *American Missionary* 7 (July 1863): 148, 154; *American Missionary* 8 (December 1864): 281, 286; W. L. Coan to S. S. Jocelyn, 3 February 1862, C. B. Wilder to Dear Brethren, 16 December 1862, L. A. Brown to W. E. Whiting, 23 February 1864, S. Hine to Dear Sir, 26 February 1864, S. J. Tappan to W. Whiting, 12, 25 January, 1

February 1865, AMAA; L. Tappan to B. Parkhurst, 26 January 1864, Lewis Tappan Papers.

6. *American Missionary* 7 (July 1863): 159; *American Missionary* 8 (May 1864): 129–31; K. A. Dunning to S. Hunt, 29 December 1865, C. B. Wilder to Dear Brethren, 16 December 1862, S. A. Hosmer to G. Whipple, 13 April 1864, AMAA; Jones, "'A Glorious Work,'" 11–12.

7. *American Missionary* 7 (October 1863): 233–34; *American Missionary* 8 (June 1864): 141; D. Todd to G. Whipple, 4 June, 4 July 1864, S. S. Nickerson to G. Whipple, 6 Janaury 1865, Ella Roper, "Wants of the Freedmen," 5 August 1864, AMAA.

8. *American Missionary* 8 (April 1864): 95–96; *American Missionary* 9 (March 1865): 58–59.

9. Sherwood, "Journal of Miss Susan Walker," 20; D. T. Allen to G. Whipple, 1 March 1864, S. G. Wright to H. Cowles, 16 November 1863, W. O. King to S. S. Jocelyn, 11 April 1863, T. P. Jackson to G. Whipple, 7 April 1863, C. B. Wilder to W. E. Whiting, 10, 15 April 1863, C. P. Day to W. E. Whiting, 14 April 1863, AMAA; *American Missionary* 7 (August 1863): 180, (September 1863): 203.

10. J. Oliver to S. S. Jocelyn, 17 December 1862, 14 January 1863, AMAA; *American Missionary* 7 (May 1863): 108, (September 1863): 202–3; *American Missionary* 10 (September 1866): 195; J. T. Trowbridge, *A Picture of the Desolated States: and the Work of Restoration* (Hartford, 1868), 287.

11. *National Freedman* 1 (1 June 1865): 166–67; Jacksonville *Florida Union*, 16 September 1865; M. L. Campbell to T. W. Osborn, 21 February 1866, Bureau Records, Ed. Div.; James H. Whyte, *The Uncivil War: Washington During Reconstruction, 1865–1878* (New York, 1958), 32.

12. *American Missionary* 10 (September 1866): 204, (December 1866): 276, (April 1866): 87; *American Missionary* 11 (April 1867): 84, (March 1867): 64; Miss E. B. Isham to T. W. Osborn, 6 March 1866, Bureau Records, Ed. Div.; Jones, "'A Glorious Work,'" 7.

13. H. M. Phillips statement (Atlanta), 30 June 1866, AMAA; Howard N. Rabinowitz, *Race Relations in the Urban South, 1865–1890* (New York, 1978), 129; *American Missionary*, 11 (April 1867): 84; *American Missionary* 13 (December 1869): 270.

14. E. P. Smith to M. E. Strieby, 27 March 1866, AMAA; *American Missionary* 9 (May 1865): 101–2; *American Missionary* 10 (June 1866): 139–40.

15. Richard B. Drake, "The American Missionary Association and the Southern Negro, 1861–1888" (Ph.D. diss., Emory University, 1957), 14–15; L. Tappan to G. Duffield, 21 September 1864, Lewis Tappan Papers.

16. J. F. Sisson to Dear Bro., 16 July 1863, J. F. Sisson to S. S. Jocelyn, 23

July 1863, J. Doxey to W. E. Whiting, 14 November 1863, R. G. C. Patten to W. E. Whiting, 28 January 1864, W. O. King to G. Whipple, 30 April 1864, AMAA; *American Missionary* 8 (July 1864): 175.

17. Jones, "'A Glorious Work,'" 17; *American Missionary* 10 (April 1866): 74.

18. *American Missionary* 10 (April 1866): 74, (September 1866): 198–99, (December 1866): 276; *American Missionary* 11 (October 1867): 219, (September 1867): 197.

19. Drake, "American Missionary Association," 114; *American Missionary* 11 (February 1867): 28; R. M. Kinney to S. Hunt, 2 July 1866, AMAA.

20. The Adrian orphanage apparently never had more than seventy orphans at any one time. Individual teachers placed children in northern homes, and on at least one occasion the AMA furnished transportation North for "many of our little ones" from the Shaw orphans' asylum in Charleston, South Carolina. The director of the Shaw asylum thanked the association for providing transportation and added: "To get them from this miserable place to nice homes in the North is indeed a work of charity and great good to the poor orphans." They were not to be sent North as servants, but to live in and be raised by selected families. C. P. Wolhampter to E. P. Smith, 19 June 1868, E. Boarn to E. P. Smith, 10 September 1868, AMAA.

21. R. Craighead to E. P. Smith, 25 April, 5 May 1867, AMAA; Jones, *Soldiers of Light and Love*, 152.

22. J. T. Newman to C. H. Thompson, 25 January 1873, J. Lynch to E. M. Cravath, 9 January 1874, AMAA; Drake, "American Missionary Association," 115.

23. R. M. Kinney to S. Hunt, 2 July 1866, AMAA; *American Missionary* 10 (September 1866): 198–99, (December 1866): 276; *American Missionary* 11 (September 1867): 197, (October 1867): 219; *American Missionary* 17 (September 1873): 206; Jones, *Soldiers of Light and Love*, 152.

24. S. W. Laidler to AMA, 14 March 1866, AMAA; *American Missionary* 9 (December 1864): 292; *Freedmen's Advocate 1* (March 1865): 9; Jones, "'A Glorious Work,'" 27.

Chapter 5. Friends and Allies

1. E. L. Pierce to S. P. Chase, 2 March 1862, Port Royal Correspondence; "History of Benevolent Organizations," Bureau Records, Ed. Div.; G. Atkinson to W. E. Whiting, 19, 22, 27 January, 10, 23, 24 February, 4, 8, 11, 29 March, 5, 22, 28 April 1864, AMAA.

2. F. Gleason to G. Whipple, 3 January 1865, L. A. Woodbury to W. E. Whiting, 15 April 1865, AMAA; *National Freedman* 1 (1 June 1865): 151, (15 November 1865): 331–32; Horace James, *Annual Report of the Superintendent of Negro Affairs in North Carolina 1864* (Boston, 1865), 42; R. B. Foster to J. W. Alvord, 8 February 1867, Bureau Records, Ed. Div.

3. Charles S. Smith, *A History of the African Methodist Episcopal Church* (Philadelphia, 1922), 58, 60, 75; De Boer, "Role of Afro-Americans," 413–28; S. L. Hammond to M. E. Strieby, 23 August 1864, D. A. Payne to G. Whipple, 4 September 1865, J. M. Brown to G. Whipple, 1 May 1867, proposed plan of the Executive Committee of the Parent M. Society of the A.M.E. Church for cooperation with the Executive Committee of the A.M. Association, AMAA; *Missionary Reporter* 1 (July 1867), 1.

4. "History of the Benevolent Organizations," Bureau Records, Ed. Div.; De Boer, "Role of Afro-Americans," 428; Morris, *Reading, 'Riting, and Reconstruction*, 116.

5. Rivalry among the various societies led John Eaton, superintendent of freedmen for the Department of Tennessee, to establish in 1864 a central authority to coordinate their efforts. Eaton, *Grant, Lincoln and the Freedmen*, 203; Unsigned, undated letter in handwriting of Hannah E. Stevenson to Reuben Tomlinson, State Superintendent of Education Letters, South Carolina Department of Archives and History, Columbia; L. Tappan to My Dear Sir, 21 December 1868, AMAA.

6. Morris, *Reading, 'Riting, and Reconstruction*, 13, 43; Richard B. Drake, "Freedmen's Aid Societies and Sectional Compromise," *Journal of Southern History* 29 (May 1963): 177; *National Freedman* 2 (1 June 1865): 170–71; W. E. Boardman to O. O. Howard, 1 July 1865, O. O. Howard Papers; Butchart, *Northern Schools, Southern Blacks, and Reconstruction*, 77.

7. Morris, *Reading, 'Riting, and Reconstruction*, 3; Drake, "Freedmen's Aid Societies," 177; E. L. Boring to E. P. Smith, 26 January 1868, W. D. Harris to G. Whipple, 6 April 1865, AMAA.

8. McPherson, *Struggle for Equality*, 402; *American Missionary* 11 (May 1867): 108–9; *American Freedman* 2 (April 1867): 194.

9. L. Abbott to O. O. Howard, 23 July 1867, O. O. Howard Papers; *American Freedman* 1 (August 1866): 66, (January 1867): 146–47; G. Whipple to J. Ogden, 26 February 1868, AMAA.

10. McPherson, *Struggle for Equality*, 402–3; B. F. Jackson to G. Whipple, 18 February 1868, AMAA.

11. When its officers recommended that the AFUC be terminated on 1 July 1869, they said it would end not because work with black education was over "but because the existence of a national organization for this purpose, will have ceased to be either necessary or expedient."

12. George R. Bentley, *A History of the Freedmen's Bureau* (Philadelphia, 1955), 63; Howard, *Autobiography,* 2:269–70, 390.

13. G. Whipple to J. W. Alvord, 5 September 1865, Bureau Records, Ed. Div., R. Bacon to Dear Father, 17 March 1869, Bacon Family Collection, Sterling Library, Yale University; Howard, *Autobiography,* 2: 272.

14. Drake, "American Missionary Association," 42–44; G. Whipple to J. W. Alvord, 17 May 1865, J. W. Alvord to G. Whipple, 8 September 1865, AMAA; Morris, *Reading, 'Riting, and Reconstruction,* 37.

15. O. O. Howard to C. P. McIlwaine, 4 March 1867, O. O. Howard to G. Whipple, 27 November 1865, Bureau Records, A.A.G. Office, National Archives; O. O. Howard to G. Whipple, 28 June 1871, G. Whipple to O. O. Howard, 7 July 1866, O. O. Howard Papers; Drake, "American Missionary Association," 44, 175; William S. McFeely, *Yankee Stepfather: General O. O. Howard and the Freedmen* (New Haven, 1968), 269.

16. In many ways Alvord was able to favor the association. He recommended it both to prospective teachers and to philanthropists, and the AMA assisted him in return. Alvord wanted to start a bank for blacks and persuaded Whipple to accompany him to New York to lobby for such an institution. When the Freedman's Savings Bank was incorporated, Alvord tied it as closely to the AMA on the local level as possible, often appointing association personnel as cashiers. At least nine AMA men were at one time cashiers. H. C. Percy superintended association schools in Portsmouth and Norfolk, Virginia, and also served as cashier of the bank. Two-thirds of his salary was paid by the AMA. The association also supported the bank by using it to handle its financial affairs in several cities. Carl R. Osthaus, *Freedmen, Philanthropy, and Fraud: A History of the Freedman's Savings Bank* (Urbana, Ill., 1976), 4, 60–62.

17. Elizabeth S. Peck, *Berea's First Century, 1855–1955* (Lexington, Ky., 1955), 28; E. M. Cravath to O. O. Howard, 23 November 1866, G. Whipple to O. O. Howard, 1 December 1866, O. O. Howard to G. Whipple, 21 May 1867, O. O. Howard Papers.

18. E. P. Smith to G. Whipple, 11 October 1866, B. F. Whittemore to G. Whipple, 5 October 1866, AMAA.

19. Kiddo was eventually relieved as assistant commissioner—apparently, in part, at AMA request. G. W. Honey to J. R. Shipherd, 20, 30 October 1866, G. W. Honey to M. E. Strieby, 27 January 1867, AMAA; S. S. Jocelyn to O. O. Howard, 2 November 1866, O. O. Howard Papers; J. R. Shipherd to O. O. Howard, 22 January 1867, Bureau Records, A.A.G. Office.

20. *Flake's Weekly Bulletin* (Galveston), 20 December 1865; G. W. Honey to M. E. Strieby, 3 April 1866, D. T. Allen to J. R. Shipherd, 14 January 1868, AMAA.

21. A. M. Sperry to J. W. Alvord, 29 January 1867, Bureau Records, Ed.

Div., G. Griffin to O. O. Howard, 15 April 1867, O. O. Howard Papers; J. R. Shipherd to O. O. Howard, 9, 25 April 1867, G. Whipple to A. P. Ketchum, 19 August 1867, O. O. Howard to G. Whipple, 20 August 1867, O. O. Howard to G. Griffin, 23 April 1867, Bureau Records, A. A. G. Office; D. T. Allen to J. R. Shipherd, 10 April 1867, O. O. Howard to J. R. Shipherd, 20 August 1867, AMAA.

22. J. W. Alvord to G. Whipple, 23 July 1867, A. H. M. Taylor to G. Griffin, 1 August 1867, AMAA; Joseph Welch, Texas School Report, 4 March 1869, Bureau Records, Ed. Div.

23. E. W. Mason, Louisiana School Report, 1 July 1869, 3 June 1870, E. W. Mason to J. W. Alvord, 5 August 1870, W. M. Colby, Arkansas School Report, 1 July 1869, Bureau Records, Ed. Div., E. A. Ware to W. E. Whiting, 10 March 1868, G. L. Eberhart to S. Hunt, 28 November 1865, C. B. Fisk to J. R. Shipherd, 25 October 1866, E. M. Cravath to E. P. Smith, 22 October 1866, AMAA; H. R. Pease, Mississippi School Report, 1 November 1868, Bureau Records, Ed. Div.

24. C. H. Howard to Whipple & Strieby, 16 December 1868, W. Fowler to O. Brown, 1 March 1866, AMAA; H. M. Whittelsey to E. P. Smith, 26 February 1870, Bureau Records, A.A.G. Office.

25. Ralph E. Morrow, *Northern Methodism and Reconstruction* (East Lansing, 1956), 164; James B. Simmons to O. O. Howard, 18 February 1869, Bureau Records, Ed. Div.; J. B. Simmons to O. O. Howard, 7 March 1871, O. O. Howard to J. B. Simmons, 11 April 1871, Bureau Records, A.A.G. Office; John A. Carpenter, *Sword and Olive Branch* (Pittsburgh, 1964), 163–64.

26. The Bureau aided Episcopalians on several occasions, and one of the strongest protests came from AMA agent S. S. Ashley. An Episcopal priest had asked the Bureau for money to build a schoolhouse. Ashley protested on the grounds that government funds would be going for sectarian purposes. He complained that denominations could get money from the Bureau when the AMA could not. "Is the AMA treated as it is in N.C. because it is not a sectarian body?" he asked. S. S. Ashley to J. W. Alvord, 26 August 1867, Bureau Records, Ed. Div., O. O. Howard to G. Whipple, 29 August 1867, AMAA.

27. O. O. Howard to J. M. McKim, 26 July 1866, 6 March 1867, G. Whipple to O. O. Howard, 20 May 1867, L. Abbott to O. O. Howard, 17 July 1867, O. O. Howard to L. Abbott, 19, 30 July 1867, O. O. Howard Papers.

28. Drake, "American Missionary Association," 22–23; J. W. Alvord to F. A. Seely, 11 May 1867, Bureau Records, Ed. Div.; Andrew E. Murray, *Presbyterians and the Negro* (Philadelphia, 1966), 169.

29. Howard, *Autobiography,* 2: 271–75; Carpenter, *Sword and Olive Branch,* 159; R. M. Craighead to E. P. Smith, 9 May 1866, G. L. Eberhart to W. E. Whiting, 20 February 1867, AMAA; O. O. Howard to G. Whipple, 26

March 1867, Bureau Records, A.A.G. Office; J. W. Alvord to C. W. Buckley, 4 May 1867, Bureau Records, Ed. Div.

30. Bureau-AMA correspondence reveals that the Bureau spent at least $298,000 on construction, repairs, and property for the AMA. It is impractical to determine the exact amount since expenditures of association schools were not always separated from gross Bureau expenditures. Figures above gleaned from AMA and Bureau correspondence, 1865–71.

31. E. P. Smith to J. W. Alvord, 5 April 1869, G. Whipple to J. W. Alvord, 9 April 1869, Bureau Records, Ed. Div.

32. Figures compiled from Rental Accounts, Bureau Records, Ed. Div.

33. *American Missionary* 10 (December 1866), 269; G. Whipple to O. O. Howard, 21 May 1866, O. O. Howard Papers; Beard, *A Crusade of Brotherhood*, 170–71.

Chapter 6. Administration and Fund Collecting

1. In 1883 the Executive Committee was replaced by a board of directors which established policy and the corresponding secretaries became its agents. Direction was still sometimes entrusted to particular officers, but the days of personal leadership ended. Drake, "American Missionary Association," 77–78.

2. Johnson, "American Missionary Association," 95, 97, 106, 117.

3. Wyatt-Brown, *Lewis Tappan*, 87, 102, 142, 293; Swint, *Northern Teacher in the South*, 155.

4. James H. Fairchild, *Oberlin: The Colony and the College, 1833–1883* (Oberlin, 1883), 289; Drake, "American Missionary Association," 40–41; Osthaus, *Freedmen, Philanthropy, and Fraud*, 60; Horace Mann Bond, *Black American Scholars: A Story of Their Beginnings* (Detroit, 1972), 50 51; Johnson, "American Missionary Association," 107–8; Brownlee, *New Day Ascending*, 265; R. M. Craighead to G. Whipple, 16 September 1867, G. Whipple to M. A. Burnap, 29 August 1864, AMAA.

5. For a detailed treatment of Lewis Tappan's early antislavery activities, see Bertram Wyatt-Brown's excellent *Lewis Tappan and the Evangelical War Against Slavery*.

6. Wyatt-Brown, *Lewis Tappan*, viii, 118, 152–54, 329–30; Lewis Tappan, *Is It Right to Be Rich?* (New York, 1869), 4.

7. L. Tappan to S. S. Jocelyn, 31 July, 4 August 1862, L. Tappan's undated suggestions for improved office operation, AMAA; Johnson, "American Missionary Association," 112, 115–16.

8. In 1866 Tappan said he had received $5,500 as salary for nineteen years' work. Of that amount, he had given $2,500 back to the AMA. The balance he

had given to establish an orphanage for freedmen. L. Tappan to G. Whipple, 30 August 1866, in unidentified newspaper clipping, AMAA.

9. L. Tappan to G. Whipple, 26 August 1862, L. Tappan to My Dear Sir, 25 February 1862, L. Tappan to M. E. Strieby, 14 January 1864, AMAA.

10. In 1870 Jocelyn and Strieby began a collection to buy a house for Whipple. Tappan quickly agreed to give $500. S. S. Jocelyn and M. E. Strieby statement, 28 March 1870, AMAA.

11. Jocelyn continued to assist in the office occasionally, avidly collected funds for the AMA, and served on the Executive Committee until his death in 1879.

12. Strieby definitely did not have Jocelyn and Whipple's ability to dismiss teachers gently and retain their loyalty. When J. A. Adams was forced out at Straight University, he wrote Strieby: "Your letter is decidely insulting & unjust, but about in keeping with some other things from your office, & in which you had an unclean hand." Adams was hurt and angry, yet his letter reflected the views of several teachers. J. A. Adams to M. E. Strieby, 20 November 1877, AMAA.

13. Fairchild, *Oberlin*, 144–45; M. E. Strieby to G. Whipple, 6 January, 22 February, 16 March 1864, AMAA; Roy, *Pilgrim's Letters*, 55.

14. L. Tappan to A. Townsend, 1 November 1865, Lewis Tappan Papers; Beard, *A Crusade of Brotherhood*, 171–72; *American Missionary* 10 (January 1866): 11; S. Hunt to J. A. Rockwell, 24 February 1866, John A. Rockwell Papers, Amistad Research Center; Drake, "American Missionary Association," 91.

15. Ketchum, a prominent New York attorney and collector of internal revenue for the District of New York, served as treasurer until 1879. Whiting, a great-grandson of Jonathan Edwards and a member of the executive committee since the AMA was organized, became assistant treasurer in 1865. He probably had direct contact with more teachers than any other official during Reconstruction. He sent their salaries, supplied their needs when possible, and patiently listened to their frequent complaints.

16. Hunt, a longtime AMA supporter, was full of advice and schemes but was not a particularly good administrator. He did not handle teachers well, was not tactful, and he often wrote scolding letters when gentle persuasion would have been more successful. In mid-1866 Cravath pleaded for the appointment of a field secretary because Hunt was "not doing for the field work what is required." In Cravath's view, Hunt seemed to be a clerk when a man of experience and organizing ability was needed. Hunt's downfall, however, was probably caused by his bickering with Strieby. In May 1866 he reprimanded Strieby for "'lazing off' and having a good time generally" when so much work needed to be done. He also complained that his ideas were not given proper

consideration. Strieby in return accused Hunt of not doing his work well. Hunt was replaced by Edward Smith in 1866. He resigned the following year, blaming Strieby for his difficulties. Firm direction by Whipple probably could have prevented the Hunt-Strieby squabble. S. Hunt to M. E. Strieby, 17, 24 May 1866, E. M. Cravath to M. E. Strieby, 16 July 1866, S. Hunt to G. Whipple, 2 July 1866, S. Hunt to Dear Brethren, 4 July 1866, J. A. Shearman to E. P. Smith, 14, 24 January 1867, AMAA; Drake, "American Missionary Association," 90.

Hunt may have been relieved without sufficient cause. Shipherd was retained long after he should have been fired. The association enthusiastically appointed Shipherd to the Chicago secretaryship because he was former secretary of the Chicago branch of the American Freedmen's Union Commission. But he proved to be vain, demanding, quarrelsome, inattentive of his duties, and a constant irritant to Whipple and Strieby. In addition to AMA work he ran a news bureau and an advertising agency and was correspondent for several papers. When he failed to attend an Illinois meeting of Congregationalists in 1866, Strieby wrote: "I am very much afraid that a man who edits so many papers will hardly find time to do our work properly." Teachers complained about Shipherd's mismanagement, he offended Bureau officials, and the Reverend S. H. Platt, an AMA minister in Kansas, accused him of defrauding the Freedmen's Bureau. After considerable urging, Shipherd resigned in late 1868. Whipple said he resigned not because of Platt's charges of dishonesty and falsehood but because he and other AMA officers had "a decided, radical & unreconcilable difference in relation to methods of transacting business, or specifically as to what was or was not justifiable in them." Drake, "American Missionary Association," 89, 93; E. M. Cravath to G. Whipple, 13 October 1866, M. E. Strieby to G. Whipple, 11 June 1866, L. A. Montague to G. Whipple, 5 December 1867, J. R. Shipherd statement, 27 December 1867, M. E. Strieby to S. H. Platt, 9 October 1867, 18 February, 14 July 1868, G. Whipple to J. Shipherd, 29 August 1868, G. Whipple to S. H. Platt, 29 August 1863, 3 April 1869, M. E. Strieby to J. Shipherd, 20 October 1868, AMAA; Butchart, *Northern Schools, Southern Blacks, and Reconstruction*, 90.

17. Drake, "American Missionary Association," 96–98.

18. Drake, "American Missionary Association," 98.

19. E. Boyce to AMA, 9 October 1861, C. Browne to AMA, 8 October 1861, P. Montague to L. Tappan, 28 November 1861, J. Coffin to Dear Friend, 8 January 1862, G. Smith to W. E. Whiting, 16 July 1863, Smith to G. Whipple, 28 November 1863, Smith to L. Tappan, 12 March, 1 July 1864, AMAA; G. Smith to L. Tappan, 23 November 1862, L. Tappan to J. P. Williston, 21 November 1863, 23 January 1864, I. Washburn to L. Tappan, 7 November 1863, L. Tappan to G. Whipple, 30 August 1866, Lewis Tappan Papers.

20. C. Crain to Dear Sir, 27 April 1864, R. W. Lyman to G. Whipple, 19 January 1864, A. Parmele to M. E. Strieby, 8 December 1876, B. B. Curry statement, 7 March 1862, AMAA.

21. J. E. Roy to Dear Brethren, 10 June 1861, D. Thurston to L. Tappan, 15 March, 22 May, 2 September 1861, 16 May 1862, 14 February 1865, Thurston to G. Whipple, 24 June, 10 July, 12 October 1861, 13 April 1863, 22 October 1864, Thurston to W. E. Whiting, 12 June, 16 September, 11 November 1863, 7 March, 6 December 1864, AMAA.

22. C. L. Parmele, Jr. to W. E. Whiting, 27 April 1864, E. Loomis to L. Tappan, 27 April, 6 May 1864, S. Lee to W. E. Whiting, 9 May 1864, L. Tappan to S. S. Jocelyn, 27 May 1862, H. Dodge to S. Giddings, 3, 28 September 1866, J. A. Hall to W. E. Whiting, 4 October 1866, Hall to G. Whipple, 16 November 1866, J. Giddings to G. Whipple, 17 November 1866, AMAA.

23. Jones, *Soldiers of Light and Love*, 98; Beard, *A Crusade of Brotherhood*, 319–20; J. S. Peck to Dear Brother, 14 January 1862, C. L. Ray to ? Duncan, 2 August 1864, G. R. Entler to M. E. Strieby, 8 March 1866, E. L. Pierce to Dear Sir, 16 May 1864, S. S. Jocelyn to G. Whipple, 7 August 1862, AMAA; G. Whipple to H. Eddy, 16 January 1866, John A. Rockwell Papers.

24. J. L. Millerd to W. E. Whiting, 7 June 1861, S. S. Jocelyn to A. Lincoln, 27 November 1861, G. Whipple to S. S. Jocelyn, 10 March, 20 June 1862, AMAA.

25. Engs, *Freedom's First Generation*, 16–17; W. L. Coan to Dear Brethren, 16 January 1862, Coan to S. S. Jocelyn, 8 May 1862, L. Tappan to S. S. Jocelyn, 31 May, 4 June 1862, AMAA.

26. W. L. Coan to S. S. Jocelyn, 18, 21 March 1862, 10 February 1863, A. P. Mason to S. S. Jocelyn, 5 February 1862, AMAA.

27. M. E. Strieby to G. Whipple, 11 January 1864, Statement of contributions, no signature, 4 August 1864, AMAA.

28. Jones, "'A Glorious Work,'" 192; S. Love to L. Tappan, 2 December 1861, H. S. Beals to W. E. Whiting, 16 January 1865, W. H. Brown to W. E. Whiting, 9 April 1864, E. Highgate to M. E. Strieby, 15 December 1864, AMAA.

29. H. Pitts to G. Whipple, 20 April 1864, M. French to G. Whipple, 12 October 1864, A. Pierce to Dear Sir, 3 March 1864, AMAA; L. Tappan to L. Foster, 23 December 1864, Lewis Tappan Papers; Drake, "American Missionary Association," 280; M. E. Strieby to E. L. Perry, 3 November 1864, AMAA; *American Missionary* 7 (July 1863): 156.

30. Brownlee, *New Day Ascending*, 21, 85; Drake, "American Missionary Association," 121.

31. The National Council recommended that $300,000 be raised for the American Home Missionary Society and $200,000 for the American Congrega-

tional Union. J. E. Roy to Dear Brethren, 17 June 1861, S. S. Jocelyn to Dear Brethren, 13 September 1865, M. E. Strieby to G. Whipple, 6 January 1864, AMAA; Drake, "American Missionary Association," 28, 99; *American Missionary* 10 (August 1865): 179.

32. Ganius G. Atkins and Fred L. Fagley, *History of American Congregationalism* (Boston, 1942), 304; Brownlee, *New Day Ascending*, 214.

33. In 1865–66 the following groups also agreed to open channels for collection among their members: the Congregational Union of England and Wales, the United Presbyterian Church, the Free Church of Scotland, the Church of Scotland, the Synod of the Canadian Presbyterian Church, and the General Synod of the Reformed Dutch Church. Other denominations sometimes supported the association also. *American Missionary* 10 (August 1866), 179.

34. S. S. Jocelyn to Dear Brethren, 13 September 1865, S. Hunt to M. E. Strieby, 25 May 1866, S. S. Jocelyn to M. E. Strieby, 16 July 1866, G. Whipple to Dear Brother, 17 May 1866, Whipple to M. E. Strieby, 12 May, 13 July 1866, AMAA; G. D. Pike to O. O. Howard, 19 April 1869, O. O. Howard Papers.

35. The Reverends J. C. Holbrook, W. W. Patton, James A. Thorne, H. M. Storrs, and Levi Coffin also represented the AMA in England and Scotland.

36. L. Tappan to W. Armistead, 17 May 1865, Tappan to J. Sella Martin, 3 July 1865, Lewis Tappan Papers; Drake, "American Missionary Association," 100; M. E. Strieby to Messrs. Holbrook, Patton, and Martin, 21 May 1866, AMAA.

37. S. S. Jocelyn to N. Wright, 8 August 1866, W. E. Whiting statement, n.d. September 1866, AMAA.

38. G. Whipple to M. E. Strieby, 1 April 1867, I. Pettibone to W. E. Whiting, 10 June 1867, E. P. Smith to W. E. Whiting, 10 April 1868, M. E. Strieby to G. Whipple, 7 June 1867, AMAA; *Freedmen's Record* 4 (July 1868): 107; *American Missionary* 11 (May 1867): 106; L. Abbott to O. O. Howard, 10 December 1867, O. O. Howard Papers; J. W. Alvord to O. O. Howard, 10 August 1868, R. D. Harper, Alabama School Report, 22 June 1868, Bureau Records, Ed. Div.; Drake, "American Missionary Association," 1, 101, 275–79; Brownlee, *New Day Ascending*, 271.

39. Charles Avery of Philadelphia donated $10,000 to Avery Institute in Charleston. Emerson Institute was named after Ralph Emerson of Rockford, Illinois. J. P. Williston of Northampton, Massachusetts, and Ichabod Washburn of Worcester had their names attached to schools in North Carolina. Storrs School in Atlanta was named after the Reverend H. M. Storrs of Cincinnati, who helped raise the original $1,000. List of benefactors compiled from *American Missionary;* Joe M. Richardson, *A History of Fisk University, 1865–1946* (University, Ala., 1980), 41; J. Pierce to E. M. Cravath, 13 May 1874, AMAA.

40. B. B. Edward to S. Hunt, 29 September 1865, C. E. Jackson to G. Whip-

ple, 5 October 1865, E. Mills to Whom it May Concern, 20 September 1865, G. D. Pike to E. P. Smith, 25 October 1867, AMAA.

41. E. P. Smith to G. Whipple, 2 April 1869, W. C. Ward to M.E. Strieby, 8 November 1876, AMAA; *American Missionary* 13 (June 1869): 130.

42. In 1868–69 Emerson Institute at Mobile was accepted as part of the public system. A draft for $1,000 was given to AMA agent George L. Putnam to pay W. I. Squirer, the principal. Putnam gave Squirer only $420. Squirer did not accuse Putnam of using the money for himself, but said, "I do claim that he has by virtue of sharp practice chiseled me out of the amount and that it is now being used daily for A.M.A. expenses." The association response indicates that Squirer was correct. W. I. Squirer to Secretaries of A.M.A., 15 February 1869, Squirer to G. Whipple, 21 February 1869, H. W. Cobb to M. E. Strieby, 22 March 1869, M. E. Strieby and E. M. Cravath statement, 6 April 1869, G. L. Putnam to E. P. Smith, 14 September 1869, 15 March 1870, AMAA.

43. The Jubilee Singers had just begun their tour to earn money for Fisk University and were in Chillicothe, Ohio, when the Chicago fire occurred. Although the Singers were in debt, they donated their entire proceeds of about fifty dollars to the Chicago relief fund.

44. John Sproat, *The Best Men: Liberal Reformers in the Gilded Age* (New York: 1968), 31–34; C. M. Blood to M. E. Strieby, 11 November 1875, AMAA; *American Missionary* 20 (June 1876): 24; Beard, *A Crusade of Brotherhood*, 203.

45. Lifelong Friend to W. E. Whiting, 18 July 1876, C. Ely to Dear Sir, 11 December 1861, Ely to G. Whipple, 24 June 1864, Ely to AMA, 23 June 1874, 25 September 1875, AMAA.

46. Bull's major offense seems to have been selling tobacco and snuff to freedmen. Thomas thought that an insufficient excuse and reprimanded the AMA for firing Bull without making a personal investigation. She also reminded Cravath that Bull had spent some of his own money on the school and that the AMA should "stand fair in its dealings" and repay him. Jones, "'A Glorious Work,'" 163; M. Thomas to E. M. Cravath, 28 August 1873, AMAA.

47. M. Thomas to W. E. Whiting, 3, 10 March, 10 July, 5, 27 August 1871, 26 January, 17 July, 21 August 1872, 30 April 1873, 2 January 1874, 5 July 1876, Thomas to E. M. Cravath, 16 October, 2 November, 6 December 1871, 25 November 1872, 3 June, 10 July, 28 August 1873, 20 April 1874, 10 July, 3 December 1875, Thomas to M. E. Strieby, 27 June 1871, 13, 20 July 1877, 3 August 1878, AMAA.

48. Richardson, *Fisk University*, 28; J. W. Healy, Statement of Donations to Straight University, 1870–1871, AMAA.

49. *History of the American Missionary Association*, 52; S. S. Ashley to G.

Whipple, 18 August 1873, T. N. Chase to E. M. Cravath, 26 December 1874, AMAA.

50. Brownlee, *New Day Ascending*, 274; Beard, *A Crusade of Brotherhood*, 256–59.

51. The Freedmen's Bureau expended more than $5 million. The Bureau and the association easily provided more than one-half of the sum spent on freedmen's education between 1860 and 1888. Drake, "American Missionary Association," 1; Brownlee, *New Day Ascending*, 271.

Chapter 7. Public Schools and Teacher Training

1. Wesley A. Hotchkiss, "Congregationalists and Negro Education," *Journal of Negro Education* 29 (Summer 1960): 291; *American Missionary* 9 (August 1865): 180–81.

2. Amory D. Mayo explained the AMA's cooperation with public schools by saying that although the association was supported by various denominations these groups eventually withdrew and organized on a more sectarian basis, which left the AMA virtually controlled by the Congregationalists, longtime supporters of common schools. "That original interest in and connection with the common school by the Congregational clergy and laity," he said, had not been forgotten. A. D. Mayo, "Work of Certain Northern Churches in the Education of Freedmen, 1861–1900," *Report of the United States Commissioner of Education for 1901–1902*, 2 vols. (Washington, D.C., 1902), 1:292–93.

3. E. A. Ware to ?, n.d. 1868, AMAA; *American Missionary* 12 (April 1868): 84; *American Missionary* 13 (November 1869): 241; *American Missionary* 11 (September 1867): 209; Drake, "American Missionary Association," 189–90; Brownlee, *New Day Ascending*, 114.

4. The Freedmen's Bureau, a strong supporter of public schools, commended the AMA stance on public education by writing: "We are glad to see that the Association works through common schools already in operation and stimulates and directs the opening of others." Quoted in Brownlee, *New Day Ascending*, 115.

5. Most of the secular societies assumed that their work was temporary. The North would help build school systems in the South that would eventually be supported by southerners. Butchart, *Northern Schools, Southern Blacks, and Reconstruction*, 26–27.

6. The Baltimore transaction hardly represents common AMA practice. The association was strongly concerned with the type of education. It cooperated with the Baltimore society because it had few schools there and because

education would continue to be religiously oriented. Brownlee, *New Day Ascending*, 114.

7. *American Missionary* 12 (December 1868): 269, (April 1868): 84; Louisiana, *Report of the State Superintendent of Public Education for the Year 1874* (New Orleans, 1875), L; Margaret L. McCulloch, *Fearless Advocate of the Right: The Life of Francis Julius LeMoyne, M.D., 1798–1879* (Boston, 1941), 208; Jones, *Soldiers of Light and Love*, 192; Dorothy Orr, *A History of Education in Georgia* (Chapel Hill, 1950), 305.

8. E. P. Smith to W. E. Whiting, 10 April 1868, J. D. Warner to E. P. Smith, 1 June 1868, E. M. Hubbard to E. P. Smith, 2 June 1868, M. E. Sands to E. M. Cravath, 2 May, 5 June, 14 October 1873, W. D. Williams to E. M. Cravath, 4 June, 5 September 1873, A. D. Gerrish to E. M. Cravath, 29 November 1873, F. Haley to E. M. Cravath, 11, 28 August 1874, J. Silsby to E. M. Cravath, 7 September 1874, B. M. Zetter to E. M. Cravath, 3 June 1875, Committee of Colored Citizens of Macon to M. E. Strieby, 1 July 1875, AMAA.

9. A. Rowe to G. Whipple, 31 August, 5, 14 October 1874, A. N. Niles to E. M. Cravath, 15 January 1875, S. S. Ashley to Bro. Woodworth, 1 February 1878, AMAA; C. T. Wright, "The Development of Education for Blacks in Georgia, 1865–1900" (Ph.D. diss., Boston University, 1977), 85–86.

10. H. M. Turner quoted in R. F. Markham to M. E. Strieby, 12 November 1875, AMAA.

11. Jones, "'A Glorious Work,'" 121–22; S. S. Ashley to G. Whipple, 29 January 1869, AMAA.

12. Copy of Alabama Board of Education statement, n.d. 1868, Bureau Records, A.A.G. Office; U.S. Commissioner of Education, *Report for the Year 1873* (Washington, D.C., 1875), xiii; T. C. Steward to E. M. Cravath, 1 March 1871, A. A. Safford to M. S. Cook, 25 January 1871, AMAA.

13. By the end of Reconstruction, state and local officials usually refused to employ white northern teachers. In 1869 the AMA arranged to give Selma free use of Burrell School. The association nominated the teachers and the city paid for their services. By 1875 the local board began to balk at hiring northern teachers. In 1877 the city assumed full control of the school. Local blacks and the AMA were so displeased with its operation that the association reopened Burrell as a private school in 1889. *Burrell Record* (May 1890): 1; E. C. Silsby to M. E. Strieby, 10 January 1877, M.F. Wells to E. M. Cravath, 15 May 1874, AMAA.

14. The AMA received far more public funds from Alabama than from any other state. Money paid to AMA teachers in public schools include the following: Tennessee $16,217, Mississippi $14,655, Georgia $13,072, North Carolina $6,082, Arkansas $1,598, South Carolina $661, Texas $180, and Louisiana $95.

These funds include teachers' salaries and rental of buildings. They do not include the black share of funds from the Morrill Act of 1862. Hampton Institute, Atlanta University, and Tougaloo College received considerable monies from the Morrill Act. Drake, "American Missionary Association," 286–87; List of contributions to AMA listed in various issues of *American Missionary.*

15. The number of common schools increased somewhat when Democrats began to discriminate more and more against black schools, and of course some elementary pupils continued to be trained at high schools, normal schools, and colleges.

16. It is difficult to determine which schools were secondary only. Normal schools and colleges offered secondary work, and some secondary institutions taught normal classes. In this study the distinction has been made by name. *American Missionary* 15 (January 1871): 3, (December 1871): 257; *American Missionary* 18 (December 1874): 272; *American Missionary* 11 (November 1867): 242; *American Missionary* 12 (December 1868):269; *American Missionary* 16 (December 1872): 267; U.S. Commissioner of Education, *Report for the Year 1889–90*, 2 vols. (Washington, D.C., 1893), 2:1083.

17. Hotchkiss, "Congregationalists and Negro Education," 292; L. A. Woodbury to S. S. Jocelyn, 7 September 1863, S. Hunt to Mrs. Hodgeboom, 30 November 1866, E. M. Cravath to G. Whipple, 7 March 1867, R. Tomlinson to O. O. Kinsman, 15 March 1866, AMAA; Joe M. Richardson, "Christian Abolitionism: The American Missionary Association and the Florida Negro," *Journal of Negro Education* 40 (Winter 1971): 41.

18. Daniel A. Payne, free-born in Charleston, college educated, sometime president of Wilberforce University, became a bishop of the African Methodist Episcopal Church in 1852. Payne worked closely with the AMA during the war years.

19. W. H. Woodbury to G. Whipple, 7 November 1863, G. Candee to G. Whipple, 15 April 1864, S. W. Magill to AMA, 10 June 1865, AMAA: Jones, "'A Glorious Work,'" 226–29.

20. *American Missionary* 11 (November 1867): 242; *American Missionary* 12 (September 1868): 202, (December 1868): 269; *American Missionary* 16 (December 1872): 267; E. Whittlesey to E. P. Smith, 10 December 1868, Bureau Records, A.A.G.

21. Among the best-known AMA normal and secondary schools in the 1870s and 1880s were Williston School, Wilmington, North Carolina; Avery Institute, Charleston, South Carolina; Brewer National Industrial and Agricultural Institute, Greenwood, South Carolina; Lewis High School, Macon, Georgia; Beach Institute, Savannah, Georgia; Storrs School, Atlanta, Georgia; Stanton Normal School, Jacksonville, Florida; Emerson Institute, Mobile, Alabama; Swayne School, Montgomery, Alabama; Howard School, Chattanooga,

Tennessee; LeMoyne Institute, Memphis, Tennessee; Ely Normal, Louisville, Kentucky; Normal School, Lexington, Kentucky; Ariel Academy, Camp Nelson, Kentucky.

22. Robert G. Sherer, "Let Us Make Man: Negro Education in Nineteenth Century Alabama" (Ph.D. diss., University of North Carolina, 1970), 312; Edwin Beecher, Alabama School Report, 13 July 1864, Bureau Records, Ed. Div.; Memorandum of Mrs. Annette Anderson, 1 March 1937, copy in Amistad Research Center, New Orleans; Huntsville *Gazette*, 26 November 1881, 10 June 1882.

23. Monthly school reports, Lincoln School, 1870–73, AMAA; Bond, *Black American Scholars*, 41–42.

24. U.S. Commissioner of Education, *Report for the Year 1877–78* (Washington, D.C., 1880), xxix; *Report for the Year 1887–88* (Washington, D.C., 1889), 997; *Report for the Year 1889–90*, 2:1086.

25. Marina Wikramanayake, *A World in Shadow: The Free Black in Antebellum South Carolina* (Columbia, S.C., 1973), 16; Lerone Bennett, Jr., *Black Power U.S.A.: The Human Side of Reconstruction, 1867–1877* (Chicago, 1967), 9, 136, 138–39; William J. Simmons, *Men of Mark: Eminent, Progressive and Rising* (Cleveland, 1887), 428–29; F. L. Cardozo to M. E. Strieby, 13 August 1866, AMAA; Joe M. Richardson, "Francis L. Cardozo: Black Educator During Reconstruction," *Journal of Negro Education* 48 (Winter 1979): 73.

26. F. L. Cardozo to G. Whipple, 21 October 1865, Cardozo to M. E. Strieby, 13 August 1866, Cardozo to S. Hunt, 2 December 1865, AMAA; R. Tomlinson, 7 October 1865, J. M. and Esther Hawks Papers, Library of Congress; R. Tomlinson, South Carolina School Report, 4 October 1865, 10 December 1866, Bureau Records, Ed. Div.

27. Black Charlestonians who taught for Cardozo in 1865–66 were William O. Weston, Richard S. Holloway, Catherine Winslow, Amelia Ann Shrewsbury, Harriet Holloway, Rosabella Fields, and Charlotte Johnson.

28. F. L. Cardozo to S. Hunt, 2 December 1865, 13 January, 3 November 1866, Cardozo to G. Whipple and M. E. Strieby, 2 December 1865, AMAA; Richardson, "Francis L. Cardozo," 75–76.

29. Whether deliberately or not, Hunt created considerable problems for Cardozo. Before sending Wall and Alexander to Charleston he told them that Cardozo had requested that no black teachers be sent. Cardozo vigorously denied the charge. Later Hunt sent teachers whom Cardozo deemed inferior. Hunt refused to withdraw the teachers, but informed them that Cardozo was disappointed in them. The latter was puzzled by Hunt's actions, since the teachers were not being withdrawn and such a statement would only make them unhappy in the situation. Hunt had a remarkable ability to alienate

teachers and principals with whom he dealt, but his dealings with Cardozo almost suggest that he had greater difficulty in dealing with blacks, though he did advocate training black teachers. F. L. Cardozo to S. Hunt, 2 December 1865, 30 October 1866, AMAA.

30. Avery Institute was originally called Saxton School. In 1868, when Cardozo transferred his students to a new two-story building, it was renamed in honor of Charles Avery of Philadelphia, who had made a $10,000 donation to the school.

31. Martin Abbott, *The Freedmen's Bureau in South Carolina* (Chapel Hill, 1967), 92; S. C. Hale to S. Hunt, 11 June 1866, F. L. Cardozo to S. Hunt, 10 March 1866, AMAA.

32. F. L. Cardozo to M. E. Strieby, 13 June 1866, AMAA; Richardson, "Francis L. Cardozo," 78–80.

33. F. L. Cardozo to E. P. Smith, 4 November, 7 December 1867, AMAA; Richardson, "Francis L. Cardozo," 82–83.

34. While Avery Institute was considered unique for its superior training, a black educator claimed it was unique in still another way. "The little proud school was shot through with the spirit of caste and class based merely upon the mechanics of color," wrote Lewis K. McMillan. "A reactionary white Charleston must certainly have seen in a reactionary Avery Normal Institute its most effective instrument of keeping the mass of Negroes forever in their place." While McMillan criticized Avery vigorously for its exclusiveness, he added, "What leadership the Negro in Charleston has had since the civil war, Avery Institute has provided it." Lewis K. McMillan, *Negro Higher Education in the State of South Carolina* (Orangeburg, S.C., 1951), 3–4, 6.

35. J. W. Alvord to O. O. Howard, 11 January 1870, Bureau Records, Ed. Div.; E. M. Cravath to M. A. Warren, 30 March 1872, AMAA; Jackson, "The Educational Efforts of the Freedmen's Bureau and Freedmen's Aid Societies in South Carolina," 25; McMillan, *Negro Higher Education*, 2; W. L. Gordon to W. A. Courtenay, 9 April 1881, in *City of Charleston Yearbook, 1880*, 126; Josephine W. Martin, "The Educational Efforts of the Major Freedmen's Aid Societies and the Freedmen's Bureau in South Carolina, 1862–1870" (Ph.D. diss., University of South Carolina, 1971), 188–90.

36. Emerson was named after Ralph Emerson of Rockford, Illinois, "who made a generous contribution toward the necessary purchase money." Beard, *A Crusade of Brotherhood*, 179; H. M. Bush, Alabama School Report, February 1868, C. H. Howard to J. W. Alvord, 6 May 1869, Bureau Records, Ed. Div.; H. M. Kelsey to AMA, 6 May 1869, E. R. Dickerson to Dear Sir, 12 September 1871, AMAA.

37. E. P. Lord to E. M. Cravath, 11 January 1873, Lord to M. E. Strieby, 11 January 1876, A. J. Holton to M. E. Strieby, 18 April 1876, AMAA; *American Missionary* 20 (June 1876): 127.

38. T. N. Chase to M. E. Strieby, 12 January 1878, W. H. Ash to M. E. Strieby, 26 February, 13 March 1878, AMAA; U.S. Commissioner of Education, *Report for the Year 1878* (Washington, D.C., 1880), xxix; Willis G. Clark, *History of Education in Alabama, 1702–1889* (Washington, D.C., 1889), 279–80.

39. C. E. Compton to J. W. Alvord, 17 July 1870, B. P. Runkle to J. W. Alvord, 22 June 1870, Bureau Records, Ed. Div.; U.S. Commissioner of Education, *Report for the Year 1878*, xxix; *American Missionary* 40 (October 1888): 304; Drake, "American Missionary Association," 186–87.

Chapter 8. The AMA Colleges

1. T. N. Chase to M. E. Strieby, 11 September 1877, AMAA.

2. The AMA urged the founding of Howard and paid the salary of its first teacher. Later it was the chief supporter of the Howard theological department, since the government would not support theological studies. For a time the board of trustees was dominated by AMA representatives and their friends. Dwight O. W. Holmes, "Fifty Years of Howard University," *Journal of Negro History* 3 (October 1918): 369, 373; New Orleans *Weekly Louisianian*, 10 July 1875; *American Missionary* 15 (January 1871): 2; James M. McPherson, *The Struggle for Equality: Abolitionists and the Negro in the Civil War and Reconstruction* (Princeton, 1964), 406. For a detailed study of Howard, see Rayford W. Logan, *Howard University, 1867–1967* (New York, 1967).

3. Hotchkiss, "Congregationalists and Negro Education," 291; Beard, *A Crusade of Brotherhood*, 146–50; Holmes, *The Evolution of the Negro College*, 95; *American Missionary* 32 (January 1878), 1.

4. Carpenter, *Sword and Olive Branch*, 161; Hotchkiss, "Congregationalists and Negro Education," 290; E. P. Smith to M. E. Strieby, 28 April 1866, AMAA.

5. The seven AMA-chartered colleges were Berea, Berea, Kentucky; Hampton, Hampton, Virginia; Fisk, Nashville, Tennessee; Talladega, Talladega, Alabama; Tougaloo, Tougaloo, Mississippi; and Straight, New Orleans, Louisiana.

6. Richardson, *Fisk University*, 2–4.

7. Mrs. C. S. Crosby to M. E. Strieby, 1 May 1866, Miss E. A. Easter to M. E. Strieby, 12 February 1866, E. M. Cravath to G. Whipple, 13 February 1866, Monthly School Reports, January, February, April 1866, J. Ogden to E. P. Smith, 25 November 1867, AMAA; Articles of Incorporation of Fisk University, Register's Office, Davidson County, Tennessee, Book 38, p. 339.

8. Richardson, *Fisk University*, 13–15; Horace Mann Bond, *The Education*

of the Negro in the American Social Order (New York, 1934), 131; *Fisk University and Normal School* (pamphlet, 1869).

9. *Fisk University Catalog, 1868–70*, pp. 20–21, *1871–72*, pp. 18–20; "Minutes of the Union Literary Society," 31 January 1868, 1 January 1876, Fisk University Library.

10. C. Crosby to E. P. Smith, 12 January 1867, E. M. Cravath to G. L. White, 6 January 1868, AMAA; *Twenty-second Annual Report of the American Missionary Association and the Proceedings at the Annual Meeting . . . 1868* (New York, 1868), 55; *Harper's Weekly* 20 (22 June 1876): 73; *Rules and Regulations of Fisk University* (flyer, 1868); *Fisk Herald*, November 1883: 5.

11. Richardson, *Fisk University*, 20–21; *Fisk News*, 27 June 1947, 2; *Twenty-fourth Annual Report of the American Missionary Association and the Proceedings at the Annual Meeting . . . November 9th and 10th, 1870* (New York, 1870), 40; Henry Hugh Proctor, *Between Black and White: Autobiographical Sketches* (Boston, 1925), 31–33.

12. Richardson, *Fisk University*, 22–24.

13. Richardson, *Fisk University*, 25–39; Gustavus D. Pike, *The Jubilee Singers and Their Campaign for Twenty Thousand Dollars* (New York, 1873); "Jubilee Day," an address by James Weldon Johnson, 7 October 1933, James Weldon Johnson Collection, Fisk University Library.

14. Virginia E. Walker became a teacher and missionary in Tennessee. America Robinson, one of the Jubilee Singers, devoted her life to teaching. In 1890 she was principal of the Macon Public School, Macon, Mississippi. James Burrus did graduate work in mathematics at Dartmouth and became a college professor and businessman. At his death he left $120,000 to Fisk. John Burrus became an attorney, businessman, and college president.

15. *Fisk University Catalog, 1877*, p. 8; *Fisk Herald*, July 1893, pp. 4, 14; *Fisk University News*, April 1922, pp. 2–3; W. E. B. DuBois, "My Evolving Program for Negro Freedom," in *What the Negro Wants*, ed. Rayford W. Logan (Chapel Hill, 1944), 36–39; W. E. B. DuBois, *Dusk of Dawn: An Essay Toward an Autobiography of a Race Concept* (New York, 1940), 30–31; W. E. B. DuBois, *The Autobiography of W. E. B. DuBois: A Soliloquy on Viewing My Life from the Last Decade of Its First Century* (New York, 1968), 122–24.

16. Savery was an incorporator and trustee of Talladega. Joe M. Richardson, "'To Help a Brother On': The First Decade of Talladega College," *Alabama Historical Quarterly* 37 (Spring 1975): 22; W. Swayne to O. O. Howard, 12 September 1866, O. O. Howard to W. Swayne, 24 June 1867, Bureau Records, Ed. Div.; Brownlee, *New Day Ascending*, 195–96.

17. Beard, *A Crusade of Brotherhood*, 73–74; Brownlee, *New Day Ascending*, 197; H. M. Bush to J. W. Alvord, 17 November 1868, Bureau Records, Ed. Div.; Talladega *Sun*, 1 April, 15 July, 21 August 1869; H. E. Brown to E. M. Cravath, 11 August 1869, AMAA.

18. Holmes, *Evolution of the Negro College*, 99.

19. *Circular of the Normal and Preparatory Department of Talladega College 1870–1871* (1871), pp. 5, 7–8, 10–11.

20. *Catalog of Talladega College, 1873–74*, pp. 14–18, *1874–75*, pp. 6–14, *1875–1876*, pp. 26–28.

21. Colleagues reported that Brown was full of projects but "deficient in systematic effort" and that he was the "weakest preacher" in a southern pulpit. G. Stanley Pope to M. E. Strieby, 10 July 1874, G. W. Andrews and Pope to M. E. Strieby and G. Whipple, 9 August 1875, AMAA.

22. W. G. Marts to M. E. Strieby, 2 May 1876, A. A. Safford to M. E. Strieby, 11 May 1876, AMAA.

23. E. P. Lord and G. W. Andrews to M. E. Strieby, 12 June 1877, G. Stanley Pope to M. E. Strieby, 13 July 1877, Mrs. H. W. Andrews to M. E. Strieby, 7 June 1878, AMAA.

24. Richardson, "The First Decade of Talladega," 34.

25. G. W. Andrews to M. E. Strieby, 28 February, 26 April 1876, AMAA; Richardson, "The First Decade of Talladega," 35.

26. Childs and his companion were the only blacks who had seated themselves in the area reserved for whites.

27. J. F. Childs to M. E. Strieby, 3 July, 14 August 1877, E. P. Lord to M. E. Strieby, 30 July, 12 September 1877, H. C. Bullard to D. E. Emerson, 17 July 1877, AMAA.

28. Even George Andrews condemned Lord for his unwise action. H. E. Andrews to M. E. Strieby, 29 June 1878, G. W. Andrews to M. E. Strieby, 29 June 1878, AMAA.

29. The fall 1879 issue of the school newspaper, the *Southern Sentinel*, claimed that the previous year's experience with industrial education had proved that the best results were not attained by allowing students to earn all their school expenses by working as it left too little time for academics. *Southern Sentinel* 2 (September 1879): 4.

30. *Southern Sentinel* 2 (October 1879): 4; Huntsville *Gazette*, 20 August 1881.

31. The initial impetus for Straight came from the Reverend J. W. Healy, AMA agent for the Southwest, who convinced local merchant Seymour Straight that a black college was needed in New Orleans. Together Healy and Straight persuaded the association and the Freedmen's Bureau. The AMA purchased the land, and the Bureau constructed the buildings. The school was named for Straight, who was its principal benefactor for the next several years. S. Straight to G. Whipple, 24, 29 March, 31 December 1869, 5 April 1870, J. W. Healy to my Dear Brethren, 25 June 1869, AMAA; C. H. Howard to J. W. Alvord, 6 May 1869, E. W. Mason, Louisiana School Report, 1 July 1869, Bureau Records, Ed. Div.; *American Missionary* 14 (May 1870): 104.

32. Teacher's Monthly School Reports, February, April 1874, S. S. Ashley to E. M. Cravath, 11 August 1873, AMAA; *American Missionary* 18 (January 1874): 9; *American Missionary* 20 (August 1876): 176; John W. Blassingame, *Black New Orleans: 1860–1880* (Chicago, 1973), 126–28; Richardson, "The American Missionary Association and Black Education in Louisiana," 160–61; New Orleans *Louisianian*, 8 October 1871, 26 October 1872.

33. *Straight University, Charter, Board of Trustees and Faculty* (1870); Blassingame, *Black New Orleans*, 126–27; New Orleans *Louisianian*, 8 October 1871, 26 October 1872; S. Straight to G. Whipple, 5 April 1870, J. T. Newman to E. M. Cravath, 27 October 1873, 22 July 1874, J. T. Newman to C. F. Hart, 26 November 1873, AMAA.

34. Five notable black men—Aristide Mary, Lieutenant Governor Oscar J. Dunn, Fabious Dunn, John R. Clay, and G. H. Fayerweather—served on the board of trustees. Two local black ministers—John Turner, chaplain of the state Senate, and L. D. Satchell—were also on the board. Dr. Louis Charles Roundanez and J. Willis Menard were on the Examining Committee. In 1874 five of the seven members of the trustees' Executive Committee were black.

35. Blassingame, *Black New Orleans*, 129; C. H. Howard to J. W. Alvord, 6 May 1869, E. W. Mason, Louisiana School Report, 1 January 1870, Bureau Records, Ed. Div.; S. S. Ashley to E. M. Cravath, 3 September, 27 December 1873, J. A. Adams to E. M. Cravath, 8 March 1875, J. A. Adams to M. E. Strieby, 15 August 1877, J. W. Healy to My Dear Brother, 9 March 1871, AMAA.

36. J. T. Newman to C. H. Thompson, 25 January 1873, AMAA; New Orleans *Louisianian*, 25 December 1870, 19 February, 16 March, 25, 28 May, 1871, 26 October 1872, 14 December 1878, 5 June 1880, 4 June 1881, 27 May 1882; *American Missionary* 18 (January 1874): 9.

37. C. C. Antoine to M. E. Strieby, 6 February 1877, AMAA; Richardson, "Black Education in Louisiana," 159–60.

38. Charles Dudley Warner, *Studies in the South and West with Comments on Canada* (New York, 1889), 17; Beard, *A Crusade of Brotherhood*, 146–48, 182; Edwin W. Fay, *The History of Education in Louisiana* (Washington, D.C., 1898), 152; New Orleans *Weekly Louisianian*, 4 June 1881.

39. For a detailed study of Atlanta University, see Clarence A. Bacote, *The Story of Atlanta University: A Century of Service, 1865–1965* (Atlanta, 1969); *American Missionary* 13 (November 1869): 245; *American Missionary* 15 (August 1871): 181, 184–85; *American Missionary* 16 (August 1872): 179; *American Missionary* 19 (March 1875): 53–54; Georgia, *Journal of the House of Representatives, 1873*, 31–32; E. A. Ware to E. M. Cravath, 21 January 1874, AMAA; U.S. Commissioner of Education, *Report for the Year 1889–90*, p. 1078.

40. Brownlee, *New Day Ascending*, 185; Suzanne C. Carson, "Samuel Chapman Armstrong: Missionary to the South" (Ph.D. diss., Johns Hopkins University, 1952), 151, 170, 179.

41. Agriculture, blacksmithing, wagon-making, carpentry, tinning, and general home economics were taught. See Clarice T. Campbell, "History of Tougaloo College (Ph.D. diss., University of Mississippi, 1970); Vernon L. Wharton, *The Negro in Mississippi, 1865–1890* (Chapel Hill, 1947), 255; A. D. Mayo, "Industrial Education in the South," *Bureau of Education, Circular of Information No. 5* (Washington, D.C., 1888), 59; Beard, *A Crusade of Brotherhood*, 187.

42. Later Bereans denied that Berea was an AMA school. It had been organized by Fee and Rogers on land donated by Cassius M. Clay, the Kentucky abolitionist. However, Fee and Rogers were both AMA agents, the association paid faculty salaries for years, constantly advertised it as worthy of support, and claimed it as its school. At least the association was a cofounder. J. A. R. Rogers, *Birth of Berea College: A Story of Providence* (Berea, 1933), 24–25; E. Henry Fairchild, *Berea College, Kentucky: An Interesting History* (Cincinnati, 1883), 86.

43. Fee, *Autobiography*, 148–49, 185–87; Peck, *Berea's First Century*, 1–25; John G. Fee, "The Induction of Colored Pupils into Berea College," John G. Fee Papers; John G. Fee to Gerrit Smith, 3 May 1873, G. S. Miller Collection, Syracuse University Library, Syracuse, N.Y.

44. Berea remained coracial until 1904, when Kentucky Law required segregation in all state schools. The segregation statute was appealed to the United States Supreme Court, which decided in favor of Kentucky. Berea then became a white college. Brownlee, *New Day Ascending*, 94.

45. After the Slater Fund was organized, all of the AMA schools introduced some industrial training and they benefited substantially from Slater money. However, such training was generally in addition to rather than in lieu of academic education and was given primarily to intermediate and secondary rather than college students. Between 1883 and 1890 Fisk, Atlanta, Straight, Talladega, Tougaloo, and Tillotson received $52,675 from the Slater Fund. During the same period Hampton received $18,000. Figures taken from the annual *Proceedings of the Trustees of the John F. Slater Fund for the Education of Freedmen, 1884–1890.*

46. Beard, *A Crusade of Brotherhood*, 179; Drake, "American Missionary Association," 205–7; Hotchkiss, "Congregationalists and Negro Education," 291; August Meier, *Negro Thought in America, 1880–1914; Racial Ideologies in the Age of Booker T. Washington* (Ann Arbor, 1963), 88.

47. Even when there was continuity, leadership was often poor. Principals often had little experience in running schools. A colleague of E. A. Ware, head

of Atlanta University, told Ware that he would not remain unless he had definite assigned responsibilities. But he was not optimistic, writing, "As his [Ware's] system is so destitute of system I am afraid he won't appreciate my wishes." T. N. Chase to G. D. Pike, 22 August 1879, AMAA.

48. A. A. Safford to E. M. Cravath, 30 October 1871, AMAA; Campbell, "History of Tougaloo College," 135; "A Brief Statement of the Financial Relation of the American Missionary Association to Fisk University, One of Its Chartered Institutions, 1865–1898," Fiskiana Collection, Fisk University; "Minutes of the Board of Trustees of Fisk University, 21 September 1875," Fisk University.

49. *American Missionary* 13 (December 1869): 270; G. Whipple to E. M. Cravath, 18, 19 August 1874, AMAA.

50. K. S. Mattison to E. M. Cravath, 7 October 1870, A. A. Safford to E. M. Cravath, 14 February 1871, M. T. Ware to E. M. Cravath, 27 April 1874, AMAA; *Fisk News* 5 (February, 1932): 5; I. Welborne Mollison to M. E. Spence, 19 February 1938, S. Brown to Mrs. A. K. Spence, 25 February 1877, Mary E. Spence Collection, Fisk University.

51. DuBois, *Dusk of Dawn*, 30; H. S. Bennett to M. E. Strieby, 30 August 1869, A. K. Spence to D. E. Emerson, 5 September 1874, J. N. Brown to E. M. Cravath, 19, 26 September, 13, 15 October 1870, J. J. Strong to E. M. Cravath, 14, 21 August 1871, B. C. Townsend to AMA, 21 February 1877, AMAA; Drake, "American Missionary Association," 225–26.

52. G. D. Pike to E. M. Cravath, 5 December 1874, AMAA; Brownlee, *New Day Ascending*, 178–80.

53. McPherson, *Abolitionist Legacy*, 66, 80, 201–2; *American Missionary* 20 (January 1876): 2; Jones, *Soldiers of Light and Love*, 138; Litwack, *Been in the Storm So Long*, 478.

54. McPherson, *Struggle for Equality*, 407; *American Missionary* 19 (January 1875): 3; U.S. Commissioner of Education, *Report for the Year 1889–90*, 2:1082.

55. Richardson, *Fisk University*, 160–61, Warner, *Studies in the South*, 17; *American Missionary* 16 (August 1872): 169; Roy, *Pilgrim's Letters*, 170.

56. A total of 1,540 blacks had graduated from southern and border-state colleges by 1890, 577 of them from AMA schools. Of this number, at least 265 were doctors, 28 were ministers, 12 were physicians, 90 were attorneys, and 4 more editors. Others were merchants, government employees, bookkeepers, graduate students, and housewives. At least one, Samuel A. McAlwee, was elected to the Tennessee legislature in 1882. U.S. Commissioner of Education, *Report for the Year 1889–90*, 2:1082; New York *Globe*, 2 February 1884; Bond, *Black American Scholars*, 23.

57. Brownlee, *New Day Ascending*, 181.

Chapter 9. The AMA and the Black Church

1. *American Missionary* 5 (August 1861): 178–79; S. S. Jocelyn to G. Whipple, 20 June 1862, AMAA.

2. *American Missionary* 7 (July 1863): 162; *American Missionary* 8 (October 1864): 234; F. L. Williams to S. S. Jocelyn, 28 April 1863, AMAA; Jones, *Soldiers of Light and Love*, 67; Joe M. Richardson, "The Failure of the American Missionary Association to Expand Congregationalism Among Southern Blacks," *Southern Studies* 18 (Spring 1979): 55.

3. M. E. Burdick to Dear Sir, 4 March 1864, AMAA; Beard, *A Crusade of Brotherhood*, 245; *American Missionary* 12 (January 1868): 8; *American Missionary* 13 (February 1869): 29; Swint, *Dear Ones at Home*, 21–22; Morrow, *Northern Methodism and Reconstruction*, 148.

4. De Boer, "Role of Afro-Americans," 427–28; Stanley, *The Children Is Crying*, 26–27, 40.

5. Stanley, *The Children Is Crying*, 40–41; *American Missionary* 9 (September 1865): 203; W. S. Bell to M. E. Strieby, 24 March 1865, S. W. Magill to Executive Committee, AMA, 3 March 1864, AMAA.

6. L. Tappan to S. C. Peck, n.d. 1864, Lewis Tappan Papers; Morris, *Reading, 'Riting, and Reconstruction*, 64; New York *Tribune*, 25 June 1873.

7. *American Missionary* 10 (July 1866): 155–56; Stanley, *The Children Is Crying*, 52–54.

8. *American Missionary* 11 (September 1867): 204, (January 1868): 1–2; Jones, *Soldiers of Light and Love*, 18.

9. Both Strieby and Whipple had supporters among AMA personnel. In 1865 the Reverend J. E. Roy complained that an AMA missionary had started a Presbyterian church for blacks and accused the association of planting Presbyterian churches with Congregational funds. On the other hand, John G. Fee, an AMA missionary since 1848, was enraged when the association accepted the endorsement of the National Council of Congregationalists in 1865 because, he said, it forsook those who had aided it—in part, because it was undenominational. J. E. Roy to Secretaries Whipple and Strieby, 25 December 1865, AMAA; Fee, *Autobiography*.

10. M. E. Strieby to T. Lyman, 14 February 1865, G. Whipple to M. E. Strieby, 8 June 1867, M. E. Strieby to G. Whipple, 11 June 1867, G. D. Pike to G. Whipple, 11 May 1868, AMAA; *American Missionary* 11 (January 1868): 1–2, 11.

11. *Freedman* 1 (September 1864): 36; T. W. Conway to My Dear Brother, 5 April 1864, AMAA; *American Missionary* 12 (August 1868): 178.

12. The Chattanooga conference also inaugurated the creation of Congregational associations to coordinate churches in the South. The first such associa-

tion was the Louisiana Congregational Association, established in 1870. By 1888 there were nine Congregational conferences in the South. Drake, "American Missionary Association," 125–26; A. N. Niles to E. M. Cravath, 22 September 1874, AMAA.

13. *American Missionary* 15 (July 1871): 147, (December 1871): 276–77, 279.

14. The AMA was admittedly sectarian by the 1870s, but it was not formally joined with the Congregationalists until 1913. Stanley, *The Children Is Crying*, 49; *History of the American Missionary Association*, 45–46.

15. *Advance* 7 (5 February 1874): 12; M. F. Wells to E. M. Cravath, 19 January 1874, J. K. Nutting to E. M. Cravath, 13 May 1873, J. T. Ford to E. M. Cravath, 4 April 1873, AMAA.

16. E. P. Smith to G. Whipple, 11 April 1870, C. H. Thompson to E. M. Cravath, 23 October 1871, S. S. Ashley to E. M. Cravath, 24 September 1873, AMAA.

17. C. W. Sharp to E. P. Smith, 7 January 1869, E. E. Rogers to E. M. Cravath, 10 April 1871, AMAA.

18. Richardson, "The Failure of the American Missionary Association to Expand Congregationalism Among Southern Blacks," 60–61; *American Missionary* 14 (February 1870): 34.

19. F. Haley to E. M. Cravath, 26 September 1874, M. E. Sands to E. M. Cravath, 27 September 1874, W. A. L. Campbell to E. M. Cravath, 1, 14, 20 October 1874, Petition to M. E. Strieby, 10 May 1876, W. A. L. Campbell to M. E. Strieby, 27 May 1876, AMAA.

20. Jones, *Soldiers of Light and Love*, 34; H. Mobley to C. H. Howard, 29 August 1873, L. Mobley to E. M. Cravath, 11 December 1874, AMAA.

21. L. Mobley to E. M. Cravath, 28 October, 8, 11 December 1874, H. Mobley to E. M. Cravath, 15 May, 4, 24 June, 8 July, 17 August, 15 October, 17 November 1874, 22 February 1875, S. S. Jocelyn to E. M. Cravath, 22 May 1875, L. J. McGaffey and S. Keller to E. M. Cravath, 12 February 1875, S. Keller and 17 others to AMA, 1 March 1875, AMAA.

22. *American Missionary* 15 (December 1872): 276.

23. Straight, Talladega, Fisk, and Howard trained most of the theological students. Tougaloo never had many students, and in 1876 President E. A. Ware closed the theological school at Atlanta because he wished to illustrate the nondenominational character of the university.

24. The association made no pretense of producing well-educated theological students. Most were unable to attend the college, but they were given "just as much of books as they can get & yet in addition an idea, a willingness, yea a desire to do anything they can by way of self support." In the fall of 1874 several young ministers intended to enter the theological class as soon as they

could pick and sell their cotton. They would have to leave at planting time. The theological departments were designed to meet insofar as practical a present need. H. E. Brown to E. M. Cravath, 20 January, 29 October 1874, J. N. Brown to E. M. Cravath, 31 October 1874, ÁMAA.

25. O. O. Howard to G. Whipple, 2 August 1870, O. O. Howard Papers; *American Missionary* 15 (June 1871): 133; *American Missionary* 16 (June 1872): 128, (December 1872): 278; *American Missionary* 18 (December 1874): 273; De Boer, "Role of Afro-Americans," 400; *Advance* 7 (5 March 1874): 8; *Advance* 8 (12 November 1874): 199.

26. T. N. Chase to G. D. Pike, 30 July 1877, J. E. Roy to M. E. Strieby, 10 December 1878, AMAA; Richardson, "The Failure of the American Missionary Association to Expand Congregationalism Among Southern Blacks," 64.

27. L. A. Roberts to E. M. Cravath, 11 January 1873, L. A. Roberts to M. E. Strieby, 7 April 1876, R. F. Markham to M. E. Strieby, 24 December 1877, 14, 15 January, 22 March 1878, AMAA.

28. *American Missionary* 15 (December 1871): 175; *American Missionary* 22 (December 1878): 355; Drake, "American Missionary Association," 132–33; David M. Tucker, *Black Pastors and Leaders, 1819–1972* (Memphis, 1975), 41; W. E. B. DuBois (ed.), *The Negro Church* (Atlanta, 1903), 79.

29. In 1890, of the 2,673,997 black church members, only 6,908 were Congregationalists. DuBois, *The Negro Church*, 38.

30. A. N. Niles to M. E. Strieby, 17 February 1876, AMAA.

31. W. A. Golding to M. E. Strieby, 3 December 1875, AMAA; Brownlee, *New Day Ascending*, 219–20.

32. E. P. Smith to M. E. Strieby, 1 July 1865, AMAA; *American Missionary* 14 (March 1870), 58–59.

33. Joseph Washington, Jr., "How Black Is Black Religion?" in James J. Gardiner and J. Deotis Roberts, Sr. (eds.), *Quest for a Black Theology* (Philadelphia, 1971), 31; W. J. Gaines, *The Negro and the White Man* (Philadelphia, 1897), 187–88.

34. DuBois, *The Negro Church*, 58; Tucker, *Black Pastors and Leaders*, 21; Morrow, *Northern Methodism*, 143; Gaines, *The Negro and the White Man*, 187–88; J. Church to E. M. Cravath, 2 March 1874, T. N. Chase to M. E. Strieby, 9 November 1878, AMAA; Litwack, *Been in the Storm So Long*, 461; Jones, *Soldiers of Light and Love*, 142.

35. Morrow, *Northern Methodism*, 146; Tucker, *Black Pastors and Leaders*, 6–7; A. N. Niles to E. M. Cravath, 15 November, 9, 12 December 1873, J. D. Smith to M. E. Strieby, 20 September 1876, J. E. Roy to M. E. Strieby, 18 November 1878, AMAA.

36. Brownlee, *New Day Ascending*, 222–23; C. Wilkins to E. M. Cravath, 21 October 1870, Resolution passed by Plymouth Congregational Church,

Montgomery, Alabama, 17 October 1870, AMAA; Jacqueline S. Haywood, "The American Missionary Association in Louisiana During Reconstruction" (Ph.D. diss., UCLA, 1974), 204; De Boer, "Role of Afro-Americans," 413.

37. *American Missionary* 18 (March 1874): 60–61; *American Missionary* 20 (January 1876): 1–2; *American Missionary* 22 (June 1878): 162.

38. J. A. Shearman to E. P. Smith, 2 December 1867, A. N. Niles to E. M. Cravath, 24 April 1871, R. F. Markham to M. E. Strieby, 18 November 1875, G. W. Andrews to M. E. Strieby, 22 May 1876, AMAA; Stanley, *The Children Is Crying*, 17–18.

39. Morrow, *Northern Methodism*, 132–33; L. A. H. Montague to G. Whipple, 25 August 1865, C. C. Copeland to M. E. Strieby, 1 January 1866, S. W. Stansbury to E. P. Smith, 19 November 1869, S. W. Stansbury to E. M. Cravath, 6 February 1871, J. N. Brown to E. M. Cravath, 30 November 1874, G. W. Andrews to M. E. Strieby, 9 August 1878, AMAA.

40. Joseph Washington, Jr., *Black Religion: The Negro and Christianity in the United States* (Boston, 1966), 30–34.

41. DuBois, *The Negro Church*, 57; Jones, *Soldiers of Light and Love*, 76; Litwack, *Been in the Storm So Long*, 471.

42. E. P. Smith to M. E. Strieby, 21 July 1865, S. W. Magill Report, 10 June 1865, AMAA; A. G. Beaman to G. Whipple, 25 February 1867, Amos G. Beaman Papers, Yale University.

43. L. M. Hagood, *The Colored Men in the Methodist Episcopal Church* (Cincinnati, 1890), 168–69; Morrow, *Northern Methodism*, 136–37; *Flake's Daily Bulletin* (Galveston), 9 June 1867; Washington, D.C., *New Era*, 17 March 1870.

44. Stanley, *The Children Is Crying*, 31.

Chapter 10. Yankee Schoolteachers

1. For recent balanced pictures of Yankee schoolteachers in the South, see Morris, *Reading, 'Riting, and Reconstruction*, 54–84; Butchart, *Northern Schools, Southern Blacks, and Reconstruction*, 115–34; Jones, *Soldiers of Light and Love*, 30–38; Jones, "'A Glorious Work,'" 169–91.

2. Tuscaloosa *Observer*, 21 July 1866; Atlanta *Daily Opinion*, 5 September 1867, quoted in E. Merton Coulter, *The South During Reconstruction, 1865–1877* (Baton Rouge, 1947), 82; Talladega *Alabama Reporter*, 12 July 1866; Alexandria *Louisiana Democrat*, 14 August 1867, quoted in Leon O. Beasley, "A History of Education in Louisiana During the Reconstruction Period, 1862–1877" (Ph.D. diss., Louisiana State University, 1957), 105; W. E. B. DuBois, *The Souls of Black Folk* (New York, 1903), 100; Joseph Earnest, Jr., *The Religious Development of the Negro in Virginia* (Charlottesville, 1904), 113.

3. That only fifteen could be identified as active abolitionists from their applications does not definitely indicate that others were not. Nevertheless, the proportion is probably fairly accurate for AMA teachers. Peck, *Berea's First Century*, 4; B. C. Church to M. E. Strieby, 15 November 1876, AMAA; J. G. Fee to G. Smith, 21 February 1854, G. S. Miller Collection; A. K. Spence to G. Whipple, 6 April 1864, J. Silsby to G. Whipple, 23 May 1865, AMAA; McPherson, *Abolitionist Legacy*, 155.

4. J. Lowrey to S. S. Jocelyn, 22 March 1863, J. F. Sisson to S. S. Jocelyn, 19 May 1863, R. B. Veazie to G. Whipple, 23 March 1864, H. Arnold to S. S. Jocelyn, 24 August 1863, J. Silsby to G. Whipple, 23 May 1865, AMAA.

5. H. S. Beals to S. S. Jocelyn, 26 January, 19 February 1862, H. S. Beals to G. Whipple, 14 April 1865, S. B. Treat, testimonial for Marcia Colton, 26 February 1864, Caroline Wheeler, testimonial for Susan Drummond, 7 January 1863, Emma G. Wood to G. Whipple, 6 November 1863, C. A. Drake to G. Whipple, 5 July 1864, AMAA; Henry L. Swint, *The Northern Teacher in the South, 1862–1870* (Nashville, 1941), 43.

6. William S. McFeely, *Grant: A Biography* (New York, 1981), xiii; J. A. Rockwell to S. Hunt, 26 December 1865, AMAA; S. Hunt to J. A. Rockwell, 13 January 1866, John A. Rockwell Papers; M. J. Conkling to M. E. Strieby, 23 September 1864, G. L. Putnam to E. M. Cravath, 25 December 1871, E. M. Wright to E. M. Cravath, 23 April 1870, AMAA; Jones, *Soldiers of Light and Love*, 8, 42.

7. C. Temple to Dear Brethren, 14 January 1864, L. A. Montague to S. S. Jocelyn, 13 February 1864, AMAA; C. A. R. Briggs to J. W. Alvord, U.S. Army Commands, RG 105, filed under Missouri, Letters received by the Chief Disbursing Officer, National Archives.

8. Jones, "'A Glorious Work,'" 160–64; *American Missionary* 8 (December 1864): 284; *American Missionary* 10 (July 1866): 152; G. Whipple to S. Hunt, 21 June 1866, G. Whipple to S. C. Armstrong, 20 May 1868, AMAA.

9. Maxine D. Jones found that the women teachers in North Carolina averaged thirty-one at the time of their application. Jacqueline Jones determined that in Georgia 76 percent of the female teachers were under thirty-six. Almost 62 percent were thirty-one or under. Jones, "'A Glorious Work,'" 166; Jones, *Soldiers of Light and Love*, 211; A. N. Niles to ?, 16 December 1870, AMAA; George A. Rogers and R. Frank Saunders, Jr., "Eliza Ann Ward, Teacher and Missionary to the Freedmen," *Bulletin of the Congregational Library* 31 (Fall 1979): 7–8.

10. Percentages of number of male and female agents gleaned from teacher lists in the *American Missionary;* Butchart, *Northern Schools, Southern Blacks, and Reconstruction*, 115, 124; *Woman's Work for the Lowly, as Illustrated in the Work of the American Missionary Association Among the Freedmen* (Boston, 1873), 11; Beard, *Crusade of Brotherhood*, 231–32.

11. Information about teaching experience has been gleaned from hundreds of letters of application in the American Missionary Association Archives. C. Little to Whom It May Concern, 20 December 1866, O. S. Dean to Whom It May Concern, 12 December 1866, P. M. Trowbridge statement, 22 December 1866, Eliza A. Summers Papers.

12. The Joneses were correct: New England teachers dominated in North Carolina and Georgia, but not for the South as a whole. New England sent more teachers to the seaboard states, while the Midwest sent more to the interior. States under the supervision of Cincinnati and Chicago offices naturally had more teachers from that area. Beginning in 1866 the *American Missionary* annually listed teachers and their home states. The numbers from each state from 1866 to 1880 are as follows: Ohio 347, Massachusetts 265, New York 229, Connecticut 136, Illinois 131, Wisconsin 93, Michigan 87, Maine 62, Vermont 43, New Hampshire 21, New Jersey 19, Kansas 3, Nebraska 2, and Oregon 1. There were a number of association teachers from the South, usually black teachers trained in AMA schools. Numbers gathered from list of teachers in the *American Missionary.*

13. H. S. Beals to S. S. Jocelyn, 19 February 1862, G. Saxe to G. Whipple, 1 March 1864, I. Pettibone to S. Hunt, 14 November 1866, J. Kimball to E. P. Smith, 23 November 1869, AMAA; Morris, *Reading, 'Riting, and Reconstruction*, 68; Sherer, "Let Us Make Men," 325.

14. Rogers, *Birth of Berea College*, 87; Richardson, *Fisk University*, 2; Statement about Enoch K. Miller in Enoch K. Miller Papers; undated statement about Ayer in AMAA.

15. J. G. Fee to G. Whipple, 3 February 1865, AMAA.

16. A. ? to E. P. Smith, 22 December 1869, A. Williams to M. E. Strieby, 16 September 1876, J. S. Spencer to E. M. Cravath, 5 July 1872, AMAA.

17. A. N. Niles to E. M. Cravath, 5 May 1871, E. A. Ware to E. P. Smith, 8 November 1867, G. N. Greene to S. S. Jocelyn, 25 July 1863, M. A. Warren to E. M. Cravath, 24 August 1872, T. N. Chase to M. E. Strieby, 3 May 1877, AMAA.

18. Others suffered from poor health before their arrival in the South. Mrs. A. H. Warren, who was sent to Missouri, claimed to have been a virtual invalid for eight years. Another was described as a "pious Christian lady, but the *flesh is* very weak." F. E. Webster to S. Hunt, 6 March 1866, S. S. Ashley to G. Whipple, 6 August 1866, A. N. Niles to E. M. Cravath, 8 February 1872, G. W. Andrews to M. E. Strieby, 11 July 1875, D. E. Emerson statement on letter from A. D. Ludlow to M. E. Strieby, n.d. January 1881, H. James to My Dear Bro., 16 January 1864, W. T. Richardson to G. Whipple, 24, 31 January, 17 June 1865, AMAA; W. A. Britton to E. K. Miller, 3 April 1867, Enoch K. Miller Papers.

19. W. T. Briggs to G. Whipple, 4 May 1864, H. James to My Dear Brother,

26 August 1864, H. D. Lyman to G. Whipple, 13 September 1864, C. B. Wilder to G. Whipple, 28 March 1864, J. S. Taylor to Dear Sir, 28 March 1864, AMAA.

20. J. F. Sisson to G. Whipple, 7 March 1864, A. Baker to S. Hunt, 31 January 1866, S. H. Champney to E. P. Smith, 29 March 1869, AMAA.

21. In 1869 Helen Leonard became too sick to remain at her post in Americus, Georgia. The AMA superintendent at Macon said, "I think the devotion at *Americus* last year permanently impaired her health." He added that last year's teachers at Milledgeville were also overburdened, "the result, the half sick overworked teachers there now." J. A. Rockwell to E. P. Smith, 9 February 1869, AMAA; E. W. Douglass to My Dear Niece, 1 April 1871, E. M. Robinson to My Dear Sister, 27 July 1875, Esther W. Douglass Papers, Amistad Research Center; J. A. Shearman to E. P. Smith, 4, 7 March 1867, T. Adams to E. Rutt, 7 May 1869, D. I. Miller to H. Hubbard, 13 November 1877, AMAA.

22. F. Campbell to G. Whipple, 9 January 1865, A. R. Wilkins and M. Burke to E. P. Smith, 31 October 1868, J. P. Bardwell to M. E. Strieby, 24 February 1865, H. F. Tradewell to E. M. Cravath, 10 March 1873, E. K. Miller to J. R. Shipherd, 15 January 1868, P. M. Lee and J. N. Cooke to E. P. Smith, 1 April 1869, M. C. Owen to E. P. Smith, 28 October 1869, J. A. Rockwell to S. Hunt, 11 April 1866, A. Baker to G. Whipple, 22 February, 1 March 1865, AMAA; A. C. Pierce to Bro. E. K. Miller, 3 May 1867, Enoch K. Miller Papers; Jones, "'A Glorious Work,'" 183.

23. E. L. Boring to E. P. Smith, 26 January 1868, S. S. Ashley to S. Hunt, 7 March, 9 January 1866, Mrs. H. S. Beals to S. Hunt, 31 January 1866, J. A. Shearman to E. P. Smith, 7 March 1867, H. M. Leonard to D. E. Emerson, 15 October 1875, C. Merrick to E. P. Smith, 24 November 1868, AMAA; George W. Clower (ed.), "Some Sidelights on Education in Georgia in the 1860's," *Georgia Historical Quarterly* 37 (September 1953): 253.

24. D. Peebles to M. E. Strieby, 1 April 1878, C. L. Woodworth to Secretaries of AMA, n.d. 1866, F. L. Cardozo to S. Hunt, 2 December 1865, E. L. Boring to E. P. Smith, 26 January 1868, AMAA.

25. C. H. Howard to E. P. Smith, 9 April 1869, J. K. Warner to W. Whiting, 13 December 1867, AMAA; E. A. Summers to My Dear Sister, 12 February 1867, Eliza A. Summers Papers.

26. Northern whites' belief that they were more vulnerable to hot weather diseases than were southerners may have been partially true in the case of malaria. Whites living in malaria-free regions are easily susceptible to all types of malaria. Evidence suggests that patients who survive a malaria attack develop a relative immunity to the particular strain which caused the infection. The immunity is incomplete and can wear off, resulting in attacks years later. And, of course, the victim may still get a different strain of malaria.

27. William P. Vaughan, *Schools for All: The Blacks and Public Education*

in the South, 1865–1877 (Lexington, Ky., 1974), 27; J. A. Shearman to W. E.
Whiting, 6 February, 13 June 1867, AMAA.

28. C. B. Wilder to G. Whipple, 23 July 1862, E. James to S. S. Jocelyn, 6
February 1864, T. A. McMasters to G. Whipple, 25 June 1864, A. R. Wilkins to
E. P. Smith, 3 August 1867, J. P. Stone to S. S. Jocelyn, 17 November 1863,
C. P. Day to G. Whipple, 22, 27 September 1864, 23 February 1865, AMAA.

29. S. A. Walker to G. Whipple, 28 September 1864, W. T. Richardson to G.
Whipple, 22 June, 23 July 1864, W. L. Eaton to G. Whipple, 10 October 1866,
H. James to G. Whipple, 14 March 1864, E. F. Rowe to M. E. Strieby, 10, 23
July 1875, M. H. Clary to E. M. Cravath, 26 December 1871, M. A. Warren to
E. M. Cravath, 19 May 1871, T. Lyman to G. Whipple, 14 October 1864, M. F.
Wells to E. M. Cravath, 20 October, 3 November 1873, B. Root to E. M.
Cravath, 26 September 1873, M. E. H. Pope to E. M. Cravath, 30 September
1873, W. H. Ash to M. E. Strieby, 31 October 1878, H. Jennie Halleck to D. E.
Emerson, 8 March 1877, AMAA; *American Missionary* 18 (January 1874): 16,
21.

30. H. Dodd to W. E. Whiting, 10 January 1864, S. S. Ashley to E. P.
Smith, 22 May 1867, AMAA; Jones, "'A Glorious Work,'" 110.

31. Rogers and Saunders, "Eliza Ann Ward," 8; Sherer, "Let Us Make
Men," 324–25; Crogman quoted in George A. Towns, "William Henry Crogman," *Journal of Negro History* 19 (April 1934): 217; Esther W. Douglass autobiography, typescript, Esther W. Douglass Papers; Huntsville *Gazette*, 6 June
1885; Swint, *Northern Teacher*, 45.

32. Room and board and travel expense cost the association more than salaries. It estimated that expense for each teacher was $200 per annum in 1863
and increased to between $300 and $500 in 1866. *American Missionary* 7 (December 1863): 275; Jones, "'A Glorious Work,'" 175.

33. S. G. Stanley to G. Whipple, 13 January 1865, H. R. Daggett to G.
Whipple, 30 January 1865, E. P. Worthington to W. E. Whiting, 9 February
1865, N. E. Parmenter to W. E. Whiting, 9 February 1865, L. M. Pinney to G.
Whipple, 1 September 1864, E. H. Alden to G. Whipple, 24 June 1864, AMAA.

34. Most teachers apparently took a salary cut to join the AMA, but often it
was quite small. Lizzie A. Gilmore was teaching in Massachusetts for fourteen
dollars a month and board. L. A. Gilmore to G. Whipple, 29 July 1864, AMAA.

35. J. Corey to W. E. Whiting, 18 August 1865, H. Leonard to M. E.
Strieby, 16 October 1875, M. D. Williams to W. E. Whiting, 5 November 1864,
M. N. Withington to E. P. Smith, 5 May 1868, S. S. Straight to G. Whipple, 5
April 1870, AMAA.

36. Jones, "'A Glorious Work,'" 175; G. Stanley Pope to M. E. Strieby, 15
February 1877, M. McAssey to M. E. Strieby, 1 June 1876, AMAA.

37. Clower, "Some Sidelights on Education in Georgia in the 1860's," 253;

Clarice T. Campbell, "The Founding of Tougaloo College" (M.A. thesis, University of Mississippi, 1967), 108–9; H. Andrews to D. E. Emerson, 24 May 1876, E. M. Pierce to E. P. Smith, 4 December 1868, J. E. Roy to M. E. Strieby, 10 December 1878, AMAA.

38. J. P. Bardwell to G. Whipple, 10 March, 11 April 1866, S. G. Wright to W. E. Whiting, 21 April 1866, E. M. Cravath to E. P. Smith, 12 July 1867, C. W. Francis to E. M. Cravath, 11 June 1874, E. M. Pierce to E. P. Smith, 30 July 1869, J. T. Ford to E. M. Cravath, 4 April 1873, G. Whipple to E. M. Cravath, 10 February 1874, AMAA.

39. C. W. Sharp to E. P. Smith, 21 January, 16, 30 April 1869, J. P. Stone to S. S. Jocelyn, 10 February 1864, AMAA.

40. G. W. Walker to E. M. Cravath, 3 May 1873, AMAA; Richardson, *Fisk University*, 20; A. Robinson to J. D. Burrus, 26 September 1876, America W. Robinson Letters, Fisk University Library.

41. J. A. Bassett to E. P. Smith, 23 December 1868, L. Tappan to G. Whipple, 16 October 1867, AMAA; *American Missionary* 11 (November 1867): 244.

42. G. L. Putnam to M. E. Strieby, 1 June 1869, T. W. Cardozo to S. Hunt, 23 June 1865, C. M. Murray to D. E. Emerson, 3 July 1876, AMAA; Jones, *Soldiers of Light and Love*, 30.

43. William T. Briggs, Annual Report of the Superintendent of Colored Schools in North Carolina, July 1865, A. Winsor to G. Whipple, 10 July 1864, M. Chase to Jennie, 14 September 1870, G. W. Walker to E. M. Cravath, 3 May 1873, AMAA.

44. Smith, *A History of the African Methodist Episcopal Church*, 93; J. F. Sisson to G. Whipple, 26 March 1866, A. Williams to M. E. Strieby, 9 September 1876, M. E. Sands to E. M. Cravath, 15 September 1873, AMAA; Carson, "Samuel Chapman Armstrong," 129, 145, 183–84.

45. Rogers and Saunders, "Eliza Ann Ward," 9; *American Missionary* 7 (October 1863): 234; George M. Frederickson, *The Black Image in the White Mind: The Debate on Afro-American Character and Destiny, 1817–1914* (New York: 1972), 101–2.

46. Frederickson, *Black Image in the White Mind*, 125; S. K. Hyde to W. E. Whiting, 28 February 1862, AMAA; McPherson, *Abolitionist Legacy*, 68–69, 201–2.

Chapter 11. Black Teachers and Missionaries

1. S. G. Stanley to G. Whipple, 4 March 1864, L. C. Lockwood to Dear Brethren, 4 October 1862, W. H. Woodbury to S. S. Jocelyn, 7, 10 December 1863, AMAA; Engs, *Freedom's First Generation*, 47.

2. L. A. Grimes to S. S. Jocelyn, 9 October 1863, J. G. Fee to M. E. Strieby, 30 May 1865, AMAA; De Boer, "Role of Afro-Americans," 228–29.

3. J. Oliver to W. L. Coan, 5 February 1862, W. L. Coan to S. S. Jocelyn, 3 May 1862, L. A. Grimes statement, 3 May 1862, L. C. Lockwood to Dear Brethren, 20 May 1862, J. Oliver to S. S. Jocelyn, 6 July, 17 December 1862, 14, 26 January, 11 May 1863, G. Whipple to T. H. Lathrop, 9 June 1863, AMAA.

4. T. DeS. Tucker to G. Whipple, 24 December 1862, G. Whipple to S. S. Jocelyn, 19 January 1864, AMAA; De Boer, "Role of Afro-Americans," 264–65.

5. W. T. Richardson to G. Whipple, 24 January 1865, J. G. Fee to M. E. Strieby, 30 May 1865, AMAA; *Twenty-fourth Annual Report of the American Missionary Association*, 4.

6. There were a number of white AMA teachers whose prejudice caused them to think that most blacks were incompetent, but the secretaries did not appear to be so afflicted. Indeed, they believed that genuinely competent teachers were rare, regardless of color. S. Hunt to Mrs. Hogeboom, 30 November 1866, AMAA.

7. E. P. Smith to M. E. Strieby, 28 April 1866, E. P. Smith to J. Ogden, 2 May 1866, AMAA; *American Missionary* 11 (April 1867): 78; *American Missionary* 13 (May 1869): 98; *American Missionary* 14 (June 1870): 123; Washington, D.C., *New Era*, 16 June 1870.

8. G. C. Booth to AMA, 28 April 1864, W. A. Jones to G. Whipple, 14 October 1868, M. E. Watson to M. E. Strieby, 20 October 1864, W. D. Harris to M. E. Strieby, 26 July 1865, AMAA.

9. H. H. Hunter and L. Hunter to Ex. Committee AMA, 25 February 1865, S. L. Daffin to G. Whipple, 1 January 1865, AMAA; Jones, "'A Glorious Work,'" 194.

10. De Boer, "Role of Afro-Americans," 406, 492–93; C. Duncan to G. Whipple, 1 March 1864, S. Stanley to G. Whipple, 19 January 1864, T. D. S. Tucker to G. Whipple, 22 February 1864, J. T. Duryea to Who It May Concern, 21 May 1864, M. P. Dascomb to G. Whipple, 19 September 1864, AMAA.

11. Horst, "Education for Manhood," 135, 149; De Boer, "Role of Afro-Americans," 110–13, 124–25, 253–62; E. Johnson and Others to Dear Brethren, 5 May 1866, C. H. Churchill to AMA, 17 October 1862, L. Tappan to G. Whipple, 5 July 1865, AMAA.

12. J. A. Adams to E. M. Cravath, 1 February 1875, C. J. Thompson to E. M. Cravath, 7 December 1874, J. T. Newman to E. M. Cravath, 22 July 1874, T. W. Cardozo to My Dear Friends in the Rooms, 17 August 1865, F. L. Cardozo to G. Whipple and M. E. Strieby, 18 August 1865, C. L. Woodworth to AMA, n.d. 1866, AMAA; De Boer, "Role of Afro-Americans," 424.

13. William Harris was ordained in 1865, at which time Bishop Daniel A. Payne of the A.M.E. church and George Whipple made an agreement that the AMA would continue to support Harris but would send him where he could also direct an A.M.E. church. This arrangement continued until he was sent to the District of Columbia in 1867. W. D. Harris to G. Whipple, 3 September 1865, 3 May 1867, AMAA.

14. W. D. Harris to G. Whipple, 3 September 1865, 3 May 1867, D. A. Payne to G. Whipple, 1 September 1865, AMAA; Westin, "The State and Segregated Schools," 28–29; Jones, "'A Glorious Work,'" 196–97, 201; Helen M. Chestnutt, *Charles Waddell Chesnutt: Pioneer of the Color Line* (Chapel Hill, 1952), 5, 8–9.

15. J. J. Wright to M. E. Strieby, 27 July, 15 August, 6 September 1865, J. J. Wright to S. Hunt, 25, 28 September, 4 December 1865, 5 February, 2 March 1866, J. J. Wright to E. P. Smith, 25 June 1869, AMAA.

16. E. G. Highgate statement, 18 January 1864, M. E. Strieby to S. S. Jocelyn, 27 January 1864, D. H. Crittenden testimonial for Highgate, 26 January 1864, E. G. Highgate to S. S. Jocelyn, 30 January 1864, E. G. Highgate to G. Whipple, 1 June 1864, C. Duncan to G. Whipple, 2 October 1864, E. G. Highgate to G. Whipple, 15 October 1864, W. E. Whiting to E. G. Highgate, 19 December 1864, E. G. Highgate to M. E. Strieby, 1 March 1865, E. G. Highgate to G. Whipple, 13 April 1865, AMAA.

17. E. G. Highgate to M. E. Strieby, 8 February, 17 December 1866, 24 September 1867, 30 January 1868, 11 May 1870, undated, unidentified newspaper clipping, AMAA.

18. J. Scollard to J. W. Healy, 1 January 1872, N. A. Ramsey to C. H. Howard, 6 October 1871, 10 January 1874, M. E. Watson to M. E. Strieby, 20 October 1864, M. E. Watson to L. Tappan, 1 September 1864, M. E. Watson to M. E. Strieby, n.d. April 1865, AMAA.

19. M. E. Watson to S. Hunt, 17 April, 6 July, 31 December 1866, J. Haines and nine others to AMA, 17 August 1868, M. E. Watson to E. P. Smith, 30 April 1869, 22 August 1870, J. Haines and six others to AMA, 10 July 1869, AMAA; W. A Low, "The Freedmen's Bureau and Education in Maryland," *Maryland Historical Magazine* 47 (March 1952): 29–39.

20. L. Tappan to G. B. Wilcox, 21 November 1864, Lewis Tappan Papers; *American Missionary* 13 (May 1869): 98; J. W. Alvord, *Tenth Semi-Annual Report on Schools for Freedmen, July 1, 1870* (Washington, D.C., 1870), 37; De Boer, "Role of Afro-Americans," 280; M. W. Martin to Editor, Washington, D. C., *New National Era and Citizen,* 29 May 1873; W. Epps and others to M. E. Strieby, 10 May 1876, W. A. L. Campbell to E. M. Cravath, 25 October 1874, A. Rowe to E. M. Cravath, 1 June 1865, J. W. Fleming to E. M. Cravath, 18 July 1875, F. Snelson to M. E. Strieby, 19 July 1875, W. A. Golding to M. E.

Strieby, 30 July 1875, J. W. Martin and others to G. Whipple, 18 August 1868, AMAA.

21. E. G. Highgate to G. Whipple, 1 June 1864, T. W. Cardozo to S. Hunt, 23 June 1865, F. L. Cardozo to S. Hunt, 13 January 1866, F. L. Cardozo to E. P. Smith, 8 June 1867, AMAA.

22. De Boer, "Role of Afro-Americans," 492; T. W. Cardozo to M. E. Strieby, 16 June, 18 July 1865, W. O. Weston to T. W. Cardozo, 24 June 1865, F. L. Cardozo to S. Hunt, 3 November 1866, AMAA.

23. W. T. Richardson to G. Whipple, 10 January 1865, J. P. Bardwell to M. E. Strieby, 5 January 1865, S. G. Wright to G. Whipple, 17 April 1865, A. Scofield to M. E. Strieby, 1 November 1864, J. G. Longley to M. E. Strieby, 18 March, 5 April 1865, M. A. Day to AMA, n.d. August 1865, AMAA.

24. J. H. H. Sengstacke to E. M. Cravath, 17 July 1875, A. Rowe to E. M. Cravath, n.d. June 1875, D. E. Emerson to M. E. Strieby, 7 December 1875, R. F. Markham to M. E. Strieby, 4 December 1876, AMAA; De Boer, "Role of Afro-Americans," 405–6.

25. De Boer, "Role of Afro-Americans," 488–91; J. T. Ford to M. E. Strieby, 16 July 1875, A. W. Farnham to Dear Brother, 5 June 1876, C. C. Scott to M. E. Strieby, 31 August 1877, E. A. Lawrence to M. E. Strieby, 31 August 1877, J. Adams to M. E. Strieby, 14 August 1877, AMAA.

26. E. Garrison Jackson to S. S. Jocelyn, 11 April 1865, E. Garrison Jackson to S. Hunt, 13 April 1866, W. Steward to E. P. Smith, 24 June 1869, AMAA.

27. T. DeS. Tucker to Dear Friends of the Association, 27 November 1862, H. S. Beals to G. Whipple, 28 February 1865, M. E. Watson to M. E. Strieby, n.d. 1865, S. A. Walker to G. Whipple, 28 March 1864, AMAA; *American Missionary* 8 (May 1864): 123; *American Missionary* 14 (December 1870): 283; W. H. Woodbury to ?, 22 March 1864, U.S. Army Continental Commands, Department of Virginia; F. L. Cardozo to W. E. Whiting, 31 August 1866, AMAA.

28. E. Garrison Jackson to W. E. Whiting, 9 May, 1 August 1866, E. Garrison Jackson to S. Hunt, 21 May 1866, W. A. L. Campbell to E. M. Cravath, 21 June 1875, W. A. L. Campbell to D. E. Emerson, 7 February 1876, AMAA.

29. S. A. Walker to W. H. Woodbury, 9 July 1864, M. M. Reed to G. Whipple, 18 July 1864, S. G. Stanley to W. H. Woodbury, n.d. July, 6 October 1864, W. H. Woodbury to G. Whipple, 28 September 1864, A. Wilkins to G. Whipple, 20 October 1864, W. L. Coan to Secretaries of A. M. Association, 27 July 1864, W. D. Harris to G. Whipple, 15 April 1864, R. G. C. Patten to G. Whipple, 14 May 1864, C. Duncan to G. Whipple, 1 April 1865, AMAA.

30. B. V. Harris to G. Whipple, 23 January, 10 March 1866, J. P. Bardwell to G. Whipple, 2, 20 March, 11, 21 April 1866, J. P. Bardwell to S. Hunt, 22 June

1866, P. Litts to S. G. Wright, 7 March 1867, S. G. Wright to G. Whipple, 26, 27 April 1866, P. Litts to G. Whipple, 27 April 1866, AMAA.

31. Jones, "'A Glorious Work,'" 207–11; S. S. Ashley to S. Hunt, 22 January 1866, AMAA.

32. R. F. Markham to M. E. Strieby, 5, 15 March, 15, 20 June 1877, J. T. Ford to E. M. Cravath, 17 April 1875, M. E. Shaw to E. M. Cravath, 25 May 1877, A. Williams to E. M. Cravath, 18 July 1873, AMAA.

33. J. T. Ford to E. M. Cravath, 17 April 1875, M. A. Warren to E. P. Smith, 3 September 1870, A. W. Farnham to M. E. Strieby, 19 August 1878, AMAA.

34. J. L. Power to M. E. Strieby, 20 July 1877, G. Stanley Pope to M. E. Strieby, 31 July 1877, J. A. Adams to M. E. Strieby, 14 August 1877, A. Lynch to M. E. Strieby, 9 November 1875, AMAA.

35. M. F. Wells to M. E. Strieby, 28 December 1876, AMAA; De Boer, "Role of Afro-Americans," 698–99; McPherson, *Abolitionist Legacy*, 273.

Chapter 12. The AMA and the White Community

1. T. E. Tate, a former Mississippi slaveholder, told General O. O. Howard in mid-1866 that the North was wrong if it thought unionism was growing in the South. Fear had created many pretended unionists, "but so soon as it was found that there was no danger whatever in sailing under the old colors they changed their bearing." T. E. Tate to O. O. Howard, 16 July 1866, O. O. Howard Papers; A. J. Evans to J. L. M. Curry, 7 October 1865, J. L. M. Curry Papers, Library of Congress; T. A. McMasters to G. Whipple, 1 November 1865, C. S. Martindale to G. Whipple, 4 December 1865, AMAA.

2. Shakspeare Allen to O. O. Howard, 8 February 1866, T. E. Tate to O. O. Howard, 16 July 1866, O. O. Howard Papers; *American Missionary* 10 (May 1866): 114; *American Missionary* 11 (February 1867): 26–27; F. Ayers to S. Hunt, 2 June 1866, W. P. Russell to M. E. Strieby, 3 August 1865, S. S. Straight to G. Whipple, 4 June 1866, AMAA; Joseph Warren, Mississippi School Report, 15 November 1865, T. K. Noble, Kentucky School Report, 1 January 1868, Bureau Records, Ed. Div.

3. U.S. Congress, *House Reports*, 39th Cong., 2d Sess., No. 30, pt. 2:99, 112, 135, 166; A. C. Pierce to E. K. Miller, 3 May 1867, Enoch K. Miller Papers; Richmond *Times*, 16 January 1866, quoted in W. Henry Brown, *The Education and Economic Development of the Negro in Virginia* (Charlottesville, 1923), 43; W. J. Purman to A. H. Jackson, 9 September 1867, Bureau Records, Florida, unentered narrative reports. A Louisiana newspaper was less playful

than the Richmond *Times* in its opposition to freedmen's education. "Nigger schools," the editor wrote, "It is worse than throwing money away to give it to the education of niggers." Livingston *Herald*, 16 February 1870, quoted in Beasley, "A History of Education in Louisiana During the Reconstruction Period," 167.

4. *American Missionary* 11 (June 1867): 133; Linda Warfel Slaughter, *The Freedmen of the South* (Cincinnati, 1869), 130–31; John P. McConnell, *Negroes and Their Treatment in Virginia from 1865 to 1867* (Pulaski, Va., 1910), 92–93.

5. Horace Mann Bond, *Social and Economic Influences on the Public Education of Negroes in Alabama, 1865–1930* (Washington, D.C., 1939), 119; Jones, *Soldiers of Light and Love*, 77; L. Abbott to O. O. Howard, 8 August 1865, O. O. Howard Papers; C. A. Briggs to Miss Dodge, 4 January 1864, M. W. Martin to M. E. Strieby, 25 December 1875, AMAA; Myrta L. Avary, *Dixie After the War: An Exposition of Social Conditions Existing in the South During the Twelve Years Succeeding the Fall of Richmond* (New York, 1906), 312.

6. A. C. Harwood to G. Whipple, 1 December 1865, H. M. Jones to S. G. Wright, 13 January 1866, S. G. Wright to G. Whipple, 24 March 1866, M. B. Hanson to E. M. Cravath, 2 March 1871, E. A. Ware to E. P. Smith, 28 November 1868, F. A. Sawlett to E. P. Smith, 1 December 1868, AMAA; H. H. Moore to T. W. Osborn, 25 February 1866, Bureau Records, Florida, letters received; M. Farrar to E. K. Miller, 2 September 1867, Enoch K. Miller Papers; U.S. Congress, *House Executive Documents*, 39th Cong., 1st Sess., No. 120, pp. 30–31; T. K. Noble, Kentucky School Report, 13 October 1868, Bureau Records, Ed. Div.; *American Missionary* 11 (May 1867): 104, (June 1867): 137.

7. F. A. Seely to J. W. Alvord, 4 November 1868, J. Warner, Mississippi School Report, 15 November 1865, W. M. Colby to J. W. Alvord, 16 July 1867, Bureau Records, Ed. Div.; O. M. Dorman, "Diary and Notes," 29 April 1865, O. M. Dorman Diary and Notes, Library of Congress; Talladega *Sun*, 19 April 1870; S. W. Stansbury to E. M. Cravath, 6 February 1871, AMAA.

8. *American Missionary* 11 (May 1867): 111; *American Missionary* 13 (July 1869): 149, (January 1869): 15–16; H. C. Foote to AMA, n.d. December 1865, S. Russell to E. P. Smith, 30 Janaury 1869, S. H. Champney to E. P. Smith, 30 January 1869, AMAA; Slaughter, *Freedmen of the South*, 142; Charles Stearns, *The Black Man of the South, and the Rebels or the Characteristics of the Former and the Recent Outrages of the Latter* (New York, 1872), 132; J. Warren, Mississippi School Report, 15 November 1865, Bureau Records, Ed. Div.

9. M. Close to S. Hunt, 31 May, 27 June 1866, AMAA; *American Missionary* 10 (September 1866): 200.

10. H. J. Ward to G. Whipple, 17 May 1864, A. Baker to S. Hunt, 31 January 1866, D. Todd to G. Whipple, 4 June 1864, AMAA; *American Missionary* 12 (June 1868): 126; E. W. Douglass to Dear Niece, 30 January 1874, Esther W. Douglass Papers; McPherson, *Abolitionist Legacy*, 182.

11. M. Farrar to E. K. Miller, 21 September, 14 November 1867, Enoch K. Miller Papers; George Teamoh Journal, 1881–1883, Carter G. Woodson Collection of Negro Papers and Related Documents, Library of Congress; M. F. Wells to M. E. Strieby, 9 August 1876, AMAA.

12. W. L. Coan to G. Whipple, 7 May 1863, L. A. Montague to S. S. Jocelyn, 28 July 1864, J. F. Sisson to G. Whipple, 7 March 1864, R. Harris to G. Whipple, 1 April 1865, C. A. Briggs to G. Whipple, 2 February 1865, AMAA; J. Ogden to C. B. Fisk, 8 March 1866, Fiskiana Collection; J. M. Bell to B. F. Butler, 3 December 1863, Benjamin F. Butler Papers.

13. *American Missionary* 11 (March 1867): 55; *American Missionary* 8 (July 1864): 174; W. Porter to M. E. Strieby, 14 October 1865, G. N. Greene to G. Whipple, 14 June 1865, W. T. Briggs to G. Whipple, 13 December 1864, AMAA; Memphis *Avalanche* quoted in *American Missionary* 10 (August 1866): 74, (June 1866): 135; U.S. Congress, *House Reports*, 39th Cong., 1st Sess., No. 101, pp. 92–93.

14. Engs, *Freedom's First Generation*, 87; *American Missionary* 11 (March 1867): 51, 56–57, (May 1867): 105; E. M. Cravath to G. Whipple, 4 December 1866, J. P. Bardwell to G. Whipple, 26, 28 April, 4 May 1866, AMAA.

15. A. O. Warren to J. P. Bardwell, 6 May 1866, AMAA; Slaughter, *Freedmen of the South*, 129–30.

16. No doubt some white southerners favored black education if kept in their own hands, but ostracism of and violence against southern white teachers of blacks was not unknown. Stetson Kennedy, *Palmetto Country* (New York, 1942), 95; M. E. Dyer to E. P. Smith, 28 December 1868, AMAA; E. A. Ware, Georgia School Report, 4 October 1867, Bureau Records, Ed. Div.

17. Joel Williamson, *After Slavery: The Negro in South Carolina During Reconstruction, 1861–1877* (Chapel Hill, 1965), 216; C. W. Buckley, Alabama School Report, 24 October 1866, Bureau Records, Ed. Div.; Harrisburg (Va.) *Rockingham Register*, 15 December 1865; Mobile *Nationalist*, 11 January 1866; Marion (Ala.) *Commonwealth*, 26 January 1871; Georgia, *Fourth Annual Report of the State School Commission Submitted to the General Assembly of the State of Georgia, at Its Session January 1875* (Savannah, 1875), 24.

18. G. L. Eberhart to S. Hunt, 4 June 1866, L. M. Peck to E. P. Smith, 21 June 1867, J. F. Caflin to E. M. Cravath, 28 January 1874, AMAA; Kenneth B. White, "Relief, Labor and Education: Some Aspects of the Alabama Freedmen's Bureau, 1865–1870" (M.A. thesis, Florida State University, 1969), 109.

19. *American Missionary* 10 (June 1866): 135; M. J. Welch to S. Hunt, 1

May 1866, G. L. Eberhart to S. Hunt, 7 May 1866, J. E. Bryant to AMA, 12 June 1866, D. Tillson to G. Whipple, 4 July 1866, W. Baker to G. Whipple, 25 February, 9 March 1865, D. N. Goodrich to M. E. Strieby, 25 February 1865, C. A. R. Briggs to My Dear Friends, 4 March 1865, AMAA.

20. Litwack, *Been in the Storm So Long*, 491–92; *American Missionary* 11 (January 1867): 19; McPherson, *Abolitionist Legacy*, 15; L. A. Darling to M. E. Strieby, 25 July 1876, E. M. Bassett to M. S. Cook, 3 May 1871, AMAA.

21. Minutes of the Berea College Board of Trustees, 1 July 1872, quoted in Loesch, "Kentucky Abolitionist," 192; De Boer, "Role of Afro-Americans," 423; S. E. Russell to G. Whipple, 7 May 1868, F. Haley to E. M. Cravath, 29 June 1874, W. Epps and twelve others to E. M. Cravath, M. E. Strieby and G. Whipple, 30 June 1874, AMAA; U.S. Commissioner of Education, *Report for the Year 1874* (Washington, D.C., 1875), 74.

22. Drake, "American Missionary Association," 220–22; De Boer, "Role of Afro-Americans," 572–73, L. Tappan to G. Whipple, 18 June 1862, C. B. Fisk to E. M. Cravath, 5 June 1872, AMAA; *American Missionary* 9 (December 1865): 273; (November 1865): 241; L. Tappan to J. Tappan, 18 March 1865, L. Tappan to W. Armistead, 17 May 1865, Lewis Tappan Papers.

23. G. Whipple to O. O. Howard, 22 December 1866, O. O. Howard Papers; S. Straight to G. Whipple, 3 March 1866, M. E. Strieby to G. Whipple, 12 May 1868, AMAA; *American Missionary* 12 (September 1868): 202, (November 1868): 250.

24. Butchart, *Northern Schools, Southern Blacks, and Reconstruction*, 159; Morris, *Reading, 'Riting, and Reconstruction*, 180; E. E. Adlington to E. P. Smith, 1 August 1868, M. B. Hanson to E. M. Cravath, 24 December 1870, M. Waterbury to E. M. Cravath, 1 April 1872, AMAA; Talladega *Sun*, 5 July 1870; *American Missionary* 10 (January 1866): 7.

25. A. A. Safford to E. M. Cravath, 7 April 1872, R. F. Markham to M. E. Strieby, n.d. November 1877, T. Lyman to S. W. Magill, 9 June 1865, I. Pettibone to W. Whiting, 31 May 1867, J. A. Shearman to E. P. Smith and G. Whipple, 24 February 1868, E. B. Eveleth to E. M. Cravath, 29 October 1872, S. M. Coles to M. E. Strieby, 22 February 1877, AMAA; *American Missionary* 14 (January 1870): 7; Washington, D.C., *New Era*, 28 April 1870.

26. James G. Hamilton, *Reconstruction in North Carolina* (New York, 1914), 616; Alabama, *House Journal 1868–1869*, 561; Alabama, *Senate Journal, 1869–1870*, 175; Marion *Commonwealth*, 27 February 1868, 19, 26 January, 13 April 1871; J. Silsby to W. Swayne, 13 April 1867, J. Silsby to W. H. Smith, 29 June 1867, General Wager Swayne Papers, Alabama Department of Archives and History, Montgomery; Mobile *Nationalist*, 11 July, 26 September, 9 January 1868; Selma *Southern Argus*, 18 August 1869; Washington, D.C., *New National Era and Citizen*, 14 August 1873; Chattanooga *Daily*

Republican, 9 January 1868; J. Silsby to E. M. Cravath, 9 April 1874, S. Blanchard to G. Whipple, 11 March 1867, E. E. Adlington to E. P. Smith, 25 December 1869, A. W. Rogers to G. Whipple, 30 September 1864, W. P. M. Gilbert to E. P. Smith, 1 November 1869, J. A. Bassett to E. P. Smith, 1 December 1869, AMAA.

27. Many assistant commissioners associated increased white violence with black political participation. See, for example, C. H. Foster to G. Whipple, 16 September 1868, AMAA; Frank R. Chase, Louisiana School Report, 19 June 1867, William M. Colby, Arkansas School Report, 1 April 1868, Bureau Records, Ed. Div.

28. The Mississippi Klan was probably the most active of any of the state Klans against schools. Apparently opposition was to paying taxes for free schools as well as hostility to northern teachers and black education. In Monroe County twenty-six schools were closed and the county superintendent was whipped by the Klan. U.S. Congress, *House Reports*, 42d Cong., 2d Sess., No. 22, vol. 1, pt. 11, pp. 282–83; Mississippi, *Biennial Report of the Departments and Benevolent Institutions of the State of Mississippi for the Year 1870–1871*, pp. 184–85.

29. *American Missionary* 13 (October 1869): 229–30; *American Missionary* 14 (January 1870): 9, (October 1870): 237; *American Missionary* 18 (September 1874): 209; J. R. Lewis, Georgia School Report, 1 January 1870, Bureau Records, Ed. Div.; R. H. Gladding to E. P. Smith, 27 September 1869, C. W. Washburn to E. M. Cravath, 24 July 1874, A. G. Marment to E. M. Cravath, 4 July 1874, AMAA; Rogers, *Birth of Berea*, 115; Austin *State Gazette*, 13 August 1874; Marion *Commonwealth*, 21 July 1870.

30. The AMA sent rifles and revolvers to Talladega and rifles to T. C. Steward in Marion, Alabama, after the Klan threatened to assassinate him and other "carpetbaggers." Steward said he conferred with his friends and they concluded that "nothing can be gained by our being murdered by these devils. We cannot see that mankind would be benefitted in the *least* by such a sacrifice, and we are not particularly anxious to gain a reputation in that manner." T. C. Steward to E. M. Cravath, 8 February, 5, 7 April 1871, AMAA; U.S. Congress, *Senate Miscellaneous Documents*, 40th Cong., 3d Sess., No. 10, pp. 1–4; Memorial of the American Missionary Association, praying the adoption of measures for the protection of loyal persons in the South in the enjoyment of their civil rights, December 1868, Sen. 40A-H10.2, U.S. Senate Records referred to Judiciary Committee, National Archives; McPherson, *Abolitionist Legacy*, 56.

31. Esther W. Douglass autobiography, Esther W. Douglass Papers; Sherer, "Let Us Make Men," 308; J. H. Simmons to E. P. Smith, 1 June 1869, 23 August 1869, J. N. Bishop to E. M. Cravath, 27 March 1871, J. N. Bishop to

M. E. Strieby, 9 November 1875, D. E. Emerson to E. M. Cravath, 6 December 1873, J. M. Cumings to E. M. Cravath, 2 January 1874, J. Silsby to E. M. Cravath, 9 April 1874, G. L. White to E. M. Cravath, 6 December 1871, AMAA.

32. J. E. Beigle to E. M. Cravath, 29 October 1870, M. F. Wells to E. M. Cravath, 21 July 1871, AMAA; *American Missionary* 19 (June 1875): 123.

33. Schools burned were: Norfolk, Virginia, school and church for second time, 1872; Emerson Institute, Mobile, Alabama, 1876; Lewis High School, Macon, Georgia, 1876; Straight University, New Orleans, 1877; Beach Institute, Savannah, 1878; Hampton Institute Academic Hall, Hampton, Virginia, 1879; Talladega College barns, Talladega, Alabama, 1880; Tougaloo College men's dormitory, Tougaloo, Mississippi, 1881; Emerson Institute, second time, 1882; and Connecticut Industrial School, Quitman, Georgia, 1885. Drake, "American Missionary Association," 225–26.

34. J. L. M. Curry to R. C. Winthrop, 14 July 1881, J. L. M. Curry Papers.

35. G. N. Greene to S. S. Jocelyn, 23 October 1863, H. S. Beals to E. P. Smith, 30 April 1867, AMAA; Jones, "'A Glorious Work,'" 259–60.

36. G. N. Greene to S. S. Jocelyn, 23 October 1863, A. Baker to S. Hunt, 18 November 1865, S. A. Hosmer to Honored Father, 1 September 1863, J. Sisson to G. Whipple, 31 December 1863, H. S. Beals to G. Whipple, 27 February 1864, E. Douglass to Secretaries of AMA, 14 January 1865, J. W. Duncan to G. Whipple, 1 April 1864, W. D. Harris Monthly Teachers Report, June 1864, T. A. McMasters to G. Whipple, 20 May 1864, AMAA; *American Missionary* 11 (March 1867): 51–52, (August 1867): 185, (September 1867): 195.

37. *American Missionary* 10 (April 1866), 78–79; H. S. Beals to E. P. Smith, 20 October 1866, H. Thompson to G. Whipple, n.d. March 1867, AMAA.

38. For a detailed treatment of the controversy over the AMA's white school in Beaufort, see Jones, "'A Glorious Work,'" 232–38, 267–72; Litwack, *Been in the Storm So Long*, 489.

39. C. B. Whitcomb to G. Whipple, 21 June 1864, J. H. Merrifield to G. Whipple, 9 June 1864, E. Gill to S. S. Jocelyn, 11 January 1864, M. C. Milligan to S. Hunt, 31 July 1866, E. B. Eveleth to E. P. Smith, 22 November, 2 December 1867, AMAA; *American Missionary* 13 (August 1869): 175–76; *American Missionary* 11 (October 1867): 223–24.

40. As long as Fee and Fairchild were in charge, equality was a goal, but Berea's racial program began to change in 1892 with the inauguration of William G. Frost as president. Paul David Nelson, "Experiment in Interracial Education at Berea College, 1858–1908," *Journal of Negro History* 59 (January 1974): 13–14.

41. J. G. Fee to M. E. Strieby, 9 June 1865, AMAA; Beard, *A Crusade of Brotherhood*, 101–4; Rogers, *Birth of Berea*, 100; *American Missionary* 10 (November 1866): 247, (December 1866): 279; *American Missionary* 11 (October 1867): 217, 228; *American Missionary* 12 (August 1868): 172; *American Missionary* 13 (January 1869): 14–15, (August 1869): 172; J. G. Fee to G. Smith, 18 November 1873, G. S. Miller Collection.

Chapter 13. The AMA and the Black Community

1. G. N. Greene to W. E. Whiting, 8 February 1864, W. T. Briggs to G. Whipple, 9 July 1864, A. Baker to S. Hunt, 17 May, 15, 30 November 1865, P. M. Lee and J. N. Cooke to E. P. Smith, 1 April 1869, P. M. Lee to W. E. Whiting, 17 April 1869, AMAA; *American Missionary* 13 (December 1869): 270; *American Missionary* 9 (March 1865): 51.

2. J. Silsby to G. Whipple, 2 November 1865, M. E. Hanson to E. M. Cravath, 5 December 1870, M. E. Lands to E. P. Smith, 5 May 1868, C. M. Semple to E. M. Cravath, 6 October 1871, AMAA; *American Missionary* 10 (February 1866): 33; Bond, *Black American Scholars*, 39.

3. L. Tappan to W. G. Kephart, 27 February 1862, S. S. Jocelyn to G. Whipple, 8 March 1862, L. Tappan to G. Whipple, 15 March 1862, C. B. Wilder to G. Whipple, 20 March 1865, G. Whipple, H. W. Beecher, W. Patton and J. C. Eldridge Petition to President Andrew Johnson, 1 November 1865, AMAA; *American Missionary* 9 (August 1865): 183, (December 1865): 266, 268–69.

4. Tappan flyer in AMAA; *American Missionary* 10 (February 1866): 28; Jones, "'A Glorious Work,'" 64.

5. Gerteis, *From Contraband to Freedman*, 47; McPherson, *Struggle for Equality*, 413; H. C. Vogell, North Carolina School Report, 16 July 1870, Bureau Records, Ed. Div.; Drake, "American Missionary Association," 118–19; *American Missionary* 16 (September 1872): 193; Sherer, "Let Us Make Man," 51; C. M. Blood to E. M. Cravath, 10 February 1874, A. Blood to C. M. Blood, n.d. May 1872, S. W. Stansbury to E. P. Smith, 29 January 1870, R. Richards to E. P. Smith, 12, 15 February, 24 May, 9 June 1870, M. D. Ayers to E. P. Smith, 13 March 1867, AMAA; Jones, *Soldiers of Light and Love*, 165–66.

6. Jones, "'A Glorious Work,'" 213–16; *American Missionary* 7 (June 1863): 139; D. Todd to G. Whipple, 31 December 1864, 1 February, 1 April 1865, AMAA.

7. *American Missionary* 11 (May 1867): 100; *American Missionary* 10 (April 1866): 75; E. Whipple to E. P. Smith, 18 July 1867, Teachers Monthly School Report, Monticello, Florida, January 1870, AMAA; Mobile *Nationalist*,

25 April 1867, quoted in Bond, *Social and Economic Influences on Public Education*, 118; G. Whipple to O. O. Howard, 30 July 1867, Bureau Records, Ed. Div.

8. E. B. Eveleth to E. M. Cravath, 25 February 1871, 27 March 1872, A. Rowe to E. M. Cravath, 7 September 1874, A. G. Marment to E. M. Cravath, 20 March 1874, 8 January 1875, AMAA; Jones, "'A Glorious Work,'" 223.

9. J. G. Fee to M. E. Strieby, 9 June 1865, H. S. Beals to S. Hunt, 30 July 1866, E. Whipple to E. P. Smith, 17 June 1867, AMAA.

10. D. Peebles to H. W. Hubbard, 23 July 1877, AMAA; Litwack, *Been in the Storm So Long*, 493; Jones, "'A Glorious Work,'" 225.

11. H. S. Beals to W. E. Whiting, 10 August 1865, AMAA; *American Missionary* 11 (July 1867): 148; Resolution at a Public Meeting of the Colored Citizens of Milledgeville, Ga. held 6 October, 1869, copy in O. O. Howard Papers; McPherson, *Abolitionist Legacy*, 194; H. M. Leonard to E. M. Cravath, 7 October 1872, AMAA; E. W. Douglass to L. C. Adams, 18 April 1872, Esther W. Douglass Papers.

12. L. A. Woodbury to S. S. Jocelyn, 10 September 1863, C. B. Wilder to Dear Brethren, 9 September 1863, AMAA; U.S. Congress, *House Executive Documents*, 39th Cong., 1st Sess., No. 120, p. 18; Engs, *Freedom's First Generation*, 77–78; Whitelaw Reid, *After the War: A Southern Tour* (New York, 1866), 144–45; "The Freedmen at Port Royal," *North American Review* 208 (July 1865): 5.

13. P. Litts to S. G. Wright, 7 March 1866, B. Harris to G. Whipple, 10 March 1866, J. A. Shearman to E. P. Smith, 2 December 1867, S. W. Stansbury to E. M. Cravath, 11 October 1871, L. A. Darling to M. E. Strieby, 22 April 1867, AMAA; Alexandria (Va.) *People's Advocate*, 10 June, 1, 29 July, 19, 26 August 1876; Washington, D.C., *People's Advocate*, 9 August 1879.

14. McPherron and his wife befriended a student in Swayne School whom they intended to send North. She visited their home often, and McPherron gave her music lessons. When in the summer of 1874 Mrs. McPherron went North, her husband remained in Montgomery and continued to give the young woman music lessons. Talk was started apparently by girls who were jealous of the attention the music student received. When confronted, the girls admitted they were lying and confessed in church. Nevertheless, a mob gathered at McPherron's house and demanded he accompany them. Finally the minister's wife and Mrs. McPherron, now returned, talked the men into leaving. Mrs. H. W. Andrews to E. M. Cravath, 17 June 1875, G. W. Andrews to M. E. Strieby, 11 July 1875, AMAA.

15. Engs, *Freedom's First Generation*, 77–78; A. Baker to S. Hunt, 1 March 1866, C. W. Francis to E. M. Cravath, 11 June 1874, T. N. Chase to

E. M. Cravath, 26 December 1874, M. E. Stewart to E. M. Cravath, 4 January 1871, AMAA; New Orleans *Semi-Weekly Louisianian*, 28 May 1871.

16. D. Burt, Tennessee School Report, 3 October 1867, C. H. Foster to J. W. Alvord, 18 July 1868, J. R. Lewis, Georgia School Report, 1 January 1870, Bureau Records, Ed. Div.; L. Parsons to E. M. Cravath, 1 March 1871, AMAA; A. G. Beaman to G. Whipple, 25 February 1867, Amos G. Beaman Papers; Richard H. Cain quoted in Litwack, *Been in the Storm So Long,* 493.

17. Jones, *Soldiers of Light and Love*, 50; M. E. Strieby to G. Whipple, 3 December 1864, W. T. Briggs to G. Whipple, 5 June 1865, AMAA; De Boer, "Role of Afro-Americans," 360–63.

18. J. L. Richardson to S. S. Jocelyn, 19 December 1863, L. A. Montague to S. S. Jocelyn, 26 April 1864, G. Candee to S. S. Jocelyn, 8, 15, 26 April, 1, 22 June 1864, AMAA.

19. W. T. Richardson to G. Whipple, 10 January, 24 February 1865, S. W. Magill to Secretaries AMA, 7, 26 February, 10 June 1865, T. Lyman to ?, n.d. August 1865, AMAA; Jones, *Soldiers of Light and Love*, 71, 76.

20. Association teachers in Macon thought blacks were responding to Frederick Douglass's 4 July 1875 speech at Hillsdale, Virginia, declaring black independence of northern benevolent associations. "We propose to cut loose from all invidious class institutions and to part company with all those wandering mendicants who have followed us simply for paltry gain," Douglass said. "And we now bid an affectionate farewell to all those plunderers, and in the future if we need a Moses we will find him in our own Tribe." Douglass wrote the AMA, saying his remarks did not apply to it. Although he differed with some of the association's religious beliefs, he said, he had always and still recognized it as laboring honestly and successfully for blacks. Douglass speech quoted in New Orleans *Weekly Louisianian*, 17 July 1875; *American Missionary* 19 (September 1875): 197–98; *American Missionary* 20 (September 1876): 208.

21. G. W. Andrews to M. E. Strieby, 11 July 1875, A. Lynch to M. E. Strieby, 26 October 1875, Macon Committee of Correspondence to M. E. Strieby, 7 December 1875, E. A. Ware to E. M. Cravath, 25 October 1870, E. P. Smith to C. H. Howard, 2 April 1870, AMAA.

22. D. Ford to E. M. Cravath, 25 September 1873, C. W. Washburn to E. M. Cravath, 20 October 1874, M. W. Martin to M. E. Strieby, 29 April 1876, M. O. Beals to M. E. Strieby, 6 November 1875, S. A. Mather to M. E. Strieby, 7 December 1875, 23 May 1876, O. O. Reynolds to G. Whipple, 23 June 1876, S. L. Smith to E. M. Cravath, 17 August, 8 September 1875, S. S. Ashley to M. E. Strieby, 31 July 1876, AMAA; Howard N. Rabinowitz, "Half a Loaf: The Shift from White to Black Teachers in the Negro Schools of the Urban

South, 1865–1890," *Journal of Southern History* 40 (November 1974): 565,
579; Larry W. Pearce, "The American Missionary Association and the Freedmen's Bureau in Arkansas, 1868–1878," *Arkansas Historical Quarterly* 31
(Autumn 1972): 252–53.

23. C. Noble to M. E. Strieby, 16 May 1876, A. Krokel to Sec. AMA, 31
August 1874, T. N. Chase to M. E. Strieby, 4 July 1878, AMAA; Washington,
D.C., *New National Era and Citizen*, 23 October 1873; *Christian Recorder*
quoted in New Orleans *Weekly Louisianian*, 21 August 1875; Butchart,
Northern Schools, Southern Blacks, and Reconstruction, 176; Jones, "'A
Glorious Work,'" 228–32; Westin, "The State and Segregated Schools," 5–6.

24. A. E. Howe to E. P. Smith, 31 March 1868, A. Baker to G. Whipple, 10
January 1865, R. F. Markham to M. E. Strieby, 7 December 1875, AMAA;
Litwack, *Been in the Storm So Long*, 453, 455; Jones, *Soldiers of Light and
Love*, 67, 143; Lawrence N. Powell, *New Masters: Northern Planters During
the Civil War and Reconstruction* (New Haven, 1980), 119–20.

25. Free blacks occasionally preferred white or light black teachers. The
Freedmen's Bureau sent a former free black community a black teacher. They
treated him "very coldly," and some refused to send their children. The Bureau withdrew the teacher and left them without a school. After a few weeks
the village leader went to the Bureau and asked for a teacher. He said he did
not care how black he was as long as he could teach children. R. M. Manley,
Virginia School Report, 1 January 1870, Bureau Records, Ed. Div.

26. Litwack, *Been in the Storm So Long*, 478; *American Missionary* 9 (September 1865): 199; H. S. Beals to G. Whipple, 28 February, 31 March 1865,
AMAA; Esther W. Douglass autobiography, Esther W. Douglass Papers.

27. D. M. Walcott to Dear Sir, 6 November 1868, D. Todd to G. Whipple, 1
February 1865, M. F. Wells to M. E. Strieby, 28 December 1876, AMAA;
Jones, *Soldiers of Light and Love*, 142; Butchart, *Northern Schools, Southern
Blacks, and Reconstruction*, 55; McPherson, *Abolitionist Legacy*, 64.

28. *American Missionary* 17 (May 1873): 108; *American Missionary* 18
(April 1874): 85.

29. *American Missionary* 19 (April 1875): 73; *American Missionary* 20
(June 1876): 123; *American Missionary* 33 (January 1879): 6; Mrs. G. W. An-
drews to D. E. Emerson, 7 November 1876, R. F. Markham to M. E. Strieby,
5 March, 5 December 1877, W. S. Alexander to M. E. Strieby, 30 March 1877,
AMAA; H. C. Morgan to Mrs. A. K. Spence, 9 November 1876, Mary E.
Spence Collection.

30. *American Missionary* 33 (January 1879): 4–5.

31. *American Missionary* 20 (January 1876): 1–2; *American Missionary* 33
(July 1879): 193, (January 1879): 1; *American Missionary* 20 (June 1876): 123.

32. McPherson, *Abolitionist Legacy*, 118–19; *American Missionary* 32

(June 1878): 162; *American Missionary* 36 (August 1882): 228–30; *American Missionary* 39 (July 1885): 189–91; E. A. Ware to D. E. Emerson, 15 June 1877, D. E. Emerson to M. E. Strieby, 26 November 1875, T. N. Chase to M. E. Strieby, 26 November 1877, AMAA; Horace Bumstead, "The Freedmen's Children at School," *Andover Review* 4 (December 1885): 555; Charles E. Jones, *Education in Georgia* (Washington, D.C., 1889), 146.

Afterword

1. Jones, *Soldiers of Light and Love,* 111; Drake, "Freedmen's Aid Societies and Sectional Compromise," 185–86.

2. Mayo, "Work of Certain Northern Churches in the Education of the Freedmen, 1861–1900," 285; De Boer, "Role of Afro-Americans," 3; Bond, *Black American Scholars,* 23–24, 41–42; Henry Allen Bullock, *A History of Negro Education in the South from 1619 to the Present* (Cambridge, 1967), 30; DuBois, *Black Reconstruction,* 667.

3. Clifton H. Johnson, "The American Missionary Association: A Short History," in *Our American Missionary Association Heritage* (New York, 1966), 38.

4. Butchart, *Northern Schools, Southern Blacks, and Reconstruction,* xii–xiii, 6.

5. Brownlee, *New Day Ascending,* 228, 236–37, 247; Johnson, "The American Missionary Association: A Short History," 37–38; Jacksonville *Florida Times-Union,* 23 October 1896.

Bibliography

Manuscripts

American Missionary Association Archives. Amistad Research Center, New Orleans.

Bacon Family Papers. Sterling Library, Yale University, New Haven, Conn.

Amos G. Beman Papers. Beinecke Library, Yale University, New Haven, Conn.

David French Boyd Papers. Department of Archives and Manuscripts, Louisiana State University, Baton Rouge.

Bureau of Refugees, Freedmen and Abandoned Lands. Educational Division. National Archives, Washington, D.C.

Benjamin F. Butler Papers. Library of Congress, Washington, D.C.

Simon Cameron Papers. Library of Congress, Washington, D.C.

Salmon P. Chase Papers. Library of Congress, Washington, D.C.

George B. Cheever Papers. American Antiquarian Society, Worcester, Mass.

J. L. M. Curry Letters in Daniel C. Gilman Collection. Milton S. Eisenhower Library, Johns Hopkins University, Baltimore.

J. L. M. Curry Papers. Library of Congress, Washington, D.C.

Esther Douglass Papers, 1865–1915. Amistad Research Center, New Orleans. Original in Rackham Library, University of Michigan, Ann Arbor.

E. H. Fairchild Papers. Hutchins Library, Berea College, Berea, Ky.

John G. Fee Papers. Hutchins Library, Berea College, Berea, Ky.

Fisk University, Faculty and Staff Letters. Fisk University Library, Nashville.

Fisk University, Letters of the Board of Trustees. Fisk University Library, Nashville.

Fisk University, Minutes of the Board of Trustees, 24 August 1867–April 1900. Fisk University Library, Nashville.

Fisk University, Minutes of the Executive Committee, 1875–1890. Fisk University Library, Nashville.

Fiskiana Collection, includes manuscripts, pamphlets, brochures, pictures, scrapbooks and newspaper clippings. Fisk University Library, Nashville.

William Godell Papers, Hutchins Library, Berea College, Berea, Ky.

J. M. and Esther Hawks Papers. Library of Congress, Washington, D.C.

C. H. Howard Papers. Hawthorne-Longfellow Library, Bowdoin College, Brunswick, Me.

O. O. Howard Papers. Hawthorne-Longfellow Library, Bowdoin College, Brunswick, Me.

Henrietta Matson Letter Press, January 1873–March 1876. Fisk University Library, Nashville.

Enoch K. Miller Papers. Arkansas Historical Commission, Little Rock.

G. S. Miller Collection. Syracuse University Library, Syracuse, N.Y.

James Pearson Newcomb Collection, 1839–1941. Barker Texas History Center, University of Texas, Austin.

Frederick Law Olmsted Papers. Library of Congress, Washington, D.C.

Records of U.S. Army Continental Commands, Department of Virginia. Record Group 393. National Archives, Washington, D.C.

Whitelaw Reid Papers. Library of Congress, Washington, D.C.

America Robinson Letters. Fisk University Library, Nashville.

John A. Rockwell Papers. Amistad Research Center, New Orleans.

Ella Sheppard Diary, 7 November 1874–14 November 1876. Fisk University Library, Nashville.

Edwin C. Silsby Papers. Talladega College Historical Collection, Talladega College, Talladega, Ala.

Thomas C. Steward Letter Press, November 1872–October 1874. Fisk University Library, Nashville.

Eliza A. Summers Papers. South Caroliniana Library, University of South Carolina, Columbia.

Superintendent of Education Correspondence, South Carolina, 1869–1876. South Carolina Department of Archives and History, Columbia.

Wager Swayne Papers. Alabama Department of Archives and History, Montgomery.

Talladega College, Minutes of the Prudential Committee, 19 December 1887–15 January 1891. Talladega College Historical Collection, Talladega College, Talladega, Ala.

Lewis Tappan Papers. Library of Congress, Washington, D. C.

Charles Henry Thompson Papers. Amistad Research Center, New Orleans.

George L. White Letter Press, September 1868–September 1871. Fisk University Library, Nashville.

Charles B. Wilder Papers in Todd Family Papers. Sterling Library, Yale University, New Haven, Conn.

Government Documents

Alabama *Report of the Judiciary Committee* to whom was Referred the "Resolution of Inquiry into Alleged Illegal Use, or Unlawful application of the Public Money, or any part of the school fund for Mobile County, or other Public Fund." Montgomery: John G. Stokes and Co., 1870.

Mayo, A. D. "Common School Education in the South from the Beginning of the Civil War to 1870–1876," in *Report of the United States Commissioner of Education for the Years 1900–1901.* 2 vols. Washington, D.C.: U.S. Government Printing Office, 1901.

————. "Industrial Education in the South," Bureau of Education, Circular of Information No. 5, 1888. Washington: Government Printing Office, 1888.

————. "Work of Certain Northern Churches in the Education of the Freedmen, 1861–1900," *Report of the United States Commissioner of Education for 1901–1902.* 2 vols. Washington: Government Printing Office, 1902.

Miller, Kelly. "The Education of the Negro," in *Report of the United States Commissioner of Education for the Year 1900–1901.* Vol. 1. Washington: Government Printing Office, 1902. Pp. 731–859.

Parmalee, Julius H. "Freedmen's Aid Societies, 1861–1871" in *Negro Education: A Study of the Private and Higher Schools for Colored People in the United States,* U.S. Department of Interior, Bureau of Education *Bulletin,* 1916. Nos. 38, 39. 2 vols. Pp. 268–95. Washington: Government Printing Office, 1917.

U.S. Commissioner of Education. *Report for the Years 1870–1890.* Washington: Government Printing Office, 1870–1893.

Newspapers

Alexandria (Va.) *People's Advocate,* 1876–1884.

Augusta *Colored American,* 1865–1866.

Augusta *Loyal Georgian,* 1866–1868.

Bee (District of Columbia), 1882–1885.

Berea Evangelist, 1885–1886.

Galveston *Flake's Bulletin,* 1865–1872.

Huntsville *Gazette,* 1881–1887.

Louisiana Sugar Bowl (New Iberia, La.), 1873–1876.

Marion (Ala.) *Commonwealth,* 1865–1871.

Nashville *Colored Tennessean,* 1865–1866.

New National Era (District of Columbia), 1870–1874.

New Orleans *Louisianian,* 1870–1872.

New Orleans *Tribune*, 1864–1869.
New Orleans *Weekly Pelican*, 1886–1889.
Richmond *Planet*, 1885–1895.
Richmond *Virginia Star*, 1877–1881.
Savannah *Weekly Echo*, 1888–1894.
Selma *Southern Argus*, 1869–1871.
Talladega *Alabama Reporter*, 1865–1869.
Talladega *Sun*, 1869–1871.

Journals

Advance. Vols. 7–14 (1873–1879).
American Freedman. Vols. 1–2 (1866–1869).
American Missionary. Vols. 1–43 (1857–1900).
Christian Union. Vols. 4–11 (1871–1875).
Fisk Expositor. Vols. 1–5 (1878–1882).
Fisk Herald. 1878–1905.
Freedmen's Advocate. Vols. 1–2 (1864–1865).
Freedmen's Record. Vols. 1–5 (1865–1868).
Missionary Reporter. Vol. 1 (1867–1868).
National Freedman. Vols. 1–2 (1865–1866).
Southern Sentinel. Vols. 1–5 (1877–1881).
Southern Workman. Vols. 2–10 (1873–1881).

Books

Abbott, Martin. *The Freedmen's Bureau in South Carolina, 1865–1872*. Chapel Hill: University of North Carolina Press. 1967.
Armstrong, M. F., and Helen W. Ludlow. *Hampton and Its Students*. New York: G. P. Putnam's Sons, 1874.
Armstrong, Samuel Chapman. *Armstrong's Ideas on Education for Life*. Hampton, Va.: Hampton Institute Press, 1940.
Atkins, Gaius G., and Fred L. Fagley. *History of American Congregationalism*. Boston: Pilgrim Press, 1942.
Bacote, Clarence A. *The Story of Atlanta University*. Atlanta: Atlanta University Press, 1969.
Beard, Augustus Field. *A Crusade of Brotherhood: A History of the American Missionary Association*. Boston: Pilgrim Press, 1909.
Blassingame, John W. *Black New Orleans: 1860–1880*. Chicago: University of Chicago Press, 1973.

Bond, Horace Mann. *Black American Scholars: A Study of Their Beginnings.* Detroit: Balamp Publishing, 1972.

———. *Social and Economic Influences on the Public Education of Negroes in Alabama, 1865–1930.* Washington, D.C.: Associated Publishers, 1939.

Broderick, Francis L. *W. E. B. DuBois: Negro Leader in a Time of Crisis.* Stanford: Stanford University Press, 1959.

Brownlee, Fred L. *New Day Ascending.* Boston: Pilgrim Press, 1946.

Bullock, Henry Allen. *A History of Negro Education in the South from 1619 to the Present.* Cambridge: Harvard University Press, 1967.

Butchart, Ronald E. *Northern Schools, Southern Blacks, and Reconstruction: Freedmen's Education, 1862–1875.* Westport, Conn.: Greenwood Press, 1980.

Carpenter, John Alcott. *Sword and Olive Branch.* Pittsburgh: University of Pittsburgh Press, 1964.

Chesnutt, Helen M. *Charles Waddell Chesnutt: Pioneer of the Color Line.* Chapel Hill: University of North Carolina Press, 1952.

Douglass, Harlan Paul. *Christian Reconstruction in the South.* New York: Pilgrim Press, 1909.

DuBois, W. E. B. *The Autobiography of W. E. B. DuBois: A Soliloquy on Viewing My Life from the Last Decade of Its First Century.* New York: International Publishers Co., 1968.

———, ed. *The Negro Church: Report of a Social Study Made Upon the Direction of Atlanta University . . .* Atlanta: Atlanta University Press, 1963.

———. *The Souls of Black Folk.* New York: A. C. McClurg & Co., 1903.

Earnest, Joseph B., Jr. *The Religious Development of the Negro in Virginia.* Charlottesville: Michie Company Printers, 1914.

Engs, Robert F. *Freedom's First Generation: Black Hampton, Virginia, 1861–1890.* Philadelphia: University of Pennsylvania Press, 1979.

Evans, Matilda A. *Martha Schofield: Pioneer Negro Educator.* Columbia, S.C.: Dupree Printing Company, 1916.

Fairchild, E. Henry. *Berea College, Kentucky: An Interesting History.* Rev. ed. Cincinnati: Elm Street Printing Co., 1883.

Fairchild, James H. *Oberlin: The Colony and the College, 1833–1883.* Oberlin: E. J. Goodrich, 1883.

Fee, John G. *Autobiography of John G. Fee, Berea, Kentucky.* Chicago: National Christian Association, 1891.

Fischer, Roger A. *The Segregation Struggle in Louisiana, 1862–77.* Urbana: University of Illinois Press, 1974.

Fosdick, Raymond B. *Adventure in Giving: The Story of the General Education Board.* New York: Harper and Row, 1962.

Fredrickson, George. *The Black Image in the White Mind: The Debate on*

Afro-American Character and Destiny, 1817–1914. New York: Harper and Row, 1971.

French, A. M. *Slavery in South Carolina and the Ex-Slaves; or The Port Royal Mission*. New York: W. M. French, 1862.

Gaines, W. J. *The Negro and the White Man*. Philadelphia: A.M.E. Publishing House, 1897.

Genovese, Eugene D. *Roll, Jordan, Roll: The World the Slaves Made*. New York: Pantheon Books, 1974.

Gerteis, Louis S. *From Contraband to Freedman: Federal Policy Toward Southern Blacks, 1861–1865*. Westport, Conn.: Greenwood Press, 1973.

Gutman, Herbert G. *The Black Family in Slavery and Freedom, 1750–1925*. New York: Pantheon, 1976.

Higginson, Thomas W. *Army Life in a Black Regiment*. Boston: Fields, Osgood & Co., 1870.

Historical Sketch of Berea College, Together with Addresses in Its Behalf. New York: David Nicholson, Printer, 1869.

Holmes, Dwight O. W. *The Evolution of the Negro College*. New York: Columbia University, 1934.

Holt, Thomas. *Black Over White: Negro Political Leadership in South Carolina During Reconstruction*. Chicago: University of Illinois Press, 1977.

Hopkins, Alphonso A. *The Life of Clinton Bowen Fisk*. New York: Funk and Wagnalls, 1890.

Howard, Gene L. *Death at Cross Plains: An Alabama Reconstruction Tragedy*. University, Ala.: University of Alabama Press, 1984.

Howard, Oliver Otis. *Autobiography of Oliver Otis Howard, Major General, United States Army*. 2 vols. New York: Baker & Taylor Company, 1907.

Howard, Victor B. *Black Liberation in Kentucky: Emancipation and Freedom, 1862–1884*. Lexington: University of Kentucky Press, 1983.

Imes, William Lloyd. *The Black Pastures*. Nashville: Hemphill Press, 1957.

Jaquette, Henrietta Stratten, ed. *South After Gettysburg: Letters of Cornelia Hancock, 1863–1868*. New York: Thomas Y. Crowell, 1956.

Jones, Jacqueline. *Soldiers of Light and Love: Northern Teachers and Georgia Blacks, 1865–1873*. Chapel Hill: University of North Carolina Press, 1980.

Levine, Lawrence W. *Black Culture and Black Consciousness*. Oxford: Oxford University Press, 1977.

Lincoln, C. Eric. *The Black Experience in Religion*. New York: Anchor Press, 1974.

Litwack, Leon. *Been in the Storm So Long: The Aftermath of Slavery*. New York: Alfred A. Knopf, 1979.

Logan, Rayford W. *Howard University, 1867–1967*. New York: New York University Press, 1969.

McCulloch, Margaret C. *Fearless Advocate of the Right: The Life of Francis Julius Lemoyne, M.D.* Boston: Christopher Publishing House, 1941.

McFeely, William S. *Yankee Stepfather: General O. O. Howard and the Freedmen.* New Haven: Yale University Press, 1968.

McKim, James Miller. *The Freedmen of South Carolina.* Philadelphia: Willis P. Hazard, 1862.

McKinney, Richard I. *Religion in Higher Education Among Negroes.* New Haven: Yale University Press, 1945.

McMillan, Lewis K. *Negro Higher Education in the State of South Carolina.* Orangeburg, S.C.: South Carolina A&M College, 1951.

McPherson, James M. *The Abolitionist Legacy: From Reconstruction to the NAACP.* Princeton: Princeton University Press, 1975.

————. *The Struggle for Equality: Abolitionists and the Negro in the Civil War and Reconstruction.* Princeton: Princeton University Press, 1964.

Marsh, J. B. T. *The Story of the Jubilee Singers with Their Songs.* 3d ed. London: Hodder and Stoughton, 1876.

Martin, Josephine W., ed. *"Dear Sister": Letters Written on Hilton Head Island, 1867.* Beaufort, S.C.: Beaufort Book Co., 1977.

Mears, David O. *Life of Edward Norris Kirk, D.D.* Boston: Lockwood, Brooks and Co., 1877.

Meier, August. *Negro Thought in America, 1880–1915: Racial Ideologies in the Age of Booker T. Washington.* Ann Arbor: University of Michigan Press, 1963.

Morris, Robert C. *Reading, 'Riting, and Reconstruction: The Education of Freedmen in the South, 1861–1870.* Chicago: University of Chicago Press, 1981.

Morrow, Ralph E. *Northern Methodism and Reconstruction.* East Lansing: Michigan State University Press, 1956.

Murray, Andrew E. *Presbyterians and the Negro: A History.* Philadelphia: Presbyterian Historical Society, 1966.

Nolen, Claude H. *The Negro's Image in the South: The Anatomy of White Supremacy.* Lexington: University of Kentucky Press, 1967.

Osthaus, Carl R. *Freedmen, Philanthropy, and Fraud: A History of the Freedman's Savings Bank.* Urbana: University of Illinois Press, 1976.

Parrish, William E. *Missouri Under Radical Rule, 1865–1870.* Columbia: University of Missouri Press, 1965.

Pearson, Elizabeth Ware, ed. *Letters from Port Royal, Written at the Time of the Civil War.* Boston: W. B. Clarke Company, 1906.

Peck, Elisabeth S. *Berea's First Century, 1855–1955.* Lexington: University of Kentucky Press, 1955.

Pike, G. D. *The Jubilee Singers and Their Campaign for Twenty Thousand Dollars.* New York: Lee, Shepard and Dillingham, 1873.

Proctor, Henry Hugh. *Between Black and White: Autobiographical Sketches.* Boston: Pilgrim Press, 1925.

Range, Willard. *The Rise and Progress of Negro Colleges in Georgia, 1865–1949.* Athens: University of Georgia Press, 1951.

Reid, Whitelaw. *After the War: A Southern Tour.* New York: Moore, Wilstach & Baldwin, 1866.

Richardson, Joe M. *A History of Fisk University, 1865–1946.* University, Ala.: University of Alabama Press, 1980.

Ripley, C. Peter. *Slaves and Freedmen in Civil War Louisiana.* Baton Rouge: Louisiana State University Press, 1976.

Rogers, J. A. R. *Birth of Berea College: A Story of Providence.* Berea: Berea College Press, 1933.

Rose, Willie Lee. *Rehearsal for Reconstruction: The Port Royal Experiment.* New York: Bobbs-Merrill Company, 1964.

Roy, Joseph E. *Pilgrim's Letters: Bits of Current History.* Boston: Congregational Sunday-School and Publishing Society, 1888.

Rudolph, Frederick. *The American College and University: A History.* New York: Alfred A. Knopf, 1962.

Slaughter, Linda Warfel. *The Freedmen of the South.* Cincinnati: Elm Street Printing Company, 1869.

Smith, Charles Spencer. *A History of the African Methodist Episcopal Church.* Philadelphia: Book Concern of the A.M.E. Church, 1922.

Smith, H. Shelton. *In His Image But . . . : Racism in Southern Religion, 1780–1910.* Durham, N.C.: Duke University Press, 1972.

Spivey, Donald. *Schooling for the New Slavery: Black Industrial Education, 1868–1915.* Westport, Conn.: Greenwood Press, 1978.

Stanley, A. Knighton. *The Children Is Crying: Congregationalism Among Black People.* New York: Pilgrim Press, 1979.

Stearns, Charles. *The Black Man of the South, and the Rebels or, The Characteristics of the Former and the Recent Outrages of the Latter.* New York: American News Co., 1872.

Stowell, Jay S. *Methodist Adventures in Negro Education.* New York: Methodist Book Concern, 1922.

Swint, Henry Lee, ed. *Dear Ones at Homes; Letters from Contraband Camps.* Nashville: Vanderbilt University Press, 1966.

———. *The Northern Teacher in the South, 1862–1870.* Nashville: Vanderbilt University Press, 1941.

Taylor, Alrutheus Ambush. *The Negro in the Reconstruction of Virginia.* Washington, D.C.: Association for the Study of Negro Life and History, 1926.

Taylor, Joe Gray. *Louisiana Reconstructed, 1863–1877.* Baton Rouge: Louisiana State University Press, 1974.

Trelease, Allen W. *White Terror: The Ku Klux Klan Conspiracy and Southern Reconstruction.* New York: Harper & Row, 1971.

Tucker, David M. *Black Pastors and Leaders: Memphis, 1819–1972.* Memphis: Memphis State University Press, 1975.

Vaughan, William Preston. *Schools for All: The Blacks and Public Education in the South, 1865–1877.* Lexington: University of Kentucky Press, 1974.

Warner, Charles Dudley. *Studies in the South and West with Comments on Canada.* New York: Harper and Brothers, 1889.

Washington, Joseph R., Jr. *Black Religion: The Negro and Christianity in the United States.* Boston: Beacon Press, 1966.

Wharton, Vernon Lane. *The Negro in Mississippi, 1865–1890.* Chapel Hill: University of North Carolina Press, 1947.

White, Howard A. *The Freedmen's Bureau in Louisiana.* Baton Rouge: Louisiana State University Press, 1970.

Wikramanayake, Marina. *A World in Shadow: The Free Black in Antebellum South Carolina.* Columbia: University of South Carolina Press, 1973.

Williamson, Joel. *After Slavery: The Negro in South Carolina During Reconstruction, 1861–1877.* Chapel Hill: University of North Carolina Press, 1965.

Woodson, Carter G. *The History of the Negro Church.* Washington, D.C.: Associated Publishers, 1921.

Wyatt-Brown, Bertram. *Lewis Tappan and the Evangelical War Against Slavery.* Cleveland: Press of Case Western Reserve University, 1969.

Wynes, Charles E. *Race Relations in Virginia, 1870–1902.* Charlottesville: University of Virginia Press, 1961.

Articles and Pamphlets

Alexander, Roberta Sue. "Hostility and Hope: Black Education in North Carolina During Presidential Reconstruction, 1865–1867." *North Carolina Historical Review* 53 (April 1976): 113–32.

"Alice Dunbar-Nelson." *Journal of Negro History* 21 (January 1936): 95–96.

Alvord, John W. *Letters from the South, Relating to the Freedmen, Addressed to Major General O. O. Howard.* Washington, D.C.: Howard University Press, 1870.

American Freedmen's Union Commission. *The Results of Emancipation in the United States of America.* New York: American Freedmen's Union Commission, 1867.

Armstrong, Warren B. "Union Chaplains and the Education of the Freedmen." *Journal of Negro History* 52 (April 1967): 104–15.

Black, Isabella. "Berea College." *Phylon* 18 (Spring 1957): 267–76.

Blanchard, F. Q. "A Quarter Century in the American Missionary Association." *Journal of Negro Education* 6 (April 1937): 152–56.

Brigham, R. I. "Negro Education in Ante Bellum Missouri." *Journal of Negro History* 30 (October 1945): 405–20.

Brown, Ira V. "Lyman Abbott and Freedmen's Aid, 1865–1869." *Journal of Southern History* 15 (February–November 1949): 22–38.

Bumstead, Horace. "The Freedman's Children at School." *Andover Review* 4 (December 1885): 550–60.

Clower, George W. "Some Sidelights on Education in Georgia in the 1860's." *Georgia Historical Quarterly* 37 (September 1953): 249–55.

Curry, Richard O. "The Abolitionists and Reconstruction: A Critical Appraisal." *Journal of Southern History* 34 (November 1968): 527–45.

Curtis, L. S. "Nathan B. Young, A Sketch." *Journal of Negro History* 19 (January 1934): 107–10.

Drake, Richard B. "Freedmen's Aid Societies and Sectional Compromise." *Journal of Southern History* 29 (May 1963): 175–86.

DuBois, W. E. B. "Of the Training of Black Men." *Atlantic Monthly* 90 (September 1902): 289–97.

Eggleston, G. K. "The Work of Relief Societies During the Civil War." *Journal of Negro History* 14 (July 1929): 272–99.

Fen, Sing Nan. "Notes on the Education of Negroes in North Carolina During the Civil War." *Journal of Negro Education* 36 (Winter 1967): 24–31.

Forten, Charlotte L. "Life on the Sea Islands." *Atlantic Monthly* 13 (May 1864): 587–96, (June 1864): 666–76.

"The Freedmen at Port Royal." *North American Review* 208 (July 1865): 1–28.

Gannett, William Channing, and Edward Everett Hale. "The Education of the Freedmen." *North American Review* 101 (October 1865): 528–49.

Green, Fletcher M. "Northern Missionary Activities in the South, 1846–1861." *Journal of Southern History* 21 (May 1955): 147–72.

Griffin, Clifford S. "The Abolitionists and the Benevolent Societies, 1831–1861." *Journal of Negro History* 44 (July 1959): 195–216.

Griggs, A. C. "Lucy Craft Laney." *Journal of Negro History* 19 (January 1934): 97–102.

Grout, Lewis. "The Relations of the Church to the Colored Race." *New Englander* 42 (November 1883): 723–30.

Hall, Betty Jean, and Richard Allen Heckman. "Berea's First Decade." *Filson Club History Quarterly* 42 (October 1968): 323–39.

Harlan, Louis R. "Desegregation in New Orleans Public Schools During Reconstruction." *American Historical Review* 67 (April 1962): 663–75.

Carson, Suzanne C. "Samuel Chapman Armstrong: Missionary to the South." Ph.D. dissertation, Johns Hopkins University, 1952.

Drake, Richard B. "The American Missionary Association and the Southern Negro, 1861–1888." Ph.D. dissertation, Emory University, 1957.

De Boer, Clara M. "The Role of Afro-Americans in the Origins and Work of the American Missionary Association, 1839–1877." Ph.D. dissertation, Rutgers University, 1973.

Haywood, Jacqueline S. "The American Missionary Association in Louisiana During Reconstruction." Ph.D. dissertation, UCLA, 1974.

Horst, Samuel L. "Education for Manhood: The Education of Blacks in Virginia During the Civil War." Ph.D. dissertation, University of Virginia, 1977.

Johnson, Clifton H. "The American Missionary Association, 1846–1861: A Study of Christian Abolitionism." Ph.D. dissertation, University of North Carolina, 1958.

Jones, Flora Mae. "John G. Fee and Berea College." M. A. thesis, Western Kentucky State Teachers College, 1934.

Jones, Maxine D. "'A Glorious Work': The American Missionary Association and Black North Carolinians, 1863–1880." Ph.D. dissertation, Florida State University, 1982.

Loesch, Robert K. "Kentucky Abolitionist: John G. Fee." Ph.D. dissertation, Hartford Seminary, 1969.

Owens, James Leggette. "The Negro in Georgia During Reconstruction, 1864–1872: A Social History." Ph.D. dissertation, University of Georgia, 1975.

Rosen, Frederick B. "The Development of Negro Education in Florida During Reconstruction, 1865–1877." Ph.D. dissertation, University of Florida, 1974.

Sherer, Robert G., Jr. "Let Us Make Man: Negro Education in Nineteenth Century Alabama." Ph.D. dissertation, University of North Carolina, 1970.

Welch, Eloise Turner. "The Background and Development of the American Missionary Association's Decision to Educate Freedmen in the South, with Subsequent Repercussions for Higher Education." Ph.D. dissertation, Bryn Mawr, 1976.

Westin, Richard B. "The State and Segregated Schools: Negro Public Education in North Carolina, 1863–1923." Ph.D. dissertation, Duke University, 1966.

Wright, C. T. "The Development of Education for Blacks in Georgia, 1865–1900." Ph.D. dissertation, Boston University, 1977.

Index

Abbott, Lyman, 81, 82, 100
Abolitionists, 102, 104, 163, 164, 169
Adams, J. A., 133, 208, 226
Adams, John Quincy, 263 (n. 1)
Adams, Mary F., 168
Adlington, Ellen E., 225, 227
Adrian Orphanage, 65–66, 278 (n. 20)
Africa: missions to, 104–5
African Civilization Society: relationship
  with AMA, 72
African Methodist Episcopal Church,
  71–72, 145, 156, 158, 249, 252; assisted
  by AMA, 72
African Methodist Episcopal Zion
  Church, 145, 158
Alabama, 45, 47, 48, 50, 62, 83, 110, 112,
  113, 115, 119, 128–31, 152–53, 157, 169,
  174, 178, 180, 203, 209, 217, 221, 223,
  225, 227–28, 229, 232, 237, 239, 241,
  243, 245, 247, 251
Alaska, 260
Alcorn, James L., 248
Alcorn Agricultural and Mechanical
  College, 139
Alden, Reverend E. H., 178
Allender, A. E., 175
Alexander, J. L., 117
Alexander, Louisa L., 193
Alexander, William S., 253
Allen, D. T., 61, 79, 242
Allen, Sarah A., 227
Alvord, John W., 43, 76, 77, 81, 82;
  relationship with AMA, 280 (n. 16)
American Anti-Slavery Society, 88
American Baptist Home Missionary
  Society, 81, 82
American Freedmen's Union
  Commission, 73, 74, 75, 76, 83, 110;

charges AMA with refusal to
  cooperate, 81; accuses Freedmen's
  Bureau of favoritism, 81, 82;
  terminated, 279 (n. 11)
American Home Missionary Society, 98
American Missionary, 9, 14, 21, 58, 60,
  64, 65, 84, 94, 97, 154, 224, 231, 251,
  252; as propaganda tool, 94
American Missionary Association: and
  Canadian missions, ix; overseas
  missions of, ix; antislavery churches,
  ix; organized, ix; early views of, ix,
  x–xi; motivations of, x; sends
  missionaries to Virginia, 3; establishes
  school for contrabands, 4–5, 10–13; and
  relief, 6–7, 10, 14, 57–67; sends farm
  managers to contrabands, 7, 23, 61; and
  recruitment of black soldiers, 9; and
  number of teachers in the field, 11, 19,
  23, 27, 31, 32, 37, 271 (n. 1); in the Sea
  Islands, 17–19; aims of, 19, 40–42;
  motives of, 20–22; and black suffrage,
  21, 252–53; and black teachers, 23, 24,
  27, 116, 132, 140, 189–93, 194–202,
  203–9; and teaching black soldiers,
  24–27; educating for citizenship, 41;
  teaches patriotism, 43; and religious
  education, 43, 44, 45, 73, 74, 125,
  145–46, 147, 148; and industrial
  education, 44, 297 (n. 45); teaches
  chastity, 46; relationship with
  Congregationalists, 46, 145, 147, 151,
  152–53, 154; and temperance, 46, 241–
  42; discipline in its schools, 46, 47;
  assists destitute whites, 63; establishes
  orphanages, 64–66, 82, 168; and other
  aid societies, 71–75, 81–82; and
  Freedmen's Bureau, 75–84;

337